Dr. Wisner. Jeremiah Evarts. Dr. Worcester. Dr. Cornelius. Dr. Armstrong.

DECEASED SECRETARIES OF THE AMERICAN BOARD OF COMMISSIONERS FOR FOREIGN MISSIONS,

FROM 1810 TO [illegible]. ENGRAVED FOR THE MEMORIAL VOLUME BY GEO. E. PERINE, N.Y.

MEMORIAL VOLUME

OF THE

FIRST FIFTY YEARS

OF THE

AMERICAN BOARD OF COMMISSIONERS FOR FOREIGN MISSIONS.

"Large designs, systematic and vigorous exertions, humble dependence on God, and entire consecration to the work, should characterize all our enterprises for the salvation of this revolted world."—RESOLVE OF THE BOARD, 1835.

FIFTH EDITION.

BOSTON:
PUBLISHED BY THE BOARD.
MISSIONARY HOUSE, 33 PEMBERTON SQUARE.
1863.

ELECTROTYPED AT THE
BOSTON STEREOTYPE FOUNDRY.

PRINTED BY
GEO. C. RAND AND AVERY.

PREFACE.

THE issue of a Memorial Volume by the Board, at the end of its first half-century, seemed a thing of course — almost as much as that of a Report at the close of the year. The only serious question was, how to produce the volume. It must obviously be prepared by one intimately acquainted with the constitution of the Board, its missions and agencies, and the modifications that have taken place in its policy and proceedings. But how could either of the Secretaries, already occupied to the extent of their ability, perform such an additional service? It was decided, however, by the Prudential Committee, that the work ought to be done, and that it ought to devolve on the senior Secretary, he having been thirty-eight years connected with the correspondence. As the subjects were familiar to him, he felt it to be his duty to undertake the work, even at a considerable risk of health. By adding, for a few months, under the pressure of the emergency, to the usual hours of daily labor — presuming that the missions would acquiesce, meanwhile, in receiving fewer and briefer letters from the Missionary House; and with such aid as he might receive from associates in the ordinary duties of his department, and from them and others in the preparation of the volume, it was supposed he might complete the work in time for its publication within the year. Through the favor of Providence, this has been done; and in a manner, it is hoped, considering the circumstances, to secure the indulgence of the Christian public.

The reader will naturally turn first to the Semi-centennial Discourse, by the President of the Board, which contributed so largely to the interest of the Jubilee Meeting. A considerable part of the volume will be found more or less illustrative of the doctrines and principles of that discourse. Those well informed in religious biography, will at once perceive the hand of the Rev. Dr. Sprague, of Albany, in the comprehensive and truthful sketches of the Founders of the Board, forming one of the chapters; and this generous contribution to the work is very gratefully acknowledged. For the admirable analysis and philosophical views of the literature of the Board and of its Missions, forming one of the chapters in the second series, the volume is indebted to the Rev. Joseph Tracy, D. D., author of the History of the Board in its first thirty years.

The work has been performed under a deep sense of responsibility for the accuracy of every statement. Very little has been taken on trust. The chapter on the difficulties experienced in procuring the charter of the Board, is an original contribution to its history; and the author was much indebted to the aid of the Hon. Charles T. Russell, of Boston, in the discoveries — for such they are to the present generation — that were made in the archives of the State of Massachusetts. The chapters on the constitution of the Board, its relations to ecclesiastical bodies, its meetings, correspondence, finances, agencies, missionaries, churches, schools, deputations, etc., were all the result of careful investigation.

Thanks are due to the Rev. Dr. Thompson, of Roxbury, and to the Rev. Isaac R. Worcester, editor of the Board's monthly publications, for their judicious criticism, extended to nearly the entire work; and also to associates in office, for their counsel and aid. But for the accuracy of the multiplied statements and opinions, it is obvious that neither they, nor the Prudential Committee, can be held strictly responsible.

This volume is the first of its kind. Other Societies may be expected, in their order, to make similar contributions to the stock of missionary experience. Should many of the facts here embodied strike the reader as not new, he will at least see them for the first time in their natural combinations. The author's prayer is, that this Memorial Volume, which he regards as among the closing labors of his somewhat protracted official life, may be accepted by the Head of the Church, and blessed to the extension of his kingdom.

RUFUS ANDERSON.

MISSIONARY HOUSE, BOSTON,
August, 1861.

CONTENTS.

THE BOARD.

CHAPTER I.

ORIGIN OF THE BOARD.

CHAPTER II.

REMINISCENCES.

CHAPTER III.

THE CHARTER AND THE LEGISLATURE.

CHAPTER VII.

MEETINGS OF THE BOARD.

CHAPTER VIII.

THE PRUDENTIAL COMMITTEE — PLACES OF BUSINESS.

CHAPTER IX.

CORRESPONDENCE — LIBRARY — CABINET.

CHAPTER X.

THE FINANCES.

CHAPTER XI.

THE AGENCIES.

CHAPTER XII.

RELATIONS TO GOVERNMENTS.

CHAPTER XIII.

THE DECEASED SECRETARIES.

THE MISSIONS.

CHAPTER I.

THEIR CONSTITUTION AND ORIGIN.

CHAPTER II.

ORIGIN OF THE MISSIONS, CONTINUED.

CHAPTER III.

DEVELOPMENT OF THE MISSIONS — THEIR LAWS OF GROWTH — THEIR COMPLETION.

CHAPTER IV.

PROGRESS OF THE WORK.

CHAPTER V.

THE MISSIONARIES.

CHAPTER VI.

THE CHURCHES.

CHAPTER VII.

SCHOOLS.

CHAPTER VIII.

PREACHING AND THE PRESS.

CHAPTER IX.

DEPUTATIONS.

CHAPTER X.

LITERATURE OF THE BOARD AND OF ITS MISSIONS.

CHAPTER XI.

FIELD AND WORK AT THE CLOSE OF THE HALF-CENTURY.

APPENDIX.

THE JUBILEE MEETING.

THE American Board of Commissioners for Foreign Missions completed its first half-century in the year 1860. As the Board had its origin in the State of Massachusetts, it was proper that the meeting commemorative of the event should be held in Boston. The people of the city and its extensive environs, connected with it by steam and horse cars, made provision for some two thousand guests; and probably a yet greater number had their own arrangements with friends or at public houses, and very many came from their homes each morning, from the distance of ten and even twenty miles, returning by late evening trains.

The names of ninety-five Corporate members, and nine hundred and seventy-four Honorary members, were entered by the Recording Secretary, though many who were present doubtless failed to report their names. The sessions were held in the Tremont Temple, commencing Tuesday, October 2, at four o'clock, P. M., and closing Friday noon, October 5.

The Temple was full at every meeting, except perhaps the opening session, and on several occasions was densely crowded. The number present to listen to the President's Historical Discourse could hardly have been less than thirty-five hundred; and nearly as many were again assembled on Friday morning at the closing meeting.

The Annual Sermon was delivered on Tuesday evening, by Dr. Samuel W. Fisher, President of Hamilton College. His text was Isaiah xlv. 1–6, and xliii. 21. On Wednesday evening, Dr. Mark Hopkins, the President of the Board, delivered the Semi-centennial Discourse, which forms an important portion of this volume. As the number of persons in attendance was much greater than could be accommodated in the spacious Temple, Park-street Church was opened in the morning, afternoon and evening of Wednesday, and in the morning and evening of Thursday, as was also Winter-street Church on Wednesday evening, for meetings that were addressed by returned missionaries and others, and very numerously attended. According to the custom of the Board, the sacrament of the Lord's Supper was observed on Thursday afternoon; and it was necessary to occupy four churches, the communicants in attendance being probably not far from forty-five hundred. Prayer meetings were held on Wednesday and Thursday mornings, at a quarter past eight o'clock, at Park-street Church; and by returned missionaries and their friends in the vestry of Tremont Temple. These meetings were fully attended, and of deep interest.

This annual meeting being specially commemorative, Thursday morning was devoted to reminiscences. It was at this session the speeches were delivered, which are for the most part embodied in the second chapter of this work. At this time, also, Pastor Fische, from Paris, representing the French Evangelical Missionary Society, Dr. Warren, Secretary of the Baptist Missionary Union, and Chancellor Ferris, from the Board of Missions of the Reformed Protestant Dutch Church, severally addressed the Board, with assurances of cordial Christian sympathy and a spirit of coöperation in the great missionary work. The President of the Board responded, heartily reciprocating the salutations and Christian sympathies of each of these gentlemen.

In consequence of the almost unexampled embarrassment of the times for the past year or two, the Board had commenced its fiftieth year with a debt of sixty-six thousand three hundred and seventy-four dollars; and its necessary annual expenditure was about three hundred and sixty thousand dollars. To place it above all embarrassment at its Jubilee Meeting, it was needful to aim at raising some four hundred and thirty thousand dollars during the year. Much gratitude and joy pervaded the meeting, that the receipts had been four hundred and twenty-nine thousand seven hundred and ninety-nine dollars and eight cents, being one thousand four hundred and sixty-six dollars and nineteen cents more than the united sum of the debt and the expenditure. This auspicious result was owing to the spirit of uncommon liberality which God was pleased to give to the friends of the enterprise generally, but more especially to a well-planned effort for the removal of the debt, suggested by a mercantile friend in Boston. The plan was to raise sixty thousand dollars among merchants and others, by subscriptions of one thousand dollars each. It was somewhat modified, but the result was secured by comparatively a small number of persons. Twenty thousand dollars were raised in Boston; as much more in New York and Brooklyn; and New England (out of Boston) responded with gratifying cordiality, Massachusetts and Connecticut each contributing more than ten thousand dollars.

The subject of missionary expenditure not being well understood in the Christian community, — the current impression being that the Prudential Committee might justly be held responsible for incurring a debt, whatever the amount of the receipts, — a brief statement was made to the meeting, showing that the Committee had but a limited responsibility for the late indebtedness. This gave rise to a protracted, earnest, and very profitable discussion. It was (as it is still) a topic for the times, and every body seemed interested. It had such an obvious bearing on the vital interests of the great cause, and also upon the personal duty of every Christian, that it did not perceptibly interfere with the spirituality of the meeting. In view of the unexpected and very grave national agitations which have since arisen, and of their depressing influence on the commercial and religious interests of the country, it was perhaps well that the main current of the meeting took this direction. That, and the disinthrallment of the treasury, may be thankfully regarded as a providential preparation for passing through the national judgments so soon to follow. The discussion did not reach its climax until the closing session on Friday morning, when the following resolution was proposed, viz.: "That the Board express the hope that the Prudential Committee will see their way clear to appropriate three hundred and seventy thousand dollars for the coming year; and that the friends of the cause will aim to raise not less than four hundred thousand dollars, that sum being desirable for the proper growth and development of the missions."

As soon as this resolution had been adopted by the Board, a wish was expressed that an opportunity might be given for the whole assembly to manifest their feelings. The President, therefore, requested those who desired to express concurrence with the sentiment of that resolution, to do so by rising. The whole great congregation rose at once; one voice unexpectedly struck the note — instantly many caught it — and a multitude of voices, like the noise of many waters, sang the well-known verse, —

"Shall we, whose souls are lighted
With wisdom from on high, —
Shall we to men benighted
The lamp of life deny?
Salvation! — O, salvation!
The joyful sound proclaim,
Till earth's remotest nation
Has learned Messiah's name."

It was a scene long to be remembered. Many an eye filled with tears, and many a bosom swelled with emotion.

The Committee and Executive Officers of the Board had contemplated a different course of thought as likely to enter into the main business of the meeting, and proposed the following resolutions to the Board; which were very cordially adopted, but with regret that there was no more time to discuss them. They have an historical importance.

"*Resolved*, That in the history of this Board, at home and abroad, from the beginning hitherto, we gratefully recognize the good hand of our God upon us; and especially on this anniversary, we would remember, with humble thankfulness, all the way which the Lord our God has led us these fifty years.

"1. We praise him for giving to the pioneers in this enterprise, on the one hand, such simplicity of faith, such earnestness of purpose, such compassion for the lost, and such love to the Saviour; and for giving to our fathers, on the other hand, such a readiness to assume the new and unknown responsibilities which were so unexpectedly thrown upon them.

"2. We praise him for inclining so many of our sons and daughters, in all the years that are past, to go forth and preach among the Gentiles the unsearchable riches of Christ; and for inspiring our churches to such a degree with the willingness so to provide for their wants, as to leave them without carefulness in the prosecution of their work.

"3. We praise him for sparing so many of our missionaries, some of them far advanced in life, to see this day; and we praise him as well for those who are not, (for the Lord hath taken them,) because of the serene trust and the radiant hope with which they passed from their earthly tabernacle to a house not made with hands, eternal in the heavens.

"4. We praise him because, in these last days, the first and chief Missionary has gone forth, glorious in his apparel, and traveling in the greatness of his strength, that he may prepare a way for his people in all the earth, by turning backward the two-leaved gates, and breaking the scepters of the mighty, and so making hundreds of millions accessible to his own life-giving word.

"5. We praise him for other achievements of unspeakable value, in that he has set his seal upon missions, as the cheapest, readiest, and truest reforming and civilizing agency; in that he has proved, beyond all contradiction, the perfect adaptation of his gospel to all classes of men, even the most degraded and the most depraved; in that he has rescued, through our instrumentality, tens of thousands from the ineffable woes of heathenism, and made them kings and priests unto God forever.

"6. We praise him, above all, for doing so much for us, and so much by us, notwithstanding our grievous unbelief, our covetousness, our indifference to the worth of the soul, our neglect of prayer, our imperfect sympathy with Christ, and our disposition to exalt ourselves; for all which we desire to humble ourselves, saying with one heart, 'O Lord, righteousness belongeth unto thee, but unto us confusion of faces, as at this day.'

"*Resolved*, That we record it as the deliberate judgment of the Board, that the churches sustaining its operations are summoned to higher obligations and higher privileges.

"1. God has committed to our spiritual husbandry some of the largest and noblest fields in the world.

"2. He has blessed our work to such a degree, that for us to remain stationary has become impossible, without a manifest and perilous disregard of duty.

"3. Having the undoubted ability to do much more than we have yet done, it will be for our spiritual enlargement, and our comfort of hope, that we place ourselves at once in harmony with the merciful designs of our enthroned Immanuel.

"4. In that season of prosperity, more dangerous than adversity, which is beginning to diffuse its cheerful light in all our borders, our best safeguard against worldliness and luxury, the love of gain and the love of pleasure, will be a ready and hearty consecration, day by day, of our property, as well as of ourselves, to Christ's honored and chosen work.

"5. The honor of our ascended Lord imperatively requires that we 'go forward,' seeing that he has opened the world so widely to his people, and placed in their hands such multiplied facilities for speedy and efficient action, and given them the silver and the gold for this very end, that now at length, when this nineteenth century is waning to its close, his people should go forth, and proclaim the acceptable year of the Lord in all the world."

Thus ended the first Half-Century of the Board, and thus commenced the second. It was well remarked, at the close of the published minutes of the meeting, "If the impressions produced during the meeting could be retained by all who were present, and if they would do all they might to extend such impressions among others, then, indeed, might the Prudential Committee expect to be enabled to sustain the missions in a healthful and vigorous growth, and to carry forward the work which the Lord has so greatly prospered during the past fifty years, to results within another half-century, more glorious, by far, than have ever yet been witnessed in connection with any missionary enterprise of the Christian church."

DR. HOPKINS'S

SEMI-CENTENNIAL DISCOURSE.

SEMI-CENTENNIAL DISCOURSE.

"THERE SHALL BE A HANDFUL OF CORN IN THE EARTH UPON THE TOP OF THE MOUNTAINS; THE FRUIT THEREOF SHALL SHAKE LIKE LEBANON." — Ps. lxxii. 16.

THERE are no contrasts like those of Christianity. The contrasts of nature are great, but nature is subordinate, and, like every subordinate system, is not only a condition of that which is higher, but serves for its illustration and prefigurement. The chief value and significance of nature are from its relation to a higher system of moral government. Great as are its contrasts, compared with those of Christianity, they are but as the shadow to the substance, but as the type to the thing typified.

In nature we have contrasts of opposition, as between light and darkness, heat and cold, life and death. In Christianity the contrasts are not merely of elements that exclude each other, but of those that conflict, and with a struggle that is conscious and intense. They are between holiness and sin, love and hatred, heaven and hell.

We have also, in nature, contrasts between beginnings and consummations. These are from growth and increase. Between the "little leaven" and the "whole lump;" between the "mustard seed," which is, indeed, the least of all seeds, and the "tree," in the branches of which "the birds of the air come and lodge;" between the "little fire" and the "great matter" it kindleth; between the fountain and the river; between the infant and the monarch; between the "handful of corn in the earth" and "the fruit thereof," the contrast is great. Every thing that grows, all organization, however huge and ponderous it may become, has its beginning in a point, often too minute for our inspection. But in Christianity the contrast is not between the leaven and the lump; it is between a single individual, on the one hand, without learning, or rank, or wealth, gathering around him his twelve disciples and teaching them; and, on the other, a whole world in ignorance and moral death, that is to be enlightened, quickened, transformed, regenerated; and, instead of being tossed by passion and turbid with sin, is to reflect over its whole surface the image of heaven. It is not between the mustard seed and the tree that reaches its limit and then decays, but between the "incorruptible seed" and a growth that shall know no end. It is not between the infant in his cradle and the general at the head of armies, or the monarch on his throne, but between the babe of Bethlehem, wrapped in swaddling clothes and lying in a manger, and the leader of the armies of heaven, having on his head many crowns, and on his vesture and on his thigh a name written —"King of kings and Lord of lords." It is between Him who stood at Pilate's bar, and Him who shall come in the clouds of heaven, and all the holy angels with him, and before whom shall be gathered all nations. It is between the Man of sorrows, expiring upon the cross, and Him who shall sit upon the great white throne, and before whose face the earth and the heaven shall flee away.

This contrast, which we thus find in the person of our Saviour, and in the beginning of his religion compared with its consummation, has been reproduced in the history of every individual Christian and of every revival of religion, and in every great movement in which Christianity has begun to reassert its purity, or its claims to universal supremacy. It is in these contrasts that we find that *method* of God by which he shows continually that the "foolishness of God is wiser than men, and that the weakness of God is stronger than men;" "that no flesh should glory in his presence."

Thus it was in the Reformation. There was a poor boy singing from house to house for bread; there was a solitary monk burdened with a sense of sin, and reading a chained Bible in his convent; and in that boy, in that monk, in that Bible was the Reformation. There were great men then — councilors, princes, emperors; bishops, cardinals, popes; but from them this light did not proceed. There were churches splendid with all that wealth could procure, magnificent cathedrals; there was St. Peter's itself; but "it was in an old wooden chapel, thirty feet long and twenty broad, whose walls, propped on all sides, were falling to ruin, that the Reformation was first preached." So, too, it was with that second and more complete reformation, when Puritanism had its rise in England, from which was English liberty; and especially with that movement which led to the exodus of our fathers. There were a few students in the universities; there were prohibited meetings for prayer in private houses of the humbler class; there were poor, but zealous and faithful men in the prisons; and there were the Mayflower and Plymouth Rock; and now there is a continent upon either shore of which the tide of emigration is setting in, where the free elements are heaving and tossing like the ocean, and where there is, as nowhere else, freedom to worship God.

So again, at a later period, four young men at the most celebrated English university formed a club. They were ridiculed as the Holy Club, and as Methodists. But persecution did its wonted work. Driven from the churches, they preached in the open air; and from them, in connection with the organizing power of Wesley and the wonderful eloquence of Whitefield, there went forth a movement that shook England and this continent, and that must go on in circles still widening till the end of time.

And what was the origin of modern Protestant missions? It was from deep poverty abounding to the riches of liberality. "When the Moravians sent out their first missionaries, in 1732, their entire congregation did not exceed six hundred persons, and the greater part of these were suffering exiles." The world knew them not; but they established numerous missions, and were doing God's work as no other people were.

How, too, did the great movement in England, sixty years afterward, originate? It was from no university, from no established church, from no distinguished man. It was in the mind of a shoemaker, the honored Carey. For years the idea was within him, as a fire shut up in his bones. When he ventured to speak of it he was regarded as infatuated; his brethren called him an enthusiast; and when they were won over, and the work was begun, literature and wit, in the person of Sydney Smith, ridiculed the "cobbler," and scoffed at the undertaking.

Of this great principle, or method of contrast, which we thus find every where, both in nature and in Christianity, we have, in the history of the American Board of Commissioners for Foreign Missions, whose fiftieth anniversary we now celebrate, a striking illustration; and this we recognize, and accept, and rejoice in, as an evidence that the movement was of God.

And not merely from the analogies of the past, do we, in this connection, find evidence of the divine origin of this work. Whenever small beginnings increase to great magnitude, or great results flow from causes and means apparently inadequate, there must be previous conditions, and concurrent agencies, which no power of man could arrange or control. The little leaven will not leaven a lump of clay. Falling at another time or place, the spark that has fired a train and blown up a fortress would have simply expired. There must be adaptation, congruity, proclivity, a meeting of some great want, a falling in with concealed tendencies, a special divine power; and if, as in this case, the results be such as only a divine power could or would produce, we must refer them to that. Historically our thoughts follow the order of visible causes, but without conditions and agencies far above these, they are of little account. Hence the chief agents in such movements are often quite as much astonished as others at the prospects which the winding and widening river of God's providence opens up, and at the results accomplished. Neither Luther, nor Wesley, nor Mills anticipated, at the beginning, what the end would be. Said Whitefield, in entering upon his work, "I have thrown myself blindfold, and I trust without reserve, into His almighty hands."

Like the movements of which I have now spoken, this for foreign missions had its origin with young men. A boy overheard his mother say, that she had devoted him to the service of God as a missionary. Here, so far as we can trace it, we find the fountain head of this broad river. When this boy was converted, his thoughts were immediately turned toward missions. He entered college, and in connection with the study of the geography of Asia, the idea of a mission to that continent was suggested and revolved. At a stated prayer meeting, held at hours when most students are either engaged in sport or are doing nothing, this idea was presented. Driven by an approaching thunder-storm from the grove where the meeting had usually been held, they took shelter behind a neighboring haystack, and there, in the language of one who was present, "Mills proposed to send the gospel to that dark and heathen land, and said we could do it if we would." The subject was then discussed, and as the storm was passing away, Mills said, "Come, let us make it a subject of prayer under this haystack, while the dark clouds are going and the clear sky is coming." So they prayed, and continued to pray and consult together through that and the following season. Then a society was formed, the object of which was, in the language of its constitution, "to effect, in the person of its members, a mission to the heathen." This was the first foreign missionary society on this continent. A similar society was soon formed at Andover, by Mills and those who went with him, and from that the proposition was made that resulted in the formation of the American Board.

What a contrast is here! On the one side is that vast continent, the cradle of the race, and of Christianity, with its myriads of people, now seen, not in the purple light of the imagination, as the Orient filled with palaces and pageants; nor with the eye of traffic, as the land of spices and of gems;

but as the abode of a perverted Christianity, of intrenched paganism, of darkness, and cruelty, and degradation; as a land where missionaries would be murdered, and fortresses could be stormed only by those who should lead a forlorn hope. On the other side are five young men, from the two lower classes in an infant college, in a place so secluded that no mail from any one direction reaches it oftener than once a week, and with an ocean and a continent intervening. They are seated by a haystack. Dark clouds are above them; but they heed not these, nor the quick flash of the lightning, nor the thunder echoing among the mountains. They are speaking of "the moral darkness of Asia;" they propose to send the gospel thither; *they say they can do it;* they kneel together in prayer; and as they pray, the heavens grow brighter, and the dark clouds roll away.

Here was "the handful of corn among the mountains." It fell in a soil prepared. What, now, has been its fruit? The American Board, devised by Drs. Spring and Worcester, was formed. At its first meeting but five persons were present, and at its second but seven. Its receipts, the first year, were but a thousand dollars. Now its meetings are like the going up of the tribes to Jerusalem; and its annual receipts are three hundred and fifty thousand dollars. Then it had no missions, and it was not known that any heathen country would be open to them. Now its mission stations belt the globe, so that the sun does not set upon them, and the whole world is open. It has collected and disbursed, with no loss from defalcation, and no suspicion of dishonesty, more than eight millions of dollars. It has sent out four hundred and fifteen ordained missionaries, and eight hundred and forty-three not ordained; in all, twelve hundred and fifty-eight. These have established thirty-nine distinct missions, of which twenty-two now remain in connection with the Board; with two hundred and sixty-nine stations and out-stations, employing four hundred and fifty-eight native helpers, preachers, and pastors, not including teachers. They have formed one hundred and forty-nine churches, have gathered at least fifty-five thousand church members, of whom more than twenty thousand are now in connection with its churches. It has under its care three hundred and sixty-nine seminaries and schools, and in them more than ten thousand children. It has printed more than a thousand millions of pages, in forty different languages. It has reduced eighteen languages to writing, thus forming the germs of a new literature. It has raised a nation from the lowest forms of heathenism to a Christian civilization, so that a larger proportion of its people can read than in New England. It has done more to extend and to diffuse in this land a knowledge of different countries and people, than any or all other agencies, and the reaction upon the churches of this foreign work has been invaluable.

But what has been done by this Board is not to be estimated by the results already realized. This is the smallest part. Foundations are laid; experience is gained; materials are gathered; the leaven is deposited and at work; fires are set.

Nor do we find the fruit of that same handful of corn only in what has been done directly by this Board. On reaching India, Judson and Rice, two of its first missionaries, became Baptists. This fact made a powerful appeal to the Baptist churches. Mr. Rice, from the class in college next after that of Mills, returned immediately, and expressly for the purpose of stirring up those churches. He went through the land with great zeal and success, and thus the Burman mission, which has been so remarkably prospered, as well as the other Baptist missions, sprung from this seed.

In 1811 " the Secretary, in behalf of the Board, suggested to the General Assembly of the Presbyterian Church the expediency of forming an institution similar to theirs, between which and theirs there might be such coöperation as should promote the great object of missions among the unevangelized nations. The Assembly, however, while they urged the churches under their care to aid in the good work, thought the business of foreign missions might probably be best managed under a single Board; and thus the undivided Presbyterian church, so long as it was undivided, coöperated with this Board. This union continued till 1837, when the Old School Presbyterians withdrew, and established foreign missions of their own, now extensive and flourishing.

In apostolic times, Paul and Barnabas had a contention and separated. In 1846, owing to a difference of views respecting the best method of dealing with slavery, numbers ceased to coöperate with the American Board, and the American Missionary Association was formed. This has prosecuted, with success, the work both of foreign and domestic missions.

Finally, in 1857, our beloved Dutch brethren, under the impression that they might thus work more effectively, formed a separate Board, and have now their own missions.

Thus are there now five Boards, through which the great mass of missionary feeling and effort on this continent finds expression; and while we joyfully recognize what is done by others, it must yet be said that they are the direct fruit of the handful of corn that was on the top of the mountains. All have conscientious and devoted laborers in the field, and self-denying and prayerful supporters at home. All recognize the authority of the last command of Christ, and the brotherhood of the race in him. Thus do they find enlargement of intellect and of sympathy, and must, we should suppose, be led, more and more, so to work in harmony, that their good shall not be evil spoken of.

Nor has the work of enlargement been confined to this continent. Through a generous appreciation of our missionaries and their work, and with a spirit of magnanimity and Christian liberality worthy of England and of this age, the Turkish Missions Aid Society was formed in 1854, and in the freest and most cordial manner has coöperated with this Board.

Is there any where a more striking illustration of the great principle of contrast adopted by God? Does not the fruit thereof shake like Lebanon? Come, O thou wind, thou strong west wind, from the great sea, sweep up the sides of Lebanon, enter into his thickets, lay hold on the boughs of his cedars. Ah, how do the forests bend, and the thickets roar, and the cedars shake! But what is all this, thou mighty Lebanon, to the shaking that now is, and that shall be, of that fruit among the nations that has sprung, and that shall spring, from the handful of corn that was in the earth upon the top of the mountains! What is it to that upon thine own sides, where the feet of him that brought glad tidings have been beautiful, and where thy children are now fed by Christian bounty, when they have fled and gathered to the house of the missionary as a refuge from death!

Having thus seen what has been done, we next look at some features of the work, and inquire how it has been done.

And here we must notice the two great elements from which this movement originated, and which have pervaded and molded the whole policy of this Board.

The first is, a transcendent estimate of what belongs to Christianity in its relation to a future life; that is, of essential and spiritual Christianity, as compared with modes and forms, and all that in which evangelical Christians have agreed to differ.

The second is, a transcendent estimate of the cross of Christ as a reformatory power, as compared with any educating, or civilizing, or reforming process, aside from that.

In virtue of the first, our aim has been simple, spiritual, grand; and we have been guarded, as fully, perhaps, as such an enterprise can be, from sectarianism and ecclesiasticism. In virtue of the second, our means have been simple and spiritual, and we have been guarded from much complication with secular schemes and side projects of partial reform.

In accordance with the first of these elements, I observe, as a first feature of the work, that what has been done by this Board has been done by honoring Christianity, and seeking to send that, without any denominational or sectarian object.

In every established religion, the grounds of interest and activity on the part of those who adhere to it, or seek to promote it, are of three kinds.

The first are those that are personal and temporal, often involving pecuniary interests, as well as those of position, and rank, and power. These are always strongest with ecclesiastics and hierarchs, and with any whose "craft" is to be furthered, or is in danger.

A second ground is found in things which are unessential, but which may, or may not, be denominational. Often, perhaps generally, these are magnified and clung to in proportion as they are distinctive, and so, unimportant. They include, sometimes, doctrines, but chiefly forms of government and modes of administration. It is here that sincere but weak and undiscriminating minds fall into bigotry, and superstition, and formalism.

It is from a combination of this with the preceding, of the Phariseeism, the Brahminism, the Ecclesiasticism of all ages, with popular credulity and superstition, that the most active and malignant opposition has always arisen when error has been attacked. From these it will arise; and its force will be the greater as the error is more incorporated into the business, the amusements, the life of a community. As opposed to evangelical religion, Sadduceeism will fall in, Herod and Pilate will be made friends. But infidelity is a Gallio. It does not care enough for these things to build inquisitions; it does not think it is doing God service.

A third ground of interest is in a rational comprehension and estimate of the essential elements of the Christian religion. If Christianity has the power to transform, elevate, and save men, it is to be valued for precisely those elements which give it that power; and the purity of efforts to promote it will be as the respect paid to those elements. It is only in the apprehension of these, and in acting from them and for them, that we can have simplicity of aim and of method; can exclude the possibility of fanaticism and malignity; and can hope for union, or for great success.

What, then, are these elements? They include those which relate to the interests of another life — to salvation from sin and its consequences. It was for these that Christ came; it is for these that we send his gospel to the heathen. They include those great but simple requisitions of Christianity, which lie between its system of doctrines on the one hand,

and its temporal results and outward forms on the other. Its system involves the whole sweep of God's moral government, and the highest questions that can arise under that government. Its results are as multifarious and complex as human life. They involve whatever pertains to the highest forms of domestic and social life, and to the most perfect civilization. In the system there are depths that the angels desire to look into, and that eternity may not suffice to fathom. Its results are like the outgoings of the morning — an outburst of beneficence that no human sagacity can follow out fully in its details. But while the system is so unfathomable, and the results so complex, the requisitions that lie between them are of marvelous simplicity; so that between these and the results that hinge upon them, there is the same great contrast of which we have already spoken.

These requisitions may all be comprised in the one word *faith*. "Believe on the Lord Jesus Christ, and thou shalt be saved." "Lord, remember me when thou comest into thy kingdom." "To-day thou shalt be with me in paradise." — It is only to feel the need of Christ, to look, and to trust. It is as when one plants a seed. It matters not that he does not comprehend the great system of nature, the whole of which is required for the growth of that seed; or the processes of its growth; or that he does not know of the waving harvests that may spring from it in future years. He performs an act of simple, I may say of sublime, faith in the system of nature, and God does the rest. "God giveth the increase." So he, be he child or philosopher, be he Greek or Jew, who simply trusts in Christ as a Saviour from sin, and so, as he must, becomes conformed unto him, plants the seed, and opens the way for the sunshine and the rain, for the processes, and growth, and results of that higher system of redemption for which the system of nature stands. Than this act nothing can be simpler. A child can do it; the heathen can do it. It is but the acceptance of a gift. "Thanks be to God for his unspeakable gift."

And as Christianity is thus simple in its requisitions when

it is to be received by the individual, calling for dependence on Christ, so is it when it is to be communicated to others, calling for dependence on the Holy Ghost; and the simplicity in the one case arises from that in the other. The simplicity of that faith in Christ, and in him crucified, which was "foolishness to the Greek," finds its counterpart in that "foolishness of preaching" by which it has "pleased God to save them that believe." Preaching, believing, salvation! this is all; and how do they correspond! Here is a gift, make it known; an offer of liberty, proclaim it; a fountain opened, stand by it and cry, "Ho, every one that thirsteth;" and he that believes will take the gift, and come out of his prison house, and drink of the living waters. So only *could* a spiritual religion be propagated.

So did the apostles and primitive Christians. Were there divisions among them? Inspiration condemned them. Did any say, "I am of Paul?" The apostle asked at once, "Who is Paul?" They were sent, and they sought simply to turn men from darkness to light, and from the power of Satan unto God, that they might — what? Belong to a sect? No; but "receive forgiveness of sins, and inheritance among them which are sanctified by faith that is in Him." In declaring that he "kept back nothing that was profitable," the apostle simply says that he "testified both to the Jews, and also to the Greeks, repentance toward God, and faith toward our Lord Jesus Christ."

When therefore the spirit of missions, which is that of Christianity, was revived, it is not strange that a desire was immediately felt to leave behind, in the onset upon heathendom, all minor questions which had divided Christians. Accordingly, in 1795, but three years after the formation of the British Baptist Society, the London Missionary Society, in which all evangelical denominations were united, was formed. In its original constitution there is an article in which "it is declared to be a fundamental principle of the Missionary Society that our design is not to send Presbyterianism, Independency, Episcopacy, or any other form of church order and government, (about which there may be a difference of opinion among serious people,) but 'the glorious Gospel of the blessed God' to the heathen; and it shall be left (as it ought to be left) to the minds of the persons whom God may call into the fellowship of his Son from among them, to assume for themselves such form of church government as to them shall appear most agreeable to the word of God."

The adoption of this principle drew the hearts of Christians together wonderfully. We are told that "the visible union of Christians of all denominations, who, for the first time, forgetting their party prejudices and partialities, assembled in the same place, sang the same hymns, united in the same prayers, and felt themselves one in Christ, rendered their meetings inexpressibly delightful;" also that the "unanimity and fervor of the assembly in entering upon this greatest of all schemes — the evangelizing of the world — created bursts of joy which nothing could express but tears." Blessed meetings! Blessed upheaval of great truths, where, as upon a high table land, Christians could walk and work together, and look down upon their differences, and claim the same promises, and with the eye of faith sweep the horizon of the whole world as their common field, and feel how much more there is that unites than there is that divides them. Such meetings, fathers and brethren, we have held; and there was in them a millennial aspect and atmosphere that could not have been without such union. In this, most of all, do we miss the brethren who have left us. Why should not we at home be united as the missionaries often are, and must be, on the foreign field? "We," says one of them, "are all one here; we can not afford to be jealous — the common foe is too strong; and the missionaries are bound together neither by creeds nor human ties, but by the fear of God and the love of Jesus." Were Christians thus united in sending and planting the gospel, the church — *the* church, in distinction from *a* church — would be carrying on the work of foreign missions.

If, indeed, there be any denomination that so claims to be exclusively the true church, that they think others are not competent to administer, or fitted to receive, all the ordinances of the church, that denomination must, so far as they thus think, work by itself. But I am unable to frame a definition of *the* church, that would meet the wants of those who accept others as Christians in full standing, as equally with themselves members of the one church of Christ, and yet insist on denominational action on the ground that it is the duty of *the* church, as such, to carry on missions. In the present state of the churches, denominational action may be more efficient, and so, expedient. Possibly it may be so from other causes, some "present distress," as Paul said of single life, but I can not believe it to be God's permanent method. No; as surely as I expect to see the sun advance in the heavens, do I expect that the hearts of Christians will be more and more drawn together in love, and that the principle of coöperation will, in some form, be more and more honored. We may not live to see it; present indications there are, not auspicious; the spring may seem to go back; but we have seen the first violet, we have heard the note of the first bird, and it will come. We may die in the wilderness, but it will come. "Swift fly the years, and rise the expected morn!"

On this great principle the American Board has always acted. What we have done here we have done simply as Christians, and we thank God for the privilege. It has been good for us thus to do it. And what we have thus done, may God give us grace always to do.

This feature of coöperation and of unsectarianism has been the more dwelt upon because it involves so fully the first great molding element mentioned above. Having faith in God as the ground of our confidence, and love to Christ and sympathy with him in saving men from their sins as our motive, our method is to send — no, not to send, but to give the means of going — to men qualified and authorized, and whom we believe the Holy Ghost sends, and to leave to them the largest discretion compatible with a faithful administration of the means intrusted to us. We say to them, So make known the truth as to bring men into a filial relation to God, and we are content to leave minor questions to the good sense of those on the ground, guided by the Scriptures and the Spirit of God.

A second feature of the work, accordant with the above, if not a necessary part of it, is the entire separation of the missionary work from any ecclesiastical organization or machinery.

This has lifted up, practically, a catholic standard; has consecrated the work in the hearts of Christians as one free from sectarian feeling and strife; and has led to united and special prayer. It has also left the missionaries free from outward ecclesiastical pressure, to take their own time and way in giving form to the new Christian communities which they have gathered from the heathen. They have been left as were the primitive missionaries, and this has often led to the precise reproduction of no one of our forms. When called upon to give their churches a name according to our shibboleths, the missionaries have declined, and have called them "apostolical." They are so. They were founded as were the apostolical churches, and going with the Scriptures instead of inspiration, the missionaries hold much the same relation to those churches that the apostles and evangelists did to the churches founded by them. They found churches; they decide in the first instance, and afterward with those churches, who may unite with them; they ordain elders, bishops, pastors; and pass on to other regions. In all this they act as ministers of Christ, amenable to the Board only as it furnishes their support, and because, having confidence in them, it does thus furnish it that they may labor for Christ. How could the missionary be more independent? We say to him, he having it in his heart, and offering to go, We have confidence in you, brother. Take the lamp of life, ask counsel if you need it, but find your own way in the darkness, and we will send you oil.

A third feature of our work, in the same line and spirit, is, that each mission is a self-governing body.

In this our missions differ from the European; but it is in accordance with the spirit of our institutions, and general habits of thought and action, both civil and religious. It is also said in the Scriptures, that " the spirits of the prophets are subject to the prophets." This makes each mission a depository of experience of great value, and forms a permanent, practical, working body, into which succeeding missionaries are received, and to which they naturally conform. It thus operates as a check upon inexperience and one-sidedness, and those excessive developments of individuality which never fail to appear where motives are stimulating and complex, and numbers are working independently for the accomplishment of a great and many-sided end.

A fourth feature of the work is directly from our estimate of the cross of Christ, and the power of that, as already mentioned.

The power is in the cross. Nothing but the mingled holiness and mercy revealed in that can quicken and regenerate the world. Holiness seen in God shows man the necessity of it to himself, and mercy renders its attainment possible. Forgiveness! Ultimate likeness to God! Let the hope of these dawn on the soul, and there is a spring of spiritual activity that will work toward its end, and in accomplishing that, will accomplish all else that we desire. The greater includes the less. Life started at the heart will work outward. Hence we make the cross of Christ the center, and value and use all else as related to that.

But can we thus reach and quicken the religious nature of the heathen? Yes, just as of others. The vital air is the same to them as to us; and so, when accompanied by the Spirit of God, are the truths revealed in the cross. He who opened the heart of Lydia can open every benighted heart, and our great hope is that he will. Hence, the conversion of men being our object, and the Spirit of God the agent, the presentation of spiritual truth and prayer must be our chief instrumentalities.

This is the spiritual side of missions; from it is their life; but with this many have no sympathy. Denying, either theoretically or practically, the efficacy of prayer, the reality of spiritual influence, and the necessity of conversion, both means and end seem to them foolishness. They either contemn the whole process and results, or, in a more dignified way, regard the missionaries and their supporters as well-meaning people, who do good on the whole ; or, appreciating candidly the outward changes wrought, they fail to connect them with their true cause.

These persons we are "not careful to answer." If we choose, we may say to them as philosophers, that we regard human destiny as turning upon *character;* that great transformations of character have been known only from the truth as it is in Jesus ; and that character being right, all desirable results of political economy and social order, and a high, pure, and permanent civilization, will follow. Or, historically, we may point them to the Sandwich Islands ; or to the Zulus in Africa ; or to unimpeachable testimony, both English and American, that our "devoted and spiritual missionaries have done more within the last twenty-five years for the enlightenment and liberty of the Turkish Empire, than all other agencies for the last fifty years ;" and we might challenge them to show similar results from other causes. But we walk by *faith.* It is enough for us that the Master has said, "Go preach my gospel." That we have done this in its primitive simplicity and power, we do not claim. There has been some diversity of views. In the different missions the general spirit and tendencies may have been somewhat different. But this has been our general aim. Experience has confirmed its wisdom, and has led and is leading us to feel more and more, that here, in distinction from all direct efforts at general enlightenment and civilization, our great strength lies.

But leaving other features of the work, we turn to the agencies — the human agencies employed, and their relation to each other. These are the Missionaries, and the Missionary Board.

Of these, the Missionaries were first. This was no scheme of men seeking agents to accomplish their own ends. The missionaries were ready and importunate to go, and the Board was formed simply as a means of sending them. From the first, missionaries have been sent only as they have offered themselves, and (with the single exception of some delay in the crisis of 1837) every one thus offering, and regarded as duly qualified, has been sent.

It is these missionaries who have done the work. All that has been done has been done by and through them. Quickened by the spirit of apostolic times, which has begun to reappear in our day, obeying the command of the Saviour, "Go ye," and sustained by his promise, "Lo, I am with you," they have not hesitated to take the one simple gospel and apply it alike to a hideous Cannibalism, to a polished Brahminism, to an Atheistic Buddhism, to an intolerant Mohammedanism, to a besotted Fetishism, and to a paganized Christianity; and, as blindness and deafness and leprosy, palsy and fever and demoniacal possession, yielded at the touch of the Great Physician, so has every form of moral evil given way before his one great remedy for the deeper maladies of man.

In thus carrying the gospel, the missionaries have exhibited the highest type of heroism, which is self-sacrifice for the highest object; while they have yet fallen so far short of Christ that there is no danger of hero-worship. Eternity alone will reveal the self-sacrifice there has been, in partings from friends and country; in exposures from climate; in privations; in standing as representatives of a foreign and antagonist system, avowing its purpose, not only, as here, to destroy all cherished wickedness of the heart, but to overthrow those external forms of religion around which the most sacred associations cluster; in the yearnings and long patience required by stolidity, by deception seemingly bottomless, by malignity; in those sunderings of affection when loved ones have died in a foreign land, and when the Christian mother, compelled to send her children from her, has turned from the shore, and with streaming eyes has said, "I do this for thee, Jesus."

For our missionaries thus devoting themselves, we claim no exemption from the common weaknesses and infirmities of men. In them, as in others, there have sometimes been strange blendings of the good and the evil; but, looking over the whole ground, this Board has special occasion for thankfulness in view of a body of missionaries so competent and efficient. I deem it no presumption to say, that in qualifications for such a work some of them have not been exceeded since apostolic times. This has been owing partly to the high qualifications demanded of candidates, and partly to the responsibility thrown upon them.

For a missionary, the two essential qualifications are, consecration and common sense. Consecration comes from piety directed into the missionary channel; but common sense, though generally supposed to be the gift of Nature, is yet her gift only in connection with the repeated and vigorous exercise of the faculties in the spheres where it is to be used, and no power is more capable of improvement. Let, then, the missionary be required, as he often has been, to provide a written language, implements, dwellings, institutions; to advance an imperfect, or to renovate an effete civilization, being thus brought into practical contact with life and man at every vital point; and whatever there is in him of a capacity for common sense will be drawn out, and the more fully the more the responsibility is laid upon him.

So have the men been formed, who, after the period of nearly a generation, have returned, and have surprised and delighted the churches by their tact, and broad experience, and thrilling eloquence, and ripe wisdom. So, as far as they have been tested, has it come to pass that the high encomium passed by the Earl of Shaftesbury upon one of our missions is not less applicable to others. This encomium, from the position and relations of its author, demands a place here. "I do not believe," says he, "that in the whole history of missions, I do not believe that in the history of diplomacy, or in the history of any negotiations carried on between man and man, we can find any thing to equal the wisdom, the soundness, and the pure evangelical truth of the body of men who constitute the American Mission. I have said it twenty times before, and I will say it again, — for the expression appropriately conveys my meaning, — that they are a marvelous combination of common sense and piety. . . . There they stand, tested by years, tried by their works, and exemplified by their fruits; and I believe it will be found that these American missionaries have done more toward upholding the truth and spreading the gospel of Christ in the East than any other body of men in this or any other age."

From the missionaries we turn to the Board. Of this the true conception is, that it is simply an instrumentality to enable Christians who can not go themselves, to fulfill by proxy the last command of the Saviour. When it does this in the best way, it answers its end; when it fails to do this, or does any thing aside from this, it does not answer its end. With every Christian the question is, or ought to be, How, soonest and best, may the gospel be preached to every creature? And, except as accomplishing this, instrumentalities and Boards are nothing. It does not appear that there were Boards of any kind in the primitive church, or that Christianity was originally propagated by any kind of associated action, whether of *a* church, or churches, or *the* church. The command to preach the gospel was not to churches as such, but to individuals. Sent by the Holy Ghost, as were Barnabas and Saul, scattered by persecution, they "went every where preaching the word;" but there was no central body with annual meetings to direct them, and to which they were required to report. It does not even appear that there was any general contribution for the spread of the gospel, the only one mentioned having been for the poor saints at Jerusalem. The method was that of individual action, with occasional consultations, as circumstances required. And this was the true method. It was this that was in the mind of Mills when he said he wished we could "break forth upon the heathen like the Irish rebellion, forty thousand strong." There is no good reason why Christian men, merchants, farmers, artisans, men of property, and men without it, should not go into heathen lands, and establish themselves there for the purpose of spreading Christianity, just as men go to California or Pike's Peak to get gold. A movement like this, spontaneous, irrepressible, requiring no agents and no Boards, would speedily do the work.

But if Boards are not required in the New Testament, neither are they forbidden. If, for the present, an intermediate instrumentality must be had, and Boards are the best, let us use them, only having them so constituted that they will be the most effective. This, this only, do we wish for this American Board. It is the pioneer and parent Board; and for the work it has had to do, and has done, perhaps it could not have been better constituted. That that work has been free from mistakes we do not claim; but we do claim that God has set his seal upon it as his; and we believe that it will stand in the past as a granite hight, looming up more and more as the distance becomes greater.

But while fifty years have but hightened our respect for that wisdom by which this Board was founded, have they not wrought silent changes in public sentiment, requiring in it some modification? If so, let it be modified. Let us have no conservatism for its own sake. When change becomes necessary to accomplish the original end of an institution, then change is conservatism. We now stand upon a hight where it becomes us to use every light of Scripture, and reason, and experience, and to be flexible to every indication of the will of God in regard to the future. Now is the time to cast off hinderances, and lay aside weights, and gird ourselves anew. We wish an organization that shall be the most efficient abroad, and work without friction at home. That we can not have till men shall be perfect. But while we would feel, economy and efficiency being secured, that the question of organization is wholly secondary, — so the water of life be only carried, it matters little how, — we would yet have, and feel that we have, the best that is practicable. We wish the churches to feel this, and would welcome — I think I may speak for the members of this Board in this — would welcome suggestions to this end. So would we work on in this imperfect way of organizations, till the hightened zeal and swelling bounty of Christians shall rise and overflow all channels of Boards, and swamp all machinery, and sweep on as a mighty tidal wave, bearing salvation around the globe.

Thus have I sought to meet the appointment of this Board, in commemorating this work of God, its features, and its instruments.

The great lessons to us of the text, and of the retrospect, are two.

The first — *that*, it may be, specially needed now — is one of humility. "Look unto the rock whence ye are hewn, and to the hole of the pit whence ye are digged." Our beginning, so feeble, was in self-consecration, in dependence upon God, in humility, and in prayer; and the method of God for the increase of his kingdom involved in such a beginning, it becomes us to weigh well. That method has not been reversed. "Except a corn of wheat fall into the ground and die, it abideth alone." The handful of corn upon the top of the mountains must germinate unseen, and give itself up to a process in which itself shall be lost, before its fruit can shake like Lebanon. So was it with Christ; so must it be with us. It is from self-sacrifice, and consecration in the very spirit of Christ, that fruit comes in this work — from these always, from these only. In carrying his gospel to others, his people *must* "fill up that which is behind of the afflictions of Christ." When the secret sympathy with him, the hidden work at the root, decays or ceases, the outward work will decay or cease. It is in vain to talk of philosophies here. The work is of God, or it is nothing; and what we have to do is to put ourselves in such a position that we can work with him. That this position is one of humility God has been fain to teach us, not by our origin alone. In various ways has he humbled us, and proved us, in all the way which he has led us these fifty years; and if now, in coming up to these hights, and looking over so great a work, there should be any of that spirit which once said, "Is not this great Babylon, that I have builded?" that spirit will be rebuked. To no place could it be more unsuited. Far rather does it become us to humble ourselves that we have done so little, to wonder at the grace that could accept of such an instrumentality, and to cry, "Not unto us, O Lord, not unto us."

Our second great lesson is one of hope. Humility and hope — these are the whole teaching of the buried seed. Seeming opposites, they are typified in nature; but Christianity alone could blend them in mutual support and augmented beauty. Humility and hope! — a hope as high as the humility is profound, because both are from our relation to the Saviour — now as crucified, now as risen. "God forbid that we should glory, save in the cross of our Lord Jesus Christ." That is humility. God forbid that we should not glory in our Lord Jesus Christ, as triumphant over the death of the cross, and as having all power given unto him in heaven and upon earth. That is hope. The work that God has begun, and to which he has pledged himself in the death of his Son, we believe that *he* will carry on. We look to a personal being; we are soldiers under the Captain of our salvation, and obey a command and rest on promises. We make a distinction, strongly pronounced, between confidence in a personal being, which is faith, and a knowledge of uniform facts and tendencies, which is philosophy; and we adopt faith as the principle of our action, not as opposed to reason, but as reason itself in its highest form. As our confidence is wholly in a personal being, it is faith; as it is confidence in God, it is also reason; and if we may but have, as we have in this work, a command that is explicit, then tendencies are no more to us than the tendency of water to a level was to the Israelites when they passed through the Red Sea. Let the waters pile themselves to the heavens, let them overarch us if they will — we move on. Let us but have such a command, and the wisdom of faith is as much higher than that of philosophy, as the wisdom and power of God are higher than those of man. Balancing tendencies alone, we should have no hope. Looking at the command and the promises, we have no doubt. We do not disregard tendencies. We think the set of the long currents is with us; but there are now, there always have been, calms, and shoals, and counter-currents, and it is only by faith that we *can* believe that the breeze shall ever spring up, and the tide rise, that shall bear us beyond them.

What the precise blending is to be of those two great elements of change, tendencies and personal interposition, or how long the unchecked current of tendencies is to run, it is not for us to say. God makes haste slowly. The bud is formed, and then winter intervenes. The baffled spring lingers. According to geology, the days were long while tendencies did their tardy work of upheavings and deposits. For four thousand years the ages were in preparation for the coming of Christ. But at length God said, "Let us make man;" at length "the Desire of all nations" came. Personality asserted a visible supremacy, tendencies were seen to be flexible to will, and special interposition reached its high-water mark, up to the present time.

But we now wait for another and broader movement. We think that prophecy and converging tendencies both indicate that we are nearing, and rapidly too, a point from which a new epoch is to open. As at the coming of Christ there were musings and forebodings, and the quickened sense caught presage of coming change, so it is now. The very air is full of its voices. The fig tree puts forth leaves. For the first time since the dispersion of men, is the world waking up to the consciousness of itself as one whole. Hardly yet do we comprehend fully the great thought of the Master, that "the field is the world." In their early dispersions, men diverged as upon a plain. That plain they now find to be a globe, upon which divergence becomes approximation and ultimate unity. The circuit of that globe, with every continent, and island, and ocean that it rolls up to the sunlight, or buries in its shadow, is now known; and this it is that we are to conquer for Christ. How wide the field, compared with that of primitive missions! How wide the work now, compared with it then! Never before was there such a theater for the action of moral forces; never before were there such forces to act; or such subordination of nature to them, giving them new facilities, and instruments of mightiest power; and never before were these forces taking their positions, and mustering themselves in such relations, as now. The old issues and specters of fear are passing. The papacy is reeling; the crescent is waning; idolatry is tottering; infidelity is shifting its ground and hesitating; the masses are upheaving. The power of those great principles of liberty and equality, which *are* Christ's gospel on its human side, is beneath them, like that of the earthquake, and oppression and slavery are seeing the hand writing upon the wall, and the joints of their loins are being loosed. And Christians are praying and giving, and when the cry comes for special help they hear it; and there is joy and thanksgiving in ten thousand hearts this night that they do; and the battalions in the great army are nearing each other, and the shout of each becomes more distinct in the camp of the other; and to-night we lift *our* shout, and hold forth the hand of fellowship in this work to all who love the Lord Jesus. And more than all, the Spirit of God is poured out, and revivals are extending, and these showers of divine grace so descend as to show what "the great rain of his strength" may be. Now the field rounds itself out into some proportion to the love of God in sending his Son; now that achievement comes up into its place for which the mighty energies that have been perverted in war and worldliness were intended; now we see the full contrast between the solitary Sufferer upon Calvary and his work; and looking upon him and upon it, we say, Yes, thou Man of sorrows, thorn-crowned and buffeted, it shall all be thine. He "shall give thee the heathen for thine inheritance, and the uttermost parts of the earth for thy possession." Looking upon him and upon it, we join our voice to that of the heavenly host, saying, "Worthy is the Lamb, that was slain, to receive power, and riches, and wisdom, and strength, and honor, and glory, and blessing."

Brethren, we rejoice that we live in this day, and may have a part in this work. It is not for us "to know the times or the seasons, which the Father hath put in his own power." It is not for the husbandman to bring on the summer. It is for him to sow and plant, and wait the movement of the heavens.

So let us, so let every Christian go forth — weeping if need be — bearing precious seed; let us sow beside all waters; let *us* see that there shall be the handful of corn upon the top of every mountain, and *God* will see that " the fruit thereof shall shake like Lebanon."

THE BOARD.

THE BOARD.

CHAPTER I.

ORIGIN OF THE BOARD.

Immediate Occasion of its Formation. — Society of "The Brethren." — The Memorialists. — Author of the Memorial. — Samuel J. Mills. — Gordon Hall. — Influence of the Andover Seminary. — Response of Leading Men in the Churches. — Institution of the Board. — Who first suggested the Idea. — Remoter Influences. — Mr. Judson's Visit to England, and its Result. — State of the Times. — Hall's Letters from Philadelphia. — Mr. Rice. — Ordination of the First Missionaries. — Previous Misgivings of the Prudential Committee.

THE American Board of Commissioners for Foreign Missions had its origin in the desire of several young men in the Andover Theological Seminary to preach the gospel in the heathen world. The four names appended to the memorial to the General Association of Massachusetts, which was the immediate occasion of forming the Board, were Adoniram Judson, Samuel Nott, Samuel J. Mills, and Samuel Newell. Mills is known to have come under a written pledge to engage in a mission to the heathen as early as September, 1808. He was a member of Williams College; and then and there a society was formed, through his agency, called "The Brethren," which had for its object "to effect, in the persons of its members, a mission or missions to the heathen." This society was transferred, with its constitution and records, to the Seminary at Andover, in the year 1809, or early in 1810, and has continued to the present time. It is distinct from the "Society of Inquiry respecting Missions," though its members are of course connected with that well-known and useful body. The memorialists were each from a different college; Judson being a graduate of Brown, Nott of Union, Newell of Harvard, and Mills of Williams. There is good reason for the belief that the hallowed flame in each of these brethren had not its origin in man. Mr. Nott distinctly avers that the "starting point and early progress" of the movement in his mind, was "without any knowledge of the existence" of those who were so soon to be his associates. He spent only one year at Andover, going thither in November, 1809. Hall, Judson, Newell, and Nott were of the class that finished its course in 1810, which was the earliest class except one in that institution. Mills was in the class of 1812. Hall was there during only a part of the last year, coming about the time of the General Association; which is presumed to be the reason his name was not on the memorial. When Judson came to Andover in 1808, he had not attained even to a confirmed belief in Christianity; but his mind was in an inquiring state, and he soon united himself heartily to the people of God. The reading of Buchanan's "Star in the East," in 1809, led him to reflect upon his duty to the heathen, and in February of the next year he resolved to devote his life to a foreign mission; not then knowing that there were others in the Seminary, or even in the country, who had come to the same resolution. The memorial to the General Association was drawn up by Mr. Judson; and his standing as a scholar and great energy of character make it quite certain that he exerted a leading influence in the measures which gave occasion to the formation of the Board at that time. But the fact that the name of Mills was attached to the memorial, though he was then in the Junior class, shows that he also was acknowledged by his brethren as a leader in this movement. Such was his shrinking from the public eye, that we may believe his name was there, and the third on the list, only at the earnest solicitation of all his associates. The names of Luther Rice and James Richards were appended to the paper, but happening to stand last, "they were struck off," as we learn from Dr. Judson, "at the suggestion of Dr. Spring, for fear of alarming the Association with too large a number." Rice was in the class of 1811. Richards had subscribed the pledge in Williams College as early as 1808, and was in the class of Mills both at college and at Andover. Hall was one of the ablest missionaries from the American churches. His graduation at Williams College — as was Judson's at Brown — was with the highest honors of his class. Mills was two years the junior of Hall in college; but, upon the conversion of the latter, in the third year of his course, the sagacity of that remarkable man singled him out for a foreign missionary; and so strong were Mills's convictions, that he declared Hall to be "ordained and stamped a missionary by the sovereign hand of God."

In the autumn of 1809, Hall received a call to become pastor of a church in Connecticut. "Then," says Dr. Ebenezer Porter, who was his theological teacher in Connecticut, — "then the heart of the missionary came out. Then was revealed the secret so long cherished between himself and his beloved brother Samuel J. Mills. These kindred spirits, associates in college, often interchanged visits afterward, mutually enkindling that holy flame which nothing but death could extinguish in their own bosoms, and which has since extended its sacred influences to so many thousands of other hearts. The general purpose of these devoted young men was fixed. Sometimes they talked of 'cutting a path through the moral wilderness of the West to the Pacific.' Sometimes they thought of South America; then of Africa. Their object was the salvation of the heathen; but no specific shape was given to their plans till the formation of the American Board of Foreign Missions. Before this period the churches were asleep. Even ministers were but half awake. To many it seemed a visionary thing in Mr. Hall, that he should decline an invitation to settle, attended with so many attractive circumstances, and so much prospect of usefulness. But I can never forget with what a glistening eye and firm accent this youthful pioneer of foreign missions, full of faith and the Holy Ghost, said, 'No; I must not settle in any parish of

Christendom. Others will be left, whose health or engagements require them to stay at home; but I can sleep on the ground; can endure hunger and hardship; God calls me to the heathen; woe to me if I preach not the gospel to the heathen.' He went; and the day of judgment, while it tells the results of his labors, will rebuke the apathy with which others have slumbered over the miseries of dying pagans."

The institution of the Andover Seminary, at the time when the Holy Spirit was interesting the minds of graduates from different colleges in the work of a foreign mission, is worthy of grateful notice. It was the only way in which they could be brought into circumstances favorable to personal acquaintance, and for associating and acting together. Nor should we omit to notice the important fact, that the missionary spirit should have been enkindled in the hearts of such men as Worcester, Spring, Evarts, and the Professors at Andover. The Seminary brought the young men where they could combine their action; and these fathers — for such they now seem, though most of them were then in the very prime of life — responded at once and cordially to their appeals. Hence the institution of the American Board of Commissioners for Foreign Missions at Bradford, by the General Association of Massachusetts, on the 29th of June, 1810. These young men and their memorial were the occasion that gave rise to the Board, but the idea and plan of it arose in other minds. The idea would seem to have first occurred to Dr. Worcester, on Wednesday morning, June 27, as he and Dr. Spring rode together in a chaise from Andover to Bradford; and the plan of it was discussed between them as they rode along. But the whole was of God, and to him be the glory.

The Rev. Kiah Bayley, writing to the Secretaries of the Board from Vermont in the year 1854, being then eighty-five years old, communicated the following incidents, which are worthy of preservation. He says, "A short time before my ordination at Newcastle, Maine, in 1797, the Rev. Alexander McLean, of Bristol, had received from his friends in Scotland the sermons delivered in London by Dr. Haweis and others at the formation of the London Missionary Society. He was charmed with them, and lent them to me. I took the pamphlet to my wife, who was then at Newburyport, and she lent it to her friends, who read it with great avidity. A subscription paper was immediately issued, and a printer engaged. The work was soon in circulation. Dr. Samuel Spring and others in Newburyport caught the sacred flame. I know not that there was any other reprint of those sermons in America. Thus I have pointed out one little rill from which your Society rose. There were others, no doubt, but I believe this was the leader. The sermons preached in London were sent to Scotland, and from Scotland to Maine, and from Maine to Newburyport. There the seed germinated, and the fruit will yet shake like Lebanon."

Messrs. Hall, Judson, Newell, and Nott completed their theological course in September, 1810, but were not able to proceed on their mission until 1812. Meanwhile, as is well known, Mr. Judson visited England to see if the London Missionary Society would arrange with the Board for a joint support of the mission; an embassy which happily failed of success. The London Directors rightly judged that two controlling powers, so widely separated, could not act with unity and decision. They also expressed the hope that as soon as the American churches became properly informed, they would furnish the means of sustaining "not only four, but forty missionaries." Those were times of non-intercourse, embargo, and commercial embarrassments in this country, and the terrible Napoleon conflicts shook the civilized world. As a passage to India seemed not likely to occur soon, Messrs. Hall and Newell went to Philadelphia, in the autumn of 1811, to pursue medical studies. Mr. Nott has shown us two letters from Mr. Hall, setting forth the feelings of himself and associates in view of their contemplated foreign mission. The first was written on the 9th of January, 1812.

"All hands upon deck! The Lord seems to be opening the door for us to enter speedily upon the mission. This even-

8

ing I providentially fell in with Captain Cumming, of the ship Amiable, of this city, who told me that his vessel would be the first to sail for India, and that by the middle of April at furthest. . . . It is currently reported that a messenger has arrived in this country from England, with a proposal to rescind the Orders in Council on a certain easy condition, to which it is said to be ascertained that our government will readily assent. But if this good news should not prove to be true, it is almost universally believed that, at any rate, the offending order will expire as soon as February, and the intelligent merchants here confidently believe that our commerce will be revived early in the spring. This is Mr. Ralston's opinion; he thinks we should get away in the spring. The prospect is such that no time should be lost. What will our Commissioners do? We shall immediately communicate this to Mr. Worcester and brother Judson. Let us bless the Lord and rejoice, but with trembling."

On the 13th of January he wrote thus: "I have seen Mr. Ralston to-day. The good man's hopes in our favor are strengthened. He has some fears. He will see the owner of the ship Amiable. Under present circumstances, we can not tell when we shall return to New England. If possible, I shall remain here until the lectures are closed, which will be the last of February. We must continue here till we learn more about a voyage to India. We should not be surprised to find that the Commissioners were not able to support us, and ourselves cast on the London Society. We have too long been in suspense."

Their suspense was relieved sooner than they expected. The Harmony, Captain Brown, proposed sailing on short notice, from Philadelphia to Calcutta, and could take the missionaries as passengers. The narration will be continued from the statement of the Prudential Committee to the Board at its next annual meeting in September.

"In the latter part of January the resolution was taken. The ordination of the missionaries was appointed to be on the Thursday of the next week — the latest day which would leave time for them to get on to Philadelphia in season. Notice was immediately given to the friends of the mission in the vicinity, and means were put in operation with all possible activity, and to as great an extent as the limited time would allow, for raising the requisite funds.

"In the mean time, Mr. Luther Rice, a licentiate preacher from the Theological Institution at Andover, whose heart had long been engaged in the missionary cause, but who had been restrained from offering himself to the Board by particular circumstances, presented himself to the Committee with good recommendations, and with an earnest desire to join the mission. The case was a very trying one. The Committee were not invested with full powers to admit missionaries, and they still felt a very heavy embarrassment from the want of funds. In view of all the circumstances, however, they did not dare to reject Mr. Rice, and they came to the conclusion to assume the responsibility, and admit him as a missionary, to be ordained with the four other brethren, and sent out with them.

"While the preparations were making, it came to the knowledge of the Committee, that the brigantine Caravan, of Salem, was to sail for Calcutta in a few days, and could carry out three or four passengers; and after attention to the subject, it was deemed advisable that two of the missionaries, with their wives, should take passage in that vessel. This lessened the general risk, and was attended with several advantages.

"According to appointment, on the 6th of February, the missionaries were ordained at the Tabernacle in Salem. A season of more impressive solemnity has scarcely been witnessed in our country. The sight of five young men, of highly respectable talents and attainments, and who might reasonably have promised themselves very eligible situations in our churches, forsaking parents, and friends, and country, and every alluring earthly prospect, and devoting themselves to the privations, hardships, and perils of a mission for life, to a people sitting in darkness and in the region and shadow of death, in a far-distant and unpropitious clime, could not fail deeply to affect every heart not utterly destitute of feeling.

Nor less affecting were the views which the whole scene was calculated to impress of the deplorable condition of the pagan world, of the riches of divine grace displayed in the gospel, and of the obligations on all on whom this grace is conferred, to use their utmost endeavors in making the gospel universally known. God was manifestly present; a crowded and attentive assembly testified, with many tears, the deep interest which they felt in the occasion; and not a few remember the scene with fervent gratitude, and can say, it was good to be there."

The Report from which this is quoted was written in September. It will illustrate the advance made by the Prudential Committee in faith and courage since the 27th of the preceding January, if we copy from their Records the results of their deliberations at that time. "The Prudential Committee met at Newburyport, for the purpose, especially, of considering the expediency of embracing, or attempting to embrace, an opportunity presented for conveying the missionary brethren to India by the Harmony, Captain Brown, of Philadelphia. After a solemn consideration of the very interesting question, they came to the following Resolves: —

"1. That, in the opinion of this Committee, the present state of the funds of the Board does not warrant the Committee to incur the expense of sending out the four missionary brethren, with their wives, with what is estimated to be an adequate sum in advance for their support. Therefore, —

"2. That, in the opinion of the Committee, under existing circumstances, it is advisable for the missionaries to go, if consistently they can, without their wives, and wait the openings of Providence for their wives to join them in the missionary field. But, —

"3. Should it be found that going without their wives would be incompatible with indispensable engagements or arrangements, the Committee will, by the leave of Providence, fit out the four brethren with their wives, and make an advance to them for their support of what is estimated to be an adequate sum for two, under the idea that, should means for supporting them all not be supplied here, a part of them may be resigned, in the last resort, to the London Missionary Society."

But what a loss of precious influence, had those wives not gone! Little was it thought by any one who saw Ann H. Judson and Harriet Newell accompanying their husbands on board the Caravan, at Salem, how soon those devoted females would both be embalmed in the memories of the church, and have an imperishable record in its history.

Referring to this meeting of the Committee, Dr. Worcester says, in one of the last letters he wrote, "When, after serious and anxious deliberation, the views of the Prudential Committee were first expressed on the question of sending the missionaries out, only one member was found decidedly in the affirmative." He does not name that member, but there is no reason to doubt it was himself. He adds, "The question was solemnly and prayerfully reconsidered. The indications of Providence, in the series of facts and circumstances which had brought the matter to that crisis, were reviewed. It seemed to be clearly the will of God that the missionaries should be sent; and the resolution was taken for the purpose, in the confidence that, by proper means, with his aid, the requisite funds could be obtained. That confidence was amply justified by the event. A lesson of immense importance was indelibly impressed upon the minds of the Prudential Committee; and on the principle then adopted, of following as Providence leads, trusting in the same sovereign Providence, with assiduous attention to the proper means for the needed supplies, have the operations of the Board ever since been conducted. From this principle may neither the Board nor the Prudential Committee ever depart. It is, I am persuaded, the vital principle of the missionary cause."

CHAPTER II.

REMINISCENCES.

Reference to Missionary Histories. — Recollections at the Jubilee Meeting. — Rev. John Keep's Recollections. — Recollections of Rev. Samuel Nott. — Recollections of Dr. Porter. — Dr. Worcester's Retrospective Address.

For more ample statements concerning the rise of the Board, the reader is referred to the Memoir of the Life and Labors of the Rev. Samuel Worcester, D. D., by his son, Dr. S. M. Worcester; and also to the Memoir of the Life and Labors of Rev. Adoniram Judson, D. D., by the Rev. Dr. Francis Wayland. In both these works, the able authors have stated the case with great fullness and accuracy.*

It will be proper, however, that we here give place for some of the recollections which were called forth by the Jubilee Meeting. There were then living only two of the members of the General Association which met at Bradford in 1810; namely, the Rev. Thomas Snell, D. D., of Brookfield, Mass., and the Rev. John Keep, now residing in Oberlin, Ohio. The infirmities of age kept the former from this meeting; but the latter was present, and the vast assembly were pleased to see how much of youthful vigor he still retained. The following statement by Mr. Keep, (from which a few passages have been necessarily omitted,) read in a firm voice audible over the whole house, added not a little to the interest of the occasion.

* See, also, an article by Dr. S. M. Worcester, in the American Theological Review for November, 1860, on the Origin of American Foreign Missions; and a Discourse by the same author at the Semi-centennial Anniversary of the Institution of the American Board of Commissioners for Foreign Missions, at Bradford, Mass., June 29, 1860.

Recollections of the Rev. John Keep.

The extremes of a half-century, at any period, furnish standpoints for surveys of marvelous interest. The extremes of fifty years back from to-day afford a contrast probably unsurpassed when judged by intervening occurrences. Of these but one claims the precedence, as characterizing the present Jubilee, viz., the rise, progress, and existing attitude of that branch of the missionary work in charge of the American Board of Commissioners for Foreign Missions.

The popular record is, that its origin was in the General Association of Massachusetts, during its sessions in Bradford, June, 1810. But, more truthfully, its birth was at an earlier period, and the Association simply wrapped it in its swaddling clothes, and appointed a nurse to collect its nutriment from the people of the country. In this there was little to attract public attention. The rise of this enterprise, like other marked movements of divine wisdom deeply freighted with good for mankind, was amid surroundings which lead us to exclaim, "Behold the stillness of God, when he rises to bless the world!"

Prayer was answered in the great revival in Yale College in 1802. Mothers were quickened to consecrate their sons and daughters to the cause of missions. Among them was the mother of Samuel John Mills, who had followed Hannah in giving her Samuel to the Lord, and whose struggling soul was at this point comforted by the conversion of her son. A child consecrated by such a mother — I knew her well — could not but experience the interfusion of her spirit. The spiritual birth of the son, then in mature age, rapidly developed the missionary equipped for service. The union of kindred spirits in Williams College, and in the Andover Theological Seminary, developed the bold, noble purpose, on their part, to begin the work of preaching the gospel to the heathen in some portion of the foreign field.

On my way to the meeting of the General Association in Bradford, June, 1810, I met, in Andover, my college classmate, Jeremiah Evarts. He invited me to be present at a gathering in the parlor of Professor Stuart, for a conference with the young men who had set their hearts upon a foreign mission, and whose memorial on the subject was to be offered for the consideration and decision of the Association. Dr. Griffin, Dr. Worcester, Rev. Mr. Sanborn of Reading, Rev. F. Reynolds of Wilmington, Professor Stuart, and Mr. Evarts, were all who had convened in answer to the appointment.* Mr. Newell gave the purpose and the wishes of the youthful missionary band. The conference was solemn, intellectual, and devotional. The conferees were not united. Mr. Sanborn expressed a deep sense of the importance of the object, and a very affectionate regard for the motives and moral courage of the young men. To him, however, the project seemed to savor of infatuation. The proposal was premature. We had work at home, more than we could do. It would be impossible to meet the expense. This was the form and substance of all opposing views in the Association. In reply, brother Worcester calmly grouped the prominent facts connected with the case. Mr. Evarts expressed his convictions that the facts justified efficient action in accordance with them. Brother Griffin, with the divine purpose deeply surging in his great soul, and God's covenant in his eye, addressed to brother Sanborn argument bathed in emotion. Professor Stuart introduced the element of faith, and brother Reynolds significantly intimated that we had better not attempt to stop God. The conference closed.

At Bradford, the statement in writing, signed by Judson, Nott, Mills, and Newell, was presented and read before the Association. It was heard with profound attention. It was a sound in the tops of the mulberry trees, and some of us held our breath.

This was followed by a frank and full statement of their views and personal experience, and the process through which

* Mr. Keep speaks from memory, after a long period. There is conclusive evidence that Drs. Spring and Snell were also present.

they reached their decision. The result was the appointment of a Board of Commissioners for Foreign Missions, and the advice that the young gentlemen put themselves under the direction of this Board. So far as I recollect, there was very little discussion. Conservatism suggested caution. All were interested in the movement; and the members generally seemed disposed to follow, in the matter, the lead of some few then present who had fully canvassed the subject. Perhaps never was the value of an intelligent leading influence more clearly seen; perhaps never was such an influence more needed or more gladly acknowledged. One thing was prominent and universal, viz., a deep sense of the sublime position and devout spiritual consecration of this missionary band. They were unpretending, modest, of a tender, child-like spirit, well understanding their aim, consecrated, a felt power. The attitude of the meeting was about this: no direct opposition, a weak faith, a genial hope, rather leaning to a waiting posture. It obviously was a relief to a portion of the body, that the subject was put into the hands of such men as those who composed the Board. In the right sense they were marked men, well suited to the emergency. This seemed to lift somewhat the pressure of the responsibility. The feeling was, *Try it;* if the project fail, it would have, from such men, an honorable burial. The kingdom of God cometh not with observation. Every feature in the opening of this great missionary movement calls us to contemplate the stillness of God. No torch-light processions, no flourish of trumpets. The kingdom of God is not in word, but in power, — the gentle footfall, the silent tread of divine love and truth to revolutionize mankind.

It is well known that the divine power, quickening the hearts of the praying people at that period, took its form, as bearing on foreign missions, in connection with the religious exercises and mutual consultations of the young men who applied to the Association. And verily they were men — tall men — in the best sense. The moral power of their position before the Association was intensified by the fact, known among the members, that Harriet Atwood, afterward the wife of Newell, and Ann Hasseltine, afterward the wife of Judson, young ladies of prominent mental culture, were bathed in the same spirit of consecration to the missionary work, and with hearts aglow with the intelligent purpose to enter the field when and where God might call them; divine Providence thus early indicating that the contemplated mission should open before the heathen with the genial influence of the Christian family. But the start of this mission lies further back, and has its origin in the spirit of prayer among the people at the opening of the present century. And here let there be no strife about names; only keep in mind that Hannah, Dorcas, and grandmother Lois are a power nearer the throne than corporate bodies and boards of managers. . . . The Lord Jesus Christ gave his life a ransom for the people, and the people heard him gladly. The people compose his church on earth, and to this very people, his church, he gave the commission to preach the gospel to all mankind. It was a significant question at Bradford, Will the churches sustain the movement? Happy was it that leading men there had well pondered this question. Griffin held his hand upon the pulse. You could read the answer in his eye — "Ay, the Church is ready!" We breathed easier. The work was begun.

Two prominent points claim the marked regard of this Jubilee Meeting: —

1. This Society sprang from the *people* — a fact which should, and which does, occupy my vision at the stand-point of 1810, where I now am.

2. Its safety in the future lies in faithfully expressing and carrying out the sentiments of the *people*.

It is for the *people*, as such, that this world was made. All its constituent parts and elements belong to mankind, to be owned, enjoyed, used, and directed with reference to the best good of the people.

I stand to-day, and here, as I never stood before. I am alone. My present stand-point is 1810. The foreign missionary enterprise an infant — but a smiling babe — prayerfully committed to the guardianship of Dwight, Treadwell, Lyman, Huntington, and others. I look across the track of a half-century, and, in the name of its primitive guardians, I hail its now colossal stature at the stand-point of 1860; and to the *present* guardians of this movement I put the question, What shall be its future? What *shall* be its future? You reply, The cross of Christ is our strength. Who but the people *support* the cross? Among the people are found the sons and daughters consecrated to missions. *Duty done gilds the future.* A present, living Christ in the soul is the inherent power. May a correct, comprehensive view, at the stand-point of 1860, infuse unction and healthful stimulants, as the coming half-century moves on, that you may reach your next Jubilee, 1910, in the fullness of the stature of perfect ones in Christ Jesus.

The Rev. Samuel Nott, now residing in Wareham, Mass., is the only survivor of the four memorialists to the General Association, and of the first company of missionaries. At the request of the Prudential Committee, he prepared the following letter, brought it with him to the meeting at which the Historical Discourse was delivered, and, not being in sufficient health for further attendance, sent it to the senior Secretary, to whom it was addressed: —

Recollections of the Rev. Samuel Nott.

Rev. and dear Sir: I proceed, according to your request, to record such memoranda of my connection with the Board as my time and strength shall permit.

The most obvious reminiscence is that forced upon me, impromptu, at my meeting with Judson in 1845, and repeated in my letter to the Rev. Mr. McCullom, at Bradford, last June, as having been for fifty years prominent in my thoughts: "All flesh is as grass, and all the goodliness thereof as the flower of the field. The grass withereth, the flower fadeth, but the word of our God shall stand forever." "You can expect but little," said Dr. Lyman to me on his way to the second meeting of the Board, "from an old man of more than three-score." It was just as true that little could be expected from the youthful agents; for youth and age were soon to vanish away as the grass, and the only just hope could be in the vital powers and divine aids which insure success to the word of God. While they perish, *it* lives and grows, indestructible and progressive.

My whole recollection of my youthful companions is, of their honest and earnest intention to publish the *word of God* — to obey the command, "Go ye into all the world, and preach the gospel to every creature." Their chief momentum seemed to me to be *a duty to be done*, and not at all a spirit of romance and adventure, or the vain conceit that they were more devoted than others who did not adopt the duty which was so plainly their own. Their perseverance through great trials to their death justifies this life-long remembrance. I may bear a like testimony to the fathers who adopted their cause. It may have been with slow steps, but they entered fully and heartily into the views and purposes of the young men, and, as it seemed to me, with the same simple intention to publish the word of God, and with the same sense of a *duty to be done*.* In both cases, it was not a mere *missionary spirit*, but rather an essential piety taking the direction of missions; not a special earnestness belonging to a special work, but Christian devotedness accepting a specific duty, as it accepts all known duties. No disparaging expressions can be just in regard to the state of religion previous to the formation of the Board. For, if there had not been a substantial Christianity ready to undertake any Christian duty, the appeal of the young men would not have been welcomed by the public, and followed by earnest and successful labors at home and

* The expression of the great moving principle — *the sense of duty* — which began the Foreign Missions, was providentially given to me in the first missionary sermon preached before the Board, at Worcester, in 1811. No arrangements had been made for a public service, and, on motion of Dr. Lyman, I was appointed to preach, because I had just delivered, at Union College Commencement, an oration illustrating the duty from our Lord's command.

abroad. The expression of Christian devotedness actually existing, was given by Dr. Woods, at the ordination at Salem, February 6, 1812, in adopting for his guide Psalm lxvii.: "God be merciful unto *us*, and bless us, and cause his face to shine upon us; that thy way may be known upon earth, thy saving health among all nations." The incidents and circumstances of the early stages of the work are superseded by the facts obvious to all, that the direct agents of fifty years ago, with a single exception, have passed away, and are of as little account as the dust of their graves; and yet, that the word which they attempted to publish has had living and glorious results. All the weakness and insufficiency are man's; all the strength and sufficiency belong to God and his word; and to God and his word all the successes of fifty years are to be humbly and devoutly ascribed.

My recollections of the course of events from June, 1810, when the Board was instituted, to October, 1815, when I left Bombay, may be summed up in Isaiah xl. 4, introducing the contrast of dying men and the ever-living word, varying it from the prophetic future to the historic past: "Every valley *was* exalted, and every mountain and hill made low; the crooked *was made* straight, and the rough places plain." I can not expect others to receive the impression made upon my own mind by difficulties which seemed impossibilities to all human skill and strength, forcing the mind to look to HIM who calleth those things which be not as though they were, and by deliverances which seemed only the work of Him "who is wonderful in counsel and excellent in working." The whole history of the five years of my connection with the Board made upon my own mind the deepest impression of the weakness and insufficiency of all human agencies, and of the divine aids and vital powers on which the progress of the word of God is acknowledged to depend.

From the first appointment of the Board, at Bradford, June 29, 1810, to the embarkation of the missionaries in February, 1812, there was every thing to discourage in the financial, commercial, and political condition of the country. The embargo had been succeeded by non-intercourse; and the war, which soon actually took place, was in the highest degree probable. Under these circumstances, the institution of the Board, and its special organization, equally adapted to the small work in hand, and the larger work which events have shown they were to do; their readiness and promptitude in sending the mission to England, and thus preparing for the unforeseen work of February, 1812; their decisive action on the arrival of the brethren Hall and Newell from Philadelphia, and fixing on February 6th as the day for ordination, with insufficient funds in prospect, — are not only evidences of their sincere desire to do their duty, but of the favor of Providence, making them equal to emergencies which only subsequent events have shown in all their importance.

A similar acknowledgment may be made in regard to the movements of the young men themselves. It was rather a guiding and overruling hand, than the foresight of an undeveloped course of events, which induced the brethren Hall and Newell to make their movement at the close of January, 1812, when there was no human prospect of funds or favor, and brought together in season the scattered missionaries within the brief time allowed. The same hand is to be acknowledged in the bequest of Mrs. Norris,* giving to the Board good hopes for the future, but requiring energetic movements for the present exigency; and in the providential arrangement, which sent forth the first mission from two places, the proper centers of the Congregational and Presbyterian churches, and united these churches in contributions sufficient for the actual necessities. The sailing of the Caravan from Salem, and of the Harmony from Philadelphia, almost exactly at the same time, and pledging both churches to the work, was an event not to have been expected; and its vast importance appears only in the light of subsequent events. How unpromising was the prospect, may be made more fully manifest by mentioning the fact, that Dr. Dwight, who was himself a member of the Board,

* Of thirty thousand dollars.

did not forbear to express himself in decided disapprobation of the action of the Prudential Committee in sending forth the mission under the actual circumstances of the case. This he did to me personally on the fourth day after the ordination at Salem; and yet, in the light of subsequent events, the rash undertaking is seen to have been wise and most important.

The course of events after the arrival of the missionaries in India was for a long time unpropitious. On the arrival of the Harmony, Mr. and Mrs. Newell were already gone to the Isle of France, and Mr. Judson was under an engagement to follow. Moreover Mr. and Mrs. Judson had already changed their sentiments on the subject of baptism, and Mr. Rice, not long after, changed his. With every conviction of their earnest sincerity, their change was deeply regretted as a hinderance to our united purpose; but it must now be acknowledged to have engaged a great denomination in the work of foreign missions, and to have blessed India beyond the Ganges with blessings above all price.

As to ourselves, remaining in connection with the Board, it is sufficient to say, that when all hope of escape from being sent to England had vanished, after we were forced to see and feel that God only could deliver us, we were delivered, as it seemed to us, by the hand of the Almighty. Our names had been already published in the Calcutta papers as passengers on the fleet, which we saw under sail for England at the mouth of the Hoogly, twelve miles in advance of the ship on which we had embarked for Bombay. On our arrival at Bombay, in February, one year after our ordination, we were met by an order from the general government that we should be sent to England from there — an order which, after friendly delays on the part of the governor of that Presidency, was upon the point of being executed, when Providence favored our escape with the intention of joining brother Newell in Ceylon, and giving up the attempt at Bombay. The same good Providence prevented the carrying out of this purpose, as it appeared afterward, that it might accomplish our original design. Arrested at Cochin, brought back to Bombay, detained under surveillance for several weeks in order to be sent by the next ship, we were delivered again, after all hope had passed, after all arrangements had been completed, and even after our baggage had been made ready for the ship, and the coolies were assembled to carry it to the boat. This deliverance, it appeared afterward, was due, under God, to the appeal to the governor of Bombay, prepared in the last extremity by Mr. Hall, and, as it seemed to me at the time, divinely fitted for the occasion. This, and all the communications of the missionaries with the governor of Bombay, were sent to the Court of Directors by the ship which was to have carried ourselves; and the result was permission from the highest authority for the missionaries to remain; but again not without the utmost hazard, and the most marked deliverance from utter defeat. This last deliverance I learned only after my connection with the mission ceased. The Court of Directors, on reviewing the papers of the missionaries, were on the point of refusing permission for them to remain, requiring their removal, and censuring all their servants who had aided them, when Mr. Charles Grant made an elaborate argument from the documents of the missionaries, which turned the vote in their favor. I regret to learn that this important paper, which Mr. Grant permitted me to copy for the Board, has been lost.

In recalling these scenes, I have reviewed several letters from our friends in India, and from Mr. Newell himself, written at the different stages of apparent defeat, on the presumption that the mission had been already defeated.

Among the providential and gracious aids to the establishment of the first foreign mission may be named the Christian death of Mrs. Newell, of which we had in Bombay full accounts from Mr. Newell. I remember its influence upon our minds in strengthening our missionary purpose, while the influence of the fuller narrative, and its wide-spread publication, is manifest to all. There may also be noticed the perfect unanimity of the two missionaries in every plan and movement; their unhesitating decision at every new and unexpected point of difficulty; their unshaken adherence to their united decisions, in the midst of objections to their course, and the counter advice of their best friends; their perseverance to extremity again and again, in the expectation of defeat and then, of censure for their rashness; and finally, their persistency in learning a language which they had no prospect of using, while yet they were intensely occupied in the most difficult affairs — all, to be ascribed to that wonder-working Providence, and I would hope to those gracious aids, which make the undertakings of frail and short-sighted men available far beyond their own foresight, expectation, or purpose. I may properly repeat, that the whole course of events, including all the decisions and movements of the leading agents at home and abroad, made upon my own mind the deepest impression of the weakness and insufficiency of all human agencies, and of the importance of the vital powers and divine aids on which the word of God entirely depends.

It was under these impressions of divine favor, making that to succeed which seemed as impossible as it was improbable, that my connection with the mission ceased, not in despondency as to the future — but, it may be, with too sanguine hopes of rapid progress to the word of God at home and abroad. Whatever disappointment has come, is partly in myself; and I can only pray that I and all may more entirely adopt the prayer given by Dr. Woods at the ordination at Salem, February 6, 1812, as the expression of the spirit which must *continue*, as well as begin, the missionary work: "God be merciful unto us, and bless us, and cause his face to shine upon us; that thy way may be known upon earth, thy saving health among all nations."

With great respect, your friend and servant,

SAMUEL NOTT.

Another testimony, which should have a place here, is that of Rev. Noah Porter, D. D., at whose house, in the year 1810, the Board held its first meeting, and where, in fact, it received its organization. The letter is dated Farmington, Conn., November 23, 1860.

Recollections of the Rev. Noah Porter, D. D.

Dear Sir: The General Association of Massachusetts, at Bradford, in 1810, designated three of the gentlemen appointed by them as "Commissioners for Foreign Missions," "to consult with other members for the purpose of appointing the time and place of the first meeting of the Board." These all belonged to Massachusetts; and it must, as I think, have been in deference to the gentlemen appointed on the Commission in Connecticut, and particularly in deference to His Excellency Governor Treadwell, that in Christian civility they appointed the place of meeting where it would best accommodate them, in Connecticut, and at Farmington, the residence of Governor Treadwell. He, as the first appointed of the whole number, was their chairman; and no doubt was chosen first in the expectation that he would be the first President of the Board. He was among the foremost of Christian laymen in New England; had been extensively known in the churches as a distinguished Christian of the Edwardean school, and an able theological writer, as well as an eminent civilian and jurist; had for many years been chairman of the Board of Trustees of the Missionary Society of Connecticut, and of its Prudential Committee; and was at that time Governor of the State of Connecticut. On receiving notice of the appointment of the meeting to be held in Farmington, foreseeing that circumstances beyond his control would make it inconvenient for the meeting to be held at his own house, he requested that it might be at mine, to which a ready consent was given. Fifty years ago, I and my wife were just starting in our course together, were in the second year after our marriage, and I was in the fourth of my pastorate. Most gladly we opened the parlor of our new house to these venerable men, and welcomed them to such hospitalities as we were able to afford. Strangers to us indeed they were not, at least in character and standing, for their praise was in all the churches, and some of them were our familiar acquaintances; but it has ever since been to us a subject of pleasing reflection, that, in a peculiar and very interesting sense, we may be said, in having received them, *to have entertained angels unawares.* Here they sat from the 10th of September, 1810, till the 12th, in prosecution of the work of their high behest — Samuel Spring, Jonathan Lyman, Samuel Worcester, and Calvin Chapin, inclusive of Governor Treadwell, five of the nine chosen at Bradford to constitute the Board. Why the other four were not present, I do not remember to have been informed, except that Dr. Dwight sent word that the concerns of the college demanded his presence, commencement being just at hand. At their invitation, I was privileged to sit with them and listen to their deliberations; to go with them, as they were feeling their way along an untrod path; to observe the very process of the formation of the American Board, — for however Commissioners had been chosen at Bradford, their formation as a Board was consummated at Farmington; to see the springing up, at the fountain head, of the little rill that in its course of fifty years has become so mighty a river, bearing life and salvation to the nations; or rather to see this angel of God pluming his wings for his flight in the midst of heaven, having the everlasting gospel to preach unto them that dwell on the earth, and to every nation, and kindred, and tongue, and people. Dr. Worcester was their scribe. Both the Constitution of the Board, and the Address which they sent out to the Christian public, while they were the fruit of the anxious deliberations and united counsels of all the members of the Board present, were, in style and form, the product of his classic pen.

Their meeting excited no general interest among the people here at the time. There was no public religious service on the occasion; nor do I remember any mention of the meeting to have been made to the congregation on the Sabbath preceding, or any notice of it to have been sent to the ministers in this vicinity. This would not have been after the customs of those times. Meetings of this kind were arranged rather for the business to be done, than for popular effect. Trustees and Committees of Missionary, Bible, and Tract Societies were accustomed to meet together in some private room, do the work assigned them, and go home, without even a knowledge of their meeting by people generally where the meeting was held. Some eight or ten years after the formation of the American Board of Commissioners, if I do not mistake the time, I was present at an anniversary meeting of the American Bible Society, in a hall of moderate dimensions, in New York, where but little was said or done for popular impression, and not more than two or three hundred people were present. There was, however, a deep-felt interest in the Foreign Missionary enterprise, here and elsewhere, at the time. The impulse that had been given to Christian feeling in our churches by the missions of the London Missionary Society, and their appeals to the Christian public in behalf of the heathen world, had not been lost; able writers on the prophecies in England and this country had brought the millennium near in the apprehension of leading men, both ministers and laymen, in the churches; and now that measures were instituted to embody them in the work, they were prepared to give these measures their ready and hearty support. A single instance, which I well remember, I may, at this distance of time, mention to you, as a specimen of what then began extensively to appear. Scarcely had the Board gone from my house, when my father, then seventy-four years old, and spending the evening of life chiefly in my family, said to my wife, "*And how much do you think I ought to give to this object?*" Her instant reply was, "*Five hundred dollars,*" which he soon afterward pledged himself to give; though, as I suppose, it was a fourth or fifth part of all that he possessed. Indeed, it seems to me that there was an enthusiasm in the missionary spirit of that day which we but rarely see now; though undoubtedly it was less diffused, and I would fain hope that it has now more of the stability and power of Christian principle and habit. In consideration of these things, I may hope to be pardoned if my attachment to the Board may seem to have something of the partiality of an early friendship; if I consider my relation to it as a member one of the highest honors that I could have received; and if, though my infirmities will probably prevent my attendance on its future meetings, I desire to die, as I have so long lived, in connection with it. I am, sir, with great personal respect and esteem, yours truly, NOAH PORTER.

Probably no one has more thoroughly investigated the early history of our foreign missions than the Rev. Samuel M. Worcester, D. D., the biographer of the Board's first Corresponding Secretary. Through his kindness we are enabled to insert portions of a speech which he delivered at the Jubilee Meeting.

RETROSPECTIVE ADDRESS OF DR. S. M. WORCESTER.

There have been great mistakes in what has often been said of the missionary spirit of those days, and of the origin of this Board. If I were at the mouth of the Mississippi, where the waters of that mighty river are emptying themselves into the Gulf of Mexico, I should not think of seeking their source by ascending to the Ohio, and thence to the fountains of the Alleghany or the Monongahela. Not any more should I refer the origin of this Board to any one individual, or to transactions in any one locality. Our God has a wide sweep in the circle of his providence, embracing manifold causes, influences, means and instrumentalities. In that providence he was pleased to lay broad and deep the strong foundations of this Board of Missions. It was once said by Dr. Lyman Beecher — and he never spoke more truly — that the American Board originated in the revivals at the end of the eighteenth and the beginning of the present century. The same testimony has just been given us by the venerable witness, [Mr. Keep,] whom God has permitted to survive to this day, and whom I am most happy to see and to hear on this occasion.

It is to me a delightful thought, that the Board thus originated not with man, but so evidently with God only wise and only good; and in such circumstances that every one, both of the missionary candidates and of the fathers and brethren who instituted this Board, should be constrained most devoutly to say, "Not unto us, O Lord, not unto us, but unto thy name give glory, for thy mercy and for thy truth's sake." I derive from this view the most animating encouragements of hope for the future. This Board, be assured, has foundations which are not soon to be moved. Whatever may be the embarrassments of the hour, there is yet a great work to be accomplished. In the fifty years to come before the Jubilee of Nineteen hundred and ten, I can not doubt, as I look back upon the fifty years now completed, there will be far more wonderful revelations of the providence of God in this glorious enterprise for the world's evangelization, than it is our high privilege this day with profoundest gratitude to acknowledge and to commemorate.

We have not the slightest reason to despond. My brother Lindley and other missionary brethren need not be troubled and alarmed, because some of us have so spoken of the importance of carefulness, that the expenditures of the Board shall not exceed the probable receipts. Let no one of them hang his harp on the willows.

When, in January, 1812, the decisive step was taken to send out the first missionaries, the first Secretary of the Board — but for whom that step would not then have been taken, and who, as his honored friend, Dr. Spring, declared, "seemed to have all the faith there was in the world" — had no adequate idea of the missionary feeling which actually existed, notwithstanding his very extensive and intimate knowledge of the state of the churches. The circulars and appeals which he sent out to different parts of New England, that if possible the means might be furnished for the new enterprise, met with a response, as I well know, even from the upper counties of New Hampshire and Vermont, which perfectly surprised and electrified his great and noble heart.

Mr. President, I hold in my hand the first subscription book ever used by an agent employed in soliciting donations. And here, sir, in the handwriting of that Secretary, is the first subscription paper circulated among the female friends of the cause. At the head of the list of names is that of Elizabeth Bartlett, with a donation of one hundred dollars; and at the end, that of Judith King, with forty dollars. There were thirty other donors, chiefly of small sums, and with no other designation than " A Friend." The whole amount subscribed by those Salem ladies was two hundred and seventy-one dollars and seventy-five cents. Mrs. Bartlett was a warm personal friend of the ever-to-be-remembered Mrs. Mary Norris, who, during the year previous, had deceased, bequeathing to the Board the munificent legacy of thirty thousand dollars. Her will was contested, and no part of the legacy was available until more than four years after her decease.

It is impossible now to realize the formidableness of the difficulties encountered in the earliest operations of this Board. Before the first missionaries had found a resting place for their feet on heathen ground, the discouragements presented to friends at home were so great and portentous, as to demand an exertion of the strongest and most heroic faith and fortitude. Let me read to you some passages from a missionary sermon, that you may see how the first Corresponding Secretary met the crisis of complicated embarrassments, which appalled so many of the sincere friends of missions, after the sailing of the Caravan from Salem, and the Harmony from Philadelphia.

The sermon was preached before the Foreign Missionary Society of Salem and the vicinity, on the first anniversary, January 6, 1813. I quote from the conclusion: —

" But, my brethren, it is not enough that you submit as the willing subjects of our glorious King; you must assist in extending his kingdom. For what purpose, indeed, do you give yourselves and all that you have to him, but to be employed in his service, that you may share in the glory of his triumphs, and sit down with him on his throne ? Do you ask how you shall assist? The answer is ready. The great work is before you — *that of giving his word to all people, in their own languages, and sending faithful men, according to his appointment, to preach it to every creature under heaven.* And every one in this house, every person in the Christian world, has an opportunity, by showing a friendly countenance to the work, by praying for its success, and by contributing as ability is given for its support and furtherance, to do something for the honor of Christ and for his possession of his kingdom.

"'*But some do not approve of this design.*' And were there not some, and of those, too, who 'made their boast in God,' who did not approve of the first publication of the gospel? In what age, indeed, in what part of the world, have the friends of Christ ever engaged in a design for the advancement of his kingdom which was not regarded with coldness by some, with jealousy by others? which was not discountenanced with derision by some, with frowns by others? which was not opposed with insidious artifice by some, with open violence by others?

"'*But it is not necessary to propagate the gospel among the heathen; they will do very well without it.*' For what purpose, then, did Christ give his blood, and command that his gospel should be preached to all people?

"'*But it is a vain attempt — the heathen will not change their religion.*' It is the word, however, of eternal truth, that all the ends of the world *shall* turn unto the Lord, and all the kindreds of the nations *shall* worship before him. Whom shall we believe? Is the arm of the Lord shortened? Is his Spirit straitened?

"'*But the missionaries will be sent back.*' That is yet to be known. But what if they are? What if some men in another part of the world, of a similar spirit with those here who hope it will be so, should undertake to obstruct the mission? Is a large and populous part of the world, for such a reason, to be blotted from the map of Christ's dominions? Or, if he permit one attempt for evangelizing a nation to fail, are his people, whose faith and perseverance he would thus try, pusillanimously to relinquish the design? Is it so, my brethren, that we have learned Christ? Then let us never more mention his name!

"'*But, if permitted to stay, they must encounter great hardships and perils.*' And pray how was it with the apostles themselves, the first missionaries of the cross? Were they not treated as the 'filth of the world — the offscouring of all things?' Did not bonds and imprisonments await them at every place? Were they not in perils continually, and in deaths oft? And did not their gracious Lord know it would be so when he sent them forth?

"'*But they are changing their sentiments.*' Men, we know, are liable to change — are liable to defection. Nevertheless the foundation of God standeth sure; nor will the grace of God fail of furnishing stable and faithful men for the missionary service.

"'*The expense must be great — it will impoverish the country.*' My brethren, how many thousands of dollars have been sent from this country to India in one year? More than enough to support, for the same time, a thousand missionaries. And for what? For articles more valuable than the souls of men? for interests more important than those of Christ's kingdom? Then, indeed, the souls of men are not worth the cost of their salvation; the kingdom of Christ is not worth the expense of extending it.

"'*But the present is an unfavorable time, for people are losing, rather than gaining property.*' Well, then, let them secure at least a small portion of what they yet have, by investing it in that kingdom which shall endure forever; by committing it to Him who will repay them with imperishable treasures. My brethren, these objections, when weighed in the balances of the sanctuary, will be found lighter than air. Men may say what they please; the profane may taunt, the pharisaical may decry, the *wise* may demur; but it is all vain. Christ will advance, and take possession of his kingdom. 'Every valley shall be filled before him, and every mountain and hill shall be made low.' The faces of those who 'make a wide mouth' shall be covered with confusion; the wisdom of the wise shall be turned into foolishness; and every opposing power shall be broken into pieces. If *you* decline the pleasure, the honor, the everlasting reward of aiding this work, others will be found

11

who will not; and the work will proceed till the shouts of salvation are heard in every clime."

I would that I could feel at liberty to proceed with some further illustrations of the events, aspects, and responsibilities of those times of trial. Indulge me a moment longer, and listen to the dying testimony of the first Secretary to the high and transcendent importance of the missionary enterprise.

"It is no light matter," he says, "to live and act for an everlasting state; and especially in public situations, connected with the momentous interests of the kingdom of God, under that eye, from which no deed, or word, or thought, or feeling is concealed, and which never loses sight of what the cross demands of every man.

"One thing is consummated, and settled in my mind; and that is, a full and delightful conviction that the cause of missions has never held too high a place in my estimation, or engaged too large a share of my attention. This is saying nothing, and less than nothing. It transcends, immeasurably transcends, the highest estimation of every created mind. And what is the sacrifice of health, what the sacrifice of life, to such a cause? Be the event what it may, recovered health, or early death, I never can regret what I have done in this work; but only that I have done so little, and with a heart so torpid." *

* Missionary Herald, 1821, p. 157.

CHAPTER III.

THE CHARTER AND THE LEGISLATURE.

Difficulties in obtaining a Charter. — Occasion of them. — The Petition. — In the House of Representatives. — Provisions of the Charter. — Proposed Amendment and its Object. — A Salem Shipmaster. — Defense by Mr. Morris. — The Bill fails. — Next Legislature. — Charter voted by the House. — Opposed in the Senate. — Mr. White's Reply. — Rejected. — Claimed by the House. — Disagreement in Conference. — Passed in Senate, with Amendments. — Amendments rejected by the House. — Mr. Crowninshield. — Charter granted. — Spirit of the Times. — Charter concurred in by Patrons. — Its Value.

No history of the proceedings by which the charter of the Board was obtained, has been written. The facts now to be given were collected from the scanty records of the Massachusetts Senate and House of Representatives, and from a few eminent men who were then in public life. Tradition relates, and the Journals of both branches of the legislature show, that the charter was obtained with difficulty, and not without some disappointment and delay. We should not greatly wonder at this, considering that the effort was made in the very year when war was declared against England, and how strong the influence of party feeling is in all such seasons of national agitation. We must also take into view the decline of evangelical doctrine and feeling in Boston and its vicinity at that period, and how large a number of professional men in the Commonwealth had received their education under influences adverse to such doctrine. Nor should we be unmindful that the great mass even of evangelical Christians were at that time slow to admit the feasibility and obligation of foreign missions.

The petition for a charter, dated February 12, 1812, and signed by Drs. Morse and Worcester, was as follows: —

To the Honorable the Senate and Honorable the House of Representatives of the Commonwealth of Massachusetts in General Court assembled:

The subscribers, for themselves and their associates, beg leave respectfully to represent: That on the twenty-seventh day of June, in the year of our Lord eighteen hundred and ten, a society was instituted "for the purpose of Foreign Missions, and for promoting the spread of the Gospel in heathen lands;" that in pursuance of the object of this association, very considerable funds have been raised; that five young gentlemen are now going on foreign missions under the directions of the said society, to the use of which missionaries they have appropriated the sum of about five thousand dollars; that the said society find it very inconvenient to manage and transact their business without an incorporation. Wherefore they pray that they may be incorporated under a suitable name, and invested with the powers and privileges usually granted to similar institutions, and authorized to do and transact business as a body politic and corporate; and as in duty bound will ever pray.

This petition was read in the House of Representatives on the 15th of February, and committed to Messrs. Rantoul of Beverly, Hathorne of Salem, and Cushman of Middleboro'. Mr. Rantoul was a gentleman of much intelligence. Though not of Orthodox sentiments, he is understood to have interested himself in the success of the petitioners, and to have enjoyed their confidence. The petition was read the same day in the Senate, and Messrs. Day and White were joined to the committee of the House. This committee recommended leave to bring in a bill, and it was granted. As the bill came originally before the legislature, it provided that the Board might hold real estate to the yearly value of six thousand dollars, and personal estate yielding an annual income of twelve thousand. These sums respectively were afterward reduced to four and eight thousand,—it is presumed to diminish the force of objections. What are now the seventh and eighth sections were not in the bill as originally reported. The first reading in the House was on the 25th of February, after which the bill was committed to Messrs. Prentiss of Roxbury, Redington of Vassalboro' (in what is now the State of Maine), and Smith of West Springfield. Dr. Prentiss was the friend and early teacher of Samuel Newell, one of the first missionaries of the Board. He lived to an advanced age, dying only a few years since, full of joy in view of the progress of the Redeemer's kingdom. It is matter of vain regret that Dr. Prentiss's early relations to the enterprise were not known until after his decease. The second reading was on the 26th, and then, or on the third reading, some one moved to add the following section: "That one quarter part of the annual income of the said Board of Commissioners shall be exclusively appropriated to defray the expense of translating the Holy Scriptures into foreign languages, and of printing and circulating the same." The object of the mover must have been unfriendly, for the act could not have been accepted in this form. So large a proportion of the entire income of the Board could not properly have been expended in translating and circulating the Scriptures in foreign languages. The amendment was greatly modified,—but whether by this or the next legislature does not appear,—so as to read that "one quarter part of the annual income *from the funds* [that is, the permanent funds] of said Board shall be faithfully appropriated to defray the expense of imparting the Holy Scriptures to unevangelized nations in their own languages;" and a clause was added, that nothing in the act should be so construed "as to defeat the express intentions of any testator or donor."

The Hon. Oliver B. Morris, of Springfield, was then a member of the House, and took part in the debate. In reply to inquiries, Judge Morris says, "I have very little recollection of the incidents attending the debate to which you refer. Nearly forty-nine years have since passed away, and almost all the particulars respecting the subject have faded from my memory. I was then a very young man, the youngest in the House, and, as I *now* think, quite too young to sit among the 'elders of the land, as a lawgiver of my people.' The debate occurred in the evening, at or very near the close of the session. A good many members participated in it, and some of them, as I thought, exhibited an illiberal spirit. A member from Salem, who had been a shipmaster trading to India, ridiculed the idea of attempting to carry the gospel to that portion of the heathen world, and said that all efforts of that kind would be worse than vain. I have no recollection of the names of other men who took part in the debate that evening. I think, however, a member from Roxbury advocated the passage of the bill. I confess I then knew nothing about foreign missions. I was induced to take the floor for the purpose of rebuking the illiberality of the opposers of the bill. I remember that I stated, on rising, my entire ignorance of the views of the petitioners, and that I had no communications from them or their friends on the subject; but I knew they were men of high standing and honest purpose, and I thought they were entitled to the favor they asked. I also remember that, while on my feet, I received suggestions from several gentlemen from Essex, friendly to the bill, so that with their aid I occupied the time of the House much longer than I intended when I first addressed the Chair. I also remember that, on the rising of the House, several gentlemen, strangers to me till then, met me and thanked me for the part I had taken. I dare not, my dear sir, after the lapse of so many years, attempt to state any thing further on the subject about which you inquire."

The gentleman from Salem, who took so active a part in the opposition, though not named by the writer, was Benjamin W. Crowninshield, afterward Secretary of the Navy under President Madison. Elbridge Gerry was at that time Governor of the State, and the ruling party in the House were in strong sympathy with him, and with the war spirit of the times, and more influenced, it may be, by the fact that the petitioners and their clerical supporters in the Commonwealth were generally on the other side, than by a feeling of direct hostility to missions. The bill failed to pass; for when the question was put, "Shall this bill be engrossed?" it was ordered "that the further consideration of it be postponed till the first session of the next General Court;" yeas, one hundred and thirty-nine; nays, one hundred and twenty. And so that House of Representatives refused to incorporate the Board.

The next legislature met on the last Wednesday of May following. Caleb Strong had been elected Governor, and there seems to have been a corresponding change in the political character of the new House, though it was otherwise with the Senate, owing to a peculiar arrangement in the senatorial districts of the Commonwealth, which the reigning party had made in the year previous. The bill was called up in the House, on the 2d of June, by Mr. Russell, of Boston, then widely known as editor of the "Columbian Centinel." It was referred to Messrs. Russell, Banister of Newburyport, and Dr. Prentiss, who reported it, somewhat enlarged, in a revised draft, which is in the handwriting of Mr. Evarts, with the names of Hon. William Phillips, of Boston, then Lieutenant Governor, and Hon. John Hooker, of Springfield, as additional corporators. Having been twice read, it was recommitted to Messrs. Dwight, Rantoul, and Hammond, and the final reading assigned for Saturday, June 6; when it passed to be engrossed, and was sent up to the Senate.

The bill seems not to have met with favor from the majority in the Senate, at least in the first instance. The Hon. Daniel A. White, of Salem, who has recently deceased,* was at that time a resident of Newburyport, and had been requested, as he informed the writer a few months since, by "his venerable friend Dr. Spring," to attend to the case. Mr. Crowninshield had been elected to the Senate, and renewed his zealous opposition to the bill, which, early in the year, had been so successful in the other body. Professing to speak from personal knowledge of missions in the East, he

* Judge White died in Salem, Mass., March 30, 1861.

represented the conduct of missionaries there as unworthy, and their labors as worse than useless. Of course the project of sending money out of the country for their support, when it was so much needed for religion at home, was to be reprobated. Mr. White replied to Mr. Crowninshield; but the newspapers made no report of speeches in our State legislature in those days, and our friend was unable to recall his argument after so great a lapse of time. In an address to the public on the subject of missions, in the year following, supposed to have been written by Mr. Evarts, it is said, that "when it was objected on the floor of the Senate of Massachusetts to the act for incorporating the Board, that it was designed to afford the means *of exporting religion, whereas there was none to spare from among ourselves*, it was pleasantly and truly replied, that *religion was a commodity of which the more we exported the more we had remaining*." There is no reason to doubt that this beautiful and suggestive reply was made by Mr. White. But it does not seem to have carried conviction to the Senate; for on the 11th of June, when the President put the question, "Shall this bill pass to be engrossed, in concurrence with the House?" the vote was in the negative. "Whereupon," says the Journal of the Senate, "Mr. White gave notice that at four o'clock in the afternoon he should move for a reconsideration of this vote." No record is preserved of such a motion, though it was doubtless made, and there is no record of the precise state of the votes in the Senate. But the other House had entered into the measure with a different spirit from their predecessors, and too deeply to give up the point; and hearing the fate of their bill, they sent a request that it might be returned to them. The Senate's Journal thus records the fact: "June 13. Mr. Knapp, of Newburyport, came up with a message from the Honorable House, to request the Senate to send down the bill entitled An Act to incorporate the American Board of Commissioners for Foreign Missions; which was sent down accordingly." After two days the House proposed a conference, — an unusual proceeding where a bill has been rejected by one branch, —and appointed Messrs. Mellen of Cambridge, Stevens of Stoneham, and Osgood of Newbury, a committee on their part. The Senate agreed to the conference, and appointed Messrs. Moody, Crowninshield, and Ripley. The conference was unsuccessful; and the Senate's committee reported on the 17th of June, — the very day when war was declared with England, — that the joint committee "could come to no agreement on the subject-matter of the difference between the two Houses, and that the Senate ought to adhere to their former vote." But the Senate, having obtained a somewhat better understanding of the case, or of the state of public opinion on the subject, rejected the report of their committee, "and the said bill, having had two several readings, passed to be engrossed, in concurrence with the Honorable House, *with amendments*." The Journal of the Senate does not inform us what these amendments were, and no one of the surviving members recollects their nature. But whatever they were, the House refused to concur in them. The Senate thereupon receded from all amendments, save one. The House Journal states, that on the 19th of June, the "Hon. Mr. Crowninshield came down from the Honorable Senate, proposing an amendment in the bill respecting Foreign Missions, and requesting the concurrence of the House, which amendment was debated, and non-concurred; and therefore Mr. Stevens was charged with a message to the Honorable Senate, stating the non-concurrence of the House." It would be interesting to know the precise ground of this last stand of the opposition, but there are no means of ascertaining it. Neither Mr. White, nor the Hon. Marcus Morton, who was then Secretary of the Senate, recollects it; though Governor Morton testifies to the fact, — which might be inferred from the Journals of the two bodies, — "that the subject excited a good deal of interest at the time." He states also his recollection, "that the opposition to the bill was very strong, and that the speeches against it were very animated and pretty violent." But the House would not recede from the stand they had taken, and so the Senate at length yielded. The Act of Incorporation, as it now stands, was passed by the House of Representatives on the 19th of June, and by the Senate on the

20th; and thus the Board acquired a legal existence, which has been of incalculable value to it, and to the cause it represents.

This narrative illustrates the opinions and spirit, which were more or less prevalent in those early times, in regard to sending Christian missionaries to the heathen. It would be gratifying to consult the debates on a measure, the importance of which not the wisest of the men concerned in it were then able to appreciate. No report, not even an abstract of the debates, probably exists. Not one of five Boston newspapers that have been consulted gives even an intimation of the discussion. Two mention the rejection of the bill by the Senate, and significantly attach a couple of exclamation points. There were then no religious newspapers, as now, to look after such matters.

On the 25th of the same month in which the charter was obtained, the General Association of Massachusetts, Drs. Spring and Morse being present, voted, "That the measures adopted by the American Board of Commissioners for Foreign Missions, in procuring the act of incorporation for securing its funds, and in the commencement of missions, meet the entire approbation of this body." In an address of the Prudential Committee, soon after, it was stated that the advantages of perpetual succession, and of holding funds under the immediate protection of the law, which could be obtained only by an act of incorporation, were highly important to secure the confidence of the American public.

This incorporation of the Board has been virtually acknowledged in all the States of our Union; and even in the remote territories of the East India Company it has been only necessary to furnish an authenticated copy of the act to secure an admission of the right of the Board to hold property in those territories. The Board has thus acquired an acknowledged legal personality, which has been found sufficient for all financial interests throughout the world. In no other way, probably, could it have gained that credit in the commercial world, which has made its bills as good as gold to its missionaries in every land.

CHAPTER IV.

CONSTITUTION AND MEMBERSHIP.

Object of the Board. — Range of its Duties. — Not a State Institution. — At first Congregational. — Proposal to the General Assembly. — Assembly's Reasons for not forming a Separate Organization. — The Board ceases to be Denominational. — Becomes National. — The Founders. — Officers. — Corresponding Members. — Honorary Members. — Number of Members. — In each State. — In Foreign Lands. — Summary. — Duties of Prudential Committee. — Working Capacity of the Board. — Wide Range of its Meetings. — Attendance of Members. — Identity of its Meetings. — Its Hold on the Affections of its Patrons.

THE "Board of Commissioners" was designed, as its name indicates, to act for others. For whom? For all who should choose to employ it; for individual Christians, churches, denominations, whoever saw fit to act through the agency it had to offer. It was created for "devising ways and means, and adopting and prosecuting measures, for the spread of the gospel in heathen lands." It was incorporated, and now exists, "for propagating the gospel in heathen lands by supporting missionaries and diffusing a knowledge of the Holy Scriptures." The Board, in its "Laws and Regulations," declares its object to be "to propagate the gospel among unevangelized nations and communities by means of preachers, catechists, schoolmasters, and the press." It thus explains its sense of the meaning of "heathen lands," in the charter, to be the same with "unevangelized nations and communities." The North American Indians are of course within its province, until they shall have been Christianized.* So are all pagan nations, and

* "This Board is limited, by charter, to the purpose of propagating the gospel in heathen lands by supporting missionaries and diffusing the knowledge of the Holy Scriptures. It hence became a serious question with the Board, whether the Indian tribes within the limits of the United States and their territories were within our limits. This question has been determined in the affirmative. The Indian tribes, but no other people of these States and Terri-

the Mohammedans. In respect to the nominal Christians of Western Asia, it is at least true, that their evangelization is an indispensable means of effecting that of the Moslems among whom they dwell. Perhaps the Board might properly have extended its missions into some of the more benighted parts of the Roman Catholic world. It did no more, however, than explore a considerable portion of South America in the years 1823–1826.*

The number of Commissioners was originally nine, all residents of Massachusetts and Connecticut, and belonging to the Congregational body. It should be noted that four of the eleven gentlemen incorporated by the Massachusetts legislature belonged to the State of Connecticut; and that the first meeting of the Board under the charter was not held in Massachusetts, but in Connecticut, under an appointment distinctly authorized by the charter. Though both of these facts would seem to have been casual, they were important. The first settled the principle, that the members of the Board need not be restricted to the State which gave the act of incorporation; and the Board has felt at liberty to elect its members from every part of the Union, and so has become a national institution. The other sanctioned the holding of its meetings in any one of the United States, and countenances the extended range of places in which they have been held — from Portland in Maine, to Detroit in Michigan and Cincinnati in Ohio.

The Board seems at first to have had no thought of becoming any thing more than a Congregational body. At its second meeting, in 1811, it suggested to the General Assembly of the Presbyterian Church the forming of a similar body of its own, with which the Board might coöperate in the work of foreign missions. The attendance of Drs. Lyman and Worcester at the General Assembly, a few months before, as delegates from the General Association of Massachusetts, may

tories, are regarded by the Board as coming within the description of heathen lands." — *Letter from Dr. Worcester*, Nov. 15, 1815.

* Missionary Herald, 1824–1826.

have prepared the way for this proposition, and perhaps also for the reply. The Assembly's response, dated June 2, 1812, was as follows: —

Having had under consideration the important and interesting vote of the American Board of Commissioners, by which they submit to the Assembly the expediency of forming an institution similar to theirs, between which and theirs there may be such coöperation as shall promote the great object of missions among the unevangelized nations, it appears proper to state, —

1. That it is matter of sincere joy, in their apprehension, to all who love the Lord Jesus Christ and the souls of men, — a joy in which the committee doubt not that the Assembly has a lively participation, — that the brethren of the American Board of Commissioners for Foreign Missions have, by the exertions they have used, and the success of these exertions, demonstrated that the churches of America are desirous to embark, with their Protestant brethren in Europe, in the holy enterprise of evangelizing the heathen.

2. That as the churches under the care of the Assembly rejoice in the foreign missions organized, and about to be organized, by the American Board of Commissioners, so, as opportunity favors, they ought to aid them, as they have in a measure already aided them, by contributions to their funds, and every other facility which they could offer to so commendable an undertaking.

3. That, as the business of foreign missions may properly be best managed under the direction of a single Board, so the numerous and extensive engagements of the Assembly, in regard to domestic missions, render it extremely inconvenient, at this time, to take a part in the business of foreign missions. And the Assembly, it is apprehended, may the rather decline these missions, inasmuch as the committee are informed that missionary societies have lately been instituted in several places within the bounds of the Presbyterian Church, which make foreign missions a particular object of their attention.

With this document before them, the Board was led to extend its membership into the Presbyterian Church; and, at the annual meeting of 1812, eight Commissioners were added from among the more prominent members of that Church, residing in the States of New York, New Jersey, and Pennsylvania. Others were also elected from New Hampshire, Vermont, and Rhode Island.

Thus did the Board prepare itself to act as a national institution in this great work; and perhaps there was never an equal number of good men associated together, for any cause, who were more deserving of general confidence. At the close of the year 1813, the Board was composed of the following persons, of whom but one now survives — the venerable Dr. Nott, of Schenectady, New York.

From MASSACHUSETTS, Samuel Spring, D. D., Samuel Worcester, D. D., William Bartlet, Esq., Joseph Lyman, D. D., Jedediah Morse, D. D., Hon. William Phillips, Hon. John Hooker, and Jeremiah Evarts, Esq.

From CONNECTICUT, John Treadwell, LL. D., Calvin Chapin, D. D., Timothy Dwight, D. D., LL. D., and General Jedidiah Huntington.

From NEW HAMPSHIRE, John Langdon, LL. D., and Seth Payson, D. D.

From MAINE, Jesse Appleton, D. D., and Gen. Henry Sewall.

From VERMONT, Henry Davis, D. D.

From RHODE ISLAND, Hon. William Jones.

From NEW YORK, John Jay, LL. D., Samuel Miller, D. D., Egbert Benson, LL. D., Eliphalet Nott, D. D., and Alexander Proudfit, D. D.

From NEW JERSEY, Elias Boudinot, LL. D., and James Richards, D. D.

From PENNSYLVANIA, Ashbel Green, D. D., and Robert Ralston, Esq.

These twenty-seven persons constituted the Board, when it actually assumed its broad, national character, and some account of them will be given in a subsequent chapter.

The charter provides for the election of a President, Vice

President, Prudential Committee, and such a number of Corresponding Secretaries and other officers as the Board shall deem expedient, who hold office till others are elected. Contracts and deeds require the signature of the chairman and clerk of the Prudential Committee, and are to be sealed with the common seal of the corporation. Members must be elected by ballot, at an annual meeting; and not less than one third of the body must be composed of respectable laymen, not less than a third of respectable clergymen, and the remaining third of "characters of the same description, whether clergymen or laymen."

At the annual meeting in 1819, a class of members called CORRESPONDING MEMBERS, was added to the Board, to be chosen by ballot, who should be composed of clergymen and laymen, residing in different, and especially in distant parts of the United States, and in other lands; and who, though it was no part of their official duty to attend its meetings, or to take part in its votes and resolutions, might yet assist in its deliberations when present, and in various ways facilitate its operations. A score of distinguished men were accordingly then chosen in the different Southern and South-western States, and about half as many in foreign lands. It soon appeared, however, that the expectations of the Board with regard to the utility of this measure were not likely to be realized; and no elections having been made in that class of members for several years, it is now nearly extinct.

The plan for another class, called HONORARY MEMBERS, adopted in 1821, has proved eminently successful. These are constituted by the payment of fifty dollars, if clergymen, or of one hundred dollars, if laymen. Though they may not vote, they have all the rights of Corporate members to move resolutions, serve on committees, and assist in the deliberations of the Board.

The following is a tabular view of the Honorary members, carefully prepared from the list in the Report of the Board for the year 1860: —

HONORARY MEMBERS.

UNITED STATES.	Clergymen.	Others.	Total.
Maine, ...	193	263	456
New Hampshire, . . .	231	453	684
Vermont, ...	208	330	538
Massachusetts, ...	790	2992	3782
Rhode Island, ...	29	119	148
Connecticut, ...	480	1095	1575
New York, ...	1034	1843	2877
New Jersey, ...	162	260	422
Pennsylvania, ...	133	264	397
Delaware, ...	8	13	21
Maryland, ...	20	20	40
District of Columbia,	16	7	23
Ohio, ...	235	266	501
Indiana, ...	43	19	62
Illinois, ...	127	148	275
Michigan, ...	85	76	161
Wisconsin, ...	38	32	70
Iowa, ...	25	16	41
Minnesota, ...	7	4	11
Missouri, ...	21	29	50
Arkansas, ...	3	9	12
Virginia, ...	64	62	126
North Carolina, . . .	20	5	25
South Carolina, . . .	18	25	43
Georgia, ...	24	45	69
Florida, ...	4	4	8
Alabama, ...	6	8	14
Kentucky, ...	18	9	27
Tennessee, ...	46	16	62
Mississippi, ...	9	14	23
Louisiana, ...	7	13	20
Texas, ...	2	1	3
California, ...	6	9	15
Oregon, ...	5	2	7
Kansas Territory, . .	3	1	4
Washington Territory	0	1	1
Choctaw Nation, . . .	8	9	17
Cherokee Nation, . .	2	3	5
Chickasaw Nation, . .	1	0	1
Unknown, ...	105	35	140
Total, . . .	4236	8520	12756

FOREIGN LANDS.*	Clergymen.	Others.	Total.
Canada, ...	37	52	89
New Brunswick, . . .	4	3	7
England, ...	23	21	44
Scotland, ...	10	13	23
Ireland, ...	5	0	5
Wales, ...	1	0	1
France, ...	6	1	7
Belgium, ...	0	1	1
Switzerland, ...	2	4	6
Italy, ...	1	0	1
Prussia, ...	0	1*	1
Russia, ...	0	4	4
Greece, ...	3	0	3
Malta, ...	1	0	1
Turkey, ...	57	40	97
Persia, ...	13	18	31
India, ...	47	25	72
Ceylon, ...	0	2	2
Siam, ...	1	0	1
Singapore, ...	1	1	2
China, ...	19	7	26
Borneo, ...	3	0	3
Australia, ...	0	1	1
Sandwich Islands, . .	35	55	90
Micronesia, ...	5	0	5
Other Pacific Isles, .	2	0	2
West Indies, ...	3	0	3
New Granada, ...	2	2	4
Chili, ...	1	4	5
Buenos Ayres, ...	1	0	1
St. Helena, ...	1	1	2
South Africa, ...	11	4	15
West Africa, ...	6	2	8
In Foreign Lands, .	301	262	563
In the U. States, . .	4236	8520	12756
Total, . . .	4537	8782	13319

SUMMARY.	Clergymen.	Others.	Total.
New England, ...	1931	5252	7183
New York, ...	1034	1843	2877
New Jersey and Pennsylvania, ...	295	524	819
Delaware, Maryland, and District of Columbia, ...	44	40	84
Virginia, and five States south, ...	136	149	285
Ohio, Michigan, Indiana, and Illinois, ...	490	509	999
Wisconsin and Minnesota, ...	45	36	81
Iowa and Missouri, ...	46	45	91
Kentucky and Tennessee, ...	64	25	89
Mississippi, Louisiana, Arkansas, and Texas, ...	21	37	58
California and Oregon, ...	11	11	22
Kansas and Washington Territories, ...	3	2	5
Indian Nations, ...	11	12	23
Foreign Lands, ...	301	262	563
Unknown, ...	105	35	140
Total, ...	4537	8782	13319

* The members in foreign lands are believed to be, for the most part, American citizens. In countries where the Board has missions, nearly all of them are missionaries.

Three hundred and fifty-eight persons have been elected Corporate members from the beginning. Of these, one hundred and fifty-three were from the New England States, one hundred and forty-one from the Middle States, forty-three from the Western States, and twenty-one from the Southern States. The number at the close of the half-century is two hundred and fourteen, distributed as follows: eighty-eight in New England, the same number in the Middle States, thirty-four in the Western States, and four in the Southern. The clergymen are one hundred and twenty-four, and ninety are laymen. As many as thirteen thousand three hundred and nineteen persons have been constituted Honorary members. One third have been clergymen, or, to speak more accurately, four thousand five hundred and thirty-seven; leaving the number of persons not clergymen eight thousand seven hundred and eighty-two. It is impossible to say how many of these are now living, but probably not far from ten thousand.

The business of originating and conducting the missions, appointing and directing the missionaries, and collecting and expending the funds, is intrusted to the Prudential Committee, who make a summary report of their proceedings to the Board at the close of each financial year. It is then the business of the Board to revise their proceedings. The duties of the Corresponding and Recording Secretaries, the Treasurer, and the District Secretaries, are distinctly and fully specified in the Laws and Regulations of the Board, and need not be stated here.

It is probable that improvements may be made in the constitution of the Board during the second half-century, as the result of experience and the progress of events. But, in point of fact, no other method of organizing missionary societies is believed to have worked with less friction, or with more power and effect than this, in the past fifty years. For an eminently experimental age of missions, for a mixed community (ecclesiastically considered) such as the Board has represented, and for the time of unsettled relations of the foreign missionary enterprise to the great moral reforms of the age, there was special need of a conservative element in the constitution of the Board; and perhaps no better method of organization could have been devised, than the one our fathers were providentially led to adopt. Of the fifty-three meetings, annual and special, forty have been held, in nearly equal proportions, in Massachusetts, Connecticut, and New York. Of the twenty-five different places of meeting, Maine, Rhode Island, New Jersey, Pennsylvania, Maryland, Ohio, and Michigan have each one, Connecticut five, Massachusetts six, and New York seven. The annual meetings, alternating between New England and the other States, have ranged from Portland to Cincinnati, a distance of more than a thousand miles. With its present organization, and the acknowledged obligation resting upon the Corporate members to attend, there is no difficulty in the Board's holding its three-days' deliberative meetings in any portion of the land. The Honorary members attending the meetings in the places most remote from each other, constitute in great measure different bodies, but it is not so with the Corporate members; and for all the purposes of trusteeship, responsibility, and an intelligent and wise administration, the incorporated Board sufficiently preserves its identity at the several meetings. Of the forty-seven Corporate members present at Cincinnati, in 1853, twenty-four were from New England and New York, and nearly forty had attended most of the meetings from the time of their election. It was so with the whole number from New England. The following table shows the attendance of the Corporate members:—

36	have each	attended	1	meeting.	13	have each	attended	14	meetings.
20	"	"	2	meetings.	11	"	"	15	"
30	"	"	3	"	9	"	"	16	"
27	"	"	4	"	2	"	"	17	"
15	"	"	5	"	4	"	"	18	"
23	"	"	6	"	4	"	"	19	"
15	"	"	7	"	1	"	"	20	"
12	"	"	8	"	8	"	"	21	"
19	"	"	9	"	3	"	"	26	"
11	"	"	10	"	1	"	"	27	"
14	"	"	11	"	1	"	"	31	"
6	"	"	12	"	1	"	"	34	"
4	"	"	13	"	52	have attended none.			

Of the thirty-six who attended but one meeting, it is certain that want of interest, in most cases, was not the reason. Of the fifty-two who never attended, fourteen were in New England, sixteen in the Middle States, eight in the Western, and fourteen in the Southern. A considerable number belonged to the Old School Presbyterian Church, which formed a Board of its own in the year 1837. In others, the southern feeling, or the infirmities of age, or early death prevented. Ninety-three of the members have averaged an attendance on fifteen meetings. The advantages afforded by such an attendance on deliberative meetings of three days' continuance, for understanding the work of missions, and acting intelligently in relation to the same, must be obvious.

Our fathers were providentially led to the existing form of organization as best adapted to their day. It was instituted solely for the spread of the gospel among the heathen, and has worked better hitherto than any one of its founders ventured to expect. The attendance and interest at its annual meetings, the responses to its appeals for funds, the number and character of the men who go as its missionaries, the success of its missions, and the standing it is permitted to hold in the estimation of Christians generally, place it on a footing with the most favored kindred institutions of modern times, whether voluntary or ecclesiastical. Nor does it appear to have less hold than any other one of the societies on the confidence and affection of its missionaries, nor upon the community to which it looks for support.

CHAPTER V.

RELATIONS TO ECCLESIASTICAL BODIES.

Relations to Contributors and to Missionaries. — To Ecclesiastical Bodies. — By the Elements of its Existence. — By Formal Recognitions. — By Donations from Churches. — By Resolutions, and other Formal Acts of General Associations, Synods, and Assemblies. — General Assembly in 1825 and 1831. — General Synod of Reformed Protestant Dutch Church. — Compact of 1832. — How understood, and the Effect. — Minute of Prudential Committee. — Objections to the Plan. — Letter to General Synod. — Synod's Response, and subsequent Proposal. — Mutual Conviction. — The Compact dissolved. — How the Connection with Missionaries was dissolved. — Mutual Tokens of Respect. — Western Foreign Missionary Society. — Old School General Assembly's Board of Foreign Missions. — The New School Presbyterians. — Relations to Ecclesiastical Bodies. — A Second Statement. — Embarrassment of Prudential Committee. — Explanatory Resolve. — The Board not an Ecclesiastical Body. — Has no Ecclesiastical Powers. — No Effect on the Ecclesiastical Relations of its Missionaries. — Scope for the two Bodies. — The Board not a Voluntary Association. — The Practical Working.

The primary relations of the Board are to its contributors, and to the missionaries under its care. To the former it is directly responsible for carrying out their known intentions; and to the latter for a wise and equitable distribution of the funds which are placed at its disposal. It is directly amenable to its patrons, and must retain their confidence and good will, or come to a speedy close. There can be no more effective control of a great working body, than the patrons of the Board silently exercise over its operations. And this controlling influence is believed to be just as effective with its present constitution, to secure conformity to the general sentiment of its patrons, as would be possible with any other constitution.

But there exist also important relations between the Board and Ecclesiastical Bodies, as such — Churches, Associations, Conferences, Presbyteries, Synods, General Assembly. Its missionaries come from these, and must receive ordination from them, and look to them for an authoritative guardianship of their ministerial faithfulness. To a great extent, moreover, these bodies are an ecclesiastical embodiment of the very people who sustain the missions; and since the Board lives on the popular Christian favor, the confidence of these bodies is indispensable to it. From the beginning, therefore, the Board has shown great deference to the ecclesiastical bodies; and it has had little reason to complain of a want of candor, kindness, and coöperation on their part.

1. It has had, from the outset, a positive connection with ecclesiastical denominations by the very elements of its existence. The original members belonged to the Congregational body, and at the first meeting after their incorporation, elected eight of the more distinguished members of the Presbyterian Church. The Board thus became as really Presbyterian as before this it was Congregational. In the following year, a member was elected from the Associate Reformed Church, along with two more from the Congregational. In 1816, one was elected from the Reformed Dutch Church, and five others within the next ten years. The membership determined, of course, the character of the institution, and connected it with these denominations. Of the present members, one hundred and five are Congregationalists, eighty-one are Presbyterians connected with the New School Church, seventeen are Presbyterians connected with the Old School Church, nine are members of the Protestant Reformed Dutch Church, and two belong to the Reformed German Church.

2. The Board has been fully and formally recognized by the ecclesiastical bodies of these several denominations, (unless the last be an exception,) as a proper foreign missionary agency for their churches. It is not necessary to speak again of its formation by the General Association of Massachusetts; of the concurrence in this act by the General Association of Connecticut; of the approval of its legal incorporation by the Massachusetts Association; of the ordination and recognition of its first missionaries by Congregational churches at Salem;

nor of the affectionate and confiding letter received from the Presbyterian General Assembly in the same year. But other kindred facts should be recorded.

(1.) A very large portion of the donations received by the Board are more or less the result of church action. The number of churches and congregations in New England, from which donations were acknowledged as the result of associated effort in the year 1839, was eight hundred and sixty-nine; and the number in the whole country, including coöperating societies, doubtless exceeded two thousand. Contributions were received, also, from not less than a thousand monthly concert meetings. The Board has been recognized and accredited as an agent in the work of foreign missions by resolutions and other formal acts of General Associations, Synods, and General Assemblies.

(2.) The amalgamation of the United Foreign Missionary Society with the Board, in the year 1825, gave occasion for a formal and emphatic recognition of the Board by the General Assembly. That Society was formed in New York City in the year 1817, by a joint committee of the General Assembly of the Presbyterian Church, the General Synod of the Reformed Dutch Church, and the General Synod of the Associate Reformed Church. The sphere of the Society's labors was among the North American Indians; and in August, 1825, it had under its care ten missionary stations, seven ordained missionaries, and twenty male and thirty female assistants. In that year, a committee from the Society attended the annual meeting of the Board at Northampton, with proposals for an amalgamation with the Board. A joint committee reported in favor of the union, and the following reasons were assigned by the commissioners from the Society: —

"That the most friendly relations and feelings now exist between the General Assembly and the Synods, and the Orthodox Associations of New England.

"That the spirit of controversy having subsided, the intelligent and candid of the Christian public are all satisfied that the same gospel which is preached in the Middle, and Southern, and Western States, is preached also in the Eastern States.

"That the missionaries of both societies preach precisely the same gospel to the heathen; and that the same regulations are adopted by both in the management of missions.

"That both derive much of their funds from the same churches and individuals; that the great body of Christians do not perceive or make any distinction between the two institutions, and consequently do not perceive any necessity for two, and regret the existence of two; and that many churches and individuals, unwilling to evince a preference for either, are thus prevented from acting promptly, and from contributing liberally to either.

"That both societies are evidently embarrassed and cramped, through the fear of collision and difficulty; and that the agents of both are discouraged, and limited in their operations by the same apprehension.

"That the objects, principles, and operations of both are so entirely similar, that there can be no good reason assigned for maintaining two.

"That the claims upon the churches are becoming so numerous and frequent, and the necessities of the destitute so urgent, that all institutions are sacredly bound to observe the most rigid economy; and that by the union, much that is now expended for the support of offices, officers, agents, &c., will be saved for the general objects of the societies.

"And, lastly, that the prevailing feeling in the churches demands a union between the two societies, and will eventually make it unavoidably necessary."

The union agreed upon at this meeting was afterward approved by the General Assembly and the General Synod; and the former, by a formal vote, commended the Board to the favorable and Christian support of the churches and people under its care. The General Synod was not ready for such a commendation at that time.

(3.) In 1831, the General Assembly appointed commissioners to confer with the Board relative to measures best adapted to enlist the energies of the Presbyterian Church more extensively in the cause of missions to the heathen. A conference was held with the Board in the autumn of the same year. These commissioners reported to the General Assembly that, in their judgment, the Board was a national institution, belonging as much to one section of the country as to another; that it fully represented the Presbyterian, Reformed Dutch, and Congregational Churches, and sustained the same relation to each; that its proceedings had been in strict accordance with this relation; that the Board, its Prudential Committee, and its missionaries, were under very high responsibility to the three denominations and to the Christian public—a responsibility peculiarly adapted to insure the purity and efficiency of the whole system; that in raising funds and in other proceedings at home, the various ecclesiastical habits of the people had been, and there was every reason to feel assured would be, regarded; that it was wholly inexpedient to attempt the formation of any other distinct organization within the three denominations for conducting foreign missions, at least until the concern should become too extensive and complicated (if that should ever be) for management by one institution; and that it was of the highest importance to their own spiritual prosperity, and to the extension of the Redeemer's kingdom on earth, that the ecclesiastical bodies and the individual churches in these connections should give the Board their cordial, united, and vigorous support.

(4.) The following year, a committee from the General Synod of the Reformed Protestant Dutch Church attended the annual meeting of the Board at New York, and proposed that a plan be arranged for the unrestricted action of that Church through the Board. Drs. Miller and Edwards, Judge Platt, Mr. Lewis, and Mr. Anderson (now the only survivor) were appointed a committee of conference. At that time, there were six members of the Reformed Dutch Church connected with the corporation of the Board, and two of its members were in the missions under the care of the Board. From the year 1816, that Church had stood in precisely the same relation to the Board as the Presbyterian and Congregational Churches, and perhaps needed only a more explicit understanding of the subject. Accordingly the report of the joint committee was chiefly occupied with explanatory statements. Having been drawn up by the writer of this, and not by the venerable chairman, he may be allowed to say, that it was not with sufficient forethought of consequences. For being understood by the Reformed Dutch Church to provide expressly for extending the distinctive organization and forms of the Church into heathen lands, that idea took such strong hold as to impair the value of the connection. Its effect was mainly to concentrate the feeling, prayers, and efforts of that Church upon the mission or missions composed exclusively of her sons. In the compact of 1832, as understood and carried out in the Reformed Dutch Church, there was another infelicity. The body responsible for the agencies at home and for procuring funds and missionaries, was not the body which appointed and directed the missionaries and was held responsible for the missions. The agencies were exclusively managed by a Board of Missions within the Church. In August, 1845, the Prudential Committee adopted a minute which was designed to be sent to the Board of Foreign Missions of the Reformed Dutch Church, unless the members of that Church present at the next annual meeting of the Board should advise to the contrary. As it is important that the working of such peculiar relations in foreign missions should be understood, a few extracts are copied from the minute. They are as follows: —

"In the opinion of the Prudential Committee, it would be favorable to the interests of the Redeemer's kingdom, were the agencies for foreign missions in the Reformed Dutch Church committed to the Prudential Committee, just as they are in respect to the churches in the Congregational and Presbyterian denominations, which furnish missionaries and funds for the system of missions under the care of the Board; but if that can not be, then it would be advisable to request the Reformed Dutch Church to assume the direction of the missionaries from that Church in the Borneo and Amoy missions; with the understanding that it shall receive every facility for so doing within the power of the Prudential Committee, the Secretaries, and the Treasurer of the Board.

"In making this movement for bringing the missions sent out from the Reformed Dutch Church, and for the nine years past under the care of the Prudential Committee, into connection with a more effective system of support, the Committee are happy to say, that their relations with their brethren of the Reformed Dutch Church have ever been most happy; while the defect they desire to see remedied is not one that can be avoided on the present system. If the home and foreign departments of the enterprise are committed to two entirely distinct Boards, it is inevitable that the missions will suffer from inadequate reënforcements, however well the different Boards are constituted, and however disposed to do their duty. The entire responsibility must needs rest on one and the same body.

"It might seem natural, after having gone through the night of adversity and trial which God usually sees fit to appoint to missions at their outset, and after the daystar has arisen at least upon a part of the enterprise, that the Prudential Committee should feel some unwillingness to have the missions go into other hands. It would not be strange if the Committee had some feeling of this sort. But they see conclusive reasons against proceeding on the present arrangement, and such difficulties may be found in the way of transferring the care of the agencies for foreign missions in the Reformed Dutch Church to the Board, that it shall be better to transfer the missions to that Church than to attempt it."

After some conference and correspondence, the Prudential Committee resolved, but not until December, that it was not then advisable to take any further action in the case. Two years later, one of the Secretaries had a personal conference with the Board of Foreign Missions of the Reformed Dutch Church, on this and other points. In the year 1851, a letter was addressed to the General Synod of that Church, stating the difficulty of obtaining missionaries. The following extracts from that letter have an historical importance: —

"If the cause of this lack of missionaries be in the nature of the connection existing between the General Synod and the Board, while we greatly value our relations to our brethren of the Reformed Dutch Church, we should still wish the cause of so great an evil removed.

"It must be obvious to the Synod, however, that the plan of operation, as agreed upon by the joint committee nineteen years ago, has been but partially carried into effect. Upon the going forth of the mission to Netherlands India, nearly the whole attention and interest of the Church appeared to concentrate upon it. It became the mission of the Church; and after the Amoy mission was commenced, the two missions were regarded as a proper and complete exponent and representative of the influence of Reformed Dutch funds and missionaries in heathen lands. The students for the ministry, and the young ministers in the Church, when pressed with the duty of becoming missionaries, have felt themselves shut up to these two missions. The appeals for new missionaries have necessarily been based upon facts belonging to these missions.

"But this was not in accordance with the joint report forming the basis of our union and coöperation. The report was designed to connect the missionary spirit and movement of the Reformed Dutch Church with the whole missionary enterprise under the care of the American Board; and by interesting Christian people in the whole, to secure their greater interest in the several parts; and especially in those portions of the system, those missions which, because they were new, for that very reason were but partially developed, and had little in themselves, excepting their necessities, to awaken an interest. We have long felt, and we feel it more and more, that the former part of this plan is important, if not essential, to the success of the latter; that the young men, especially, of the Reformed Dutch Church should realize that they are free to direct their attention to any part of the unevangelized world occupied by the missions under the care of the American Board — to Western Asia, Africa, India, Polynesia, and the Indian tribes, as well as to Borneo and China. Thus will they come under a broad and diversified system of missions, in different quarters of the world, in varied climates, religions, languages, and civilizations; and some of the missions ripening already to harvest. Thus the motive power will be greatly increased; and there is stronger probability, under the ordinary ministrations and callings of the Spirit, that the young heralds of the cross will be drawn into a favorable contemplation of the subject, and be led to a hearty self-consecration to the cause and the work of foreign missions. And thus we may expect that a greater number will be found ready to labor in the service of Christ at Amoy and in Borneo. This is the sort of scattering in missions which is sure to increase; and greatly have we desired to feel more freedom to try the effect of this plan upon the young men in the seminary at New Brunswick, and upon the younger ministers, and to see it every where in full experiment throughout the Reformed Dutch Church. Indeed, we almost despair of seeing the Borneo mission revived, as we think it should be, and the Amoy mission speedily enlarged, and a new mission established in India by missionaries from the Reformed Dutch Church, — at least through the agency of the American Board, — unless the prayers and efforts of the ministers and members of the Church are directed to a wider and more varied field than is presented by these missions alone."

The Synod, in their reply, after renewing their assurance of unabated confidence in the Board, stated that they regarded the manner in which the missionary operations had been conducted hitherto, as a proper interpretation of the wishes of the Church in respect to the future, and that they deemed it their duty to sustain their own distinctive missions.

All parties became at length convinced, that the interests of the missionary cause would be promoted by a different arrangement. As a consequence of this, the General Synod adopted the following resolutions in the year 1857: —

"1. That, considering the growth of our missions abroad; the duty of the Church, in her distinctive capacity as such, to take charge of these missions; the growing sentiment among our people in favor of such a course; and the hopeful prospect that this action will tend to call out far more largely and promptly the resources of our denomination, — we are satisfied that the time has come to dissolve the union with the American Board of Commissioners for Foreign Missions, and henceforth conduct our operations among the heathen through the exclusive agency of our own Board.

"2. That the intimate relation which has existed for a quarter of a century between the Reformed Protestant Dutch Church and the American Board of Commissioners for Foreign Missions, in the prosecution of this work, has confirmed our confidence in the wisdom, the integrity, and catholic spirit of that great and noble institution; nor shall we ever cease to feel a lively interest in the growth of its operations and the success of its plans.

"3. That, in dissolving the pleasant and useful connection we have maintained with the officers and members of that Board for the last twenty-five years, we are not influenced by any dissatisfaction with their modes of action, or any want of fidelity on their part to the terms of this connection.

"4. That we take pleasure in expressing to the American Board of Commissioners for Foreign Missions our grateful sense of the benefits derived from their experience, foresight, and enlarged views, and of the uniform Christian kindness and courtesy which have marked their intercourse with our Board.

"5. That the Board of Foreign Missions, now composed of fifteen members, be increased to twenty-four, the additional members to be chosen by the Board itself; that they be, and hereby are, empowered to arrange with the American Board of Commissioners for Foreign Missions the terms of an amicable separation, and to assume the management and control of the missions in Arcot and Amoy; and that they be authorized and directed to employ all suitable means, such as the use of the press, the appointment of agents, the holding of missionary conventions and the like, for the purpose of developing the power and exciting the interest of our churches in the great work of evangelizing the world."

These resolutions being submitted to the American Board the same year, at its meeting in Providence, the Board responded in the resolutions which follow: —

"1. That, in accordance with the proposal received from the General Synod of the Reformed Dutch Church, the Board assents to a dissolution of the compact, for the prosecution of foreign missions, which was formed with that Synod in the year 1832.

"2. That the appointment of a missionary being a personal matter, involving a mutual contract and obligation between the missionary and the Board, therefore, should the missionaries of the Amoy and Arcot missions, formed and prosecuted on the basis of this compact, request a release from their connection with the Board, the Prudential Committee is instructed to grant such a release; and also to transfer the property in those missions to the Board of Foreign Missions of the Reformed Dutch Church.

"3. That all financial questions, growing out of this business, be referred, for mutual adjustment, to the Prudential Committee and the Board of Foreign Missions of the Reformed Dutch Church.

"4. That in assenting to a dissolution of this compact, now of twenty-five years' duration, the Board gratefully acknowledges the expressions of respect, esteem, and confidence which are embodied in the resolutions of the General Synod; and it would also bear testimony to the Christian kindness and urbanity which have uniformly and eminently characterized the pastors and members of that Church, and especially the officers of its Board of Foreign Missions, in their intercourse with the officers and agents of this Board, and would give assurance of our earnest hope and prayer, that the results of the step now taken may equal the highest expectations of the Reformed Dutch Church in the promotion of the Redeemer's kingdom."

(5.) Notwithstanding the action of the General Assembly of the Presbyterian Church in 1831 and 1832, there were portions of that Church which did not act cordially through the

Board. The Western Foreign Missionary Society was formed by the Synod of Pittsburg as early as 1831. After the division of the Presbyterian Church into two bodies, called Old School and New School, in 1837, the Old School Assembly adopted that Society, under the name of The Board of For eign Missions of the Presbyterian Church. The Old School churches, however, withdrew their support so gradually from the Board, as not to occasion any serious embarrassment in the support of its missions. None of the Presbyterian missionaries withdrew from the Board in consequence of these changes; and the churches of the New School continued their relations and patronage as before.

(6.) In accordance with a recommendation from the Special Committee on the Report of the Deputation to India, in 1856, the Board gave a more definite expression to its relations to ecclesiastical bodies, in the following resolution: —

That, on the whole subject of ecclesiastical relations and organizations, the principle of the Board is that of entire non-intervention on the part of the Board and its officers; that missionaries are free to organize themselves into, or to connect themselves with, such ecclesiastical bodies or churches as they may choose, either on missionary ground or in this country; and that in organizing churches, provided the principles held in common by the constituencies of this Board be not violated, the persons to be thus organized are free to adopt such forms of organization as they may prefer.

At Philadelphia, in the year 1859, the General Assembly proposed, through a committee, that the appointments of missionaries be so disposed, whenever it is wise and practicable, as to facilitate the formation of foreign presbyteries. The report of a committee of conference, in reply to this and other propositions, was not presented to the Board until the last morning of the session; and it was afterward found by the Prudential Committee, that the portion which treated of the designation of missionaries, and the formation of foreign presbyteries, was somewhat indeterminate, and capable of a more or less enlarged application. They accordingly signified their embarrassment to the Board at its fiftieth meeting, and suggested the expediency of further conference with the General Assembly. The committee to whom this subject was referred unanimously reported, through Dr. Poor, that such conference was not called for; "it being their firm belief, that the Prudential Committee, while exercising its discretion in the appointing of missionaries, in view of all circumstances, as they may occur, and acting on the clearly-declared principle of non-intervention in ecclesiastical affairs, will be able to carry out the full intent of the phrase in question, to the satisfaction of all parties concerned."

From all that has been said concerning the constitution and ecclesiastical relations of the Board, it must be obvious that *it is not an ecclesiastical body*. This is true, notwithstanding its origin; notwithstanding its members are all in the Christian church; notwithstanding relations it may have formed with the general ecclesiastical bodies of the denominations. Appointment by an ecclesiastical body, responsibility to such a body, and individual relations sustained by members to the churches, are not of themselves sufficient to confer ecclesiastical powers on a Missionary Board. The American Board can neither organize churches, nor associations, nor presbyteries; it can not admit members to the church, nor excommunicate them; it can not ordain ministers of the gospel, nor silence them; nor can it transfer them from one denomination to another, nor change their ecclesiastical relations. The same is doubtless true of the other Missionary Boards, whether formed by ecclesiastical bodies or otherwise. Not one of them possesses ecclesiastical powers; not one of them, properly speaking, is an ecclesiastical body. All are equally powerless, in the respects above mentioned, with the American Board, which has no ecclesiastical power whatever.

Hence, if a missionary, when he comes under the direction of the Board, is connected with a presbytery, or association, that connection is not thereby in the least affected. There is no feature in the constitution of the Board which prevents the body to which he belongs from having the same authority over him after the connection has been formed, as it had before; and the ecclesiastical body is just as much bound to watch over him as a minister of the gospel, to counsel him, and to discipline him, in case there is need of it. And when his connection with that ecclesiastical body ceases, (if it ever does,) it can not be by any act of the Board, but by a regular dismission from his ecclesiastical body, that he may join some other which has grown up in the field of his missionary labors.

This is a beautiful feature in the existing methods of conducting foreign missions. For neither the churches at home, nor their ecclesiastical bodies, as such, can devote the time, nor acquire the experience, for the management of a great system of missions. It is therefore necessary to appoint trustworthy boards of agency, or else to recognize existing boards, for that purpose. The American Board has, in this respect, been signally favored, having been employed by the churches for a long course of years, and having never had its wisdom or faithfulness seriously impeached.

The Board takes ordained missionaries and lay assistants from the denominations with all their ecclesiastical relations upon them; and experience has shown that there is scope for all the direction necessary on the part of the Board, without interfering in the least with those relations, or with the performance of any of the duties growing out of them.

On the other hand, the Board is not, in the common acceptation, *a voluntary association.* A voluntary benevolent association, in the strict technical sense, is one which any man may join by paying a certain sum of money annually. Most of our national societies are constituted in this manner; and when it is alleged that the Board is otherwise constituted, it is by no means intended to imply that the mode of organization in those great societies does not combine ample means of efficiency and security. No person becomes a voting member of the Board by merely contributing to its funds. The Honorary members have the right to attend the meetings, and assist in all the deliberations; and they do attend, in far greater numbers than the Corporate members, and render most valuable assistance in the discussions at the annual meetings. But only the Corporate members vote. Hence the Board can not properly be called a voluntary association, and is not liable to the objections alleged (whether justly or not) against such. At the same time it secures most, if not all, of the advantages claimed for that class of associations, as well as most, if not all, the advantages claimed for associations created by ecclesiastical bodies.

There has been no practical difficulty, thus far, in the great ecclesiastical machinery, arising from the Board's operations. It has had only to keep within its own peculiar province. Its responsibility is for all that is legitimately involved in the collecting and use of funds. This responsibility is perfect, and is not shared with ecclesiastical bodies. It claims not to be the plenipotentiary of the churches, nor to stand in the place of the churches. Its relations are to the donors, as such, and to missionaries, as such; its responsibilities are to them. This of course involves the right and duty of judging whether a candidate is adapted to the work, and whether the missionary is faithful to his engagements. If either denies a leading gospel doctrine, as that Christ is divine, or that regeneration is by the Holy Spirit, or that everlasting punishment awaits the finally impenitent, and persists in these errors, and such as these, he may be adjudged unworthy of support, and his connection with the Board be dissolved, even though his ecclesiastical position remain unaffected. The Prudential Committee have always exercised the fullest liberty of judging as to the fitness of candidates, from whatever church, and of missionaries, however related, to receive the funds placed at their disposal. The missionaries have almost always received their appointment, necessarily, before ordination, and even before licensure. But in whatever stage they came, and from whatever quarter, in so momentous and costly an affair as sending preachers of the gospel to the ends of the earth, it was impossible to take for granted their adaptation to the missionary work; or to allow the determination of it to rest with ecclesiastical bodies, or to be adjusted by the ecclesiastical status. The Church Missionary Society of Great Britain, many years since, had occasion to assert the same right, as regards its missionaries, against the claims of certain Bishops. The Society admitted, as unreservedly as the Board does, that every missionary and candidate must be *rectus in ecclesiâ*, and that this is a point to be decided by ecclesiastical bodies; but held that the whole question of the use of the funds was exclusively for the Society to determine. It should be added, that from the first, excepting in the case of the Reformed Dutch Church, the missionaries of this Board have had their designation determined on purely missionary grounds, wholly irrespective of their denominational relations.

The experience of half a century shows, that in this there is nothing onerous. All the missions being self-governing bodies, the main responsibility rests with them. But it is for the Prudential Committee to see that the funds go, in the highest possible degree, for the propagation of the gospel. Both the missionary and ecclesiastical principles have all along worked side by side without interference.

CHAPTER VI.

EARLY CORPORATE MEMBERS.

The Character and Prosperity of Institutions affected by the Views of Founders and first Administrators. — Early Corporate Members of the Board. — From different Communities, States, and Professions. — Presidents of Colleges and Professors in Theological Seminaries. — Other eminent Ministers of the Gospel. — Eminent Civilians.

EVERY great institution takes its character, more or less, from its originators, and those who first administer its affairs. The almost unexampled prosperity of the American Board may, therefore, be safely attributed, in no small degree, to the eminently enlightened, comprehensive, and evangelical views of its founders and early members. Its leading founders were undoubtedly among the nine original Commissioners appointed at Bradford, in June, 1810. These, with a single exception, were embraced in the Act of Incorporation, and two were then added; and sixteen others were elected by the Board in 1812 and 1813. The members of the Board, thus constituted, were from several Christian communions, and from different States, professions, and walks of honorable usefulness. Without question their well-known and distinguished names, irrespective of any personal share in the deliberations of the Board, exerted a decided and auspicious influence upon its interests, by increasing its influence on the Christian public, and encouraging a more extensive and liberal coöperation, at the critical period of its inceptive or experimental enterprises. Our limits will allow us to notice them only in the most general manner. It may be most satisfactory to contemplate them in the different classes or groups, into which they naturally range themselves. We will bestow a few words upon each of them in the order of their birth.

PRESIDENTS OF COLLEGES AND PROFESSORS IN THEOLOGICAL SEMINARIES.

First on the list comes TIMOTHY DWIGHT. He was born in Northampton, Mass., in 1752, — a maternal grandson of the great Edwards; exhibited in his early years a degree of intellectual precocity almost unparalleled; was graduated at Yale College in 1774, after which he taught a grammar school in New Haven, and then was for some time a tutor in the college; was a chaplain in the army of the revolution for about a year, commencing shortly after he was licensed to preach; spent several years subsequently in his native place, dividing his time between preaching the gospel, working on a farm, conducting a school of great celebrity, and serving the State in the capacity of a legislator; was ordained pastor of the Congregational church in Greenfield, Conn., in 1783, and remained there, in the double capacity of a minister and the head of a most flourishing academy, until 1795, when he was transferred to the presidency of Yale College; which office, in connection with that of professor of divinity, he held with almost unrivaled popularity till the beginning of 1817, when he was summoned to his reward. President Dwight had a most attractive and impressive exterior — his form was erect and stately; his face finely formed, and his eye and whole expression kindling with animation and intelligence, and his movements the very perfection of grace and dignity. His mind was at once profound and brilliant, logical and imaginative; his memory was a vast and well-ordered storehouse, that suffered nothing to escape from it. In the pulpit he showed himself equally at home in the heights and in the depths: there was a majesty, a comprehensiveness, and yet a simplicity, in his presentation of Scripture truth, that left it at no one's option whether or not to listen; and there was a distinctness of utterance, and general ease, freedom, and impressiveness of manner, that formed an appropriate channel for his eloquent thoughts and expressions. As a teacher, the vast fertility of his mind, and his almost endlessly diversified stores of knowledge, combined with his graceful facility of communication, gave him a prominence which few of his cotemporaries could claim; while, as the presiding officer of the college, he was a model of thoughtfulness, dignity, firmness, and efficiency. As an author, he is quite voluminous; and his System of Theology, especially, is known and admired wherever the English language is read. There are not a few still living, who will show the estimation in which they hold him by saying, "Take him all in all, we do not expect ever to look upon his like again."

Next comes the venerable ASHBEL GREEN, another honored name, which the Church will never suffer to die. He was a native of New Jersey, and the son of an honored Presbyterian minister; was graduated at Princeton College in 1783, and afterward served his Alma Mater both as tutor and as professor of mathematics and natural philosophy; commenced preaching in 1786, and the next year was settled as a colleague of the venerable Dr. Sproat, of Philadelphia; was for several years a chaplain to Congress, and in intimate relations with General Washington; had much to do in organizing the Presbyterian Church on its present basis, as well as in establishing the Theological Seminary at Princeton; accepted a call to the presidency of the College of New Jersey in 1812, and continued in the faithful discharge of its duties until 1822, when he resigned the office and returned to Philadelphia to spend his remaining days; was occupied during his latter years in preaching up to the full measure of his ability, in writing for the press, especially in conducting a religious periodical, and in helping forward all the good objects that came within the range of his influence; and closed his eventful life, after a somewhat protracted period of decline, in May, 1848, when he had nearly completed his eighty-sixth year. Dr. Green was a man of commanding presence and intellect. He had a large frame, a fine, intellectual head, an earnest and rather stern expression of countenance, and, especially toward strangers, a somewhat stately and distant manner. His mind was logical and discriminating, his taste highly cultivated, and his knowledge extensive and varied. His discourses in the pulpit were always luminous and instructive, and delivered in an impressive manner, though his elocution was rather forcible than graceful. He had great energy and strength of purpose, while yet he was most conscientious in all his movements. Some things about him, especially in his more public demonstrations, seemed rugged and severe; but those who knew him well, knew that there was a warm and tender heart beating in his bosom. He was an eminently devout man, and his habit of devotion survived almost the entire wreck of his mental faculties. He had long been regarded as one of the fathers of the Presbyterian Church, and few had so much to do as he in the molding of its destinies.

The third on our list of worthies is JAMES RICHARDS. He was born in New Canaan, Conn., in 1767; evinced at an early period much more than ordinary intellectual tastes, but was obliged by his straitened circumstances to learn a trade; after struggling with various difficulties, became a member of Yale College in 1789, but was compelled by his poverty to withdraw at the close of the Freshman year; engaged for a while as a teacher, and then went to Greenfield and prosecuted both his academical and theological course under Dr. Dwight; commenced preaching in 1793, and was settled as pastor of the Presbyterian church in Morristown, N. J., in May, 1797; resigned his charge there, and became pastor of the first Presbyterian church in Newark, as successor to Dr. Griffin, in 1809; accepted a call to the professorship of theology in the Auburn Theological Seminary in 1823, where he remained, greatly honored and beloved, until August, 1843, when he closed his earthly career. Dr. Richards was every way a fine specimen of a man. He was upwards of six feet in height, well proportioned, with a countenance indicative of fine intellectual powers, and a most genial and kindly spirit. And his countenance was a faithful index to his character. He had a mind of great comprehensiveness and discrimination, that delighted in tracing every thing back to first principles, and especially in unraveling the intricacies of error. He was distinguished for nothing more than for practical wisdom; he saw, as if by intuition, the right and wrong of every subject that was presented to him, in connection with practical life; and hence, in all difficult and embarrassed circumstances, especially in public bodies, his presence was regarded as an element of safety. In the pulpit his manner was characterized by great solemnity and earnestness; and his discourses were full of well-digested evangelical thought, expressed in clear, forcible, simple language. As a professor of theology, he was eminently successful in conveying to the minds of his pupils the exact shade of thought as it existed in his own mind, and, while he encouraged them to independent thinking, he discouraged them, both by precept and example, from rushing into wild extremes. He adorned every relation that he sustained. He lived emphatically to bless the Church, and the Church has already testified her gratitude for his services by embalming his memory.

The name of Samuel Miller (another of this honored group) will awaken grateful and tender emotions in many hearts. His father before him, though of New England origin, was an excellent Presbyterian minister in Delaware; and there the son was born, in the year 1769. He was graduated honorably at the University of Pennsylvania, in 1789; studied theology under the direction partly of his father, and partly of the celebrated Dr. Nisbet, of Dickinson College; was ordained and installed in June, 1793, as colleague pastor of the First Presbyterian Church in New York; was transferred to Princeton, as professor of ecclesiastical history and church government in the Theological Seminary, in 1813; and after a long course of honorable usefulness in that relation, died in January, 1850. What first impressed one on meeting Dr. Miller, was his uncommonly attractive person; his face a very mirror of benevolent feeling and social refinement; his manners evincing not only great kindliness, but a degree of culture that would not have dishonored a court. In short, he was an admirable model of a Christian gentleman. His mind, though not uncommonly rapid in its operations, always moved in a luminous path, and usually reached a result which it was not easy to gainsay. His manner in the pulpit was a compound of solemnity and dignity, and was probably more thoroughly conformed to rule than is consistent with the highest efforts of pulpit eloquence. His sermons were, in a very high degree, methodical; were written always with great correctness, and sometimes with high rhetorical beauty, and were always designed and adapted to accomplish an important object. In the professor's chair, he always showed himself thoroughly at home on the subject of the recitation, though his lectures were perhaps less remarkable for bold and stirring thoughts than for well-digested and interesting details. He never tired in offices of good will to his pupils, and they in turn looked up to him with a reverence and gratitude truly filial. In his character the graces of nature beautifully combined with the graces of the Spirit to render him at once one of the most attractive of men, and one of the loveliest of God's saints.

Henry Davis (the next in order) was born at East Hampton, L. I., in 1771; was graduated at Yale College in 1796; studied theology under the direction of the excellent Dr. Backus, of Somers, Conn.; then served for several years as a tutor in the college at which he graduated; was appointed professor of divinity in the same institution in 1801; but before he felt prepared to enter upon the duties of the place, his health became so much enfeebled that he was obliged to withdraw from the college altogether; accepted the professorship of the Greek language in Union College in 1806; became president of Middlebury College in 1809, and president of Hamilton College in 1817, where he remained until 1833, when, owing to some adverse circumstances in connection with the economy of the institution, he resigned his office, though he continued to reside at Clinton till his death, which occurred in March, 1852. Dr. Davis was a man of vigorous mind, of very liberal acquirements, of ardent temperament, of heroic resolution in adhering to his own honest convictions, and of much kindliness of spirit in his social intercourse. In his preaching there was great directness, both of matter and of manner, and much to indicate that his heart was in all his utterances. He had a great distaste for all the ultraisms of the day, not caring to trust himself to any other guides than the Bible and common sense. He was the subject of a protracted decline in his latter years; but to the close of life he joined the humility and cheerful trust of the Christian with the dignity of the sage.

JESSE APPLETON (the sixth in the series we are presenting) was born at New Ipswich, N. H., in 1772; was graduated at Dartmouth College with high honor in 1792; spent nearly two years after his graduation in teaching a school, first at Dover, N. H., and then at Amherst; studied theology under the venerable Dr. Lathrop, of West Springfield; was ordained and installed pastor of the church in Hampton, N. H., in 1797; was chosen president of Bowdoin College in 1807, where he spent the residue of his life, which came to a close in November, 1819. President Appleton combined with the graces of a fine person, a striking countenance, and cultivated manners, an intellect of rare comprehensiveness and analytical power; a taste the most cultivated and exact; an exuberance of keen but delicate wit; a high sense of honor, and the most genial and kindly sympathies; and finally, a profound reverence for the great realities of religion, and a deep interest in whatever had a bearing on the spiritual welfare of his fellow-men. He was a highly attractive preacher, especially to the more intellectual portion of his audience, and his published sermons and lectures will leave no one in doubt as to the reason of it. His influence upon the college was eminently auspicious, and his name, throughout the whole region in which he lived, is a synonym at once for greatness and for goodness.

The last in this group, and the only survivor of the whole

number, is Eliphalet Nott, to whom we can now only allude, because — thanks to a gracious Providence — the grave has not yet claimed him. His birthplace was Ashford, Conn., and the year of his birth was 1773. He spent several of his early years with his elder brother, the Rev. (afterward Dr.) Samuel Nott, of Franklin, Conn.; studied for a while at Brown University, and received the degree of Master of Arts from that institution in 1795; studied theology with his brother at Franklin, and after he was licensed to preach, went as a missionary into the State of New York, and not long after became pastor of the church in Cherry Valley, where also he was the preceptor of an academy; accepted a call from the First Presbyterian Church in Albany, in 1798, where he remained till 1804, when he became president of Union College. Here he has been ever since, exerting an influence more varied and powerful than almost any other man of his generation. It will be time enough to attempt an analysis of his remarkable character when the last chapter of his eventful life can also be written.

Other Eminent Ministers of the Gospel.

At the head of this list (adopting the principle of arrangement already referred to) stands Samuel Spring. He was born at Northbridge, Mass., in 1746; was graduated at the College of New Jersey, under the presidency of the great Dr. Witherspoon, in 1771; prosecuted his theological studies partly at Princeton and partly in New England; commenced preaching in 1774, and the next year served as chaplain in the continental army; was ordained and installed pastor of a Congregational church in Newburyport, in 1777; and continued in that relation till his death, which occurred in March, 1819. He belonged to the class of ministers in New England commonly known as Hopkinsian. He had a large, well-proportioned frame, a countenance expressive at once of high intellect and great benevolence, and more than common urbanity and dignity of manners. As a preacher, he was both didactic and forcible; and on some occasions he is said to have risen to a very high pitch of pulpit eloquence. He had an almost intuitive discernment of human character — a trait which eminently qualified him for the adjudication of involved and difficult cases. When asked on his death-bed what portion of his life gave him most pleasure in the review, he replied, "That I have been permitted to preach the gospel; that I have been enabled to preach what I believe to be the system of truth; and that I have been the unexpected instrument of establishing the Seminary at Andover."

JOSEPH LYMAN was born in Lebanon, Conn., in 1749; was graduated at Yale College in 1767; served as tutor there in 1770–71; was ordained and installed pastor of the Congregational church in Hatfield, Mass., in 1772, and continued in that relation (having a colleague during his last two years) until his death, which occurred in March, 1828. Dr. Lyman had much of nobility enstamped upon his person, his countenance, his movements, his whole external bearing. His intellect was of a high order, and was especially distinguished for the bold and iron grasp which it took of every subject to which it was directed. His preaching was always sensible and logical, but never in a high degree popular. He was especially at home in deliberative bodies and ecclesiastical councils, always showing a clearness of discernment, a promptness of decision, a firmness to encounter opposition, and a perfect familiarity with parliamentary usage and rule, that were sure to make him the master-spirit of the body. He was an earnest politician, and regarded Federalism as so nearly allied to Christianity, that, in common with many other ministers of his day, he did not scruple to enter into a vigorous defense of it in the pulpit. Every thing that occupied his thoughts he saw in a strong light, and, as he was incapable of concealment, or of a temporizing policy, it was not strange that some of his deliverances did not sit easily upon every body. He had qualities that would have graced the head of a nation, and especially the head of an army. Those who have visited him at his house in old Hatfield will not need to be told that he always received his friends in a spirit of the most simple, dignified, generous hospitality.

SETH PAYSON, a son of the Rev. Phillips Payson, was born in Walpole, Mass., in 1758; was graduated at Harvard College in 1777; was ordained and installed pastor of the Congregational church in Rindge, N. H., in 1782, and continued in that charge until his death, which occurred in February, 1820. He possessed a vigorous intellect, a fertile imagination, a retentive memory, and a large fund of varied and useful knowledge. He had fine powers of conversation, and great facility at adapting himself to any peculiar circumstances into which he might be brought. He was a luminous and highly interesting expounder of divine truth, and all his services in the pulpit were characterized by great propriety and solemnity. As a pastor, he was at once eminently faithful and greatly beloved. He was for two years a member of the Senate of New Hampshire, and evinced great wisdom and tact in the business of legislation. He had a high reputation as a counselor and peacemaker, and not a few distracted congregations were indebted to his influence for their recovery of a spirit of harmony and good will. And we must not omit to state, as not the least of his distinctions, that he was the father of the late Rev. Dr. Payson, of Portland, whose life was a glowing epistle, now known and read of almost the whole of evangelical Christendom.

JEDEDIAH MORSE was born at Woodstock, Conn., in 1761; was graduated at Yale College in 1783; and from that time till 1785 taught a young ladies' school in New Haven, at the same time pursuing the study of theology under Drs. Edwards and Wales; was licensed to preach in 1785; accepted a tutorship in Yale College in 1786; spent several months preaching in Georgia and South Carolina in 1787, and returned the same year; and after occupying several different pulpits at the North for a short time, was selected as pastor of the Congregational church in Charlestown, Mass., in April, 1789.

Here he continued till the spring of 1820, when, owing to various circumstances more or less affecting his comfort, he resigned his pastoral charge, and removed to New Haven, where he continued to reside till the close of his life. Dr. Morse's life was a scene of uninterrupted labor, and was a much more than ordinarily eventful one. In the department of geography, his labors must undoubtedly be considered as marking an epoch in the science. With most of the benevolent institutions of the country that sprung up in the early part of the present century, including also the Andover Theological Seminary, he had much to do, not only in originating them, but in nursing them through the period of their infancy. In his latter years he directed much time and attention to the Christianization of our Indian tribes; and, as the result of his inquiries under a commission from the War Department, he made a report, of great and enduring interest, which was published in an octavo volume, in 1822. He was very prominent in the controversy which attended the introduction, or rather the avowal, of Unitarianism in New England; first, by publishing his "True Reasons" for opposing the election of Dr. Ware to the professorship of divinity in Harvard College; next, by projecting, and for many years sustaining, the Panoplist; and finally, by issuing a pamphlet entitled "American Unitarianism," consisting of extracts from Belsham's Life of Lindsey, which opened the controversy in which Channing and Worcester, and afterward Stuart, Woods, and Ware, were the principal writers. Dr. Morse was a man of very pleasing person and address, of great mental activity, of boundless industry, of unquenchable ardor, and of a perseverance that was proof against every thing not absolutely insuperable. He had high executive talent, as was evident from the fact of his being a prominent member or officer of so many public institutions. He was an easy, perspicuous, and classical writer, and his sermons were always evangelical and instructive, and delivered in a clear, musical voice, and with perfect simplicity of manner. Circumstances conspired to make him somewhat a man of war in his day; but it was not in that respect only that he was a man of mark. His name survives, not only in his own manifold works, but in the character and achievements of an illustrious progeny.

Calvin Chapin was born in Springfield, Mass., in 1764; was graduated at Yale College in 1788; afterward spent two years in Hartford in teaching a school; studied theology under the Rev. Dr. Perkins, of West Hartford; and, shortly after being licensed to preach, was chosen tutor in Yale College, which office he held till 1794, when he accepted an invitation to the pastoral charge of the church in Rocky Hill, Conn. In 1847, he retired from the active duties of his office; and in March, 1851, was called to his rest. He was a tall man, not very symmetrically built; very quick, and somewhat angular in his movements; shrewd, clear-headed and witty; earnest, energetic, and persevering; and caring little what others might think or say of him, so long as he was convinced that he was in the right. He was a most entertaining companion, an able preacher, and a vigorous laborer in every good cause that came within the range of his efforts or his influence. He was one of the earliest and most active promoters of the cause of temperance. He was intensely solemn in his public ministrations, but his boundless good humor in private amounted well-nigh to a passion.

Samuel Worcester was born at Hollis, N. H., in 1770; was graduated at Dartmouth College, with the highest honors of his class, in 1795; immediately after, accepted the charge of the New Ipswich Academy, at the same time pursuing his theological studies; was ordained and installed pastor of the church in Fitchburg, Mass., in 1797; resigned his charge, on account of the dislike of some of his people for his Calvinistic doctrines, in 1802; and the next year was installed pastor of the Tabernacle Church in Salem. When the American Board of Foreign Missions was formed in 1810, he was chosen its Corresponding Secretary. In 1817, finding the duties of this office, in connection with those of his pastoral charge, an overmatch for his strength, he received the Rev. Elias Cornelius as a colleague in his ministerial labors. In January, 1821, with a view to the improvement of his health, as well as to see for himself the condition of the missions in the South-west, he sailed from Boston to New Orleans, and thence passed on to the Cherokee tribe of Indians. He had the pleasure of meeting the missionaries at Mayhew and Brainerd; but by this time his health had declined so far that he was unable to proceed further; and there, among the children of the forest, he died, on the 7th of June following. He was a man of great comprehensiveness and power of mind, as well as of remarkable executive tact and ability. What he accomplished for the cause of foreign missions especially is a monument to his honor, alike noble and imperishable. There was a certain manliness and force of character, a far-reaching insight into the future, and an heroic fidelity to his own convictions, that always made his presence an acknowledged element of power. He wielded a most vigorous pen, and in controversy was well-nigh matchless. His letters to Dr. Channing, in connection with the Unitarian controversy, especially the last letter, have been considered as almost unrivaled specimens of polemic theological discussion. His published sermons are rich in evangelical thought, logically and luminously presented, and show that his ministry must have been a highly edifying one. Intellectually, theologically, practically, he might well be reckoned among the giants of his day.

ALEXANDER MONCRIEF PROUDFIT was the fourth son of the Rev. James Proudfit, who emigrated from Scotland to this country in 1754, and settled first as pastor of the Scottish Presbyterian congregation in Pequea, Pa., and in 1783 removed to Salem, N. Y., where he died in 1802. The son was born at Pequea in November, 1770. He was fitted for college partly at Salem, and partly at Hackensack, N. J., and in the latter place was under the instruction of that celebrated classical teacher, Dr. Peter Wilson. In March, 1789, he joined the Sophomore class in Columbia College, and, in 1792, graduated with the highest honors of his class. The Rev. Dr. John M. Mason was one of his early friends, and was very influential in determining the choice of his profession. He commenced the study of theology, under the direction of his father, at Salem, but after a year placed himself under the Rev. Dr. John H. Livingston, then residing in New York, and a Professor of Divinity in the Reformed Dutch Church. He was licensed to preach at Galway, N. Y., on the 7th of October, 1794, by the Associate Reformed Presbytery of Washington, of which his father was a member.

About three months after he was licensed, he was called by the congregation of Salem to settle as colleague with his father: he accepted the call, and was ordained and installed on the 13th of May, 1795. In 1802, while Dr. Mason was in Europe, soliciting funds in aid of the Theological Seminary founded by the Associate Reformed Church, Mr. Proudfit, by appointment of Synod, supplied his pulpit, laboring in the congregation with great fidelity and to general acceptance. In 1812, he was honored with the degree of Doctor of Divinity from both Middlebury and Williams Colleges. In June, 1819, he was elected Associate Professor with Dr. Mason in the Theological Seminary of the Associate Reformed Church. He accepted the appointment, but as the session commenced in November, he had little time to prepare for the arduous duties which he thereby assumed. His connection with the institution seems to have been a source of considerable disquietude to him, and it continued only during a single session. The Seminary, after suspending its operations seven years, was at length revived and established at Newburgh, and during the summer of 1833, as well as at a later period, he was occupied chiefly in endeavoring to promote its interests. In 1835, the Synod appointed him Professor of Pastoral Theology, but finding it inconvenient to reside at Newburgh, he retained the place but a short time. The same year he resigned his pastoral charge, and became Secretary of the New York Colonization Society, in which capacity he labored with untiring zeal to the close of 1842. He had one or two favorite objects yet unaccomplished when he was called to a higher sphere. He died of catarrhal fever at the house of his son, Rev. Dr. John Proudfit, of New Brunswick, in the perfect possession of his faculties, and the full confidence of entering into rest, on the 17th of April, 1843.

Dr. Proudfit was a man of a high order of intellect, of an amiable and kindly spirit, rather staid and formal in his manners, with a highly cultivated mind, and a heart always glowing with the fervors of devotion. Though his manner as a preacher was not attractive to the multitude, it was characterized by a deep sincerity and earnestness very likely to open a way to the heart. His printed discourses are of a deeply evangelical tone, sensible, pathetic, and often truly eloquent. He had great executive talents, and labored efficiently in many ways for the advancement of the cause that was most dear to him. His memory is embalmed in the gratitude and reverence of the church.

Eminent Civilians.

John Langdon was born in Portsmouth, N. H., in 1739, and was educated at a grammar school in his native place. Though the commencement of the revolution found him engaged in a profitable mercantile business, he entered with great spirit into the contest, and, at the peril of his property, and even life, he participated in the removal of the armament and military stores from Fort William and Mary, in Portsmouth harbor. In 1775, he was a delegate to the Continental Congress, but resigned his office in 1776, on account of being chosen navy agent. In 1777, he was Speaker of the New Hampshire House of Assembly; and subsequently was a member and Speaker of the State legislature, a member of the Continental Congress, a delegate to the convention that framed the constitution of the United States, and President of New Hampshire. He was one of the first United States senators from New Hampshire, and held the office until 1801.

On the accession of Jefferson to the presidency, the post of Secretary of the Navy was offered him; but he declined it. From 1805 to 1812, with the exception of two years, he was Governor of New Hampshire; and in 1812 was offered by the republican congressional caucus the nomination for the office of Vice President of the United States, which, however, on account of the infirmities of advancing age, he declined. Several of his last years he spent in retirement. During the latter part of his life, he was a member of a Congregational church, and seemed to place a high value upon Christian ordinances. His disposition was eminently social, his manners urbane, and his whole bearing exceedingly attractive.

ELIAS BOUDINOT was born in Philadelphia, in 1740, and, after receiving a classical education, studied law under Richard Stockton, one of the signers of the Declaration of Independence, and very soon became eminent in his profession. He early espoused his country's cause, and in 1777 was appointed by Congress commissary general of prisoners, and during the same year was elected a member of that body, of which also he became president in 1782, and in that capacity signed the treaty of peace. He now resumed the practice of law, but was again elected to Congress, under the new constitution, in 1789, and continued a member for six years. In 1796, Washington appointed him director of the mint of the United States, as the successor of Rittenhouse, which office he held until 1805. He was first president of the American Bible Society, and made to it the munificent donation of ten thousand dollars. He distributed his property with a most liberal hand while he lived, and by his last will bequeathed the principal part of his large estate to charitable uses. He was a man of an originally strong and highly cultivated mind, of most enlarged views, of glowing patriotism, of gentlemanly and honorable bearing, and consistent and elevated piety.

JEDIDIAH HUNTINGTON was born in Norwich, Conn., in the year 1743; was graduated with high honor at Harvard

College in 1763; and soon after engaged in commercial pursuits. He entered the continental army in command of a regiment in 1775, and in 1777 was appointed by Congress a brigadier general. After the war, he served as sheriff of the county in which he lived, and as treasurer of the State. In 1789, he was appointed collector of the port of New London, and held the office twenty-six years. He served his country honorably during the stirring scenes of the revolution, and he served his God faithfully from early manhood to the close of his life. He was not only a member, but an officer of the church, and was a fine model of a finished gentleman. God had given him not only large means, but a large heart, thus rendering him a great public benefactor.

JOHN TREADWELL was born in Farmington, Conn., in 1745; graduated at Yale College in 1767; studied law under Titus Hosmer, of Middletown, and then settled in his native town, but without engaging in the practice. He was a zealous patriot in the revolution, and was a representative of the town to the General Assembly for many years, commencing with 1776. In 1785, he was elected one of the assistants, and was annually reëlected to this office till 1798, when he was chosen Lieutenant Governor. In the autumn of 1809, on the decease of Governor Trumbull, he was chosen, by the legislature, to the office of Governor; and, by a renewal of the appointment at their session in May, he was continued in that office during the following year. He occupied also, at different periods, several respectable judicial positions, and was for a long time one of the most influential members of the corporation of Yale College. He was distinguished rather for excellent common sense and good judgment, than for any of those qualities which enter into the idea of genius. His opinions were carefully formed, and were held with great tenacity, and no temptation was powerful enough to occasion the least faltering of his fidelity to the true and the right. He was a most diligent student of the Scriptures, an earnest friend of evangelical religion, and a humble and devout worshiper of God. He died in August, 1823, aged seventy-seven years.

JOHN JAY was born in the city of New York, in 1745; was graduated at King's College in 1764, after which he studied law, and in 1768 was admitted to the bar. The high professional reputation which he very soon acquired, as well as his unyielding integrity and fervent patriotism, attracted the eyes of his fellow-citizens toward him as a suitable person to be put forward in the opening contest for independence. Accordingly, he was appointed to the first American Congress in 1774; and he was the writer of the eloquent address to the people of Great Britain, which was adopted by Congress in the autumn of that year. In 1776, he was recalled to assist in framing the government of New York. After the fall of New York and the removal of the Provincial Assembly to Poughkeepsie, his mind was constantly at work, and his pen often, in performing good service for his country. From 1777 to 1779, he was Chief Justice of the State, but resigned the office in consequence of his duties as President of Congress. In 1779, he was appointed Minister Plenipotentiary to the court of Spain. In 1782, he was appointed a commissioner to negotiate a peace with Great Britain; and he signed the definitive treaty at Paris, in September, 1783. In 1784, he returned to this country, and, even before his arrival, had been appointed by Congress Secretary of State for Foreign Affairs. In 1789, he was appointed by Washington Chief Justice of the United States. In 1794, he was appointed Minister Plenipotentiary to Great Britain, and was instrumental in effecting the famous treaty which bears his name. In 1795 he was elected, and in 1798 he was reëlected, Governor of the State of New York. In the summer of 1800, he withdrew from the cares of public life, and took up his residence in Bedford, N. Y., where, in dignified retirement, he passed the residue of his days, and died in May, 1829, aged eighty-four years. With splendid powers of intellect, cultivated by the best educational advantages, he combined the most unswerving integrity and intense devotion to the interests of his country and his race. He never held any public office but that his character reflected honor upon it. He was a devout member of the Protestant Episcopal Church, and much of his time during his last years was given to studying the Scriptures, and devout meditation on religious subjects. His patriotism was of a truly Christian type; his religion was at once calm, earnest, and consistent; and both the church and the state are pledged that his memory shall be fragrant with coming generations.

Egbert Benson was born (it is believed in the city of New York) in the year 1747. He was graduated at King's (now Columbia) College in 1765; studied law, and rose to eminence in his profession. He was a member of Congress from 1784 to 1788; and was subsequently Judge of the Supreme Court of New York, and also of the Circuit Court of the United States for the district of New York. In person he was rather short and thick-set, with an expression of countenance that betokened much kindly feeling. He was highly intellectual in his tastes, and had acquired a vast amount of general information, while he was more especially versed in literary and historical antiquities. He was for many years an exemplary member of the Reformed Dutch Church, and his life was in beautiful harmony with his Christian profession. He was a most genial and entertaining companion, having always something to impart from the vast and varied stores of facts and incidents treasured in his memory, suited to every occasion.

William Bartlet was born in Newburyport, Mass., in the year 1748. He began life in comparative poverty, and spent the years of his minority with his father, sharing with him the labors of a humble occupation; but he succeeded at length in becoming owner, in part, of a vessel employed in trade. This was the first step in the course that resulted in his becoming one of the most opulent men in the country. Though he was not a little embarrassed in his commercial pursuits by the war of the revolution, the return of peace marked a decided epoch in his pecuniary prosperity, and from that period to nearly the close of his long life, he might be said to be actively engaged in business. He was a man of a firm, athletic frame, of a vigorous and discriminating mind, of great decision, and most persevering industry. He took a deep interest in all that pertained to the well-being of society, was a warm friend to divine institutions, and a diligent student of the Holy Scriptures; but it is believed that for some reason, known perhaps only to himself, he never made a public profession of religion. But that for which he was most distinguished, was the princely munificence which he manifested in relation to the numerous and varied objects of public and private charity. His well-known liberality toward the Theological Seminary at Andover would alone be sufficient to place him among the most distinguished of our public benefactors. He died at Newburyport, where he had spent his whole life, on the 8th of February, 1841, aged ninety-three years.

William Phillips was born in Boston in the year 1750, and being prevented by a feeble constitution from receiving a collegiate education, he engaged in mercantile pursuits with his father, from whom, in due time, he inherited an immense fortune. He was for a long time a representative in the State legislature, was more than once an elector at large of the President of the United States, and was for several years Lieutenant Governor of Massachusetts. In stature, he was scarcely up to the medium height; his countenance was expressive of the utmost benignity; and his manners, though highly polished and worthy of his exalted position in society, were as simple as childhood. In his natural disposition, he was generous and affectionate; he abhorred every thing like intrigue or cunning, and in all his business relations was scrupulously exact in meeting all the claims of justice. He was thoroughly evangelical in his creed, and eminently blameless and consistent in his life. His benevolence scarcely knew a limit; for many years before his death, his annual contributions to charitable objects were from eight to eleven thousand dollars; and by his will he contributed to the same class of objects upwards of sixty thousand dollars. He died in Boston, on the 26th of May, 1827, aged seventy-seven years.

HENRY SEWALL was born in York, Me., in 1752. From his father he learned the mason's trade, and worked at it in his earlier years. He early became deeply imbued with the spirit of the revolution, and having joined the army in 1775, he continued his connection with it until the peace. As he had the title, for many years, of "General" Sewall, it is presumed that subsequently to the revolution he was connected with the militia of his own State. When the Congregational church was formed in Hallowell, in 1791, he united with it and became its deacon. He was a man of more than ordinary talents; of highly cultivated mind, considering his opportunities; of an uncommonly meek and benevolent spirit; and of most earnest devotion to the cause of Christ. He studied the Bible closely and critically, and admitted nothing as an article of his creed for which he could not give what was to himself, at least, a satisfactory reason. He was greatly respected and honored throughout the whole region in which he lived for his intelligence, benevolence, piety, and active usefulness. He died at Augusta, Me., in September, 1845, aged ninety-three years. He was brother of the venerable Jotham Sewall, whose name is so fragrant throughout all the Congregational churches of Maine.

WILLIAM JONES was born in Newport, R. I., in 1754. During the war of the revolution, he was a captain of marines, and at the capture of Charleston was made a prisoner. He was for several years the Speaker of the House of Representatives in Rhode Island, and in 1810 was chosen Governor of the State, and remained in office till 1817. He died at Providence, in April, 1822, aged sixty-seven years. He was highly respected for his talents and virtues, and acquitted himself honorably in the various posts of public responsibility and usefulness that he occupied.

ROBERT RALSTON was born in Chester County, Pa., in 1761, and, with little more than a common-school education, he engaged in mercantile business in Philadelphia, not far from the time that he reached his majority. By his bland manners, skillful management, and incorruptible integrity, he gradually rose to the highest point of commercial respectability, and accumulated a fortune which gave him a place among the most opulent citizens of Philadelphia. At the same time, his liberality was proportioned to his affluence: he was the watchful and generous friend of many of the benevolent institutions of his day; and of the Philadelphia Bible Society, the first institution of the kind on this continent, he was the acknowledged originator. He was distinguished for sterling good sense, and close observation of men and things: for uncommonly active habits; for great urbanity of manners; for the most whole-souled and graceful hospitality; and for whatever enters into the character of a devout and earnest Christian. From the year 1802 till his death, he held the office of ruling elder in the Second Presbyterian Church in Philadelphia. He was a model of dignity, consistency, and kindliness, in all his relations. He died in Philadelphia, in August, 1836, in the seventy-fifth year of his age.

JOHN HOOKER was born in Northampton, Mass., in the year 1761. His father was the Rev. John Hooker, the immediate successor in the pastorate to Jonathan Edwards, and one of the brightest lights of the New England pulpit. He was graduated at Yale College in 1782, after which he studied law with his uncle, Colonel John Worthington, and commenced the practice of it at Springfield. Here he continued till the close of life. On relinquishing the practice of law in 1810, he was appointed Chief Justice of the Court of Common Pleas, and held the office for about ten years. He was also for a long time Judge of Probate, and in various ways exerted an influence that extended much beyond his own town or county. He was a man of excellent sense, and of great practical wisdom. When thrown among strangers, he was more inclined to hear than to talk; but with his intimate friends, he was as social and genial as could be desired. His judgment was greatly confided in by men of different religious creeds and different political parties.

He possessed the most unyielding integrity, and no one ever thought to move him a hair's breadth from the line of his honest convictions. He had withdrawn from the practice of the law many years before his death, but he was always doing good by his pure and devoted example, and was ready to render efficient aid to any good object that solicited his attention. He was for many years a deacon in the First Congregational Church in Springfield, and was a steady and stanch friend to the interests of evangelical Christianity. He died in 1829, carrying with him to his grave the blessings of the community of which he had been for so many years a valued and honored member.

JEREMIAH EVARTS was born in Sunderland, Vt., in the year 1781. After going through his preparatory course under the Rev. John Eliot, of Guilford, Conn., he entered Yale College, where he was graduated in 1802. He was hopefully the subject of a revival that occurred in college early in his senior year; and he connected himself with the college church. After spending some time in teaching an academy at Peacham, Vt., he studied law under Judge Chauncy, of New Haven, and commenced practice there in 1806. In 1810, he removed to Charlestown, Mass., to take the editorial charge of the Panoplist, a monthly religious periodical, which had been originated, and for several years conducted, by Dr. Morse; and he continued to be thus engaged until 1820, when the work was superseded by the Missionary Herald, published under the direction of the American Board. In 1812, he was chosen treasurer of the Board, and the next year a member of the Prudential Committee. The former of these offices he held until 1822. In 1821, he succeeded Dr. Worcester as Corresponding Secretary, and during the next and last ten years of his life he devoted himself with a martyr-like zeal to the duties of this most responsible office, accomplishing for the cause of missions what could scarcely have been expected in an ordinary life. In the early part of 1831, his health had become so much reduced, — partly, no doubt, from his excessive labors, — that he found it necessary to intermit his active exertions, and use some special means for his restoration. He accordingly sailed for Cuba in February, and, after remaining there a few weeks, came to Charleston, S. C., where he stopped with his friend, the Rev. Dr. Palmer, and on the 10th of May entered into his rest. His personal appearance was by no means imposing, but he had a mind and a heart that made him a prince in the domain of intellect and of goodness. He was far-seeing, cautious, earnest, firm, conciliatory, — every thing, in short, to render him an eminently suitable person to conduct one of the grandest of human enterprises. His memorial is in the record of his wise plans successfully carried out, of his untiring labors cheerfully performed, of his manifold sacrifices patiently submitted to, and of the joy unspeakable and full of glory that filled his soul while the gate of heaven was opening to receive him.

CHAPTER VII.

MEETINGS OF THE BOARD.

The Earlier Meetings. — Where held. — In what Buildings. — Attendance. — Northampton, 1825. — New York, 1827. — The Lord's Supper. — Boston, 1830. — Philadelphia, 1841. — The Meeting held under Excitement of a Debt. — Of Extraordinary Interest and Influence. — Treasurer's Statement. — Mr. Hubbard's Speech. — Mr. Greene's Speech. — Session prolonged. — Affecting Scene. — The Roll called, and Members pledge themselves. — The Assembly testifies its Sympathy. — Special Meeting at New York, 1842. — Results of the Pledges. — Meeting at Norwich, 1842. — Rochester, 1843. — Dr. Chapin's Letter. — Worcester, 1844. — Brooklyn, 1845. — First Vote by Yea and Nay. — Other Cases. — Boston, 1848. — Mr. Greene's Letter. —Pittsfield, 1849. — Cincinnati, 1853. — Attendance of Members. — Tendency westward. — Hartford, 1854. — Mr. Hill's Letter. — Special Meeting, 1856. — Mr. Frelinghuysen's Letter.

THE annual meetings of the Board are held in the autumn. Dr. Porter, of Farmington, informs us that the first meeting was in his parlor. Only five members were present, and he seems to have been the only spectator. Five others of the annual meetings were in parlors; one at Worcester, in the boarding house of the Misses Kennedy, where the gentlemen all lodged; three at Hartford, all in the house of Henry Hudson, Esq.; the other at Salem, in the house of Mrs. Elizabeth Bartlett, one of the earliest large contributors to the Board. The last was in 1820. Eleven were in halls of moderate size, the last of these in 1831; nine were in lecture rooms, the last in 1839. The first business meeting in a church edifice was in 1833, and such meetings were always with a small attendance until 1842. It was long the impression that what were called business sessions could not have much popular interest.

Only seven members were in attendance at the second meeting; nine at the third; and twelve at the fourth. The writer's first attendance was at Northampton, in 1825, when the meeting was in the town hall. Eighteen Corporate and twelve Honorary members were present, who were generally seated around a long table; and his most distinct remembrance of them is in debating the question of discontinuing the Foreign Mission School at Cornwall. Mr. Evarts was the chief speaker in favor of the discontinuance, and Dr. Beecher against it, but all in the best feeling.

The meeting at New York city, in the year 1827, was remarkable for its animated and protracted discussions on the duty of a far more extended liberality. Josiah Bissell, Jr., who must still be well remembered in the interior of New York for his self-sacrificing efforts to sustain a line of Sabbath-keeping stage coaches on the great route of western travel, was present, and the moving spirit of the occasion. Some of the proceedings of that meeting are noted in the chapter on agencies. The Lord's Supper was then administered for the first time, in connection with the meetings of the Board; and so well pleased were the members with their experience on that occasion, that they voted to repeat the celebration ever after.

The meeting of 1830, at Boston, was the last which Mr. Evarts attended, as the one just ten years before was the last attended by Dr. Worcester. Thirty years have passed since that meeting. Of the twenty-eight Corporate members then present, twenty are now in their graves; and so are one third of the five-and-twenty Honorary members. The sessions were in the chapel of the Old South Church, an irregular building, of one story, in Spring Lane, since replaced by a more commodious edifice. The room was at no time more than half filled; but what an amount of character and influence! Speaking only of a few of the departed, there was Governor Smith, the President of the Board, dignified, courteous, the most accomplished of presiding officers. There was General Van Rensselaer, the "Patroon," alike distinguished for wealth, personal standing, modesty, and true dignity of character; he was the Vice President. Dr. Calvin

Chapin was there, the Recording Secretary, and then the only clerical survivor of the original members. His Records lie open before us, in two volumes, bound by himself, distinctly legible, but with not an inch of unoccupied paper. We remember him for his laconic replies, his irrepressible wit, the occasional flashes of his rigid countenance, and the interest of his conversation and familiar letters. Dr. Chapin lived to see the rule abolished giving to the Corporate members the right to draw their traveling expenses in attending the meetings; and he was apprehensive as to the measure, lest it should diminish the attendance and influence of that class. Eighteen years have passed, and those apprehensions have not been realized. Dr. Miller and Dr. Alexander, of the Princeton Theological Seminary, were there; both remarkable men, who evinced a deep interest in the deliberations. There were three lay members, successively chairmen of the Prudential Committee: William Reed, for some time a member of Congress; Samuel Hubbard, afterward a Judge of the Supreme Court; and Samuel T. Armstrong, subsequently Lieutenant Governor of Massachusetts. Each of them, through a course of years, devoted a large amount of valuable time, thought, and influence to the cause; and they too have gone from earth.* Dr. Woods, from the Andover Seminary, was there, watching the flow of the river which he was able to trace back better than almost any other one present; and Dr. David Porter, every faculty of whose great soul was enlisted in Christ's cause; Dr. Justin Edwards, whose rare grasp of the relations and powers of general principles afterward gave wonderful effect to his labors in the cause of temperance and the Sabbath; Dr. Benjamin B. Wisner, who, with his fine executive talent, was soon to be enlisted as a Secretary of the Board, alas! for so short a time; and Dr. Elias Cornelius, then approaching, as it soon appeared, the close of his brilliant and most useful career. It was at this meeting that Mr. Evarts

* A lifelike portrait of Mr. Reed, along with an equally truthful one of Dr. Worcester, now graces the committee room, and it would be well if similar memorials of the others were also there.

read the conclusion to the twentieth Report, containing a prospective view of our own country — one of the most eloquent productions that have resulted from the modern missionary enterprise.

The meeting at Philadelphia, in 1841, is worthy of an extended notice; not so much on account of the attendance of members, though that was unusual, as for its remarkable character, and its extended, powerful, and permanent influence upon the community. It was held under the excitement of a debt, which had been accumulating for several years, and had become nearly as large as the one that so occupied the attention of the Jubilee Meeting. That was one of the great pecuniary crises of the Board; and such was the effect of the meeting, through the divine blessing, that this debt was removed before the next anniversary, through the ordinary channels of contribution. An excellent account of the meeting, in the New York Observer, by the editor, Dr. S. I. Prime, contributed much to its influence on the community; and a free use will be made here of that report.

The meeting was held in the First Presbyterian Church, commencing on Wednesday, September 8, at ten o'clock, A. M. The receipts of the year had been two hundred and thirty-five thousand one hundred and eighty-nine dollars and thirty cents; the expenditure, two hundred and sixty-eight thousand nine hundred and fourteen dollars and seventy-nine cents; and the debt was fifty-seven thousand eight hundred and eight dollars and ninety-one cents. Of course more than three hundred thousand dollars would be needed the next year. The Treasurer brought the case distinctly before the Board. As to the probable receipts, he said it had been stated at the last annual meeting that three hundred thousand dollars could be raised, but it had not been; and the Committee saw no reason to suppose an equal amount would be raised in the year to come; and they considered it unsafe to go on unless means were devised for a substantial increase of the funds. "As the times are now, we can go on," continued Mr. Hill;

"but if money should be greatly in demand, and this debt be suddenly called for, we might be in most unpleasant circumstances. Our credit, a most precious jewel, that can not be too carefully preserved, would be endangered, and there would be no relief but in falling back on the permanent funds, which, by our charter, may not be touched for the ordinary expenses of the Board. And many of us have doubts whether it is right for a religious institution to contract debts to a large amount. With the prospect before us that the receipts will fall far short of the appropriations, to say nothing of the debt, we are ready to ask, *What shall be done?*" He conjured the members to speak out, and tell what ought to be done.

Dr. William J. Armstrong, the Home Secretary, submitted the views of the Prudential Committee on the necessity of greater system in efforts to raise the funds; which were ably responded to by a special committee through Chancellor Walworth. A series of resolutions was appended to the committee's report.

"After the reading of this paper," says the Observer, "there was a solemn and anxious pause of some moments. The members of the Board were called on to express their views, but no one appeared willing to break ground in this great emergency. The wisdom of the wise seemed to fail, while all were disposed to ask, 'Lord, what wilt thou have us to do?'

"The venerable Dr. Yale called the attention of the Board to a memorable declaration, made twenty-five years ago, that the energies of Christendom, wisely directed, and attended with the blessing of the Spirit, might send the gospel over the world in a quarter of a century. 'If it were my own expression,' said he, 'I would not make it; but it is not mine; it was made by a beloved man who has been resting from his labors twenty years; he died in the Cherokee country, June 7, 1821.* Nor was it *his* expression only, but that of the Prudential Committee; nor *theirs* merely, but it was formally

* Dr. Worcester.

adopted by the American Board at Hartford, Conn., September 18, 1816. Of the members then present, only three now survive; one [Dr. Chapin] is present to-day; the quarter of a century is gone, and the most of those who made the declaration are gone; but the work is not done. I feel a pang of sorrow when I reflect that since that declaration was made, six hundred millions of pagans have gone down to the grave.'

"Having said these words, Dr. Yale sat down, and the silence was again prolonged."

The impressive scene is well remembered. This report was made on Thursday, and the members had begun somewhat to realize the proportions of the impending evil. It was no time for rhetoric, and none felt able to propose a solution of the difficulty. The silence was broken by the Rev. Chauncey Eddy, one of the general agents of the Board, lately deceased. He was followed by Mr. S. T. Armstrong, a member of the Prudential Committee already mentioned, who affirmed that the Committee had acted in the fear of God, and in reference to their responsibility to the Board; and now they looked to the Board to justify their conduct, and to furnish the means for carrying on the work. And unless they should meet this emergency and furnish the means, there was a calamity coming upon us, and a shame to cover our faces which no vail could screen. The excellent remarks of Mr. Hubbard, then chairman of the Prudential Committee, are deserving of remembrance.

"Mr. Hubbard felt a deep interest in the subject, as one of the Committee. Agents who incur debts for their principal are often regarded as unfaithful, and made the subject of rebuke. And unless the Committee had had good grounds for the course they had taken, they ought to be rebuked. He then proceeded to show, from documentary history, that the Prudential Committee had been guided from year to year by the intelligent direction of the Board. In 1839, the debt was nineteen thousand one hundred and seventy-three dollars; and then the Board advised that no reduction be made, and that no missionaries be detained who were willing to be sent out.

In 1840, the debt was twenty-four thousand and eighty-three dollars, and the Committee were again authorized to continue their appropriations. Acting on these instructions, the Committee had gone on sustaining the missions, and raising the funds as rapidly as possible, and now find themselves in debt fifty-seven thousand dollars, in consequence of doing what the Board told them to do. Suppose we go on, and do as we are told during another year, while no more is contributed, and the debt is raised to one hundred thousand dollars. Do you suppose we will do it? I will resign rather than do it. The Committee feel the pressure of their responsibilities. The Secretaries are not able or willing to bear it. Their energies, health, strength, are sinking under it. It is their duty to resign unless the Church comes up to their aid. Mr. Hubbard said the subject must now be met as a matter of business. Votes and resolutions do not pay debts. They would not meet the drafts of this Board in London. Resolutions are not bills of exchange. He enforced the necessity of preserving untarnished the integrity of the Board, let it cost what it might.

"He showed, with great clearness, how there was no reason to fear that increased contributions to this cause would diminish the receipts of other benevolent institutions; they would rise or sink together. Mr. Hubbard went on to demonstrate the identity of the missionary spirit with the religion of Christ; remarking, that when a great effort was made in the city of Hartford for foreign missions, some one said there would be a revival there within a year. The prophecy was true. One thousand souls were added to the churches. Not that he would propose to purchase such blessings, but he believed they were connected as means and ends. There would be no lack of funds from Hartford the coming year; and if the Spirit was poured on the churches every where, we should not come here saying, we are in debt, and know not what to do. He then went on to illustrate his doctrine by reference to the order of nature in the production of crops, &c., and to quote the promises of God, and to show his dealings with his people in ancient days. If we use the means, God will bless them. If we neglect the work, it will nevertheless go on; the Lord will raise up friends, if need be, from the stones of the field; but we shall lose the honor and happiness of coöperating with the Son of God in giving his gospel to the world. Those of us who can not go personally to the heathen may send others; and every man who contributes bears a part with Christ in this work. No one is so poor as not to be able to do something. The lay members of the Board should put their shoulder to the wheel, and, with the active labor of all, the debt might be paid."

The subject was resumed on Friday. There is a permanent value in the speech of Mr. Greene, then one of the Corresponding Secretaries, and the reader will be pleased to see copious extracts.

"As yet, through all the remarks that had been made," said Mr. Greene, "he saw no more light than when we commenced our sessions. We have the same means proposed as in 1838, 1839, and 1840. We have calls, appeals, pledges, recommendations, but we are now deeper in debt than ever, and provisions made for an increase of funds in time past are not adequate to the present emergency. The plans, and pledges, and resolutions are all encouraging, but there are two or three difficulties in the way.

"They are not quick enough in their operation. If our system of agencies could be greatly increased, if we could cover the whole field with them at once, and they were welcomed by the churches, the work might be done. But many churches will not admit agents among them. Some churches, near to Boston, have refused to have an agent sent to them. A large association has recently passed a resolution to that effect, and addressed a letter to the various benevolent societies, informing them of the fact. We know, as well as if we saw the result, what the effect will be. There will be a falling off of thirty-three per cent. in their contributions, unless God should in a wonderful manner pour out his Spirit on some one man among them, who will see that the work is done. And if we should send a dozen more agents into the field, the churches would say they were coming too thick and too fast, and would not tolerate them.

"But where shall we find the agents? We have been looking for a year or more for the right kind of men, but we can not find them; at least, those who are willing to make the requisite sacrifices of habits of study, family relations, and local attachments, and who are, at the same time, the men we want. We must have those who have a *heart* in the work, and men of talents and tact, who are qualified for other spheres; and these are not so easily found. We might send men who would answer the purpose of a wooden clock, — to tell the people the time had come to take up a collection; but these are not the agents for us, or for the people. It is much easier to find fault with agents than it is to find the right kind of agents.

"In 1837," continued Mr. Greene, "we were compelled to curtail all branches of missionary labor. It broke the health and hearts of many of our self-denying missionaries; it led them to distrust the interest of the churches at home in their support; it brought the missionaries into discredit with the heathen, who saw them disbanding their schools and reducing their stations; but, worse than all this, the Christian community became *familiar with the idea* of curtailing missionary operations. No greater disaster than this could befall us. The Church has thought that the missionaries might retrench their expenses, or come home, or that the Prudential Committee might retrench; or, in any great emergency into which the Board might come, that some wise scheme would be devised, by which they might for a season stand still, or go back, without disgrace and disaster. There can be a breaking up of the missions; we can disband the schools; we can go back to where we were in 1810! But to *begin again;* to recover lost ground; to revive the abandoned work — is not so easy a task.

"And few realize the difficulties in the way of reaching the distant and most expensive missions with orders of curtailment. No vessel may be ready to sail. After the order is dispatched, some months must elapse before it reaches the mission; and when it does, the mission has laid out its plans for the year, has hired printers and teachers, established free schools, contracted engagements with the natives, and made known to them its plans; and would you have the faith of the missionaries dishonored in the eyes of the heathen? Must they break their pledges, and confess that the Christian world will not sustain their efforts to save the perishing?

"Suppose our missionaries in the East, who have eight thousand children around them learning to read the Bible, and through whom they have access to multitudes of natives, receive an order to curtail their operations. They return us the question, 'Do you want us to send these children back to heathenism? If we *must*, we will do it.' But shall *we*, can *we*, be so hardhearted or indifferent as to compel them to do it? If the Prudential Committee are able to make such a requirement of the missionaries, they are unworthy to fill the seats they occupy. Well did one of the missionaries say, as he disbanded the schools of five thousand children, and let them go back to the embrace of heathenism, 'What an offering to Swamy!'

"In this crisis, Mr. President, are we now placed. The trial is growing more and more severe and perplexing every day. We have heard much of praying for the Spirit, and the answer to our prayers has brought us into these straits. God has opened the way; he has given our missionaries an abundant entrance into the fields of labor; and the Church falls back! If the world was shut up as it was when Hall and Newell went out, we could not use the funds now asked, if we had them. But God has opened the door wide, in answer to prayer, and the Church falters. It is true we do not pray enough, or feel our dependence on God as we ought. But if our prayers would find acceptance with God, we must lay *ourselves on the altar* to which we come, or no incense will go up.

"It has appeared strange to me," continued Mr. Greene, "that a Church which has come up from nothing to *this*, should falter now. If in 1810 the Church had said, 'A wall as high as heaven is around the heathen world; we can not gain access to them; they are joined to idols; let them alone;' it would not have been strange. But now that the world is open, and the heathen are casting away their idols, and God calls us to come on and bear a part with him in the victory, that the Church should draw back is amazing!

"When there were none willing to go to the heathen, that the Church should be at ease, is not so strange; but when our missionaries are ready to go to distress, and privations, and death, that the Church should say, 'We are not willing to sustain you,' is indeed amazing. Why is not every one coming up with his *thank offering* for what has already been done? Why are we so indifferent about the heathen? Why is not every heart broken, and every eye a fountain of tears? O! did we realize what momentous consequences hang on the issue of this meeting, we should *feel*. Do we think that one soul will have its destiny for eternity changed by the decision to which we come? Bring that soul here, and place him in the aisle of this house, and no man dare hold up his head, no man dare go to the communion table, who has voted to withhold from that soul the means of salvation. But we know, as well as we know that we sit here, that thousands of immortal souls are suspended on the issues of this hour.

"It is very solemn business, this consulting for the souls of men, — saying whether this and that soul shall or shall not have the bread of eternal life. And yet there is no other light in which the subject is worth looking at. If this is not the true issue, call home your missionaries, appoint no more officers, pay off your debt, stop all your operations, and let the heathen alone."

Friday noon, when it is usual for the Board to terminate its sessions, there was a deeply interesting conversation as to the necessity of prolonging the meeting. After a prayer by the Rev. Mr. Danforth, the Board resolved to continue together until it should reach some more favorable result. The session in the afternoon can not be adequately described. It was unique in the manifestations of feeling. Venerable men, of eminent position, were seen weeping under their irrepressible emotions, in view of the infinite interests that seemed in jeopardy. At length Dr. Justin Edwards asked whether the Prudential Committee had any thing more to communicate. Learning that they had not, he requested that the resolutions introduced by Chancellor Walworth, the day before, might be adopted. These had pledged the Corporate and Honorary members now attending the Board, individually and collectively, to exert themselves to excite an interest in others in the cause of missions, and to contribute liberally of their substance to the support of missions.

Dr. Edwards then said he wanted something to secure personal responsibility; and he proposed that the roll be called, and that every member should answer to three questions, which were in substance as follows: —

1. Will you increase your subscription, this year, at least twenty-five per cent. above that of last year?

2. Will you endeavor to influence others, so far as in your judgment may be proper and right, to do the same?

3. Will you come to the meeting of this Board next year, and report what the Lord hath done by you? Or, if unable to attend, will you communicate by writing? This proposition he supported by a spirited and effective address.

"The proposition of Dr. Edwards was agreed to, the roll called, and each member, both Corporate and Honorary, who was present, was called upon to answer these questions; and nearly all promptly answered in the affirmative; though some few preferred not to pledge themselves explicitly, some qualified their answers, and a considerable number pledged themselves to increase their subscriptions fifty or one hundred per cent. The Prudential Committee were instructed to propound these questions to the absent members of the Board, and also to send a circular letter, embracing substantially the same, to all the churches which patronized the Board, whose ministers were not members."

Dr. Chapin has the important additional fact, in his record of the meeting, that those present, not members of the Board, were respectfully invited to answer the same questions, and that nearly or quite the whole assembly rose in an affirmative reply.

Further to insure the success of this effort, at the suggestion of Mr. Hubbard, it was resolved to hold a special meeting of the Board in New York city on the 18th of the following January. Perhaps it would have been better to have authorized the Prudential Committee to call such a meeting, in case they should deem one expedient. The apparent necessity for it had actually ceased when the time arrived, the debt being then reduced two thirds, and in a fair way for liquidation. The Prudential Committee and Secretaries were in some perplexity how to prevent the meeting from being a failure; but it was not such. Among the statements then made, it was said that besides the responses forwarded to the Committee by individual members of the Board, there had been a more informal, though perhaps not less hearty, response from an equal or greater number of ministers and laymen at meetings of ecclesiastical bodies and auxiliary societies; embracing one Synod and some Presbyteries and Associations in the State of New York, and some in the States of New Hampshire and Maine. The members had answered the first two of the three questions proposed at the annual meeting with great unanimity. At the annual meetings of nearly all the auxiliary societies in the State of Connecticut, of eight in Massachusetts, and nearly all in Vermont, — embracing most of the auxiliary meetings held since the anniversary of the Board, — the questions just alluded to were put and affirmatively responded to with great promptness and unanimity.

As one of the consequences of the meeting at Philadelphia, and of the extended and interesting notices of the same, the meeting at Norwich, in the following year, was thronged; and from that time the Board has had no occasion to lament the want of an audience, as well at its business sessions, as at those designed to be of a more popular character.

At the meeting in Rochester, N. Y., in 1843, the venerable

Dr. Chapin declined holding any longer the office of Recording Secretary. His letter, which is of permanent interest, coming from the last of the original members of the Board, and from one of the five composing the meeting to which he refers, is given here, with a few omissions. It was addressed to the President of the Board.

The undersigned would respectfully, through you, request the Board not to consider him as a candidate for any office in its power to confer. At the same time, he trusts that it will not be inexcusable presumption in him to express, retrospectively and in a word, his devout wonder and joy.

Thirty-three years ago, a meeting of the Board consisted of no more than five persons, and our much-esteemed brother Noah Porter, and his excellent family and house, afforded every accommodation. That meeting was distinguished by fervency of prayer, strength of faith, and the perfection of such hope as Christian faith warrants. At that trying moment, however, the Board had neither missionaries nor money. It seems quite remarkable, too, that every opening of access to "the dark places of the earth" was entirely conjectural and imaginary.

Just compare that meeting with the experience of the Board at Norwich, twelve months ago. In this, more than four hundred names were offered and received, of members Corporate and Honorary. Such a fact, combined with the affectionate testimony of absent members, presents invincible proof of hearty friendship and zeal in thousands, or rather in millions, for the accomplishment of the heavenly object to which the Board is religiously self-consecrated. Furthermore, truly encouraging and animating is the evidence — in numerous and widely-separated stations selected, in many missions established, and in the great success realized — that Christ superintends, approves, and blesses the benevolent enterprise.

The undersigned assumes leave to say, that, through inexhaustible grace, he feels no measured satisfaction in the clear anticipation of a speedy union with the glorified spirits of Treadwell, and Lyman, and Spring, and Dwight, and Worcester, and Evarts, and their cotemporaries and successors. Allow him to add, that while his probationary life and faculties are continued, his unceasing and affectionate prayer will be, that Zion's King may promote human well-being and Jehovah's praise, by annually increasing the means of the Board, by wisely directing its measures, and by crowning its benevolent efforts with the salvation of the world.

CALVIN CHAPIN.

The attendance at Worcester in 1844 was very large, owing to its being in the midst of a dense missionary population. There were present eighty-seven Corporate and five hundred and seventeen Honorary members; and of patrons, male and female, a far greater number. Two churches were filled with the communicants on Thursday. Many clergymen and others, not being able to find seats, assembled in still another church for prayer.

The first time in which the Board is known to have decided a disputed question by a call of the roll of members, and the formal response of "Yea" or "Nay," was at Brooklyn, N. Y., in the year 1845. It was upon the adoption of a report on the subject of slaveholding in churches under the care of missionaries of the Board, made by a committee appointed the previous year. There have been only two other occasions on which this method was resorted to, and those were in connection with the same subject — at Hartford in 1854, and Philadelphia in 1859. The reader is referred, for the more important proceedings of the Board in relation to this matter, to the minutes of the annual meetings at Brooklyn in 1845, Boston in 1848, Hartford in 1854, Utica in 1855, and Philadelphia in 1859.

The minutes of the meeting in 1848 contain a letter from the Rev. David Greene, declining a reëlection as Corresponding Secretary, in consequence of impaired health. From this letter it will be proper to make the following extract: —

I must be permitted to say, that during the almost twenty-one years of my official connection with the Board, — a period extending over more than half the Board's history from its organization, and a longer period than any other executive officer has been connected with it, except the present Treasurer and the senior Corresponding Secretary, — it has been my happiness to be associated intimately with the present Treasurer, six persons in the office of Secretary, and fourteen as members of the Prudential Committee, six of whom have been removed, as we doubt not, to the heavenly rest; and I would here record, with thankfulness to God, that in all the meetings for business held during this whole period, (and they have been, on the average, more than one a week,) and in all our mutual private intercourse, there has never been, so far as I have reason to believe, one offensive word, one uncourteous act, or one unkind feeling. Though often differing, of course, in opinion on some of the many delicate and perplexing subjects which have come up for discussion and action, in feeling all without a single exception have been harmonious and fraternal. The scenes of prayer and anxious consultation and wearisome labor, passed with these brethren in the committee room and in the private apartments of the Missionary House, have made impressions which no other scenes, nor time itself, can efface. From all my respected and beloved fellow-laborers there, including the Prudential Committee, I have received unvarying kindness and forbearance. A willingness to share in and lighten each other's burdens has ever characterized the relations and intercourse there. For all this they have my hearty thanks, as they shall ever have my affectionate remembrance, my sympathy, and my prayers.

Justice requires me further to say, that I feel confident that the interests of the Board are safe in their hands. From their systematic and laborious attention to the business intrusted to them, their singleness of aim, and their prayerfulness, the divine guidance and blessing will not be withheld. Borne down with burdens, responsibilities, and anxieties, which those who have not participated in them can but poorly appreciate, and oftentimes grieved and weakened by the suspicions, censures, and counteraction of brethren, whose wishes it would be far more easy and pleasant to conform to than to contravene by pursuing another course, which a knowledge of the facts and bearings of a case and a single regard to the interests intrusted to them demand, I most earnestly commend them to the prayers, the sympathy, the confidence, and the coöperation of all the friends of missions; and I have no doubt that the more fully their motives and proceedings are understood, the more cheerfully will this sympathy, confidence, and coöperation be accorded to them.

No one can read the speech of the Secretary, already quoted, without being impressed with the great loss which the Board experienced on this occasion. The effects of a railroad collision created the necessity. Having retired upon a farm, Mr. Greene is still living in the midst of his numerous family, and takes an unabated interest in the progress of the Redeemer's kingdom.

The meeting at Pittsfield, in the year 1849, is known to have been preceded by an extraordinary amount of prayer, owing to a prevalent anxiety lest alienating discussions should arise; and it will be remembered by those who were present, as a season of the most elevated Christian enjoyment. Other meetings had been more fully attended, and took a deeper hold on the feelings and sympathies by reason of some question of general and absorbing interest; but on no previous occasion had there been such a constant, delightful commingling of the sweetest, tenderest emotions of the Christian heart. The reflection often arose in many a breast, We are sitting in heavenly places in Christ Jesus.

The first meeting beyond the Alleghanies was in the year 1853, at Cincinnati. There were fears that comparatively few of the Corporate members would be present, on account of the distance and the expense of the journey. But there were forty-seven; twenty-six from New England, and nine from New York and New Jersey. Twelve were from the Western States. One hundred and four of the hundred and eighty Honorary members were from that side of the mountains. Not till 1843 had one of these anniversaries been held as far west as Rochester, and not till 1847 was it as far as Buffalo. And what were those three cities, and where indeed was the West, when the Board was organized? There has since been a successful meeting at Detroit, and the next is appointed at Cleveland.

The forty-fifth annual meeting of the Board at Hartford, in 1854, was perhaps the largest ever held, save the fiftieth. Ninety-nine Corporate and five hundred and ninety-six Honorary members were actually enrolled. There was a greater number of members at Boston in 1848, but not so many persons commended to the hospitality of families in the city and vicinity. At this meeting, Henry Hill, Esq., having reached the age of sixty, and having served thirty-two years as Treasurer, declined a reëlection. In his letter to the President he states, that when he entered on his official duties in 1822, the annual receipts were about sixty thousand dollars, and the whole amount in the previous twelve years was little more than three hundred thousand dollars. The annual receipts, at the date of his letter, exceeded three hundred thousand dollars, and the sum total was over six millions. The salary of the Treasurer, deducting his donations to the Board, had averaged less than fourteen hundred dollars. This was below his necessary expenses; but he had declined receiving more, though often kindly urged to do so, having an income on property acquired previous to his connection with the Board. His letter concludes thus: "A female, connected with the Gaboon mission, on her death-bed gave to the Board about fifty dollars, as a dying thank offering for having had the privilege of laboring thirteen years on the shores of Western Africa. With the same spirit, as I would hope, and in testimony of my continued confidence and interest, the Board will please accept the inclosed donation, which I also make as a thank offering that I have been so long allowed to serve the Board as its Treasurer." The check was for two thousand dollars.

The visit of a deputation to the missions in India in 1854–5, which will be spoken of in the chapter on deputations, gave rise to a special meeting of the Board at Albany, in March, 1856. Misapprehensions had arisen, at the annual meeting in the preceding autumn, as to the proceedings in India, and the

Prudential Committee was requested to call the Board together when the deputation should have returned. The special meeting was necessarily held in the most inclement season of the year; and its size, while evincing an apprehension that grave errors had been committed, showed the strong hold of the cause upon the best feelings of the community. Eighty-two Corporate and at least two hundred Honorary members were in attendance. A special committee of thirteen, appointed on this occasion, presented a printed report to the Board at its next annual meeting in Newark, the main result of which will be stated in the chapter treating on deputations.

In the year 1857, at the meeting in Providence, the Hon. Theodore Frelinghuysen, President of the Board, retired from office on account of the withdrawal of the Reformed Dutch Church, of which he was a member, from its connection with the Board. In a letter to the Prudential Committee and Secretaries, subsequent to the meeting, the esteemed and beloved President, speaking in behalf of that branch of the missionary community, as well as for himself, thus gave expression to his feelings: —

In parting from you, I feel as a child parting from a venerated and beloved mother. Like a mother you have cherished us, when we were few and feeble. You took us under the wings of your care, and linked our interests together. We thank you for all your kindness. We thank God for the precious seasons of Christian privilege that we have enjoyed together. We have often gone up to the heights of Zion, and looked down upon this dark world, and traced the footsteps of our wonder-working God and Redeemer. And from these "heavenly places" we have together hailed the first streaks of the morning, the sure tokens of that coming glory which the Sun of Righteousness shall shed upon this benighted and sin-stricken world. These hallowed seasons will be for grateful thanksgiving in that blessed world where partings never grieve, and the past shall be recalled only to augment the pleasures of a sanctified memory.

CHAPTER VIII.

THE PRUDENTIAL COMMITTEE — PLACES OF BUSINESS.

Members. — Constitution of the Body. — Growth of the Meetings. — Attendance of Executive Officers. — Manner of doing Business. — Duties of the Committee. — Place of Business, 1821. — Pressure of Duties. — Place of Business, 1822. — New Laborers. — Place of Business, 1826. — Destroyed by Fire. — Place of Business, 1830. — The Missionary House. — Its Cost and Advantages.

THE PRUDENTIAL COMMITTEE.

THE Prudential Committee has now twelve members, one of whom is from the city of New York, and one from Brooklyn. No member receives compensation for his services. The stated meetings are held weekly, on Tuesday, at three o'clock, P. M., and occupy the afternoon. Five members are a quorum for business. There is a remarkable uniformity in the attendance. Of the eight from Boston and its vicinity who were in the country, the past year for instance, the average attendance was seven at the fifty-two meetings. Gentlemen in full city business will appreciate this sacrifice of time, which was cheerfully made.

The meetings of the Prudential Committee had a very small beginning. There were but three members at the outset — Dr. Worcester, of Salem, who was the Corresponding Secretary, and Dr. Spring and Mr. Bartlet, both of Newburyport. For years the meetings were migratory. Only two are recorded in 1810, the same number in the second year, six in the third, two in the fourth, and four in the fifth. There were eight meetings in 1815, ten in 1816, twelve in 1817, the same number in 1818, and nineteen in 1819, which was the year preceding Dr. Worcester's death. Mr. Evarts came into the Committee in 1812, and Dr. Morse in 1815. Both resided in Charlestown. Until the close of 1816, the places of meeting seem to have been casual. Newburyport and Salem had each eight of the thirty-four meetings, Charlestown seven, Boston and Andover four each; the remaining three were at Worcester and Hartford, in connection with meetings of the Board. Mr. Reed, of Marblehead, entered the Committee in 1818, and Dr. Woods, of the Andover Theological Seminary, in 1819. About that time, the meetings began to be held usually in Boston. At this early period, when principles were unsettled, when the business was tentative and not usually urgent, when the members were scattered, and the time for railroads had not come, the Secretary would often seek a solution of his missionary problems by correspondence, or by conference with individual members whom he chanced to meet. The meetings began to be held weekly in the year 1832.

The meetings have been attended for many years by the Corresponding Secretaries, the Treasurer, and the Editor of the monthly publications, in virtue of their office, but they do not vote. The Chairman is appointed from among the members, and the Senior Secretary has been Clerk. A long table, in the center of the committee room, allows the whole seventeen to gather around it, each one with pen and paper before him. After an opening prayer, and the reading of the minutes of the previous meeting, for correction (if need be) and approval, the Foreign Secretary, the Home Secretary, the Secretary for New York City (if present), and the Treasurer, are called upon successively to bring forward the business needing attention in their several departments. They are expected to state it clearly, and to be prepared for a concise and accurate presentation of all the documents and facts needful for its elucidation. This is their business; and when this is done, the Chairman calls upon each person present to express his opinion; then gives his own; and, should a result have been reached, he declares it, or a formal vote is taken.

The discussions, in this small deliberative body, are in the conversational tone, — the members being seated, — are seldom protracted, almost never controversial. There is often a diversity of opinion at the outset, and a point is regarded as unsettled until there is a substantial unity. If there be not, the case is reserved for a future meeting, perhaps referred to a sub-committee for a written report. The large number of reports now on file form a valuable repository of facts and experience. Sometimes these reports are extended and elaborate. Where there are such diversity of mind and disposition and such varied and delicate interests, as in an extended system of foreign missions, intricate cases must needs arise, requiring careful investigation and nice discrimination. A single case has been known to occupy the chairman of a sub-committee all the time he could spare for it, which was a portion of almost every day, for some five or six weeks. Such cases, however, occur but seldom. It might be hard to find a body of Christian men in our own land, of different professions, and so largely occupied with business of their own, who devote such an amount of time to the oversight of a benevolent enterprise. The by-law, prescribing their duties, is as follows: "It shall be the duty of the Prudential Committee to carry into effect all resolutions and orders of the Board, the execution of which shall not have been assigned to some other committee; to cause the more inviting fields for missionary enterprise to be explored, if necessary; to appoint the places where missions shall be attempted, and to determine the scale upon which they shall be conducted, and to superintend them; to appoint, instruct, and direct all the missionaries of the Board; to prescribe where the Treasurer shall deposit the moneys of the Board, and the times and modes of investments and remittances; to draw orders authorizing the payment of moneys from the treasury; to ascertain the state of the treasury at least twice a year, and as much oftener as they see cause; to appoint agents at home and abroad, with such powers and duties as they may think are demanded by the best interests of missions; and, generally, to perform all duties necessary, in their opinion, to promote the objects of the Board; provided the same shall not be contrary to any resolution or by-law of the Board, nor to the Act of Incorporation.

They shall annually elect a chairman and clerk, the former of whom shall keep the bond of the Treasurer."

PLACES FOR TRANSACTING THE BUSINESS.

Coming from the Theological Seminary at Andover, in 1821, shortly after the decease of Dr. Worcester, to assist Mr. Evarts during a vacation, the writer found that the executive business of the Board was all transacted in one small room in the basement of Mr. Evarts's dwelling house. Here that invaluable man was well-nigh prostrated by the combined duties of Treasurer, Corresponding Secretary, and Editor. It seems, indeed, looking back after near forty years, that all these duties could not, at that time, have equaled those of either one of the departments in the present secretaryship. But this view is in some respects illusory. The missionary work is peculiar in its nature, and these pioneers had every thing to originate, learn, and settle. There are embarrassments enough now, and they are painful enough, and doubtless always will be, for the trial of faith and patience; but there has been great progress in simplifying and systematizing the modes of operation. Problems and cases which caused those men protracted and anxious deliberations, have long since been settled, and now serve as precedents, like adjudicated cases in courts of law.

In the spring of 1822, the writer was required to spend a few months at what were then called the Missionary Rooms, while Mr. Evarts visited the Indian missions. These Rooms were in the second story of a tenement in what is now known as Cornhill. The Correspondence and Treasury had each a separate apartment, and the editing was connected with the former, which devolved upon the writer; while Mr. Levi Chamberlain, an intelligent and successful young merchant of Boston, who had relinquished his business for the missionary service, had the temporary charge of the latter. Mr. Chamberlain's health requiring a milder climate, he joined the Sandwich Islands mission in 1823, and, until his death in

1849, was the able and faithful secular agent in that mission. These two young men were of course under the general oversight of the Prudential Committee; but it illustrates the infancy of the work, that, for half a year, it could be committed to such inexperienced hands. Mr. Evarts returned in the following summer. Henry Hill, Esq., entered upon his long and faithful service as Treasurer in the autumn. Mr. Hill was born in Newburgh, N. Y.; received his mercantile training in the city of New York; and, after one or two business visits to Europe, he was for some years a merchant in Chili. Having acquired a moderate competency, he returned to the United States, resolved to devote himself to a life bearing more directly on the cause of Christ. The knowledge of this fact led to his election by the Board. At that time, also, the writer, having completed his course in the Seminary, became a permanent laborer at the Missionary Rooms.

The building of an edifice in Hanover Street, in 1826, for the church under the pastoral care of Dr. Lyman Beecher, furnished more convenient apartments for the Board. These were in the basement story, and were secured to the Board, by the liberality of a few individuals, free of rent for five years. The rooms were three in number, one for the Treasury, and two for the Correspondence; and into them the offices of the Board were removed in the spring of that year. Early in the morning of February 1, 1830, the Hanover-street Church was consumed by fire. A part of the property of the Board was insured; and through the kindness of Providence, and the laborious exertions of friends, nearly all the account books, records, correspondence, and other valuable papers in the offices of the Secretary and Treasurer, which no insurance could have made good, were saved; together with a considerable portion of the Annual Reports, and of the back volumes of the Missionary Herald.

The offices were again removed to Cornhill; and here the business of the Board was transacted until the erection of the Missionary House on Pemberton Square, in the year 1838.

The Prudential Committee had increasingly felt the need

of a house to be owned by the Board, and better adapted to its business. A record of the desirableness of such a building appears as far back as the year 1823. The national Bible, Tract, and Sunday School Societies had erected such buildings. The inconvenience and loss resulting from repeated removals were not small, and must needs increase with the property at the Rooms. The general depression of business in the year 1837 afforded a good opportunity for building, since the expense was not to be met by donations, nor by a loan, but simply by a change in the investment of a portion of the permanent funds. The lot and building cost some thousands less than they would have done before, or probably at any time since. The Missionary House stands on one of the corners of Pemberton Square, and is built of brick, thirty-one feet by fifty, with two one-story offsets in the rear, some forty feet in length. The hight of the building is three stories, exclusive of basement and attic; and it is economically and neatly finished throughout. In the basement are offices for the agent for publications, and the purchasing agent, with storerooms for every kind of article on the way to the several missions, and also an ample safe-room for the archives. The offices of the Treasurer and Corresponding Secretaries are in the first and second stories, each having a room of convenient size, with a small retiring room contiguous to it; and there is a safe in each of these stories. The Library and Cabinet occupy the third story, and the meetings of the Prudential Committee are held in the Library, which is also called the Committee Room. The attic is mostly devoted to pamphlets, chiefly publications of the Board. The Missionary House is central, quiet, airy, and near the great horse-car lines running through and out of the city. The cost of the house and land was twenty-two thousand six hundred and thirteen dollars and sixty-one cents. The house, besides greatly facilitating the operations of the executive officers in their various departments, has given to the Board the appearance of stability and permanence, and has had the effect to strengthen its hold on the public mind, and also its credit in the commercial world.

CHAPTER IX.

CORRESPONDENCE — LIBRARY — CABINET.

Early and Later Correspondence. — Postage. — Manuscript Volumes. — Copying of Letters. — Advantage of this Practice. — Freedom of the Correspondence. — Responsibilities of the Secretaries. — Instructions to Missionaries. — Number of Secretaries. — Library of the Board. — Missionary Cabinet.

THE CORRESPONDENCE.

THE correspondence of the Board is carried on by the Secretaries and Treasurer. The District Secretaries have, of course, a correspondence of their own. Thirty years ago, the cost of postage at the Missionary House was nearly six hundred dollars, very little of which was for sea-letters, — those to missions in foreign lands being nearly all sent by ship from the port of Boston, and the greater part received from them being first deposited on their arrival in the Boston post office. There were then no ocean mail-packets, and of course there was no ocean postage.

Seven years later, the number of sheets received from the missions in one year exceeded fifteen hundred. The number of letters in the domestic correspondence, during a year, was about twelve hundred. The annual postage on letters and pamphlets was nearly a thousand dollars, though a large portion of the letters from beyond sea was subject to little or no charge.

For many years after the Board commenced its operations, the rates of postage were high. Up to July, 1845, a single sheet, under thirty miles, cost six cents; from thirty to eighty miles, ten cents; from eighty to one hundred and fifty miles, twelve and a half cents; from one hundred and fifty to four hundred miles, eighteen and three fourths cents; and over four hundred miles, twenty-five cents. From 1845 to 1851, the postage was five cents the half ounce under three hundred miles, and ten cents for a greater distance. The present standard of three cents for any distance short of three thousand miles, and six cents beyond that, was adopted in 1851. The postage on letters to the missions beyond sea, by the "overland" mails, is from thirty-three to forty cents for every half ounce; excepting to the Sandwich Islands, where it is seventeen cents. The postage, in periods of ten years, was as follows: —

First period,	$330 74	Fourth,	8,215 79
Second,	3,920 33	Fifth,	8,951 72
Third,	8,270 23	Total,	$29,688 81

The letters and other documents received, during thirteen years, from the Armenian mission alone, were somewhat more than three thousand sheets. The proportion was not so great from the other missions. The missionaries are expected to write to the Missionary House on paper furnished for the purpose, and always with a proper margin for the binding of the letters and journals. Manuscripts of every kind are bound in volumes convenient for reference, which are deposited in a room secure from fire, forming the archives of the Board. An inventory of the contents of this room gives the following results, viz.: —

	Volumes.
Letters and other Documents received from Missions and Missionaries,	157
Miscellaneous Foreign Letters,	4
Autograph Letters from Officers of the Board, chiefly the Secretaries,	9
Letters from Candidates, and Testimonials,	30
Letters from Persons in the United States,	59
Documents,	17
Copies of Letters, made by letter press, to Missionaries and others in Foreign Lands,	47
Copies of Letters, made by letter press, to the Indian Missions,	22
Copies of Domestic Letters, made by letter press, sent from the Missionary House,	58
Copies of Letters in Folio Volumes, made by pen, viz.: —	
Foreign and Domestic,	5
Domestic and Indian,	4

	Volumes.
Foreign,	4
Indian,	2
Domestic,	9
Agencies,	1
From the Treasurer,	8
Foreign Letters, copied from the letter-press volumes, since the year 1837,	25
Instructions to Missionaries,	1
Records of the Board, (including duplicates of the first two volumes,)	6
Minutes of the Prudential Committee,	3
Records of the Prudential Committee,	11
Whole number of volumes,	482

Letters from the Missionary House are always copied before being sent. Since the year 1835, the copies have been taken by a press; and the foreign letters are afterward fairly copied out by hand. This is found needful for a distinct and permanent record; and the advantages of it to the Board have appeared on several occasions; as, for instance, in the investigations of the special committee on the proceedings of the deputation to the India missions. That committee reported themselves to have read twenty-five hundred pages of the correspondence, extending through many years.

As all that is written from the Missionary House, and all that is received there, are thus preserved and arranged, it will be readily seen that there is an historical value in the collection.

The correspondence of the Secretaries with particular missions has been more or less extended, at different times, according to circumstances; and great freedom has always been awarded to them in reasoning upon all subjects, on which they believed it useful to correspond with their brethren,— always observing the radical distinction between suggestions, opinions, and arguments, on the one hand, and decisions, instructions, and rules, on the other. The like freedom is awarded to the missions and missionaries. On subjects resolvable only by experience, an interchange of views has sometimes extended through several years, before the opinions of the Prudential Committee and their brethren have become settled and consentaneous; and not unfrequently, as the result of this free correspondence, the sentiments at first entertained on both sides have been considerably modified.

Correspondence is very far from having been the whole duty of the Secretaries. Until within a few years past, they edited the Missionary Herald. They have always been responsible for the preparation of the Annual Report, though of late they have sometimes had aid in writing it. They have written appeals, circulars, and most of the missionary tracts. The whole intercourse with candidates for missionary employment, up to the time when their papers come before the Prudential Committee, belongs to the Secretaries; and so, afterward, until their embarkation. The Secretaries have also, at different times, been at great pains to prepare and deliver Instructions, on behalf of the Prudential Committee, to missionaries about going forth to their several fields. The writing of these has been useful in various ways, but especially as it required a thorough research into the condition of the countries whither the missionaries were going. The Instructions were usually delivered in the presence of crowded assemblies, in cities or in central places; though some of the most elaborate of them, developing the missions to the Oriental Churches, were given in the presence of theological students at some one of the Seminaries. Dr. Worcester's Instructions to Messrs. Parsons and Fisk, in the year 1819, who were then "bound in spirit to Jerusalem," and also those to the first missionaries to the Sandwich Islands in the same year, are among his most eloquent productions. Not far from sixty of these documents are preserved at the Missionary House, in a printed or written form. About two thirds of them belong to the period between 1830 and 1847. It will suffice to give extracts from two or three of these official documents when treating of the rise of the missions, in the second part of this volume. To the Secretaries it belongs to see the numerous visitors to the Missionary House; and it is important that they give personal attention both to missionaries coming home on a visit, and to those who are going forth to their distant fields. It is, moreover, their duty and pleasure to give attention to the returned children of missionaries on their arrival. There are also missionary conventions and meetings of auxiliaries, which it is often desirable for them to attend, in connection with district secretaries and returned missionaries. Add to this the personal visits to the missions, — of which an account will be given in a subsequent chapter, — and the reader will have some idea of the multifarious and onerous duties connected with the secretaryship. Still, without a nearer view than these pages give, there can not be an adequate impression.

At first, and until 1832, there was but one Corresponding Secretary. An assistant was employed in 1822, who was formally appointed Assistant Secretary in 1824, and a second Assistant Secretary was appointed in 1828. These were really the editors of the Missionary Herald; and one of them acted as Assistant Secretary for the foreign correspondence, and the other for the Indian and home correspondence. They were appointed Corresponding Secretaries in 1832; one for the foreign correspondence, the other for the Indian, and for editing the Missionary Herald; and a third Secretary was then appointed to take charge of the home correspondence.

In compliance with the earnest desire of patrons in the city of New York, a Corresponding Secretary, to reside in that city, was appointed in 1852, and the appointment has been continued until the present time. The care of the departments of correspondence is necessarily put upon the Secretaries residing in Boston. There being an Editor for the monthly publications, the Board has now but two Corresponding Secretaries in Boston, who respectively have charge of the Foreign and Home Departments.

Library of the Board.

In November, 1821, the Prudential Committee directed, that notice be given of an intended collection of a Missionary Library, and that the public be invited to contribute books, not only for the Library, but for the use of the various missions of the Board. Such a notice was given, and this was the first step toward collecting the present Library of the Board, which now more than fills the sides of the large Committee Room. It is perhaps the most valuable collection of works in what may be called the literature of benevolence, that is any where to be found. The Library has ever been an object of interest to the executive officers. It is largely made up of the reports and periodicals of benevolent societies in America and Europe, received for the most part by donation or exchange; and possesses, of course, the more important domestic and foreign serials, and the standard works in missionary biography, travels, and history. It has been found promotive of economy to possess some, at least, of the more reliable works on the countries where the Board had planted, or was expecting to plant, its missions. One illustration of this is well remembered. Many years since, yielding to strong advice from India, the Prudential Committee went so far as to appoint two missionaries for commencing a new mission among the Rajpoots of Western India. It was afterward deemed advisable to consult Lieutenant Colonel James Tod's Annals and Antiquities of the Central and Western Rajpoot States, in two quarto volumes, then recently published. Accordingly the work was imported from England, and showed conclusively that a mission to Rajpootana would then be premature. The enterprise was relinquished, and subsequent events amply proved the correctness of this conclusion. As an aid in editing the monthly publications of the Board, and in preparing the annual reports, addresses to the public, and instructions to missionaries, as well as in the correspondence, this Library has been of great value.

The collection is nearly complete in respect to foreign and domestic Missionary Societies, and Bible, Tract, and other benevolent institutions of this country, and also in the similar publications of kindred societies in Great Britain. Mr. Evarts bequeathed to it a valuable portion of his own library. The present number of volumes is six thousand one hundred and fifty-two.

The Cabinet.

The Cabinet, to which a room in the Missionary House has been devoted, is a collection of articles from heathen countries, illustrative of their religions, manners, and customs. It is open to the public, and its influence has doubtless been good. The Cabinet owes its existence more to the care exercised to preserve the articles of curiosity which have naturally come to the House from the different missions, than to any set purpose to create such a thing. The number of articles might easily be enlarged, were there room for more. The most interesting object in this room is a revolving case, containing more than four hundred daguerreotype, ambrotype, and photographic portraits of missionaries and assistant missionaries of the Board, male and female, many of whom are now no longer in the land of the living. This collection of portraits was begun in the year 1845, and has been attended with little cost.

CHAPTER X.

THE FINANCES.

Obtaining Funds the greatest Difficulty. — Means employed. — Worth of an Exigency. — Striking Fact. — Receipts in Periods of Four Years. — In Periods of Ten Years. — General Summary. — Whence derived. — Gradual Increase. — Expenditure in Periods of Four Years. — Comparative View. — The Expenditure almost necessarily Progressive. — Influence of faith on Missionary Confidence. — On the Cost of the Missions. — Limitation necessary. — Dissent of Missionaries. — Duty and Powers of the Prudential Committee. — Estimates and Appropriations. — New Responsibilities. — On the Cost of the several Agencies. — Remittances. — Investments. — Permanent Funds. — Indebtedness, and the Responsibility for it. — Not prevented by Ruinous Reductions.

THE financial history of the Board admits of great expansion, yet must be briefly treated. The greatest difficulty in propagating the gospel through the world is believed to be obtaining the funds. The chief root of all the evils that have come upon the enterprise from the beginning until now, has been "the love of money" in the professed people of God. Who can tell how much of thought, feeling, and labor, of solicitude, fatigue, and disappointment, how many convocations, speeches, and resolutions, journeyings, consultations, and pledges, and how much of prayer and faith, it has required to obtain only a few hundred thousands? And what frequent haltings for lack of pecuniary means — what backward marches — what territory lost that had been gained for the King of Zion! This is one view of the subject. A more reasonable and hopeful view is, to regard the enterprise as in its infancy and inexperience, and its economic nature as yet imperfectly understood. Perhaps it is true, that as large funds have been providentially committed to Missionary Societies in the past fifty years, as they had the knowledge to administer judiciously; and that it is impossible to have the necessary steadiness and increase of contributions until there shall be a more intelligent, pervading conviction of the essentially progressive nature of the work, and of the wasteful, destructive consequences of not providing for it. This knowledge is extending and increasing; and the very exigencies, by creating anxiety and alarm, tend to awaken thought and inquiry, and so increase this knowledge. Hence the first Corresponding Secretary used to say, that an exigency was worth a thousand dollars to the Board. It is worth much more now; but this presupposes a faithful and wise administration, that will bear a searching investigation as to the cause of the exigency.

It is believed to be a fact, that the great permanent advances in the receipts of the Board all stand in immediate connection with its larger debts, and would seem to have resulted from the effort to throw them off. But indebtedness has thus proved useful only as it could not be avoided.

The subject of missionary finance naturally divides into receipts and expenditures. The former are mainly from donations and legacies; but inasmuch as these are sometimes required by the donors to be invested, there comes at length to be an income from permanent funds. Moreover, in the prosecution of foreign missions, houses and lands must sometimes be owned, and printing-presses, and other property; and hence another, though very limited source of income, in the sale of books and other properties.

The expenditures are for the missions, for collecting the funds, and for the administration. Estimates, appropriations, remittances, regulations for the expenditure, investments, and the whole subject of indebtedness, come under the second division, as does the discussion of the various permanent funds, and of the economical questions which develop those laws of missionary finance, that are as really beyond the control of missionaries, and the directors and patrons of missions, as the laws of nature. A proper treatment of all these topics would require more space than can be afforded in this volume.

RECEIPTS IN PERIODS OF FOUR YEARS.

Years.	Periods.	Receipts.	Periods of 4 Years.	Increase.	Av. An. Rec'ts.	Increase.
1811		$999 52				
1812		13,611 50				
1813		11,361 18				
1814		12,265 56				
1815	1	9,493 89	$46,732 13		$11,683	$10,684
1816		12,501 03				
1817		29,918 63				
1818		34,727 72				
1819	2	37,520 63	114,698 01	$67,966	28,674	16,991
1820		39,949 45				
1821		46,354 95				
1822		60,087 87				
1823	3	55,758 94	202,151 21	87,453	50,537	21,863
1824		47,483 58				
1825		55,716 18				
1826		61,616 25				
1827	4	88,341 89	253,157 90	51,006	63,289	12,752
1828		102,009 64				
1829		106,928 26				
1830		83,019 37				
1831	5	100,934 09	392,891 36	39,734	98,222	34,933
1832		130,574 12				
1833		145,847 77				
1834		152,386 10				
1835	6	163,340 19	592,148 18	199,257	148,037	49,815
1836		176,232 15				
1837		252,076 55				
1838		236,170 98				
1839	7	244,169 82	908,649 50	316,501	227,162	79,125
1840		241,691 04				
1841		235,189 30				
1842		318,396 53				
1843	8	244,254 43	1,039,531 30	130,882	259,882	32,720
1844		236,394 37				
1845		255,112 96				
1846		262,073 55				
1847	9	211,402 76	964,983 64	74 547	241,245	18,637
1848		254,056 46		Less than in	the preceding	period.
1849		291,705 27				
1850		251,862 28				
1851	10	274,902 21	1,072,526 22	107,543	268,131	26,886
1852		301,732 70				
1853		314,922 88				
1854		305,778 84				
1855	11	310,127 77	1,232,862 19	160,336	308,215	20,084
1856		307,318 69				
1857		388,932 69				
1858		334,018 48				
1859	12	350,915 45	1,381,185 31	148,323	345,296	37,081
1860		429,799 08				
	Total,	8,632,315 55				

The balance in the treasury, at the close of the above period, was $1,466 19. The footing of this table should, therefore, have been greater by $2,531 64. The discrepancy arose from the use of some early tables of receipts, prepared to show the amount of donations and legacies.

RECEIPTS IN PERIODS OF TEN YEARS.

1.

Year.	Donations.	Legacies.
1811	$975 96	
1812	13,597 40	
1813	11,209 90	
1814	11,791 91	$15 00
1815	9,122 54	291 00
1816	10,412 51	101 83
1817	24,505 66	2,620 00
1818	31,712 53	80 00
1819	33,676 25	290 37
1820	35,224 49	973 15
	$182,229 15	$4,371 35

2.

Year.	Donations.	Legacies.
1821	45,433 65	363 83
1822	57,625 87	1,816 61
1823	48,509 70	5,054 52
1824	44,657 55	1,642 18
1825	50,624 03	3,101 45
1826	57,645 75	2,075 36
1827	82,435 25	4,088 03
1828	95,784 00	3,721 88
1829	94,870 90	9,671 34
1830	75,408 73	5,379 43
	$642,995 43	$41,285 98

3.

Year.	Donations.	Legacies.
1831	89,068 26	9,235 76
1832	117,392 00	10,349 93
1833	132,565 68	8,828 85
1834	138,919 00	6,709 66
1835	148,896 35	6,997 25
1836	164,817 55	8,757 84
1837	233,443 39	14,030 32
1838	227,338 11	5,491 35
1839	223,987 84	17,700 24
1840	228,777 55	11,813 53
	$1,705,205 73	$99,914 73

4.

Year.	Donations.	Legacies.
1841	$213,236 39	$20,506 65
1842	277,495 04	39,088 31
1843	222,014 90	20,761 32
1844	217,902 66	16,446 85
1845	220,863 92	32,437 01
1846	195,208 37	63,436 90
1847	192,816 92	16,548 29
1848	225,595 01	26,157 49
1849	261,431 41	28,271 29
1850	217,839 26	31,474 84
	$2,244,403 88	$295,128 95

5.

Year.	Donations.	Legacies.
1851	244,521 43	28,169 36
1852	263,683 46	36,020 44
1853	269,899 42	35,156 16
1854	264,951 97	32,238 89
1855	256,855 57	44,482 60
1856	250,486 22	48,730 36
1857	321,432 98	55,035 12
1858	269,827 29	34,248 76
1859	276,597 38	49,963 03
1860	373,241 72	52,597 53
	$2,791,497 44	$416,642 25

SUMMARY.

Periods.	Donations.	Legacies.
1811–1820	182,229 15	4,371 35
1821–1830	642,995 43	41,285 98
1831–1840	1,705,205 73	99,914 73
1841–1850	2,244,403 88	295,128 95
1851–1860	2,791,497 44	416,642 25
Total,	$7,566,331 63	$857,343 26

Legacies to the Permanent Funds are not included in the preceding tables of receipts. These funds are two — the General Permanent Fund, consisting of $64,715, and the Permanent Fund for Officers, amounting to $39,840.

GENERAL SUMMARY.

From Donations,	$7,566,331 63
From Legacies,	857,343 26
From Other Sources,	208,640 66
Grand Total,	$8,632,315 55

An inquiry, prosecuted some twenty years since, made it seem highly probable, that not more than two thirds of the church members, even in the State of Massachusetts, then gave any thing for the cause of foreign missions. It appeared, moreover, that eight parts out of nine of all that was given, was by church members. In most districts of country, the proportion of giving church members must be considerably less, and the proportion contributed by the visible church more. It is matter for grateful acknowledgment, however, that from the beginning there has been, on the whole, an upward tendency in the receipts. Dividing the time of the Board's existence into periods of four years, in every one of these periods, with but a single exception, there has been an increase of receipts. That exception was owing to the extraordinary impression made on the Christian community by the meeting of the Board in Philadelphia, in the year 1841, which, through the divine blessing, carried the income of the following year up to the unprecedented amount of three hundred and eighteen thousand dollars. The table presents a striking illustration of the advance of the mighty cause of the gospel, slowly, but steadily, surely, from period to period, as by invincible laws.

EXPENDITURES IN PERIODS OF FOUR YEARS.

Years.	Periods.	Expenditures.	Periods of 4 Years.	Increase.	Av. An. Exp's.	Increase.
1811						
1812		$9,699				
1813		8,611				
1814		7,078				
1815	1	5,027	$30,415		$7,603	
1816		15,934				
1817		20,485				
1818		36,346				
1819	2	40,337	113,102	$82,687	28,275	$20,672
1820		57,621				
1821		46,771				
1822		60,474				
1823	3	66,380	231,246	118,144	57,811	29,536
1824		54,157				
1825		41,469				
1826		59,012				
1827	4	103,430	258,068	26,822	64,517	6,706
1828		107,676				
1829		92,533				
1830		84,798				
1831	5	98,313	383,320	125,252	95,830	31,313
1832		120,954				
1833		149,906				
1834		159,779				
1835	6	163,254	593,893	210,573	148,473	52,648
1836		210,407				
1837		254,589				
1838		230,642				
1839	7	227,491	923,129	329,236	230,782	82,309
1840		246,601				
1841		268,914				
1842		261,147				
1843	8	256,687	1,033,349	110,220	258,337	27,555
1844		244,371				
1845		216,817				
1846		257,605				
1847	9	264,783	983,576	*49,773	245,894	*12,443
1848		282,330				
1849		263,418				
1850		254,329				
1851	10	284,830	1,084,907	101,331	271,226	25,333
1852		257,727				
1853		310,607				
1854		322,142				
1855	11	318,893	1,209,369	124,462	302,342	31,115
1856		323,000				
1857		355,590				
1858		372,041				
1859	12	376,418	1,427,049	217,680	356,762	54,420
1860		361,958				
	Total,	$8,633,381				

* Less than in the preceding period.

There was an excess of the expenditure over the receipts in seven of the twelve periods, and in five of them the receipts exceeded the expenditure. The difference formed the debt, as it stood July 31, 1859, which was so happily removed in the following year. The annual increase in the Board's expenditure from the beginning, has averaged about seven thousand six hundred dollars. During the last six periods, the annual increase was about eight thousand eight hundred dollars. Considering the prosperity and extent of the system of missions, as a whole, perhaps it is not more than their natural growth, under the ordinary blessing of Heaven. Foreign missions are essentially progressive, as much so as a family. The analogy is most striking. The children advance physically, intellectually, morally, making increasing demands for food, clothing, and education. This is the family constitution, and violence is done to the laws of domestic life whenever the growth is resisted, or even not promoted. Up to a certain period, it involves a regular increase of expense, which no enlightened parent would withhold, except from necessity. Thus we see in a mission a regular growth and development up to a certain period of its life. But experience shows, that an invariable yearly increase in the receipts is not to be expected. There was a decrease in fifteen of the past fifty years. There have been vacillations analogous to those in the business of the country, and more or less resulting therefrom; and it is one of the unsolved problems in foreign missions, how to provide against these. Perhaps our only solution is in the principle of faith. The main ground of confidence in the success of missions to the heathen world, is in that principle. Our hopes and expectations concerning their progress and final triumph are sustained by the command, promise, faithfulness, power, and agency of Almighty God.

The experience of the Board in its first twenty-five years did not warrant any serious apprehension of danger in leaving the several missions to exercise a discretion, under general directions from the Committee, as to the amount of their annual expenditures. But in the year 1836, the expenditures of the Board rose from one hundred and sixty-three thousand dollars — which was the expenditure of the previous year — to two hundred and ten thousand dollars; and the debt from four thousand six hundred dollars to thirty-eight thousand eight hundred dollars. The expenditures of the year 1837 were two hundred and fifty-four thousand dollars, or ninety-one thousand dollars more than the receipts of the previous year, and the debt forty-one thousand dollars. Had not the receipts of the Board, in that year of general gloom and bankruptcy in the country, exceeded those of the previous year by more than seventy-five thousand dollars, the Board would have met at Newark under an overwhelming load of debt. Had no more been contributed in 1837 — that year of commercial disaster and distress — than in the two years of plenty immediately preceding, the missions, without a miracle of mercy, would have suffered all but starvation and ruin! For how could the Board, in such circumstances, have had credit in the commercial world to draw its bills of exchange on London in sums sufficient to supply their wants? or, resorting to the only other mode of remittance, where could it have procured specie, when there was none in the market? Moreover, had not the Committee, in the summer of 1837, reduced the expenses of the missions some forty thousand dollars, the debt, instead of being only thirty-five thousand dollars, would have risen to seventy-five thousand dollars.

The Prudential Committee attributed no blame to the missions for this increase in their expenditures. At the commencement of every mission, circumstances for a time prescribe narrow limits to a judicious expenditure. The missionaries do not know the language, and have no press, no schools, no native helpers. They need money only for food, clothing, shelter, occasional tours, and for procuring instruction in the language. But with advancing time there are changes. Beginning to preach, they need preaching houses of some sort, which, at the least, the natives must have help in providing. They prepare books, and require a press.

They have a printing establishment, readers, a demand for books, and need paper, ink, workmen. They have free schools, training schools, native helpers, preaching tours, and calls for new stations, more laborers, more and more extended and vigorous operations. In such circumstances, it might be judicious, if the funds can be obtained, to increase the expenditures considerably. Nay, to the missionaries on the ground, a great increase may seem a matter of obvious necessity, and not to make it they may feel to be a neglect and exposure of the harvest in the field no better than a waste of money, labor, and influence. And yet, in the actual state of the treasury, — as better known to the Committee at home than it can be to them, — such an increase of expenditure may involve other and greater evils, which ought on no account to be incurred.

About the years 1835 and 1836, many of the missions felt impelled to enlargement by motives like these; and the number of the missions had now become such, that a small increase of expense in each made a large sum in the aggregate. So distant were the missions from each other, that they could not act in concert; and so distant from the seat of the Board, that a long time was required to modify their expenditures in an emergency. There was no way, therefore, to prevent the evil of an overdrawn treasury, but by assigning bounds to the annual expenditure of each mission. Indeed, so great was the exigency, in the early part of 1837, as to constrain the Committee at once to put a limit upon the expenses of each mission, making use of such facts as they had in deciding what it ought to be. This they did in a circular letter, which, though it did not require reductions, served to effect them in many cases. The missions generally appreciated the motives which governed the Committee, and conformed to their instructions. In one mission, however, a portion of the missionaries called in question the right of the Prudential Committee so to restrict their expenses. They resolved, that, in their opinion, it was the duty of the Board fully to sustain the schools, or be chargeable with a dereliction of Christian and missionary duty fatal to the best interests of the people. They also passed the following, among other resolutions: —

That as the Board, in their late letter, seem to withhold from the schools that aid which we had reason from their instructions to expect, therefore we can not but feel deeply grieved at such a procedure, without a full knowledge of our circumstances, and the difficulties in which such a measure might involve us.

As a vital principle was here involved, which needed settlement before going further, the case was referred to the Board at its meeting in 1838. The response of the Board was as follows: —

1. That our missionaries, in passing these resolutions, evidently acted under a misapprehension as to the facts in the case; and we have good reason to believe that had they possessed more definite information on the subject, they would not have adopted the resolutions.

2. That it is, and always will be, the duty of the Prudential Committee, under the superintendence of the Board, faithfully to employ all the means furnished by the charities of the community in providing for the comfortable support of the missionaries, and for the enlargement and success of their operations.

3. That, both as a right and a duty, it unquestionably belongs to the Prudential Committee, under the supervision of the Board, to regulate the expenses of every mission, and of every missionary; that this principle is clearly implied in the standing rules of the Board, and that the uniform practice has been in accordance with it, ever since the commencement of our foreign missions; that the Board deem this principle of vital importance in the prosecution of missions; and that it can not be overlooked or neglected without opening the door for great irregularities and embarrassments in their pecuniary concerns, and thus forfeiting the confidence of the public.

4. That it is the indispensable duty of all the missionaries of the Board to govern themselves, in regard to their expenditures, and all their proceedings as missionaries, according to the directions of the Prudential Committee.

5. That although in ordinary cases it is altogether proper, and a matter of course, that the Prudential Committee should have free consultation with the missionaries in every station before making important changes in relation to expenditures, or other subjects pertaining to the conduct of missions, yet they have a perfect right, and are bound in duty, to make any changes at once, without such consultation, whenever the circumstances of the case render it necessary.

Thus it was that the present system of Estimates and Appropriations arose. The missions are expected to make out a carefully prepared estimate of the expenditures needed for the next year in every department of their labors, going as much as possible into detail, and to forward it in time to reach the Missionary House before October; and upon these estimates the appropriations for the following year are made out by the Prudential Committee; and by these the Treasurer of the Board is governed in his remittances. As the missions are expected to be governed by them, it might seem that nothing more is needful to keep the expenditure within the appropriation. The success has not been complete. The appropriations are to be made beforehand. The missions are in distant countries; and it is not possible for the Board to proceed on the principle of remitting only as the funds are actually in the treasury. No foreign missionary society is able to do this. Those distant expenditures must be authorized months before they are actually incurred; and of course with reference to the probable and not the actual receipts. In the working of an extended system of foreign missions, this is the wisest economy. Suppose it possible to obtain the funds beforehand for a six months' or a year's outlay: on such a financial system, there must be large sums constantly on hand, with the difficulties of safe investment, with interest, with losses, and with the uncongenial reputation of a money-lending institution. The Christian public will not make such advances to a missionary society, nor are they desirable. It has been, however, the tacit understanding of the missions, that the Board is to make good to them the nominal value of all the appropriations. Had this applied in practice only to losses on exchange, the evil would not have been great. But the principle once admitted, naturally had a broader application; and so the year has been apt to close with a considerable excess of the expenditure above the appropriations. Losses, war prices, extra appropriations, etc., instead of being met on the ground by modifications in the enterprise itself, have come home upon the central treasury; and, if no special fund had been reserved for such contingencies, they of course created a debt, and went out in that repulsive form and aspect to the churches. The inconvenience of this has been seriously felt. It has seemed desirable, therefore, so to arrange the appropriations that the missions will go through the year, and meet all their outlays, with the money actually appropriated. This would necessarily involve the right of the missions to modify the several departments of expenditure. A sum being placed at their disposal,—all the Board is able to assign for the year,—the missions will so manage as to make it meet all the exigencies of the year in immediate connection with their field. The Board is too remote from the missions for prompt intervention; but the missions are in the midst of their work and expenditure, and so can stop short at any time, where they must. Skill, thought, resolution, painstaking, will be required; but, if this be carried out in all the missions, it will leave the Board, at the close of its year, with nothing extra to meet, except the possible excess of the appropriations above the receipts.

The Agencies will be treated historically in a subsequent chapter; but this is the place to remark upon their cost. The salaries of the district secretaries are necessarily larger in some districts than in others. For obvious reasons, this class of laborers need to reside in central places, where railroads and post-routes meet, and from which they can most readily visit and communicate with the different sections of their respective districts; and it is found that such men as pastors and churches will gladly welcome, are not obtainable at less salaries than are paid by the Board. The traveling expenses form no part of the salary. These represent the amount of travel performed in prosecuting the agency. The one thousand seven hundred and seventy-nine dollars paid last year on this score, if all for the road expenses alone, would represent some sixty thousand miles of travel. The distance traveled can be scarcely less than fifty thousand miles. The roads are often long and wearisome. As with postages in the case of secretaries, so with road expenses in respect to agents, the greater the amount, the greater, almost of course, the labor performed.

The value of the PRESS, as a missionary agent, is inestimable. The Board has relied much on the self-supporting religious newspapers and periodicals of the day, which form so prominent a feature in the religious life of the age. But every large society finds it necessary to have channels of its own for communicating with the public. It has been so with the Board during the greater part of its existence. The Missionary Herald has been its main reliance. That publication was once more than supported by subscribers paying a dollar and a half for the volume. The question arose at length, whether the cause would not be promoted by sending the Herald gratuitously to every donor of ten dollars and upward who did not prefer taking it as a subscriber, to every collector of not less than fifteen dollars, to treasurers of associations contributing not less than twenty dollars, and to pastors in congregations which statedly contribute to the treasury of the Board through the monthly concert or otherwise. Such was the opinion of the Board; and these donors, collectors, treasurers, congregations, are justly reckoned among the supporters of the Missionary Herald. Somewhat more than two thousand copies are paid for by subscribers, who are often, by the rule, entitled to gratuitous copies, and about thirteen thousand copies go as is stated above. Similar remarks would apply to the gratuitous distribution of some forty thousand copies of the Journal of Missions and Day Spring.

The cost of printing the Annual Report has ever been regarded as a judicious expenditure. The Report would not have been elaborately written if it were not to be printed; the motive would not have been sufficient. It would have been little more than the brief general abstract usually read at the annual meeting. A thorough digest was the thing needed, a careful résumé, an intelligent exhibition, of the proceedings and events of the year; and such has been the Annual Report. It has put the Board and the churches in communication with the executive and the missions. Its influence upon the officers in preparing it, has been like taking an account of stock with the merchant. It has been the winding up of the mainspring. The Board would not have felt that it understood or could understand the business, but for the Report. The document is believed to be no larger than is needful for an intelligible account of such extended and prosperous operations; nor is the edition greater than the number of associations and donors who rightfully expect to receive it.

The MISCELLANEOUS expenditure scarcely needs remark. The payment for postage represents a large amount of correspondence. Within our own country, it is paid for letters written at the Missionary House. With the missions, and individuals in foreign lands, it is only for communications from or to the executive officers of the Board. More than five hundred dollars, not in the treasurer's account, was paid for letters passing through the Missionary House from missionaries or their personal friends, and of course charged to the private account of the missionaries. As to salaries, it may be proper to say, that the Secretaries have never been able to live upon their salaries alone; though, having always received as much from the Board as they themselves deemed expedient, they have never seen reason to complain.

Remittances.

The remittances to the missions, previous to the year 1830, were usually in specie. The exception was in the years 1826 and 1827, when an arrangement was kindly entered into by Edward A. Newton, Esq., — now of Pittsfield, Mass., then a merchant in Calcutta, — to advance funds for the expenses of the India missions, for which bills were to be drawn payable in London. Since 1830, the Board has made its remittances through Messrs. Baring, Brothers, & Co., the well-known bankers in London. The Treasurer draws no bills until authorized by the Prudential Committee, and a certified copy of their vote is required by the agent of the bankers, before he gives the sanction of his house. During the thirty years past, the Board has remitted nearly four and a half millions of dollars through the Messrs. Barings to the several missions. From fifteen to twenty-five thousand pounds sterling have generally been out at one time, but there has never been a time when any security was demanded.

Almost all the missions are thus sustained. These bills of exchange form a better remittance than specie, as they can be sent by mail, oftener, in smaller sums, with less trouble, without the cost of insurance and freight, and without the loss of interest. In general they are remitted monthly, and about the same amount is sent from month to month. The bills are sold by the missions, and thus are converted into money. The monthly remittance is equal to a twelfth part of the annual allowance to the mission. Of course the bills do not accumulate in the hands of the treasurers of the missions, and those which arrive and become due in London are about the same in amount from month to month with those which are sent from Boston. After these bills of exchange have once completed a revolution in their appointed orbits, it makes little difference in the amount of the Board's indebtedness, at what period in their revolution they are charged in the Treasurer's accounts; for they are scattered along through every month in the year in nearly equal proportions, and while new bills of exchange commence their revolution and are entered to the debit of the Board, the like number terminate theirs, and come up for final adjustment. While, therefore, this mode of remittance continues undisturbed, it makes little difference, on the debit side of the accounts, whether the bills are charged when remitted, or on reaching the mission, or on coming to maturity in London.

The usage of the Treasurer is to charge the bills as soon as they are remitted. This is due to the banking house in London, which, through its agent in Boston, makes itself responsible for the payment of these bills of exchange before they are sent. This is due also to the community; for these bills of exchange are as truly a remittance of money as the sending of so many bank bills from Boston to New York, and the Board is held firmly bound to redeem them in specie, or its equivalent, and the community ought to know the extent of the liabilities. Moreover, — and this consideration alone would be decisive, — if the bills were not charged until they had completed their circuit, and a war, or any other cause, should break up the present arrangement, and compel the Board to resort again to the remittance of specie, all the missions which are sustained by this means would inevitably be charged with double their actual expenditure for the greater part of a year following this event; and the Board would suddenly fall into arrears, and that too, probably, in circumstances very inauspicious. For not only would specie have to be bought to take the place of the bills of exchange in the monthly remittance, (which of course would have to be charged at once,) but for months the bills that were performing their revolution would be arriving in London, and demand payment there.

Investments.

The Permanent Funds of the Board are divided into two classes — the General Permanent Fund, and the Fund for Officers. The former amounts to sixty-four thousand seven hundred and fifteen dollars, as has been stated, and the latter to thirty-nine thousand eight hundred and forty dollars. The foundations of the General Fund were laid in Mrs. Norris's legacy of thirty thousand dollars, at the outset of the Board's history. It is chiefly made up of legacies bequeathed for it expressly, and embraces the Missionary House. The Fund for Officers, the income of which goes to pay part of their salaries, had its origin many years ago in the dissatisfaction which some excellent patrons, living in rural districts, felt at the amount it was needful to give the officers for their support. It was made up in part by contributions for this specific object, and in part from the profits of the Missionary Herald, when the paying subscription list was much larger than it is at present. It is deemed prudent to retain such permanent funds as are now held by the Board, in order that there may be a sure reliance in case of emergency. The credit of the Board might otherwise, under circumstances of unexpected difficulty, be impaired, which would prove an incalculable evil.

At the meeting of the Board in Utica, in 1855, the committee on the Treasurer's report proposed that a select committee be appointed to consider the propriety and expediency of making some permanent provision for the support of superannuated and disabled missionaries, and also to inquire into the expediency of revising the present rules respecting the children of missionaries, and that the said committee report at the next meeting of the Board. Such a committee was appointed, and presented a written report at the following meeting, which was ordered to be printed for circulation among the members, and to come up for consideration at the meeting in Providence in 1857. Two able reports were then presented; one by the majority, in favor of establishing a fund for the relief of superannuated and disabled missionaries, and the children of missionaries. The other was a minority report against such a fund. After considerable discussion, the following resolutions were unanimously adopted as a substitute for those proposed by the committee: —

1. That it is highly desirable to cherish and strengthen a warm Christian sympathy in behalf of those who have been

disabled in their work as missionaries, and toward their widows and children, and that it is desirable to open all suitable channels for the practical expression of such sympathies.

2. That the Prudential Committee will receive and cheerfully appropriate, according to the same principles which have hitherto governed them in the premises, whatever legacies or contributions may be made from year to year, and designated by their donors for this specific object.

The subject will be treated somewhat more largely in the chapter on missionaries.

Indebtedness.

The Board has been obliged often to report a debt, greater or less in amount; but this has not been because its annual expenditure in so many instances exceeded its income. When a debt is once incurred in a great system of operations, and where the demand on the treasury is constant and increasing, it is not easily removed; because there must be a sum large enough to pay both the current expenses and the debt. In truth, the missions have grown faster than the habit of giving in the churches. The expenditure has consequently pressed hard upon the receipts. In two or three instances, owing to unusual prosperity in some of the missions, and it may be to commercial distress at home, the indebtedness has become such as to occasion some uneasiness. But it has always been paid without impairing the credit of the Board, or bringing any damage on the Christian community. Taking one time with another, the expenditure has probably been no more in advance of public sentiment, than to operate as a really healthful stimulant. It is quite certain that the restriction upon the expenditure has always been as stringent as seemed to comport with a proper observance of the law of continued progress, which God has prescribed for the missionary enterprise. The missions can not be healthy, contented, prosperous, without a free growth and expansion. And it has ever been the policy of the Board to protect, as far as possible, the results of labor in the missions.

The public admission of debt, on the part of the Board, has never affected its credit. When the debt has become large, effectual measures are taken to reduce it. The banking house in London, however, on whom its bills of exchange are chiefly drawn, appears to be aware that Christian benevolence, directed to a commanding religious object of enduring interest, like the conversion of the world to God, is more to be depended on than mere skill in trade. It is also a fact, that the permanent funds of the Board are greater than the debt has ever been; and, as a last resort, even that portion of them which the Board has no power to spend, because the donors gave only the interest to be expended, might, doubtless, by a process of law, be made available to the discharge of its liabilities. A permanent fund to a certain amount, that can not be applied to current expenses, is an important, if not an indispensable, safeguard to the credit of the Board in the commercial world. It has been deemed proper always to state the accounts of the Board so that the community may see just how far the institution is within the line of safety.

The Prudential Committee has often had but a very limited responsibility for the balance, which the closing year has left standing against the Board. The elements composing it were perhaps scarcely within their legitimate control. Only by an exercise of power, it may be, in disregard of the laws of missionary finance, could they have done any thing effectual to prevent it. Reducing missions, and holding back missionaries, besides being contrary to the command of Christ, are not found to exert a beneficial effect on the treasury. They have a disastrous influence on the missionary spirit in our colleges and theological seminaries, and indeed every where. If new missionaries fail to come forward, and there is actually a decline in the number of missionaries abroad, it is found to be hard to induce the churches to advance in the amount of their subscriptions. In consequence of an error of this sort in 1837, the Board, ten years afterward, stood in its receipts nearly where it did at that time. Here it is emphatically true, that "there is that withholdeth more than is meet, but it tendeth to poverty."

CHAPTER XI.

THE AGENCIES.

The Two Branches. — Agents early in the Half-Century. — Growth of System. — Brookfield Auxiliary. — Laws of Benevolent Giving. — Productiveness of Agencies. — Organizing of Associations and Auxiliaries. — A Model Collector. — Causes of Decline in Associations. — Missionaries as Agents. — Action of the Board on Deputations to Auxiliary Meetings. — General Agents. — District Secretaries. — Proper Sphere of Agencies. — Cost of the Agents. — Home Publications of the Board, and their Cost. — Cost of the Two Branches of Agency.

THE Agencies, or means for raising funds for the support of missionaries, are of two kinds — the living agent, and the publications. The outlay for these two departments is nearly the same. The cost of working a large missionary system does by no means increase in proportion to its extension; neither does the comparative cost of the agencies.

THE AGENTS.

The Board has always found it necessary to employ agents. The first was the Rev. John Frost, from the Andover Seminary, who performed a successful work in New England and New York toward the close of 1811, and early in 1812. Agents were afterward employed from year to year, as their services were needed, and they could be obtained. It is known that about seventy have been thus employed who pursued their theological studies at Andover. Pastors of churches have also engaged in temporary agencies. Among the most noted of these was the Rev. Dr. Edward Payson, of Portland, Me.; and this service he performed more than once. The nature of his agency in the year 1816, is thus indicated by Dr. Worcester: "The Prudential Committee request you, Rev. and Dear Sir, to spend as much time in the agency, during the present year, as may be consistent with your other engagements and duties. They wish you to visit the principal places, first in the District of Maine, and then in other parts of the country; to animate and strengthen the associations already formed for aiding the Board; to promote the forming of societies wherever it may be suitable, and to do what you can to unite and engage the hearts of ministers and people in the heavenly design of imparting the knowledge of salvation to the many millions who are perishing in pagan darkness and corruption."

In July of the same year, the late Dr. Elias Cornelius began his agency for promoting the objects of the Board, and especially for improving the character and condition of the Cherokee, Choctaw, Chickasaw, and Creek Indians. After conferring with the government at Washington, he was to visit Mr. Kingsbury's station in the Cherokee country, afterward called Brainerd, and to do what he could to encourage that infant establishment.

In the year 1821, the Prudential Committee recorded the fact, "that the clergy belonging to the Brookfield Association (in Massachusetts) have generally entered upon a plan for receiving the regular and systematic contribution of a small stipulated sum from each member of the church, who may be disposed thus to contribute, at a stated season frequently recurring, the aggregate of which contributions is to be applied to the support of missions among the heathen." Whereupon it was resolved, "That the Committee highly approve of this method of increasing and concentrating the benevolent exertions of the professors of godliness; and that they respectfully suggest to their brethren who have manifested a peculiar interest in the success of this plan, the utility and propriety of making it known to ministers of the gospel extensively, and of inviting their coöperation." The Auxiliary Society, subsequently formed within the bounds of this Association, adopted the practice, in 1826, of printing not only their Annual Report and proceedings, (which they had done before,) but also the names of all the subscribers and donors, and the amount of their several contributions; and this they have continued to do, annually, to the present time. The Library of the

Board contains a collection of the Reports of this Auxiliary, from 1825 to 1859. The volume is of value, as affording means for determining the laws which govern benevolent giving in rural districts. Such a use was made of these Reports in a Statistical History of Benevolent Contributions, laid before the Board at its meeting in 1852. The Auxiliary then embraced sixteen churches, each with its own male and female Missionary Associations. The following tables, constructed from the Reports for 1838 to 1841 inclusive, and for 1847 to 1850, show the number of subscribers under several sums, from six cents up to ten dollars.

SUMMARY FOR THE YEARS 1838–1841.

Years.	Dollars.						Fractional parts of a dollar.											No. of contributors.	Amount contributed.
1838.	10	5	4	3	2	1	75	60	50	40	37	30	25	20	12	10	6		
Gentlemen,	20	41	2	39	75	279	7	1	153	2	1	2	75		19	5	4	725	$1,184 15
Ladies, . . .	4	10	4	21	64	246	27	7	415	6	9	14	441		144	30	51	1,493	917 39
	24	51	6	60	139	525	34	8	568	8	10	16	516		163	35	55	2,218	$2,101 54
1839.																			
Gentlemen,	20	36	4	43	77	283	18		176	1	1	4	120	6	43	5	19	856	1,211 45
Ladies, . . .	3	8	5	15	58	264	45	8	450	2	13	11	528	27	140	37	41	1,655	1,019 39
	23	44	9	58	135	547	63	8	626	3	14	15	648	33	183	42	60	2,511	$2,230 84
1840.																			
Gentlemen,	37	29	13	46	98	324	11		225	1	1		137	7	42	18	24	1,013	1,571 13
Ladies, . . .		15	8	20	69	281	24	5	478	3	11	11	535	42	161	37	67	1,767	942 64
	37	44	21	66	167	605	35	5	703	4	12	11	672	49	203	55	91	2,780	$2,513 77
1841.																			
Gentlemen,	34	44	11	41	92	267	21	3	184	1	1	6	144		28	6	19	902	1,526 85
Ladies, . . .		27	7	19	85	290	54	28	424	8	15	23	556		163	49	74	1,822	1,169 37
	34	71	18	60	177	557	75	31	608	9	16	29	700		191	55	93	2,724	$2,696 22

GENERAL SUMMARY.

Years.	Dollars.						Fractional parts of a dollar.											No. of contributors.	Amount contributed.
	10	5	4	3	2	1	75	60	50	40	37	30	25	20	12	10	6		
1838 . . .	24	51	6	60	139	525	34	8	568	8	10	16	516		163	35	55	2,218	$2,091 54
1839 . . .	23	44	9	58	135	547	63	8	626	3	14	15	648	33	183	42	60	2,511	2,230 84
1840 . . .	37	44	21	66	167	605	35	5	703	4	12	11	672	49	203	55	91	2,780	2,513 77
1841 . . .	34	71	18	60	177	557	75	31	608	9	16	29	700		191	55	93	2,724	2,696 22
	118*	210	54	244	618	2,234	207	52	2,505	24	52	71	2,536	82	740	187	299	10,233	$9,532 37
Average	29	52	13	61	154	558	51	13	626	6	13	17	634	20	185	46	74	2,558	$2,383 09

* This should be stated $10 and upward; thirty-five of the subscriptions were over $10.

1838, Contributions at the Monthly Concert, ...	$465 31	
1839, " " " "	647 97	
1840, " " " "	584 45	
1841, " " " "	509 82	
		$2,207 55
Amount of Subscriptions, ...		$9,532 37
From other sources, ...		276 14
Contributions from 1838 to 1841 inclusive, ...		$12,016 06

SUMMARY FOR THE YEARS 1847–51.*

Subscriptions.	No. of subscribers.	Subscriptions.	No. of subscribers.
Under ten cents, ...	333	One to two dollars, ...	151
Ten cents, ...	315	Two dollars, ...	484
Twelve and a half cents, . .	448	Two to three dollars, . . .	50
Twelve to twenty-five cents, .	173	Three dollars, ...	250
Twenty-five cents, ...	2,343	Three to five dollars, . . .	52
Twenty-five to fifty cents, . .	133	Five dollars, ...	233
Fifty cents, ...	2,088	Five to ten dollars, ...	63
Fifty cents to one dollar, . .	177	Ten dollars, ...	113
One dollar, ...	1,624	Over ten dollars, ...	83

Whole amount from Subscriptions, ...	$10,525 58
From Monthly Concerts and other sources, ...	3,396 40
Total, ...	$13,921 98
Whole amount for four years, including Monthly Concert, . . .	$13,921 00
Average annual amount, ...	$3,480 00

* The following results were obtained from an examination of the valuable statistics published by the Brookfield Auxiliary: —

While the number of subscribers diminished on the whole, the amount of the subscriptions increased. In the first period, the whole amount raised in these towns, including monthly concert contributions, was eleven thousand seven hundred and seventeen dollars and ten cents; in the last period, it was thirteen thousand nine hundred and twenty-one dollars and ninety-eight cents, or three thousand four hundred and eighty dollars and fifty cents annually, upon the average. This is about one dollar and thirty-six cents to each church member. In the former period, the average annual amount was about one dollar and three cents to each church member. One town increased in its contributions one hundred and forty-two per cent., another one hundred and five per cent. The increase in the whole Association was about eighteen and a half per cent.; though, according to the number of church members, it was thirty-two per cent.

The figures show that many members of these churches did nothing for the

Number of church members in 1850,	2,403
Average annual amount to each,	$1 36
Amount raised by the Gentlemen's Associations,	$6,027
Average annual amount,	$1,506
Male members of the church in 1850,	702
Average number of male subscribers,	763
Average annual amount to each,	$1 96
Average annual amount to each male member of the church,	$2 14
Amount raised by Ladies' Associations,	$4,208
Average annual amount,	$1,052
Female members of the church in 1850,	1,701
Average annual number of female subscribers,	1,433
Average annual amount to each,	$0 73
Average annual amount to each female member of the church,	$0 62

Board. In fourteen of the churches, the number of members in 1850 was two thousand four hundred and three, but the average annual number of subscribers in the last period, in these towns, was but two thousand one hundred and ninety-six. Now, many subscribers were not members of the churches. In one parish, the number of subscribers was more than twice as great as the number of church members. There must, then, have been several hundreds of professing Christians in these churches who did nothing for this society. How large a part of them contributed to the cause of missions through other channels, is not known.

The average annual number of male subscribers in these fourteen towns, in the latter period, was seven hundred and sixty-three — sixty-one more than the number of male members of the churches in 1850. The female members of the same churches in 1850 were one thousand seven hundred and one, and the female subscribers in these towns were, on the average, only one thousand four hundred and thirty-three annually, for this period — two hundred and sixty-eight less than the number of female church members. In the former period, the whole average annual number of subscribers in the same fourteen towns was two thousand three hundred and fifty-three: viz., males, eight hundred and twenty-six; females, one thousand five hundred and twenty-seven; number of church members in 1840, two thousand six hundred and thirty-two: males, eight hundred and fifteen; females, one thousand eight hundred and seventeen.

In both periods, therefore, the annual number of male subscribers slightly exceeded the number of male members of the church, while the annual number of female subscribers was considerably less than the number of females in the churches.

The figures show, also, an increase in the number of large contributions. In the former period of four years, there were but thirty-five subscriptions

The receipts of the Board were more than doubled in 1817, though it was a year of scarcity and pressure, the agencies having been considerably enlarged. The number of agents employed in the Eastern, Middle, and Southern States was eight. Mr. Cornelius was one, and Samuel J. Mills another, the latter laboring in Maryland and Virginia. A similar result followed the use of the same means in 1822. In 1823, there was a falling off in the receipts. This deficiency was not attributed, at the time, to any diminution of interest in the missionary work, but to the want of agents. In the year

exceeding ten dollars in amount, and eighty-four of just ten. In the latter period, there were eighty-three exceeding ten dollars, and one hundred and thirteen of just ten. The number of subscriptions exceeding two dollars, in the former period, was six hundred and twenty-six; but in the latter it was eight hundred and forty-four, though the whole number of subscriptions, as stated above, had diminished. But though the number of large subscriptions increased, it was still painfully small.

Again. The figures show that, though some had gone forward, a very large part of the subscribers still did but very little. Of nine thousand one hundred and thirteen subscriptions, — the whole number, in the last period, omitting some juvenile associations, — three thousand six hundred and twelve were in sums not exceeding twenty-five cents each; and six thousand and ten, or one thousand five hundred and two annually, in sums of less than one dollar each.

The figures show, also, quite too conclusively, that the amount subscribed, generally, was by no means regulated by the exact ability of the subscribers. Subscriptions were in *convenient* sums — in sums which constitute a kind of units in our currency. Thus there were three hundred and thirteen subscriptions of ten cents, and four hundred and forty-eight of twelve and a half cents, but only one hundred and seventy-three between twelve and a half and twenty-five cents, and then two thousand three hundred and forty-three of twenty-five cents. There were only one hundred and thirty-three between twenty-five and fifty cents, but two thousand and eighty-eight of fifty cents; one hundred and seventy-seven all the way between fifty cents and one dollar, and one thousand six hundred and twenty-four of one dollar. From one dollar, the general rule was to go to two; from two, to three; from three, not to four, but to five; and from five, to ten. So that people need not be urged to *double* their subscriptions, but only to increase. If they increase, they will at least double, in a large majority of cases. The twenty-five cent subscribers will not go to twenty-eight or thirty-one cents, nor will the one dollar subscribers often go to one dollar and twelve and a half, or one dollar and twenty-five cents. Men do not calculate so closely upon what they can give. Some, who give by hundreds or thousands, may make such a proportionate increase, but not the great number of small contributors.

1839, the Board declared, that the contributions of the public generally would not be called forth, unless agents were employed to make personal applications, and bring the matter home to all classes of people.*

The effort to raise funds has, from the first, assumed more or less an organized form. The Missionary Herald for 1818 opens with an address to Foreign Mission Societies, other Associations auxiliary to the Board, and individual patrons and contributors, signed by Dr. Worcester. He says there were then fifty Foreign Mission Societies, as auxiliary societies of the first rank were styled, some embracing entire counties, but the greater part established in large towns, including the vicinities. There were also about two hundred and fifty Associations — smaller bodies, male and female, composed of persons who could not conveniently belong to the county or district society, but were willing to do something for all or for some of the objects of the Board.

In the first two months of the year 1821, donations were acknowledged from as many as seventy-eight organized bodies, in about one third of the towns from which donations were received. These Associations contributed just one half of the amount received in those months; and not far from one half of what came through these Associations came from forty-eight composed exclusively of females.

In the year 1823, an important effort was commenced to systematize and extend the organization for raising funds, which was prosecuted through several of the subsequent years. A plan of organization was carefully considered by the Prudential Committee, and published in the Missionary Herald for 1823. Two kinds of societies were desired, one large, the other small, the larger to include the smaller. The larger societies were for cities, collections of towns, or counties. They were immediately auxiliary to the Board, and called Auxiliary Societies. The smaller were for towns, parishes, school districts, and were immediately auxiliary to the larger

* Report for 1839, p. 36.

societies, and called Associations. The Auxiliary Societies were the medium of communication between the Associations and the Board. It was also deemed expedient that every town or parish should have two Associations, one of males, the other of females. The reason for this arrangement was, that in most places greater funds would thus be secured, and in the manner least objectionable.

The Auxiliary Society was composed of the members of the several Gentlemen's Associations within certain prescribed limits. It should have included also ladies. The contribution of any sum annually, from a gentleman or lady, was all that was needful to membership in the Association. The main object of this local organization was to secure the annual appointment of a sufficient number of collectors, male and female, to present the application to every suitable person within the limits of the Association. This was the essential thing; and it was proposed to have both male and female collectors, and separate societies of ladies.

The subscription, if subscriptions were taken, was only for the year, and of course would have to be repeated annually. Supposing an active, faithful body of collectors, this was the best arrangement. It would tend to create a feeling of responsibility in the collectors; unless they acted, the Association died. It secured a good share of action, which would conduce not a little to the life and perpetuity of the Association. It might fairly be presumed that the standard of liberality would rise from year to year in a place where this system was in operation; and persons would be likely to subscribe more liberally, where the subscription was to be made for one year only, than where it was for several years.

The first Associations organized were by ladies in the Old South, Park-street, and Union Churches, of Boston, in November, 1823. From this time, the work of organization was prosecuted rapidly in New England, by means of agents employed for the purpose; and a monthly statement of the exact progress of the work was made in the Missionary Herald. The greater part of the organization was effected in the four subsequent years. The result of this effort, in 1839, is exhibited in the following tabular view: —

STATES.	Gentlemen's Associations.	Ladies' Associations.	Whole number.	STATES.	Gentlemen's Associations.	Ladies' Associations.	Whole number.
Maine, ...	63	45	108	Pennsylvania, ...	69	18	87
New Hampshire, . . .	92	86	178	Maryland, ...	3	0	3
Vermont, ...	91	83	174	District of Columbia,	5	0	5
Massachusetts, ...	222	209	431	Virginia, ...	10	4	14
Rhode Island, ...	0	1	1	Ohio, ...	81	35	116
Connecticut, ...	151	152	303	North Carolina, . . .	0	1	1
New York, ...	96	26	122	South Carolina, . . .	3	2	5
New Jersey, ...	36	17	53	Georgia, ...	1	1	2
Number of the Associations, ...					923	680	1603

To a great extent, these sixteen hundred Associations were embodied in near fifty larger associations, called Auxiliaries. Supposing each Association to have had, on an average, four collectors, then more than six thousand local agents were thus designated, by their own people, for the service of collecting funds.*

* A description of one of these collectors, a fine specimen of his class, has been furnished by Dr. A. C. Thompson: —

"Deacon Lewis M. Norton, of Goshen, Conn., commenced acting as a collector the second year after the formation of the Litchfield County Auxiliary, and continued in the service more than thirty years. He performed this entire work for the town alone, and every year, with one exception when he was sick. His son then acted for him. He commenced his work in season, at least one week before the county anniversary, and was always ready to report in full at the general meeting. His private affairs required great activity on his part, yet he devoted an entire week, annually, to this business. His visits to families were always pleasant, and he laid out his routes in such a way as would enable him to dine where he expected to get no money. His subscription lists, receipted by the treasurer of the Auxiliary, are all still on file among his papers. The treasurer was for many years the venerable Colonel Talmadge, of Litchfield, at whose house the collectors and their wives were expected to dine on the day of the anniversary. My impression is, that that Auxiliary was, at least in its earlier years, one of the most successful of the kind; and that, in proportion to property and population, more was contributed in Goshen than in any other town in the county or state. I have at least heard that affirmed, but have no data for substantiating the same."

After the lapse of twelve or fifteen years, in the year 1839, it was found that remittances were made by only one fourth of the Gentlemen's Associations, while more than two thirds of the Associations composed wholly of ladies gave proof of an actual and healthful existence. The system had naturally suffered from the lapse of time, but more from the fact that other benevolent societies, seeing its efficacy, had adopted it in many places; and so many objects were thus presented in some districts, as to bring the use of collectors into disrepute. In some of the best portions of New England, pastors interfered, and insisted that only the more expensive departments of benevolence should send collectors through their parishes; and there the system still exists substantially, and works to general satisfaction.

The Prudential Committee early declared their conviction that it was useful to the cause, and to missionaries under appointment but not yet entered upon their work, that they serve in agencies at home, until ready to go forth on their mission. From forty to fifty were thus employed in the first thirty years of the Board's history, and with all the advantages anticipated by the Committee. In process of time, however, this species of agency lost much of its power to interest and move the churches. The mere fact of missionary consecration ceased to confer the prestige it did at first, and the general diffusion of information concerning missions and the heathen world had greatly abated the power of this class of agents to impart novelty to their addresses. Thenceforward the chief demand for the services of missionaries in the churches was during their visits to their native land, after years of toil in the foreign field; and their reports of what they had seen of the Lord's doings among the heathen seem not yet to have lost any of their interest.

At the meeting of the Board in New York city, in the year 1827, — one of its more influential meetings, — a committee was appointed to consider the duties of members of the Board. That committee made the following report: —

"As far as has come to our knowledge, it is the opinion of the friends of missions generally, and decidedly the opinion of your committee, that the plan now in operation, of keeping alive the missionary spirit in this country and supplying the treasury of the Board through the instrumentality of Associations and Auxiliary Societies, is the most simple, effective, and desirable that has been devised for this purpose; that all previous measures have been abandoned as unsatisfactory, and could not easily be reverted to, even were they desirable; and that the most serious ill consequences are to be apprehended, should the favor of the community toward the Auxiliary Societies be lost, or in any great degree diminished.

"It is the common belief, that this Board has become pledged to its Auxiliaries to send them a deputation of persons to be present at their anniversary meetings, with the view of encouraging and stimulating to continued exertions, and of communicating such useful and interesting intelligence in respect to the missionary enterprise, as is always received with satisfaction, and commonly with advantage.

"The persons, in time past, who have been deputed for this purpose, when Auxiliaries were few in number and confined within narrow limits, were missionaries returned from foreign stations, members of the Prudential Committee, and members of the Board.

"It is understood, that persons of the first description will always be employed for this object, when obtainable; that the pressing and increasing employment of the Prudential Committee renders it wholly impossible that much of their time should be spared for the purpose; and that it remains, therefore, for the members of the Board to assume this important duty, which, in the opinion of your committee, they should assume, and discharge with punctuality and care.

"It will of course be expected of the Prudential Committee, that they make those requisitions upon the members as generally, and appoint them to places of meeting as near to their residences, and otherwise study their convenience, as circumstances will allow."

This report was adopted, with the following resolutions:—

1. That it shall be the duty of the Corporate members of the Board to attend the anniversary meetings of Auxiliary Societies when required by the Prudential Committee, as a deputation from this Board; and that the traveling expenses of such members, in going to and returning from the places of meeting, be paid out of the treasury of the Board.

2. That the Prudential Committee be authorized and requested to take such measures as they may think proper to engage the active exertions of the Honorary members of the Board, and of such other clergymen and laymen as they may consider disposed and qualified to promote the interests of the Board, either at the meetings of Auxiliaries, or on any other occasions.

Historical truth requires the admission, that far less came from these proceedings of the Board than was anticipated by the remarkable man with whom they originated, Josiah Bissell, Jun., and by those kindred spirits who acted with him.

The Rev. George Cowles was the first of the General Agents, receiving his appointment in 1826. After him, at different times, until the year 1848, and in different parts of the country, were more than a score of agents sustaining the same appellation, which are here named in the order of their appointment, viz.: Rev. Ornan Eastman, Rev. Artemas Bullard, Rev. Horatio Bardwell, Rev. Chauncey Eddy, Rev. David Magie, Rev. William J. Armstrong, Rev. Richard C. Hand, Rev. Harvey Coe, Rev. Edwin Holt, Rev. Jacob D. Mitchell, Rev. William M. Hall, Rev. Erastus N. Nichols, Rev. William U. Foote, Rev. William J. Breed, Rev. Frederick E. Cannon, Rev. William Clark, Rev. Harvey Curtis, Rev. David Malin, Rev. Orson Cowles, Rev. Isaac R. Worcester, Rev. Ira M. Weed, Rev. Samuel G. Spees, and Rev. James P. Fisher.

In the year 1848, the General Agents received the appellation of District Secretaries, as best comporting with their official duties. That portion of the country from which the Board derived its funds was divided into thirteen districts, each of which was to have its secretary. The number was afterward reduced to eleven, and ultimately to eight. The following persons have held or now hold this office, viz.: Rev. Messrs. William Clark, Isaac R. Worcester, Orson Cowles, David B. Coe, James P. Fisher, Frederick E. Cannon, D. D., David Malin, Harvey Coe, A. S. Wells, Ira M. Weed, S. G. Clark, H. A. Tracy, O. P. Hoyt, J. H. Pettingill, William Warren, John McLeod, A. Montgomery, and Calvin Clark. Ten District Secretaries were under appointment in the year 1849: the number has been somewhat reduced.

Whatever name may be given to the agency, it is strictly auxiliary to the pastoral office, and to be employed only where it can operate with advantage to the cause. Some look for the day when agents will no longer be necessary; but that day is still in the future. A great and good change, however, has long been in progress among the agencies employed by the Board. Since the year 1823, the effort has been to throw responsibility for raising the funds upon parochial agencies, upon collectors appointed by the people themselves, and of course upon those also whose duty it is to see that collectors are appointed. The whole responsibility ought, evidently, to rest there. The difficulty has been to create and sustain a sufficient local feeling of responsibility. Adverse events are constantly occurring. Pastors and active church members die, or are removed; there are ebbings in the missionary spirit; adverse influences arise; the minister is in need of aid. Just in these circumstances, and such as these, the District Secretary finds his vocation; and, with a large district, the best talents will have ample scope. Even his indirect usefulness, in quickening the piety of the churches into a more active and vigorous life, may be more valuable to the cause of Christ at home, than his pastoral labors could be if in charge of a congregation; and the experience of the Board has been very decisive as to the necessity for such labors in the present state of the churches, as a means of sustaining the missions.

The annual cost of agencies employed by the Board in its second decade, varied with great irregularity from two hundred and forty to three thousand three hundred and twenty-five dollars; in the third, from one thousand one hundred and four to eight thousand nine hundred and seventeen dollars, the largest outlays being in the middle years; and in the fourth, from six thousand two hundred and forty-one to fifteen thousand seven hundred and three dollars. The fifth and last decade began with fourteen thousand one hundred and ninety-one, and ended with ten thousand six hundred and eleven dollars. The amount of agency, from year to year, was determined by the exigencies of the cause. Regarding each decade, however, as a whole, the increased expense of the agencies is quite noticeably proportioned to the increase of the receipts.

The cost of the agencies, as compared with the gross receipts of the Board from the beginning of its operations, is a little more than three and one third per cent.

The Press.

The home publications, in this department of the Agencies, have been Annual Reports; Annual Sermons; the Missionary Herald; the Day Spring, for fourteen years; the Journal of Missions, for the last eleven years; Quarterly and Monthly Papers, for a few years subsequently to 1831; occasional Missionary Sermons; Missionary Tracts; Appeals in times of exigency. The number of these publications, (not including Appeals, of which there is no record,) so far as issued at the cost of the Board, is as follows: —

Annual Reports,	166,750	copies.
Missionary Sermons,	115,250	"
Missionary Tracts,	1,582,879	"
Missionary Heralds, (gratuitous copies in the eighteen last years; the number in the previous distribution is not known,).	199,074	"
Day Springs, gratuitous copies,	616,854	"
Journal of Missions, gratuitous copies,	416,320	"
Total,	3,097,127	"

The titles of the more important of the Missionary Tracts are given below.*

* Conversion of the World; or, The Claims of Six Hundred Millions, and the

The Panoplist was the medium of communication with the Christian public in the first years of the Board. The Missionary Herald was first issued in connection with the Panoplist, and

Ability and Duty of the Churches respecting them. 1818. By Rev. Gordon Hall and Rev. Samuel Newell.

Hints to Collectors. 1824. By a Secretary.

Missions will not Impoverish the Country. 1826. By Rev. David T. Kimball and Lyman Beecher, D. D.

Duty of Christians to support Missionaries to the Heathen. 1826. By Rev. Stephen Frontis.

Vindication of American Missionaries at the Sandwich Islands. 1828.

The World to be Reclaimed by the Gospel. 1828. By Archibald Alexander, D. D.

Letters of William Penn. 1829. By Jeremiah Evarts, Esq.

The Future Destinies of America, as affected by the Doings of the Present Generation. 1830. By Jeremiah Evarts, Esq.

A Comparison of the Apostolic Age with the Present, in respect to Facilities for Conducting Missionary Operations. 1832. By Lyman Beecher, D. D.

Trials of Missionaries. 1832. By Eli Smith, D. D.

Essay on the Right Use of Property. 1832. By William G. Schauffler, D. D.

Character and Condition of Females in Heathen Countries. 1833. By Rev. Henry Lyman.

The Spirit of Primitive Christianity. 1833. By Rev. Samuel Munson.

A Call to Personal Labor as a Foreign Missionary. By William S. Plumer, D. D.

The Extent of the Missionary Enterprise. By Gardiner Spring, D. D.

The Moral Condition and Prospects of the Heathen. 1833. By B. B. Wisner, D. D.

Duty to the Heathen. 1833. By Rev. Ira Tracy.

When a Christian may be said to have done his Duty to the Heathen. 1834. By Rev. David Greene.

The Saviour's Injunction to his Disciples. 1834. By Rev. Isaac Bird.

On Deciding early to become a Missionary to the Heathen. 1834. By a Secretary.

Letters on the Constitution of the Board. 1836. By a Secretary.

What will you do for the Heathen? 1837. By Rev. Reuben Tinker.

Pray Less, or Do More. 1838. By Rev. Hollis Read.

Appeal to Physicians. 1838. By Asahel Grant, M. D.

Missionary Schools. 1838. By a Secretary.

The Work of Missions to be Progressive. 1840. By a Secretary.

Abstracts of Donations for 1839, 1840, 1844, 1856.

Manual for Missionary Candidates. By the Secretaries.

The Promised Advent of the Spirit. 1841. By a Secretary.

Proposals for raising up a Native Ministry. 1841. By a Secretary.

On the Use of Maps at the Monthly Concert. 1843. By Edward W. Hooker, D. D.

both were edited by Mr. Evarts. It became a separate publication in 1819, and the property of the Board in 1821. Owing to difficulties, delays, and cost in distributing the Herald, be-

Christian Public Spirit; or, Living for the Kingdom of Christ. By Rev. David Greene.

Report of a Visit to the Levant. 1844. By Drs. Rufus Anderson and Joel Hawes.

Refutations of Charges against the Sandwich Islands Missionaries. 1844. By Rev. Joseph Tracy.

The Theory of Missions to the Heathen; or, Office and Work of the Missionary to the Heathen. 1845. By a Secretary.

Divine Method of raising Charitable Contributions. 1845. By Elisha Yale, D. D.

Control to be exercised over Missionaries and Mission Churches. 1845. By a Secretary.

Cultivation of the Spirit of Missions in Literary and Theological Institutions. 1845. By Edward W. Hooker, D. D.

Letters to Pious Young Men. 1846. By Rev. John Scudder, M. D.

The Agency devolving on White Men in Missions to Western Africa. 1848. By Rev. John Leighton Wilson.

Labors and Hinderances of the Missionary. 1846. By Rev. David Greene.

On Missions to the Jews. 1849. By a Secretary.

The Missionary Age; or, The Time for the World's Conversion come. 1851. By a Secretary.

Missionary Responsibilities of Pastors. 1851. By S. L. Pomroy, D. D.

Grand Motive to Missionary Effort. 1852. By S. L. Pomroy, D. D.

Statistical History of Benevolent Contributions in the past Sixteen Years. 1853. By a Secretary.

Claims of the Missionary Work upon the Mental Strength of the Ministry. 1855. By Rev. David Bliss.

The Oriental Churches and Mohammedans. By Cyrus Hamlin, D. D.

Ought I to become a Missionary to the Heathen? By Rev. Reuben Tinker.

Outline of Missionary Policy. 1856. By Rev. S. B. Treat.

Letters on Polygamy. 1856.

Oahu College. 1856. By a Secretary.

Report of the Deputation to India. 1856. By R. Anderson and A. C. Thompson.

Report of the Select Committee on the Deputation to India. 1856.

Can the Board be kept out of Debt, and in what Manner? 1859. By a Secretary.

Historical Sketch of the Board. 1860. By Rev. Isaac R. Worcester.

Value of Christianity at the Sandwich Islands. By Rev. Ephraim W. Clark.

Missionary Schools. (Second Tract on the subject.) 1861. By a Secretary.

It is proper to add, that the Author of this volume is responsible for the tracts which are attributed to a Secretary.

fore the existence of railroads, the experiment was made, in 1823 and some subsequent years, of printing an edition of the work at Utica, N. Y., and in 1853 at Cincinnati, O.; but it was not wholly satisfactory in either case. In a special report made to the Board at its meeting in 1841, the Prudential Committee thus remarked upon this work, and on the importance of a wider dissemination of missionary intelligence: —

"Aside from the Missionary Herald," they say, "there is no vehicle by which missionary information is systematically and widely disseminated among the patrons and friends of this Board. Of this periodical, not more than twenty-two thousand have ever, in one year, been circulated in this country. This number, if they were all equally distributed among the three thousand churches from which the Board may look for its funds, would give only about seven copies to a church. But the manner in which these are distributed leaves many whole churches without a single copy, and oftentimes many contiguous churches, not poor nor small, nor in parts of the country remote or difficult of access, with not more than one or two copies each on an average. Yet considerable effort has been made to extend the circulation of this work. It is well received, and nearly twice as many copies of it are issued as of any similar periodical in this country, or England. Still, probably less than a tenth part of those from whom, if they were well informed on the subject, the Board might expect to receive patronage, ever see the Missionary Herald, or in any other manner obtain regular and full information on missionary subjects. Hence, with regard to the nature and objects of the missionary work, the manner of proceeding in it, the history, success, or present state of the several missions, there is, even among those friendly to the cause, a want of information greatly to be lamented, and which must be removed before this work can be expected to move on vigorously and rapidly." *

This gave rise to a small monthly publication called the Day Spring, designed to be an auxiliary to the Missionary

* Report for 1841, p. 39.

Herald; and, after some years, that gave place to a monthly paper somewhat larger, called the Journal of Missions.

The cost of the publishing branch of the Agency, for the past fifty years, as compared with the gross receipts, has been exactly three per cent.; which is also the cost of it in the year 1860. To this cost of publications add the cost of the agents, and it is found that the entire cost of the Agency — that is, of all the means for cultivating the missionary spirit in the churches and procuring the funds — has been between six and one third and six and one half per cent. on the gross receipts. Who that has had experience of the reluctance with which even good men give their money, will not have a feeling of gratitude that the cost has been no more?

CHAPTER XII.

RELATIONS TO GOVERNMENTS.

Massachusetts and the Charter. — English Admiral in the War with England. — The Alligator. — East India Company. — Charles Grant. — Sir Evan Nepean and the Effective Appeal. — Relations of American Missionaries to their own Government. — Not affected by the Nature of their Mission, nor by their Circumstances and Relations. — Dispatch of Daniel Webster declaring the Equal Rights of Missionaries. — Subsequent Declarations. — Government of Holland. — Netherlands India. — French Government. — Result as regards Supreme Governments, and as regards Local Governors, Embassadors, Consuls, and other Officials. — Duty of Praying for Governments.

THE difficulty experienced by the Board in procuring its charter from the legislature of Massachusetts, in the year 1812, has been already explained with sufficient fullness. The war with England commenced in that year, and the merchants of Salem, having a large trade with India, were desirous of sending an agent to Calcutta, for the purchase of goods to be sent to the United States on the return of peace. Knowing that the Board was anxious to forward letters, books, and supplies to its missionaries who had embarked early in the year, they offered to send out a small vessel that would take gratuitously whatever the Board wished to transmit, if Dr. Worcester would procure a license from the British Admiral, Sir John Borlase Warren, commanding on the coast. This license he succeeded in obtaining. A note from the Admiral gives the contents of his letter of protection, which ascribed to the Alligator — a coasting schooner or pilot-boat of only seventy tons — more of a missionary character than had been claimed for her. On reaching Calcutta, the little vessel was seized and condemned; but the letters and parcels for the missionaries were forwarded, after some delay. The Calcutta agents freely acknowledged the mercantile objects of the voyage, and it is understood that in these the shrewd merchants were successful;

but the Company's government suspected, or professed to suspect, some political plot concealed under the guise of religion, and were consequently the more severe upon the missionaries.* Doubtless the Secretary and the Admiral were led, in their interest for a better cause, to overlook the evidences of a commercial speculation, which were upon the very face of the enterprise.

The East India Company have been quite as tolerant of American as of English missionaries. Even from the first, there have been true-hearted and influential persons, both in India and England, upon whose friendly intervention the Board and its missions have been wont to rely. Such were William Wilberforce and Charles Grant in England. The latter, when a resolution seemed about to pass in the Court of Directors, excluding the first American missionaries from the Company's possessions, presented a written argument in their defense, showing that the governments in India had assumed powers not authorized by the laws of the British empire, nor by the law of nations. The Directors avowed their belief that the object of the missionaries was simply the promotion of religion, and authorized the Governor to allow them to remain. Such friends, too, were the Rev. Thomas T. Thomason, Dr. William Carey, and George Udney, Esq., of Calcutta, and William T. Money, Esq., of Bombay. Among these should be numbered also Sir Evan Nepean, Governor of Bombay in 1813, to whom, at the close of that year, Messrs. Hall and Nott addressed their eloquent and successful plea for liberty to remain and preach the gospel in India. No wonder that such an appeal as the following overcame the official scruples and fears of a man so well disposed toward their object as Sir Evan.

"It is our wish, that your Excellency would compare, most seriously, such an exercise of civil authority upon us with the general spirit and tenor of our Saviour's commands. We most earnestly entreat you not to send us away from these heathen.

* Life of Dr. Worcester, vol. ii. p. 237. Tracy's History of the Board, 2d edition, p. 40.

We entreat you by the high probability that an official permission from the supreme government for us to remain here will shortly be received; and that something more general, and to the same effect, will soon arrive from England. We entreat you by the time and money already expended on our mission, and by the Christian hopes and prayers attending it, not utterly to defeat its pious object by sending us from the country. We entreat you by the spiritual miseries of the heathen, who are daily perishing before your eyes, and under your Excellency's government, not to prevent us from preaching Christ to them. We entreat you by the blood of Jesus, which he shed to redeem them. As ministers of Him who has all power in heaven and on earth, and who, with his farewell and ascending voice, commanded his ministers to *go and teach all nations*, we entreat you not to prohibit us from teaching these heathen. By all the principles of our holy religion, by which you hope to be saved, we entreat you not to hinder us from preaching the same religion to these perishing idolaters. By all the solemnities of the judgment day, when your Excellency must meet your heathen subjects before God's tribunal, we entreat you not to hinder us from preaching to them that gospel, which is able to prepare them, as well as you, for that awful day. We entreat your Excellency not to oppose the prayers and efforts of the Church, by sending back those whom the Church has sent forth in the name of the Lord to preach his gospel among the heathen; and we earnestly beseech Almighty God to prevent such an act, and now and ever to guide your Excellency in that way which shall be most pleasing in his sight."*

England and America were then at war, but these two missionaries were recognized by the Governor in their higher relations to the peaceful kingdom of the Lord Jesus.

Circumstances led to a formal discussion of the relations of American missionaries to their own government, at the meeting of the Board in 1842. The question affected the rights

* Report of the Board, 1814.

of persons. It was argued, that there is nothing in the nature of a foreign mission to weaken the missionary's claims as an American citizen, and the argument was thus stated: —

1. The Christian ministry, besides having an express divine appointment, is an original and essential element of all Christian society. It forms a portion of the community, — a distinct profession, having its peculiar and appropriate employments, — as much so as any of the secular professions, whether of law, or medicine, or commerce. In the practice of its appropriate duties, the clerical profession is as much entitled to claim the protection of the government of its country, as any of the other classes composing the body politic. If the views which, as a citizen, he has a right to take of the duties appertaining to his profession, lead him to go and preach the gospel abroad, wherever he may go, he is as much entitled to the protection of his government, while demeaning himself like a good citizen, as if he were a merchant.

2. The Christian ministry exists for a twofold object, viz.: to sustain the institutions of the gospel in evangelized nations, and to propagate them in nations that are unevangelized. This has been the common opinion in all ages. Indeed, the propagation of the gospel by the ministry has a special prominence given to it in the Scriptures, as well as by the moral condition of the world hitherto.

3. Those clergymen who engage in foreign missions not only pursue a business which belongs appropriately to their profession, and in performing which they may, of their own right, claim the protection of their country, but they are also the agents, in this business, of a very numerous and respectable body of citizens. There are many hundred thousands in our community who have an interest more or less in this enterprise of Christian benevolence. They contribute for its support. The missionary is their agent. Their rights are involved with his. They are partners with him in this business.

4. The Act of Incorporation given to the Board in the year

1810, by the legislature of Massachusetts, recognizes missions to unevangelized nations as a lawful and proper work for American citizens to engage in. The Board is incorporated and made a body politic by the name of the American Board of Commissioners for Foreign Missions, — for the purpose of propagating the gospel in heathen lands by supporting missionaries and diffusing a knowledge of the Holy Scriptures. This is the language of the charter. The Act, though given by a single State, is practically recognized by all the States in the Union, as giving the Board an unquestionable right to receive and hold funds for the purpose of sending Christian missionaries to heathen nations. Though this fact may have no direct bearing on the question of a missionary's citizenship, it must be regarded as legalizing his business.

5. Our national government is accustomed to give passports to missionaries, knowing them to be missionaries, when they are about going forth to their work. The passports given to missionaries are the same as are given to other citizens, certifying that they are American citizens, and commending them, as such, to the representatives of the nation abroad, and to the governments of the world. Nor could these documents with any propriety be refused.

Nor is there any thing to destroy these claims in the circumstances and relations into which the foreign missionary is brought.

1. The first fact that meets us, is his dependence on his native land. He derives his support from thence. He looks to those whose agent he is for the means of living from year to year. To these patrons, or rather to the Missionary Board acting in their behalf, he looks also for direction in his labors ; and between him and his directors there is an active and intimate correspondence as long as he lives. In point of fact, his relations to his native land are as fresh and strong, so far as feeling, interest, and dependence are concerned, at the end of twenty years, as at the outset of his mission.

2. Another fact is this — that the government of the country

to which the missionary goes, never recognizes him in any other relation than that of a missionary or American citizen. He never becomes a citizen of the country. Indeed, no missionary of the Board could conscientiously comply with the conditions on which citizenship is conferred upon aliens in the British empire; and in barbarous pagan countries there would be folly in the attempt to procure it. He never sustains any other relation to the land of his sojourn than that of a missionary. He is neither banker, nor merchant, nor trader, nor cultivator of the soil. He does not own even the house he inhabits. He has the fewest possible ties to the country, the least possible hold upon it, that will comport with the performance of his missionary work. It would perhaps conduce more to the prosperity of the cause of missions, if facts were, in some respects, less favorable to the strength of this case — if missionaries, for instance, find it easier to gain rights and privileges in the countries where they labor, and have more inducement to aim at the permanent settlement of their families. The facts must be stated as they are. Even his children he regards as having their home in the fatherland; he looks upon them as Americans, though the laws of our country in relation to children born out of the country are not what they should be.

3. It is important to consider the theory of foreign missions in determining the relations which missionaries sustain to their native land. Regarded theoretically, missions are not permanent institutions. They are movable, itinerant. As soon as their object is accomplished in one place, or country, they are to be transferred to another. They are designed to plant the institutions of the gospel, and then they leave them to the conservative influences that have been gathered about them. This is true theoretically, and it will come out in fact, as soon as the Church shall prosecute the work with becoming vigor. Missions are not colonies; they are not settlements; they are mere temporary instrumentalities, employed indeed to accomplish permanent results, but having a foreign origin, and a foreign support, and to be withdrawn as soon as they can be

spared. Hence the missionary is emphatically, in the essential principle of his calling, a sojourner, pilgrim, stranger, having no continuing city.*

Early in the year 1842, it was found necessary to bring the subject to the notice of Daniel Webster, then Secretary of State, and he kindly furnished a copy of a dispatch which he sent, under date of February 2, to the Minister Resident at Constantinople, who had taken too restricted a view of the purport of our treaty with the Ottoman government. As this is believed to have been the first formal declaration of our government on this important subject, it is due to that eminent statesman that the dispatch should be quoted. It was as follows: —

"It has been represented to this Department, that the American missionaries and other citizens of the United States, not engaged in commercial pursuits, residing and traveling in the Ottoman dominions, do not receive from your legation that aid and protection, to which, as citizens of the United States, they feel themselves entitled; and I have been directed by the President, who is profoundly interested in the matter, to call your immediate attention to the subject, and to instruct you to omit no occasion where your interference in behalf of such persons may become necessary or useful, to extend to them all proper succor and attentions, of which they may stand in need, in the same manner that you would to other citizens of the United States, who, as merchants, visit or dwell in Turkey.

"Inclosed is a letter addressed to me this day, by Ex-Governor Armstrong, of Massachusetts, a gentleman of high character, which will explain to you the nature of the representations that have been made upon this subject, and which it appeared due to you, as well as to those interested in the cause it is the object of the representation to shield and to promote, frankly to communicate; and the Department believes, that it will only be necessary to invoke your attention to its contents,

* Report of the Board for 1841, p. 36.

to insure from you, in future, to the individuals described, what this government expects from its representatives abroad, in all cases where citizens of the United States are concerned."

Edward Everett and Lewis Cass, when afterward in the same high office, distinctly recognized this claim of the foreign missionary. Mr. Marcy did the same, virtually, in measures for a decisive rescue of Dr. Jonas King from unjust oppression by the Greek government at Athens.

It has sometimes, though rarely, been found expedient for the Board to seek relief from grievances by direct appeals to foreign governments. In the year 1839, the Rev. Dr. Robert Baird, who was then living in Paris, made, at the request of the Prudential Committee, a very satisfactory visit to Holland in relation to the restrictions imposed on missionaries from the Reformed Protestant Dutch Church, whom the Board had sent to Netherlands India in the preceding year.

Two years later, as a means of obtaining information, and of conciliating the government of Holland, the Committee, in concurrence with the Board of Foreign Missions of the Reformed Dutch Church, sent the Rev. Isaac Ferris, D. D., to that country. Dr. Ferris reached Rotterdam in June, and was received with great kindness and respect by Mr. Ledeboer, Secretary of the Netherlands Missionary Society, and by the Board of Directors of that institution. He found that society not a little embarrassed by a late restriction of the government, requiring them to send to Netherlands India only native Dutch missionaries, of whom few were to be obtained. A committee had gone to the seat of government to effect the removal of this restriction; and the Directors instructed them to seek the removal of the restrictions imposed on the missionaries from the Reformed Dutch Church of the United States. The committee no doubt pleaded the cause of their American brethren with ability and faithfulness; but the result was unfavorable in every respect. Dr. Ferris now went to the Hague, and had an interview with the Minister for the colonies, who expressed the most friendly regard for the American branch of the Dutch Church, and confidence in its missionaries; but stated that the exclusion of foreigners from their interior possessions in the Indian Archipelago was a principle of settled state policy. The American missionaries would be restricted to Borneo, and required to spend some time in Batavia before going thither. The Minister, however, assured Dr. Ferris that the colonial authorities would be instructed to give countenance and facilities to our mission in Borneo, both on the coast and in the interior.* The mission of Dr. Ferris, though not successful in its main object, led to the transfer of the Chinese branch of the Borneo mission to Amoy, in China, and threw light upon the subsequent duty of the Board with respect to Netherlands India. In June, 1843, the members of the Borneo mission, being no longer able to endure the embarrassments thrown in their way by the Dutch Resident at Pontianak, addressed a memorial to the Governor General of Netherlands India, in which their missionary office appears to good advantage in their respectful but dignified and decisive appeals.

The Queen of Louis Philippe, King of France, is understood to have been a woman of strong religious sentiment, and to have taken an interest in the success of Roman Catholic missions. Missionaries of the Board in Western Africa were led to believe, from their intercourse with French naval officers, that some of them looked for advancement through her influence, as a consequence of the zeal they should manifest for these missions; and that much of the annoyance of Protestant missions in the Pacific Ocean from French naval officers, during the reign of Louis Philippe, was from this cause. To diminish, if possible, the evils resulting from such interference at the Sandwich Islands, the Rev. Dr. Baird, being in Paris in 1841, was requested to convey to the king, if possible, a letter from the Prudential Committee in relation to the disastrous visit of Captain La Place and the frigate L'Artemise at the Sandwich Islands. Aided by General Cass, the American Minister, Dr. Baird obtained the desired interview, presented the letter, and stated to the king its more important points.

* Report of the Board, 1842, p. 167.

His Majesty promised to read the letter, and its accompanying documents, and to give the whole subject his most serious attention; but it was evident that he had previously heard the statements of the Romish missionaries as to their unpleasant relations to the government of the islands. Dr. Baird afterward saw Guizot, the Prime Minister, and stated the case to him. The Minister heard with evident surprise and regret, and promised, with every appearance of sincerity, to have the whole matter investigated and equitably adjusted.

While the experience of the Board favors the fewest possible direct communications by Missionary Societies to national governments, — where, however, it has never had occasion to complain of disrespect, — it has had abundant occasion gratefully to acknowledge kind and generous acts from the colonial authorities of Southern Africa, from local governors and official men of every grade in British India, from the successive English embassies in Persia, and in a notable instance from a Russian embassy at that court. The same may be emphatically said of Lord Stratford de Redcliffe, for many years English Embassador in Turkey, whose comprehensive and enlightened views as a statesman led him always to advance the interests of his own great nation by means of skillful national reforms and religious toleration in the Turkish empire. Nor has there been occasion, since Mr. Webster's dispatch, to complain of our own representatives at the Porte; though their power to protect has been less than it would have been were their mission raised, as it should be, to the embassadorial grade. English consuls in Turkey and Persia have generally been as kind and obliging to our missionaries as if they had been of the same nation. In Western Africa, even French admirals and their subalterns, after the first rough experience about the year 1844, have been gentlemanly in their deportment, and ready to oblige. Excepting the disgraceful scenes connected with Lieutenant Percival and the United States schooner Dolphin at the Sandwich Islands in 1826,* the visits of our own

* Annual Report for 1827.

national ships have every where contributed to the respectability and safety of our missionaries, and added not a little to their happiness.

All who desire the success of missions should make continual "supplications, prayers, intercessions, and giving of thanks," "for kings and for all that are in authority," that missionaries, in the several countries where they labor, "may lead a quiet and peaceable life, in all godliness and honesty." The unevangelized world is in great part subjected to the control or paramount influence of governments that are with us far more than they are against us, and that may be expected to extend to us a reasonable protection. What a progress in the past half-century! "This is the Lord's doing, and it is marvelous in our eyes."

CHAPTER XIII.

THE DECEASED SECRETARIES.

Dr. Worcester. — Mr. Evarts. — Dr. Cornelius. — Dr. Wisner. — Dr. Armstrong.

Dr. Worcester and Mr. Evarts were among the founders of the Board; and the well-drawn outline of their lives and characters in the sixth chapter will suffice for a notice of them in that relation. But it will be proper to speak somewhat more fully concerning them as Corresponding Secretaries; and also to commemorate the three other deceased Secretaries — Cornelius, Wisner, and Armstrong. This will be done as far as possible in the language of their immediate associates, who were in circumstances to know them thoroughly.

Samuel Worcester, D. D.

Excellent and useful as Dr. Worcester was in ecclesiastical controversy, and as a preacher, pastor, and councilor, his greatest claim on the gratitude of posterity is in the official relation he sustained to foreign missions. The failure of great and good enterprises, or at least the disasters which befall them, are often the inevitable consequence of some radical error in the incipient stages; and the absence of fatal errors in the scheme and working of the Board must be attributed, under God, to the admirable sagacity of the first Secretary, acting in fraternal understanding and sympathy with Mr. Evarts. Moreover, while not many of the great missionary problems of the Board were actually wrought out and demonstrated until after his death, he put not a few of the more important in the most hopeful way of being resolved. The Board itself was shaped for a wise and steady policy, as if the great disturbing influences of fifty years had all been foreseen. The missions beyond sea were also made deliberative, self-governing bodies, with entire freedom in ecclesiastical matters, and with all the discretionary power, and consequent responsibility, in the use of funds, that comported with the wishes and claims of the donors. Had the master builder been enabled to look down through the ages, he would not, perhaps, have done so well. Human wisdom is less a matter of foreknowledge, than a correct perception of the present relations of things, and a simple conformity to the present indications of Providence. It is being correct in the step next to be taken. With this instinctive perception, this heavenly tact, Dr. Worcester was eminently endowed. There were hardly facts enough then for constructing a theory of missions to any great extent; and where the Board did act, as it must needs have acted more or less, upon the popular notions of the times, it found great occasion for subsequent modifications; as in the value of direct civilizing agencies in missions, the influence of the higher education on savage minds, and the training of heathen youth amid the civilization of our own country. But then these experiments were the way to come at the truth, and they led to the more correct experience, upon which the missions are now being prosecuted. Mr. Evarts, writing under the influence of Dr. Worcester's recent decease, shall say what more is necessary concerning that great and good man.

The faithful pen of our revered associate — Mr. Evarts writes — has recorded, in the last letter of considerable length which he ever wrote, the formation and the early history of this society. He recorded it as an act of gratitude to God for his favor to the rising institution, and as an attestation (the event has proved it to be his dying attestation) to the great truth, that trust in God is the only safe principle of the missionary enterprise.

When the Board was first organized, it was little suspected by any one that its concerns would soon become so weighty and complicated as they actually became, or that the duties of the Corresponding Secretary would be so arduous as they actually were. Yet the choice was just as it would have been had all these things been foreseen. Before the embarkation of the first mission, in February, 1812, there had been little opportunity for active labor. No funds had been received, no plans of extensive operations had been adopted. The Secretary, however, had not been slumbering at his post. Always an observer of missions, and well acquainted with the modern history of attempts to propagate the gospel, he applied himself with new diligence to obtaining a correct knowledge of the heathen world; to learning the difficulties and discouragements which every missionary society must expect to encounter; and to the consideration of those great motives to action which the steady view of a world lying in wickedness will impress upon a pious mind.

From 1812 to 1817, the concerns of the Board were increasing in number and in interest. Several cases of great delicacy occurred, and the occasions of anxious deliberation were much more numerous than any person, not intimately acquainted with matters of this kind, would ever imagine. The labor of maintaining a correspondence with the missionaries; with others, who were preparing to be employed in various departments of the missionary work; with the officers of similar societies, at home and abroad; and with patrons and friends in our widely-extended country, must have occupied much of his time. Add to this the weight and responsibility of planning and commencing new missions; of providing for the comfort and usefulness of numerous families already employed or to be employed; of preparing for meetings of the Board and of the Committee; and of laying before the public, at stated intervals, the proceedings and results, the hopes and prospects, the occurrences, both adverse and favorable, which had any bearing on this great concern, — and no one can doubt that great courage and industry were necessary to carry a man through these efforts, amidst the cares inseparable from the oversight of a large congregation, and the public consultations to which reference has been made. Yet a vigorous exertion was continually sustained, that, while the general operations of the Board were going forward, parochial duties and services should not be neglected.

At the annual meeting of the Board in September, 1817, the Secretary informed his associates that he could no longer continue to labor as he had done, intimating, at the same time, that it would be a great relief to him if some other person could enter upon the duties of his office. The concerns of the Board were constantly multiplying and enlarging. He had for a long time been obliged to give up all seasons of relaxation, all that species of intercourse which is commonly denominated social and friendly, in distinction from the details of important business, and the performance of solemn professional duty.

To dispense with his services was out of the question; and the best that the Board could do was to propose a measure which, if acceded to by himself and his people, should release him from the greater part of his parochial duties. This measure could not go into immediate operation, and it was not till the summer of 1819 that the Rev. Elias Cornelius was settled as colleague pastor of the Tabernacle Church and congregation, with the express provision that the senior pastor might devote three quarters of his time, without interruption, to the missionary cause. In the mean while, occasional relief had been obtained by means of candidates for the ministry, and the kindness of his clerical brethren, who appreciated the value of his services. It was a matter of no small difficulty to gain the consent of an affectionate people to an arrangement which should deprive them of so large a share of a beloved pastor's labors; and we are warranted in asserting that nothing but an enlarged regard to the interests of the Church, and a firm persuasion that the cause in which he was embarked might well demand great sacrifices from every professed Christian, could have gained so complete a victory over private attachments and personal friendship. To the honor of the deceased it should be added, that he was never urged to continue in the office of Secretary, and to consent to a modification of the pastoral relation, by any other arguments than such as require the followers of Christ to surrender their own ease and advantage at the call of their Master. It was clearly seen by many, and not less clearly by our departed friend than by others, that a continuance of his labors, on the plan proposed, would render the support of his family more precarious than if he were simply a parish minister; that it would fasten upon him unceasing care and toil, exhaust his strength, probably shorten his life, and leave his family without those claims upon the kind and generous feelings of his people, which would be promptly acknowledged were his undivided services bestowed upon them. All this he saw, and then cheerfully made the sacrifice.

During the remainder of his pilgrimage, though able to accomplish much, and that in a very effectual manner, his body seemed gradually falling a prey to disease. In very few instances, we apprehend, have the mental powers been preserved in so vigorous exercise, to the very close of life, amidst pain, weariness, extreme debility, and the indications of approaching dissolution.

Jeremiah Evarts, Esq.

The Rev. David Greene came into the correspondence of the Board in 1824, six years before the death of Mr. Evarts, and married his eldest daughter. He has communicated the following estimate of Mr. Evarts's character, and of his public services in the missionary cause: —

Mr. Evarts labored for the Board twenty years, — the first ten as its Treasurer, and afterward, upon the death of Dr. Worcester, ten years as Secretary. Indeed, during the ten years that he was Treasurer, Dr. Worcester residing at Salem, while the business of the Board was transacted at Boston, no inconsiderable portion of the correspondence and other labors pertaining to the Secretary's department was performed by Mr. Evarts. Excepting the individual efforts of the Eliots and Mayhews, the Brainerds and Edwardses, and a few others of former generations, this was at the very commencement of the foreign missionary enterprise in this country. There were no precedents to guide the executive officers of the Board, no examples to be followed. Whether for raising funds and obtaining missionaries at home, or for conducting operations in missionary fields abroad, principles were to be established, methods of procedure devised; in short, the very foundations were to be laid for operations so extended as to correspond with the rising abilities of the American churches, and as permanent as the wants of the unevangelized nations. Into this work Mr. Evarts entered with all his heart, taking a leading part from its very beginning; and for it he was well qualified. Probably no man in the country was better informed, or had thought more earnestly, on the subject of missions than he. As editor of the Panoplist and Missionary Magazine, he had collected and become familiar with all the accessible publications in this department of beneficence; and by the intelligence from the English missions, which he, as editor, had disseminated through the churches, he had done much to prepare the way for the organization of the Board in 1810.

Mr. Evarts came early into public life; and though, at the organization of the Board, he was not thirty years of age, he was widely known as a leading man in the Christian community; and wherever known was beloved and confided in as a man of sterling integrity, wise as a counselor, liberal and candid in his judgments, sober and conservative in his views, and yet eminently enterprising, public-spirited, and in all respects trustworthy. Plans and measures which came under his consideration were carefully studied till he was confident that he understood their bearings and results, and in his conclusions he had great self-reliance. Hence he seldom or never had to renounce crude or hastily-formed opinions, or to abandon ill-concerted plans or measures. Few public men have laid themselves open so little to the charge of indiscretion. He was a laborious business man. Work, any kind of work, which would honor Christ and do good to men, was a pleasure to him. His mind was so well furnished and so thoroughly disciplined to habitual effort, that, though possessing little bodily vigor, he could perform a great amount of intellectual labor, especially with the pen, without weariness. He was not fastidious as to the particular labor assigned him. It was a remark of his, that while he would not wish to direct what sphere of labor Providence should assign to him, he would prefer to be employed in the foreign missionary work; but in what department of it, — whether as Secretary, Treasurer, Agent, or Editor, at home or as a missionary, — he cared little, only let him be employed for Christ and the heathen. This expressed the spirit which he manifested through the twenty years of his connection with the Board. Whether as accountant and financier, or in correspondence, or addressing the friends of missions, or defending the Indian tribes against meditated wrongs, or as an officer of a church, or a promoter of temperance, or of the observance of the Sabbath, he was always the earnest, laborious man; never declining labor because it did not belong to him, or because he was doing more than his share. The motto in the books of his library, "*Nil sine magno labore vita dedit mortalibus*,"* well exhibits his view of life; and he cheerfully accepted and acted upon the arrangement.

The social qualities of Mr. Evarts contributed not a little to his influence and success in his work. His ability to adapt himself to all classes of persons — to be the intelligent, affable, kind, sympathizing, Christian friend of persons of all habits, and at all stages of life — eminently fitted him to hold intercourse with the friends and patrons of the Board, and with missionaries and their families, while his intelligence, manliness, and gentlemanly deportment gave him welcome access to men in all the highest stations.

In those early periods of the Board's history, when almost the whole Christian community, both ministers and laymen, doubted the wisdom of entering the foreign field, and thought

* It is the lot of mortals to accomplish nothing without great labor.

the time for such a work had not come, little sympathy and encouragement from beyond their own circle could be expected by those who assumed the responsibility of carrying it forward. Then there was need of trust in God, of faith in his promises, and in the power of gospel truth and motives. These graces Mr. Evarts possessed. In those dark times, when helpers were comparatively few and timid, and their views contracted, when doubters and objectors were many and bold, and multiform difficulties were to be encountered both at home and abroad, Mr. Evarts's courage never failed. His trust was in God's purpose and promise to convert the world. However numerous were the opposers, or formidable the obstacles, or faint-hearted the friends, he was not disappointed; for he had taken all this into account, and was still hopeful, assured that what God had promised he was able to perform, and that his time and manner of carrying his purposes into effect were the best.*

Elias Cornelius, D. D.

Dr. Cornelius was born at Somers, N. Y., July 31, 1794, and hopefully converted while in Yale College, where he was graduated in 1813. He studied divinity under the direction of President Dwight, and afterward with Dr. Lyman Beecher, and was licensed to preach June 4, 1816. Immediately after this he was commissioned to act as an agent of the American Board. After performing a highly successful agency in the States of Connecticut, Massachusetts, and Rhode Island, on the 9th of April, 1817, he received ordination as an evangelist. He was then sent on a special mission to the Indian country in the south-west, in aid of the now venerable pioneer of the Indian missions, Dr. Cyrus Kingsbury. At Washington he had repeated interviews with the heads of departments, as to the best means of meliorating the condition of the aborigines, by

* A Memoir of the Life of Jeremiah Evarts, Esq., Corresponding Secretary of the American Board of Commissioners for Foreign Missions, by E. C. Tracy, 8vo., pp. 448, was published by Messrs. Crocker & Brewster, Boston, 1845.

schools, husbandry, and the mechanic arts. Arriving at Brainerd, he was joyfully welcomed by the missionaries, and his services to the mission were various and important. He subsequently spent three months in New Orleans, principally in the service of the Missionary Society of Connecticut. At the close of his useful and highly acceptable sojourn in that city, he presented the subject of foreign missions to the consideration of the people, and obtained more than a thousand dollars.

The following touching passage is from a sketch of Dr. Cornelius's life and character, by Dr. Bela B. Edwards, afterward a professor in the Theological Seminary at Andover, who was associated with the subject of this brief notice while Secretary of the American Education Society. The occurrences were on his homeward journey from New Orleans.

"In one of his letters, Mr. Cornelius thus pours out the fullness of his feelings in reference to the American Board: 'If there be an institution in the world which I love most, I speak the sincere sentiment of my heart when I say, it is the American Board of Commissioners for Foreign Missions. I have all that confidence in their wisdom, their efficiency, and their piety, which excites to the most vigorous exertion in their behalf of which I am capable; and I need not add, that these remarks apply most emphatically to the Prudential Committee, and their indefatigable Secretary and Treasurer. To forward their views, I have toiled two years, and never anticipate greater happiness in my life than has been associated unceasingly with those toils.' The following animated description of the interview of Mr. Cornelius with Mr. Evarts, forcibly reminds us of that more sublime and rapturous meeting which they have since enjoyed in the temple not made with hands, where they shall hunger no more, neither thirst any more, where tears are wiped from off all faces, and where the Lamb, who is in the midst of the throne, is leading them to living fountains of water. 'After great fatigue and considerable impediment from ill health in the low country, I had the indescribable joy of arriving at the missionary station [Brainerd] on the 14th of May, twenty-two days from the time

I took leave of Natchez. I know not that it is possible for a human heart to beat with higher joy than did mine, in once more meeting the precious brethren and sisters of the mission. This joy was rendered more intense by the presence of Mr. Evarts. It seemed as if the ends of the country had come together. It far more than repays one for the most fatiguing journey; and such is the reward of Christian missionaries.'"

In this tour of eight or nine thousand miles, Mr. Cornelius preached three hundred times in behalf of the Board, and collected seven thousand two hundred dollars. He was present at the formation of a church at Brainerd — the first of the Indian churches.

To enable Dr. Worcester to devote the greater part of his time to official duties as Secretary of the Board, Mr. Cornelius was installed colleague pastor of the Tabernacle Church in Salem, July 21, 1819. His services as a pastor, and subsequently in connection with the American Education Society, do not come within the range of this notice. Yet it should be said that, in the service of the Education Society, he traveled from fifteen to twenty thousand miles, and raised funds to the amount of between one hundred and twenty and one hundred and fifty thousand dollars. Upon the decease of Mr. Evarts, he was elected Corresponding Secretary of the Board, but did not see his way clear to accept the office till near the close of the year. He came to Boston in the January following to consult on future operations, preached on the cause of missions in several churches, and early in February left for New York, where was his family. At Hartford, he was prostrated by a fever on the brain, which terminated his invaluable life, February 12, 1832, when he was scarcely thirty-eight years of age.

Dr. Cornelius was not spared to enter upon his work as Secretary of the Board, and nothing can be said of him in that relation. He died on reaching the middle period of life. His powers were developed very early; he was not twenty-two when sent on his special agency to the Indians. With great versatility of powers, there was a remarkable harmony in his character. His talents for business were extraordinary; his integrity was beyond all suspicion; his rare energy of character was founded on a thorough knowledge of his duties; and his early removal occasioned great lamentation in the churches.*

BENJAMIN B. WISNER, D. D.

Benjamin Blydenburg Wisner was born September 29, 1794, in Goshen, Orange County, N. Y.; was graduated at Union College in 1813, where he performed the duties of tutor from 1815 to 1818; afterward went through a course of theological studies in the Seminary at Princeton; and was ordained pastor of the Old South Church in Boston, February 21, 1821. In 1832, he was elected one of the three Corresponding Secretaries of the American Board, and continued in the discharge of the duties of that office till his death, which occurred, after a brief sickness, February 9, 1835, in the forty-first year of his age.

The author can not give a better delineation of Dr. Wisner, as he appeared to his associates in office, than the one, substantially, which he communicated to Dr. Sprague, in the year 1851, for his "Annals of the American Pulpit."

Dr. Wisner became one of the three Corresponding Secretaries of the Board in the autumn of 1832. His was the home department in the correspondence, — having special charge of the system of means for raising funds and procuring missionaries. This was before the General Assembly's Board for Foreign Missions was formed, and the entire broad field covered by the Congregational, Presbyterian, and Reformed Dutch Churches was open to him. In fact, the Presbyterian churches of the South were organized for action in aid of foreign missions in direct connection with his official agency. He had been four years a member of the Prudential Committee of the Board previous to his election as Secretary,

* A Memoir of the Rev. Elias Cornelius, by B. B. Edwards, was published by Messrs. Perkins & Marvin, Boston, 1833, pp. 360.

and was thus enabled to enter at once on his duties with the advantage of a large stock of appropriate information.

Dr. Wisner had the rarest qualifications for a secretaryship in a great missionary institution. His spirit, naturally somewhat overbearing, had been softened by a partial failure of health and pastoral trials. Cheerful, social, rejoicing in the usefulness of his associates and of all about him, his fine conversational powers made him a most agreeable companion. His public spirit made him ready for every good work; and such was his love for work, that he seemed never to grow weary in well-doing. He did every thing promptly and thoroughly, and little things and great things equally well; not with eye service, or to have glory of men, but because he loved to be doing good, and because nature and grace made him happy in doing with his might what his hand found to do. So it was always and every where; and this made him the man for committees and sub-committees, on which he was generally to be found, when work was to be done trenching largely upon the hours usually appropriated to rest and sleep. He was a model of a business man — wakeful, cheerful, collected, judicious, laborious, devoted, disinterested. It was no mere official interest he had in his duties. The public welfare was his own. He felt a responsibility for the course of events. His heart was in the great cause of missions — in every part of it.

His forte was executive. But he had great power also in debate in deliberative bodies. As a writer, he did not readily adapt himself to the popular mind. There was a lack of fancy and imagination, of the discursive and illustrative power, and of flow in thought and style — defects that may have been owing to some infelicity in the manner of his education. But, as an extemporaneous debater, he would have commanded attention on the floor of either House of Congress. At the very outset of the discussion, he seemed to have an intuitive perception of the leading points, in their natural relations and order, and to be at once prepared for a logical, instructive, convincing argument. This always gave him influence in deliberative bodies, where his tact and ability seemed never to be at fault.

His mental powers came early to maturity; and comparing his labors and influence with those of other men, he needed not threescore years and ten to stand with the more favored men in the impression made upon his age. Yet his early death has ever seemed among the greater mysteries of God's holy providence.

William Jessup Armstrong, D. D.

The biographical sketch of Dr. Armstrong, which appeared in the Missionary Herald soon after his decease, was prepared by Mr. Greene, one of his associates in the correspondence of the Board. It is necessary very much to abridge this account, in order to find it place in this volume.

Dr. Armstrong was born at Mendham, N. J., October 29, 1796. He became hopefully pious while a member of the college at Princeton, where he was graduated in 1816. After a course of theological studies, under the direction of his father and in the Seminary at Princeton, he devoted two years to a home mission in Albemarle County, Va., laboring principally in Charlottesville and its vicinity, near the residence of President Jefferson. Infidelity and irreligion greatly prevailed at that time. No church had been organized there, and the Lord's Supper had never been administered. With the young missionary's ardor and singleness of aim, and with the peculiar pathos of his eloquence, he could not but command attention. Success attended his labors. A number of interesting conversions occurred even among infidels. A Presbyterian church was gathered, which still exists, and the face of society was much changed for the better. He afterward labored three years as pastor of the First Presbyterian Church in Trenton, N. J. In the spring of 1824, he succeeded Dr. John H. Rice in the First Presbyterian Church in Richmond, Va., where he remained ten years, his Christian influence all the while extending through the State.

Dr. Armstrong had a large share of public spirit. He prayed much for the success of missions; uniformly prepared for the monthly concert of prayer; was an example of liberality in his contributions; endeavored to awaken and foster a missionary spirit among his people; and had the satisfaction of seeing a number of his spiritual children go on missions to the heathen. He was repeatedly invited to engage in agencies for promoting a missionary spirit in that part of the country. But the time when his soul seemed peculiarly moved for the heathen, and he was, as it were, newly baptized with the missionary spirit, was at a union meeting for prayer for the conversion of the world, held on the first Monday in January, 1833. Standing among the ministers, and before the assembled churches of Richmond, with a countenance glowing with love, he said, "My brethren, I am ashamed that there are so many of us here in this Christian land. We must go to the heathen." "That day of prayer," says one who was present, "made an impression on many hearts which was deep and lasting." This was doubtless the way in which God was preparing him to perform the labors to which he was soon to be called in connection with the foreign missionary work. When the Central Board of Foreign Missions, embracing the Presbyterian friends of missions in Virginia and North Carolina, was formed in 1834, to act through the American Board, Mr. Armstrong was elected its Secretary. This involved the dissolving of his pastoral relations, which was a sacrifice he made at much expense of feeling.

Dr. Wisner attended the first meeting of this Society, going by invitation; and Mr. Armstrong was soon after appointed General Agent of the American Board for the States of Virginia and North Carolina. The contributions within the sphere of his agency, in fourteen months after he commenced his work, were about ten thousand dollars. This was before the division of the Presbyterian Church and the formation of the General Assembly's Board of Foreign Missions. On the death of Dr. Wisner, in 1835, Dr. Armstrong was elected a Secretary of the Board for the home correspondence. In this office he remained till November 27, 1846; when, on his way from Boston to New York, in the steamer Atlantic from Norwich, in a furious tempest, the vessel was dashed in pieces upon the shore, and among the lifeless bodies found on the beach was that of this excellent servant of God. His watch had stopped soon after four o'clock, and it was probably at that time, on Friday morning, he entered the haven of rest. Survivors relate that he was conspicuous among the passengers throughout the day and evening of Thursday, as a minister of Christ, addressing to his companions in danger appropriate religious instruction and consolation, and commending them to God in prayer. Some of the passengers, seeing the dread crisis rapidly approaching, drew near and stood by his side, "because," as one remarked, "it seemed safer to be near so good a man." Just before the wreck broke upon the reef, and the falling deck and the overwhelming waves swept him lifeless into the sea, he said to one, "I hope we may be allowed, if God will, to reach the shore with our lives; but if not, I have perfect confidence in the wisdom and goodness of Him who doeth all things well." This was his dying testimony to the goodness of God and his own faith in him. The vital spark was probably extinguished instantly by the falling timbers. The same expression of calm confidence in God remained enstamped on his features in death, significant of that heavenly peace with which he closed life here, and entered on that life where are no perils, anxiety, suffering, or death. His remains were forwarded to New York, where was his bereaved family, and where the funeral solemnities were attended in Dr. William Adams's church, November 30, a vast assembly testifying how greatly he was beloved.

Dr. Armstrong excelled in the pulpit, and his labors as a preacher, during the twelve years he was connected with the Board, were incessant, and every where acceptable. He was truly a faithful Christian brother, sympathizing with his associates in all their perplexities and trials; endeavoring to alleviate their burdens; bearing with them, counseling them, and praying for them; never tenacious of his rights, and always scrupulously careful not to wound their feelings. A plesanter man to coöperate with they could not desire. His wisdom did not arise from uncommon grasp of mind or sagacity; but its elements were goodness of heart, honesty and singleness of purpose, and trust in God. His love of what was right and Christian, his guilelessness and frankness, led him, as it were, instinctively, and almost intuitively, to discern and aim at the best results, and to pursue them by means and in a manner which could hardly fail to conciliate and secure approbation. This, with his promptness and assiduity, enabled him to accomplish his objects more surely and effectually than most other men.*

* A volume was published in 1853, entitled Memoir and Sermons of Rev. William J. Armstrong, D. D., late Secretary of the American Board of Commissicners for Foreign Missions. Edited by Rev. Hollis Read. 12 mo. pp. 411.

THE MISSIONS.

THE MISSIONS.

CHAPTER I.

THEIR CONSTITUTION AND ORIGIN.

What constitutes a Mission. — Stations and Outstations. — Natives not Members of Missions. — Relations of Missionaries to the Native Churches. — Territorial Extent of Missions. — The Missions conformed to the Habits of the American People. — Their Responsibility. — Origin of the Missions. — Missions in India. — Religious Destitution of India. — Missions to Western Asia. — Instructions to the first Missionaries. — Growth of the Enterprise.

THE by-laws of the Board declare, that "a majority of missionaries and assistant missionaries in any mission shall, in their regular meetings, decide all questions that may arise in regard to their proceedings and conduct, in which the mission is interested; the decision being subject to the revision of the Prudential Committee. At such meetings, every male missionary and assistant missionary present, having arrived at the age of twenty-one years, is entitled to a vote." The missions are designed, therefore, to be self-governing communities; and there is of course a necessity for their assembling for business. The meeting may be of the whole body, or of delegates from the stations. A station is a local establishment, occupied by one or more missionaries. An outstation is occupied by a native helper, who may be a preacher, or only a catechist. A catechist is a native evangelist not formally licensed. No native helper has a vote in the missions. He is employed, paid, supported by the mission, and accountable directly and only to the mission. The mission and the native Christian community are kept organically distinct, that the work of the mission may be completed in the shortest possible time. The Board sends forth and sustains missionaries, evangelists, as founders of the gospel institutions. The most important of these institutions is the native church, with its pastor and office-bearers; and its value is enhanced by its being homogeneous with the people. Its ministry is expected to be of the people as soon as may be, in race, social condition, sympathies, and style of living. The better educated native helpers, on becoming preachers and pastors, have sometimes aspired to the rank, if not to the salary, of missionaries. But it has been deemed vital to success, in rearing a self-governing, self-supporting native community of Christians, not to separate the preachers and pastors from their own people, as would be done by admitting them to membership in the foreign missionary body. Their direct relations never extend to the Board. Readers, catechists, preachers, pastors, they may be, but not in a technical sense missionaries to their own people. Missionaries are on the ground only for a time. Hence they are dissuaded from becoming permanent pastors of native churches, lest those churches should never feel able to stand alone. For the same general reasons, it has been deemed undesirable that missionaries should become members of native ecclesiastical bodies.

Regard for convenience has had much to do with the territorial extent of missions. Three missions are now on the ground once occupied by the Armenian mission, called the Western, Eastern, and Central Missions to Turkey. The three Mahratta missions, owing in part to increased traveling facilities, have been combined in one. The missionaries in China are divided into three missions, because of the difficulty of meeting for business. For the same reason there are three missions among the Tamil people of Southern India and Ceylon.

The missions derive their organization from the taste and habits of the American people; and persons of foreign birth and education have found it somewhat difficult to work happily and well in them. The missions are held to be responsible for the proceedings of the several stations and members, but can not set aside instructions received from the Prudential Committee. These must accord, however, with the laws and regulations of the Board, and the doings of the Committee are subject to revision by the Board. The several missionaries have the right of appeal from the missions to the Prudential Committee; and both the missionaries and the missions may appeal from the Committee to the Board. This right has seldom been exercised by individual missionaries, and never yet by a mission.

Origin of the Missions.

The first mission of the Board, as is well known, was that to the Mahrattas of Western India. The first station was at Bombay. Here Hall and Newell lived and died. It is noticeable that neither of the fields now occupied by the Board in India seems to have been contemplated by the Prudential Committee, when they sent forth the first missionaries. Birmah, the only country named in their Instructions, was reserved by Providence for our Baptist brethren. The three missionaries who retained their connection with the Board, driven westward by the persecutions of the East India government, obtained a footing in Bombay. At that time, from Cape Comorin through the whole western coast of India to Bussora, Mocha, Mozambique, Madagascar, Mauritius, and on to the Cape of Good Hope, there was not one Protestant missionary. Gordon Hall, in an appeal to the churches of his native land, in February, 1826, just before his lamented decease, takes this affecting view of the moral desolations of the world at that time: —

"From Bombay we look down the coast for seventy miles, and we see two missionaries; and fourteen miles further on, we see two more. Looking in a more easterly direction, at the distance of about three hundred miles, we see one missionary, chiefly occupied, however, as a chaplain among Europeans. In an eastern direction, the nearest missionary is about one thousand miles from us. Looking a little to the north of east, at the distance of thirteen hundred miles, we see ten or twelve missionaries in little more than as many miles in length on the banks of the Ganges. Turning thence northward, at nearly the same distance from us, we see three, four, or five more, separated from each other by almost as many hundred intervening miles. And looking onward beyond these distant posts, in a north-east direction, through the Chinese empire and Tartary, to Kamschatka, and thence down the north-western coast of America to the River Columbia, and thence across the mountains to the Missouri, the first missionaries we see, in that direction, are brethren Vaill and Chapman among the Osages.

"Again we look north, and at a distance of one hundred and eighty miles, we see two missionaries; but from thence, with two or three doubtful exceptions, through all the north of Asia to the pole, not a single missionary is to be seen. In a north-western direction, it is doubtful whether there is now one missionary between us and St. Petersburg. Westerly, the nearest is at Jerusalem or Beirût. South-west, the nearest is at Sierra Leone; and more to the south, the nearest may be among the Hottentots, or on Madagascar." *

The only Mahratta station which the Board now has on or near the coast, is in Bombay, a city containing half a million of inhabitants. Stations were formerly occupied at Mahim and Tannah, on the adjacent continent, but only for a short time. In the Deccan, or great upland east of the Ghauts, is one of the most interesting clusters of missionary stations to be found in India, with Ahmednuggur for its center.

The missions to the Tamil people, in Northern Ceylon and Southern India, grew out of Mr. Newell's wanderings, subsequent to his visit to Mauritius with his admirable wife. Coming to Ceylon, which was under the English government and not the East India Company, and finding the governor favora-

* Missionary Herald for 1826, p. 313.

ble to a mission, he recommended sending one to the District of Jaffna, where the Tamil language was spoken. It was thus the Board was led to commence its Ceylon mission, in the year 1816, — Messrs. Richards, Poor, Meigs, and Warren being the first missionaries. Out of this grew the missions to Madura, Madras, and Arcot.

The first movement of God's people in this country for the spiritual renovation of the countries of Western Asia, was directed toward Jerusalem, and primarily to the Jews of Palestine. The best exposition of the views and feelings with which this enterprise was commenced, is in the Instructions already mentioned, delivered by Dr. Worcester to Messrs. Parsons and Fisk, in the Old South Church, Boston, October 31, 1819. It falls in with the object of this volume to make copious extracts from these Instructions. They were printed at the time, but have long been inaccessible to the public. To the first of the American missionaries to Western Asia the Prudential Committee spoke as follows: —

Your mission is to be regarded as a part of an extended and continually extending system of benevolent action for the recovery of the world to God, to virtue, and to happiness. In the prosecution of it, respect is to be had, not merely to what may be effected by your own efforts directly, but also to the lights and facilities, the aids and inducements, which you may afford to the efforts of others, either acting cotemporaneously with you, or successively to come after you. Facts are lights; clear inducements are lights; fair results of experiments are lights; correct notices of evils and of remedies are lights. To lay open to the view of Christians the state of the world, or of any portion of it, and to point out ways and means of melioration, is to do much toward the accomplishment of what is possible.

Yours is a field of no ordinary description. It comprises, either within itself or by intimate association, all that is most affecting to Christian feeling, or most interesting to Christian hope. There patriarchs, and prophets, and apostles, and martyrs,—and He who is their Lord and ours,—lived, and labored, and died. There the revelations of heavenly mercy were given, the sacrifice for the world's redemption was offered, and the commandment of the everlasting God, that the gospel should be made known unto all nations for the obedience of faith, was delivered; and there the first churches of the exalted Redeemer, which once shone with his glory in all its brightness resting upon them, now lie in ruins. The candlesticks have long since been removed,—the light has been, for dismal centuries, almost totally extinguished, and the powers of darkness have triumphed and trodden down and led captive at their pleasure. "But the Lord will arise and have mercy upon Zion; for the time to favor her, yea, the set time, is come. For his servants take pleasure in her stones, and favor the dust thereof." Her old waste places are to be builded, and the foundations of many generations to be raised up.

That the hearts of all Christians may be engaged in this mighty work, that the exertions for its accomplishment may be wisely directed, and the proper means in the best manner applied, the scene must be laid open in as clear a light as possible, and every thing comprised in it must be examined with care. The doing of what you can for this purpose will constitute no small share of the business, the interest, and the utility of your mission. For a lucid illustration of what we here mean we refer you to the Christian Researches of Dr. Buchanan, who desired to see the things which you are sent forth to see, and into whose design, with a like activity of benevolence and diligence of inquiry, it may be your privilege to enter.

From the hights of the Holy Land—from Calvary, from Olivet, and from Zion—you will take an extended view of the wide-spread desolations and variegated scenes presenting themselves on every side to every Christian sensibility, and will survey with earnest attention the various tribes and classes of fellow-beings who dwell in that land, and in the surrounding countries.

At Jerusalem and in Judea you will find people of many nations, — Jews, Arabs, Turks, Asiatics, and Europeans, — of different and distant countries, and of various religions — Judaism, Paganism, Mohammedanism, and Christianity. The professed Christians are not only of different nations, but of various communions and names — Romanists, Grecianists, Armenians, Nestorians, Jacobites, and Protestants. With this mingled people, in all its varieties, you will endeavor, by attentive observation and diligent inquiries, to make yourselves as thoroughly acquainted as possible in regard to their general state, their religious opinions and rites, their moral and civil habits and manners, their means of improvement — in a word, the circumstances favorable and unfavorable to the propagation of the gospel, in its purity, and with its blessings, among them.

The two grand inquiries ever present to your minds will be, What good can be done? and, By what means? What can be done for the Jews? What for the Pagans? What for the Mohammedans? What for the Christians? What for the people in Palestine? What for those in Egypt? In Syria? In Persia? In Armenia? In other countries to which your inquiries may be extended?

The fruits of your researches, consisting of facts, descriptions, notices, reflections, comparative views, and suggestions of methods and means of usefulness, you will regularly enter in your journals, and transmit to us as opportunities are afforded. Possibly also you may be able to send home some books or ancient manuscripts, interesting to the student in the Scriptures, in ecclesiastical history, or in general literature, or at least gratifying to a laudable veneration for antiquity, or to a reasonable curiosity.

This business, however, of procuring and communicating information, interesting and important as it will be, is not all that you are to attempt. You go to that land, still of promise, as Christian missionaries — as ministers of Christ commissioned to testify the gospel of the grace of God to Jews and Gentiles, — to people of every nation, and name, and condition. This character you are sacredly to maintain in every place, and this commission you are faithfully to execute as you have opportunity.

The abettors of those different religions, and the adherents to the different sects, regard each other with mutual jealousy; and you will not think it strange if they all regard you with something more than suspicion. You will take all prudent care that you do nothing rashly, nothing inconsiderately or unadvisedly; that you do not inadvertently or needlessly expose yourselves to resentments, rapacities, stratagems, or acts of violence; startle prejudices, excite suspicions, or offend against laws, or customs, or ceremonies, or opinions; and that, by avoiding all appearance of earthly wealth or distinction, by Christian courtesy and kindness, and meekness and gentleness, and by all fair and lawful means, you conciliate civility, confidence, favor, and respect.

The Jews have been for ages an awful sign to the world. But the period of their tremendous dereliction and of the severity of God is drawing to a close. You are to lift up an ensign to them, that they may "return and seek the Lord their God, and David their king." They will return. The word of promise is sure, and the accomplishment of it will be as life from the dead to the Gentile world. The day is at hand. The signal movements of the age indicate its dawn. It may be your privilege to prepare the way of the Lord. It may be your felicity to see some of the long-lost children of Abraham returning with dissolved hearts, and confessing, with unutterable emotions, that the same Jesus whom on that awful spot their fathers crucified, is indeed the Messiah, the Hope of their nation, and of all the nations of the earth. It may be your distinguished honor to be leadingly instrumental in "building again the tabernacle of David, which is fallen down, and the ruins thereof, and in setting it up, that the residue of men may seek after the Lord, and all the Gentiles upon whom his name is called." It will be our unceasing prayer, and the unceasing prayer of many, that your mission may be crowned with all this joy and all this glory.

Since the Instructions were delivered, from which the foregoing extracts are made, a little one has become a thousand, a small one a strong nation. From that mission to Jerusalem, which it was not found expedient to continue long, arose the missions to Syria, to Greece, to the Jews of European Turkey, to Assyria, to the Nestorians, and to Western, Eastern, and Central Turkey, all of which, excepting those to the Greeks and the Jews, are now in operation.

The mission to the Nestorians resulted from the explorations of Messrs. Smith and Dwight. While employed in drawing up Instructions for these brethren, the eye of the writer casually fell upon the mention of a people in North-western Persia called "Chaldeans," by Dr. Walsh, chaplain of the English embassy at Constantinople; and this occasioned the visit to Oroomiah, and the interesting revelations concerning the Nestorian people, which led the Board to institute the successful and prosperous mission among them. Thus are events of the most unequal magnitudes often providentially connected together as cause and effect.

CHAPTER II.

ORIGIN OF THE MISSIONS, CONTINUED.

Missions to the Islands of the Pacific. — Missions to Africa. — Missions to China. — Missions to the North American Indians.

MESSRS. BINGHAM, Thurston, and others composing the first mission to the Sandwich Islands, received their Instructions in Park-street Church, Boston, from Dr. Worcester, October 15, 1819. Only that part of this official document will be copied, which illustrates the nature of the compact of the members of the mission with each other, and with the Prudential Committee.

The kingdom of the Lord Jesus is a kingdom of order. Missions for the advancement of this kingdom are to be maintained by a regular, though simple and free polity. The free-will offerings of many churches and many thousands of individuals are cast into one treasury, and committed, for application to the intended objects, to persons duly appointed to the high trust. Upon these sacred funds, and under this constituted direction, approved persons, freely offering themselves for the holy service, are sent forth to evangelize the heathen. The compact, explicit or implied, engages to them affectionate and provident patronage, maintenance, and aid, so long, and only so long, as they conform themselves to the instructions and regulations of the service. Contempt or disregard of the instructions and regulations would tend to confusion and every evil work. The humble and devoted missionary, therefore, will consider a due observance of the directions of those who are intrusted with the weighty concerns of the mission, as a point of sacred duty, on which much is depending. If in his judgment the service might be benefited by an alteration or modification of any part of the system, or any special order, he may reasonably confide that his representations, made in a proper manner, will receive kind and considerate attention; for, of all men in public trust, the managers of missionary concerns have evidently the least inducement to treat those who act under their direction with unkindness or neglect, and the strongest motives to render them every facility, encouragement and aid in the faithful prosecution of their work.

Like the members of other missions, you will find it convenient and necessary to form yourselves into a body politic, having rules and regulations of your own, but conformable, or not repugnant, to the directions of the Board, or Prudential Committee, for the orderly management of your joint concerns; for the due distribution of your means of support, your trusts, and your labors; for the keeping of regular records and journals; for your correspondence with the Secretary and accounts with the Treasurer of the Board; and for various purposes, important to the welfare and success of the mission.

The Micronesian mission, commenced in 1852, was an offshoot of this mission, and is composed in part of natives of the Sandwich Islands.

The first missionary of the Board to the African continent was the Rev. John Leighton Wilson, who spent twenty years on the western coast, near the equator, first at Cape Palmas, and then on the Gaboon River. The Instructions of the Prudential Committee to Mr. Wilson were delivered in the First Presbyterian Church in Philadelphia, September 22, 1833, by Mr. Anderson, Secretary for the Foreign Correspondence. The reader may be interested to observe with what animating hopes the first mission to these dark countries was commenced.

Eight years ago, the Board, by a formal resolution, enjoined

32

it upon the Prudential Committee to embrace the earliest opportunity for establishing a mission in Africa. Nor have the Committee been unmindful of this injunction, but have attentively observed the indications of Providence unto this day, not only in reference to Western Africa, but also to the northern and eastern shores of that continent. In the year 1829, a missionary of the Board made a visit of inquiry to two of the principal cities on the northern shore. But on the eastern, until within a few months past, no cloudy pillar was seen to invite our labors. Through the space of forty degrees of latitude, from the port of Natal to the Strait of Babelmandel, it seems quite impracticable for the Board to establish and sustain a mission. At length, after the Committee had directed one of their Secretaries to address a letter of inquiry to the Rev. Dr. Philip, of South Africa, light gleamed unexpectedly from the south-eastern shore, and laid open to our view a promising and accessible field; and now we wait for nothing but suitable men for the service to commence a series of stations on the eastern, as well as the western coasts of Africa. And from De la Goa Bay we may hope to advance northward upon Mozambique, and perhaps ascend into the interior.

But it has been toward Western Africa that the Committee have looked with the most intense desire to labor for the spiritual good of that benighted continent. Soon after the resolution just referred to was passed by the Board, which had special reference to Western Africa, a colored Presbyterian clergyman, in one of our Western States, was appointed a missionary of the Board to the native tribes within the colony of Liberia. He has since died in that colony; but, for reasons which it is not important to relate, did not go thither as a missionary of the Board.

Since that time, until your disposition to consecrate yourself to the liberation of Africa from her thralldom of ignorance and sin became known to the Committee, no man offered his services to the Board, whose constitution and habits were thought to be adapted to the climate. But now the time appears to have come for us to enter the arena of that spiritual conflict, which is to extend itself with invincible power, until Africa shall rejoice under the peaceful reign of Jesus Christ.

The Committee will now briefly advert to the probable course of the mission in future years.

It is generally admitted that the churches of this country owe to Africa a debt which nothing except the gospel of the grace of God can ever cancel. This evening we acknowledge that debt to the full extent, and promise to coöperate with our brethren of other kindred associations in paying it. Though it be greater than the debt which England owes, it must be paid — not with silver and gold, but with the gospel. Through all her vast extent, Africa must hear the glad tidings — her

> "mountain tops
> From distant mountains catch the flying joy" —

and all her plains and valleys become vocal with the high praises of God.

Within twenty years, the coasts around the Gulf of Guinea will probably be occupied, to a great extent, by colonies of colored emigrants from different parts of this western world. These colonies will take the place of the chain of forts that were reared long since to protect that most nefarious commerce by which the coast of Guinea has been signalized. These colonies will be important auxiliaries to Christian missions in Western Africa. Without them, the blighting influences of climate and of the slave trade, combined, would wither all the missions we might plant upon the coast, and we could scarcely proceed at all into the interior. They will serve for landing places, for places of rest and refreshment, for defense, and for posts of observation and inquiry; and by the information they collect, the roads they open, and their commercial intercourse, they will greatly facilitate our entrance among the several tribes and nations of the interior.

An object of primary importance, in respect to the inland parts of Western Africa and the central portions of the continent eastward of the Niger, is the exploration of the country with a view to missionary operations. None of this vast region has been thus explored, unless it be some districts immediately behind the colony of Sierra Leone. It was the solution of geographical problems, that governed the inquiries of most of the travelers in Western and Central Africa. Now that the problems of chief interest have been solved, and the Niger has been traced to the sea, mere curiosity may subside; but Christian benevolence will awake, and investigate the intellectual and moral condition of the whole people. Between the coast of Guinea and the Desert of Sahara there may, perhaps, be twenty-five millions of souls. Concerning most of these, our knowledge is exceedingly vague and general. We can distinguish, however, two races of men, viz.: the original inhabitants of the country, and the descendants of Arabs and other emigrants from Asia. The latter are daily advancing southward, and carry with them the religion of the false prophet.

The great region now before us is broken in the center by a chain of mountains extending east and west. The southern slope toward the sea is occupied by several barbarian states, of which Ashantee and Dahomey are considerably known to the civilized world. The great, fertile, and populous valley of the Niger extends along the northern side of these mountains, through twenty degrees of longitude; then, breaking the chain of mountains, it pours the united floods of two majestic rivers into the Gulf of Guinea.

Two steamboats are now upon the Niger, and it is the intention of the company to which they belong to keep them there, if it be possible. In process of time we may expect to ascend that river, and, entering the Tshadda, we may advance toward the rising sun. Eastward of the Niger, the mountains ascend to a loftier hight than on the west, and are known as the Mountains of the Moon. What sort of a country and what kind of people we shall find in our progress eastward, is uncertain. Geographers suppose that the central regions rise and spread out into a vast table land, extending from the Mountains of the Moon southward. Possibly this, like the high central regions of Asia, affords an extensive range to wandering hordes; but whether they be mild or savage, pagans,

Mohammedans, or nominal Christians, is yet wholly unknown. Indeed, it is true, that almost the whole of Africa is yet to be explored by the Christian missionary, before missions can be prosecuted on that benighted continent with intelligence and efficiency.

Having made a successful beginning among the tribes of the coast, around the colonies, we shall, as our laborers increase and the roads are opened, advance into the interior with our permanent establishments. The native races promise the speediest results, and the progress of the Mohammedans must be checked. From the English fort on the Gold Coast, we may enter the country of the Ashantees; and when the Niger is open, we may ascend to the kingdom of Borgoo, northward of the Kong Mountains.

Wherever we go, schools must be opened for educating schoolmasters, catechists, pastors, and preachers. The languages must be learned and reduced to writing. Printing-presses must be erected, and the natives taught to work them. Constellations of Christian churches must be called into being, and shine around these. The preacher must revolve in his orbit, and truth from the pure word of God come down upon the people, like rain upon the mown grass, and showers that water the earth.

From these illuminated districts the light will radiate, the heavenly influence will spread, and God the Holy Spirit will bless the means of his own appointing when used in obedience to his command.

Meanwhile, the mission which we hope soon to commence on the south-eastern coast may be expected to extend its outposts more and more, and ascend the coast, and advance upon the central highlands. Our European brethren, also, of different denominations, whose line of march already extends across the continent on the south, will advance from that quarter; the English Episcopal missions will advance from the Mountains of Abyssinia, and our brethren of the same denomination at Sierra Leone, and those of various names at Liberia, will move with us from the west; and our children may hear of the meeting of these upon some central mountain, to celebrate in lofty praise Africa's redemption. O, what a meeting, what a day! And it will surely come; and Africa, all Africa, shall rejoice in the liberty wherewith Christ maketh his people free.

The mission to Southern Africa was the immediate result of strong representations from Rev. Dr. Philip, of Cape Town, superintendent of the London Missionary Society's mission in that part of the continent, along with a desire for a more healthful African climate than was to be found in the equatorial regions. Two missions were sent thither in the year 1834; one composed of brethren from the Southern States, destined to the interior; the other of brethren from the Northern States, whose field of labor was to be among the Zulus of the south-eastern coast. The interior mission, after traveling twelve hundred miles from Cape Town, was soon after broken up by the wars of the Dutch Boers upon the natives, and its members joined the Zulu mission. This mission also came near being discontinued, the Prudential Committee at one time having resolved to abandon it; but its establishment was ultimately effected through a series of providences, clearly indicating the duty of retaining that field.

The attention of the Board was drawn to China by a well-known Christian merchant, the late D. W. C. Olyphant, Esq., then a resident at Canton. His vessels were always open and free for missionaries to China. One, named the Morrison, of four hundred tons, — a large vessel for those times, — was almost a missionary ship. Her exploring voyage to Japan in 1837, with Mr. King, a partner, and Dr. Peter Parker and Mr. S. Wells Williams of the mission, will entitle her to a place in all the histories of missions to those remarkable islands. Since then, the operations of divine Providence, with the apparent design of opening not only China but also Japan to the gospel, have been upon a grand scale. While we are writing, it is credibly reported that not only the chief cities of the coast, but the great rivers of China, are rendered accessible to the commerce of Christendom, and of course to its Christianity. The Board has established missions at Canton, Amoy, Fuhchau, and Shanghai; and at last it has a missionary residing at Teintsin, near the metropolis of the Chinese empire.

The rise of the missions among the North American Indians will be sufficiently indicated when treating on deputations to the missions, and in the historical catalogue of missions, at the close of a subsequent chapter.

CHAPTER III.

DEVELOPMENT OF THE MISSIONS — THEIR LAWS OF GROWTH — THEIR COMPLETION.

Object of Missions to plant the Gospel Institutions. — Apostolical and Modern Missions. — Development in Preaching and Schools. — Missions necessarily progressive. — Evidences of Progress. — Progress essential to their Prosperity. — Consequences of disregarding this Law. — Early Preëminence given to Preaching. — Schools and the Press. — Subordinate Agencies falling into their Places. — How the Work may be completed. — An Unsettled Problem. — Difficulties in Native Churches. — Similar Difficulties in the Apostolic Churches. — Allowance for Failings in Mission Churches. — Hard to reach the Self-sustaining Point. — Necessary Modifications. — A Fixed Limit to the Ability of Missionary Societies. — A Limit to the Number of Missionaries. — The Native Agency should have Room for Growth. — Too much required of Missions. — A Mission may grow, and yet not increase its Cost to the Society. — When the Work of a Mission is completed.

Enough has been said to illustrate the origin of the missions, in their larger extent. It will now be in order to treat of their development, and laws of growth.

Development of the Missions.

Experience has shown, that the great object of missions — the introduction of the gospel among the unevangelized — can be effectually accomplished only by a course of measures fitted to secure the establishment of the gospel institutions. These the apostles introduced wherever they went, but with far less difficulty than we experience. Were the heathen countries of our times like Asia Minor, Macedonia, and Achaia, we should need to provide only for the personal and family expenses of missionaries, and for printing the Scriptures and religious books and tracts; and even a part of this expense, and soon the whole, would be defrayed by the converts. Moreover, owing to the present state of the heathen nations, we have found stronger reasons than the apostle Paul had at Corinth and Thessalonica, for not looking to converts for the personal support of missionaries. The most we can expect from them is, that they shall support their own native teachers and preachers, and gradually assume the support of their schools, and of the press.

Among the developments common to the missions, the most important has been in the matter of preaching. While this has by no means been restricted to the Sabbath, there has been a tendency to give more and more significance to the day, by regular preaching in some one place. It has generally required long time and patience to collect and sustain even a small adult congregation, but not otherwise has it been possible to keep up the tone of the enterprise. The missionary has needed the preparation for such a duty, as well as its reacting influence upon his own mind and heart. He has needed a service where he could speak authoritatively as an embassador, without the humiliation of rude objections and foul abuse. The native Christians have also needed regular, well-studied exhibitions of the plan of salvation, and of their duty as Christians. They could not be adequately informed and elevated to the self-governing, self-sustaining basis by means of mere conversational preaching. They required the benefit, indeed, of every one of the auxiliary means of grace, but could never reach their full stature as Christians without the regular, stated, formal preaching of the word. The heathen then saw the missionary in his true place and dignity. If they did not often go to hear him, they knew there was a day which he regarded as specially set apart by the God of heaven for declaring and for hearing the truths of the Christian religion; and also a time when the missionary assumed authority to speak, and when it was the sole business of all others to hear.

Not only has he preached the gospel orally, statedly, formally on the Sabbath, and more familiarly during the week, but as a good Protestant Christian he has sought to give the Bible to the people. And as that could benefit them only as they were able to read, he found it needful to open schools; not with the expectation of teaching the whole population to read, nor even a considerable portion of it,—that being impossible,—but to form such a public sentiment as in the end would insure this result. A demand was thus created for school books and for the press. The schools served as an introduction and a tie to the people at the outset of the work, and as a means of infusing Christian ideas into the language. As converts multiplied, it became an interesting question how to provide native pastors for them, and how to convert the more promising of the pious youth into evangelists and teachers. Without such, the mission could never finish its work; hence institutions arose for training both males and females. When natives had thus been prepared to be helpers in the different departments, it became needful to aid in their support until the native churches should be able and willing to sustain them; otherwise some of the most valuable and costly results of missionary labor would be wholly sacrificed and lost.

Laws of Growth.

The more important indications of progress in the missions have been these—collecting hearers, reducing languages to writing, translating the Scriptures, forming Christian schools, creating a desire for education, awakening anxiety to learn the way of life, multiplying converts, gathering churches, training up a native ministry, and leading the people to support it; and whatever else goes to improve and elevate the domestic, social, civil, and religious life of the people. And this leads to the remark, that continued progress has been found essential to the prosperity of the missions. Regarded in their spiritual nature, missions seem to be under the same laws with individual Christians, in whose spiritual life there is no such thing as standing still, but advancement is the condition of health. A living mission must needs grow and spread its branches, like a tree. It increases in its demands for labor, oversight, nutriment, and expenditure. We learn this from experience. The greater the disposition to hear, the greater is the need of preaching and of preaching houses. The more diffused and earnest the desire for schools, the greater is the demand for teachers, school houses, and school books. In proportion to the progress of mind and feeling upward from barbarism, has been the cost of printing, (if the means were at hand,) and the demand for the lights and advantages of general knowledge. But the most urgent among the growing expenses in a prosperous mission have been those for the training and support of helpers in the higher classes of native agency; and the measures for rearing this agency having been commenced, they have been found essentially progressive, but with this redeeming feature, that at length they begin to diminish the demand for foreign laborers.

A reference to the varying expenditure of the Board would not invalidate this statement; because the expenditure has been more or less subject to arbitrary limitations, — determined by the amount of receipts, rather than by the actual necessities of the missions. Who can tell what an amount of good in missions has been thus annually sacrificed? Who has not sympathized with the disappointments and griefs of the missionaries? It is melancholy to think of the waste of influence thus occasioned in the missions, since they reached the stages of manifest success. The churches have not seemed prepared for rapid progress. Instead of glad praises to God for thus answering prayer for the extension of his kingdom in foreign lands, the officers of the Board have often been put upon the painful task of showing that they have labored to the utmost to check the speed of their missionary trains.

There has been a growth of experience and skill in the conduct of missions during the past half century. It is indeed true that our fathers, at the outset, gave the preëminence to the preaching of the gospel, in their theory of missions, as really as do their successors. Thus they wrote as far back as the year 1813, and nothing stronger can be said now: "Important as the distribution of the Scriptures among the heathen in their own language, is held to be by us and by the Christian public generally, it should never be forgotten, that the *preaching of the gospel*, in every part of the earth, is indispensable to the general conversion of mankind. Though the Scriptures alone have, in many individual cases, been made the instrument of regeneration, yet we have no account of any very extensive diffusion of Christianity except where the truths of the Scriptures have been preached. Were the heathen generally anxious to receive the Scriptures and to learn divine truth, they would, like the Ethiopian eunuch, apply for instruction to those who had been previously acquainted with the same Scriptures, and, when asked if they understood what they had read, would reply, 'How can we, except some man should guide us?' The distribution of the Bible excites inquiry, and often leads those who receive that precious book to attend public worship in the sanctuary. But the preaching of the gospel is, after all, the grand means appointed by Infinite Wisdom for the conversion and salvation of men. Without this, the Scriptures, however liberally distributed, will have comparatively little effect among any people, whether Pagan or nominally Christian." And again, in 1817: "The translation and dispersion of the Scriptures, and schools for the instruction of the young, are parts, and necessary parts, of the great design. But it must never be forgotten, or overlooked, that the command is, to 'preach the gospel to every creature,' and that the preaching of the word, however foolish it may seem to men, is the grand mean appointed by the wisdom of God for the saving conversion of the nations."

From this practical view of the work, taken by the Board at the opening of its career, there has been no intentional departure, either by the Prudential Committee or by the missions. Schools and the press have always been regarded as subordinate to preaching. When agriculture and the mechanic arts have also been taught, as in the Indian missions, and at first on the Sandwich Islands, it has been as a subordinate means. At the same time, there has been a tendency in the more important of the auxiliary influences to transcend their proper limits. Book-making has sometimes acquired an undue prominence, especially in the early periods, when some brethren may have found it easier even to translate the Scriptures, than to preach in a foreign tongue, and when preaching yielded little apparent fruit, and schools were easily multiplied, and tracts and books could be circulated to any extent. In the chapter on the difficulties in obtaining the Board's charter, it was seen how translating and circulating the Scriptures then preponderated, in the public mind, over preaching as a means of converting the heathen.

The subordinate agencies have been gradually falling into their places, and it is reasonable to expect, under the lead of the Great Captain, that the progress of the gospel will be more rapid in the second half-century than it has been in the first.

How the Work may be completed.

It is an unsettled problem how the work of missions may be so finished, that the missionary force can safely withdraw, leaving the new Christian community to take care of itself. There are spiritual, intellectual, and social difficulties to be first overcome; and these are often much aggravated by adverse influences from abroad. Out of what depths of moral and social degradation is every heathen convert raised before he is fitted for membership of the church of Christ! "And such were some of you," — "fornicators, idolaters, adulterers, effeminate, abusers of themselves with mankind, thieves, covetous, drunkards, revilers, extortioners." (1 Cor. vi. 10, 11.) But though "justified in the name of the Lord Jesus," they are sanctified only in part, "babes in Christ," continually needing to be taught "which be the first principles of the oracles of God." Who can realize what it is, and what it must be, for an entire community of Christians to have had their home, for a long course of years before conversion, where truth had fallen in the street, and equity could not enter, without rule or protection of law, with no standard of morality, no domestic virtue, no culture of the affections, no correct public sentiment, and almost no conscience? And who, that has closely observed the weaknesses and imperfections of human nature in its most favored conditions, is not prepared for occasional and violent outbreaks of ingratitude, passion, waywardness, and wickedness, in churches gathered from the lower, and sometimes the lowest, depths of humanity? That such churches should live, thrive, and ever reach the self-sustaining point, is a miracle of grace.

Causes such as these had their influence in churches gathered by the apostle Paul, as we see in his Epistles. At Corinth he had occasion to lament the many who had been carried away by false teachers, their disorderly worship, their irregularities at the Lord's Supper, their negligent discipline, their party divisions, their litigations, debates, envyings, wraths, strifes, backbitings, whisperings, swellings, tumults. And how soon were the Galatians seduced from their loyalty to the truth, so that the apostle feared he had labored among them in vain! He exhorts the Ephesian church members to put away lying, to steal no more, to have nothing more to do with covetousness and fornication. Four years after this he speaks of his helpers in Lesser Asia as all turned away from him. That he had not full confidence in all the native pastors appears from his address at Miletus. At Rome, there were those who preached Christ of envy and strife, supposing to add affliction to his bonds; and at his first arraignment before Cæsar, not a member of the Roman church had the courage to stand by him. To the Philippians he declares his belief that many professed Christians were enemies of the cause of Christ, and gloried in their shame, minding earthly things. In this same Epistle he speaks in desponding terms of his native helpers, who sought their own, and not the things of Jesus Christ. He thought it needful to exhort the Colossians not to lie one to another, and the Thessalonians to withdraw from such as walked disorderly. He cautions Timothy against fables, endless genealogies, and profane babblings, as if such were prevalent in some of the churches; and speaks of preachers destitute of the truth, with corrupt minds, ignorant, proud, addicted to controversies that engendered envy, strifes, disputations, and railings; and of some who had even made shipwreck of the faith, and added blasphemy to their heresies. The apostle John, somewhat later, declares that many "antichrists" had gone out from the church, denying the Father and the Son.

Yet it is generally supposed that the Apostolical Churches possessed as much piety as the best portions of the visible Church of our times. Indeed, the great apostle speaks of Roman Christians, only a few years before the date of his Epistles to Timothy, as being noted for their faith throughout the world. At the very time of his censures on the Corinthians, he declares that church to be "enriched by Jesus Christ in all utterance and in all knowledge," so that it came behind in no gift. While he so seriously cautions the Ephesians, he ceases not to give thanks for their "faith in the Lord Jesus, and their love unto all the saints." He thanked God upon every remembrance of the Philippians; and when he wrote to the Colossians, he gave thanks for their faith in Christ Jesus, and their love in the Spirit, and to all the saints. And how remarkable his testimony in behalf of the Thessalonians! He remembered, without ceasing and with constant gratitude, their work of faith, and labor of love, and patience of hope in the Lord Jesus Christ, wherein they had become followers of him and of the Lord, having received the word in much affliction, with joy of the Holy Ghost, so that they were examples to all that believed, in Macedonia and Achaia.

The fact undoubtedly is, that visible irregularities and disorders, and even certain immoralities, are more to be expected in churches gathered from among the heathen, than in the churches of Christendom; and they are, at the same time, more consistent with grace in the church, than in countries that have long enjoyed the light and influence of the gospel. While the primitive converts from paganism were remarkable for the high tone of their religious feelings, and the simplicity and strength of their faith, they were wanting in respect to a clear, practical apprehension of the ethical code of the gospel.

It is obvious, that Paul found the burden of his "care of the churches" much enhanced by the thoroughly wicked character of the age. His manner of treating the native pastors and churches is a model for missionaries and their supporters in our day, who ought to expect greater manifestations of ignorance, weakness, and sin in churches that are gathered in Africa, India, and the Sandwich Islands, than at Ephesus, Colossé, and Corinth, in the palmy days of Roman civilization.

This imperfect state of the native churches, and the circumstances in which they exist, have made it difficult for the missions to reach a point where these churches might be safely left, even after the native community had become Christianized. There is a limit beyond which it has not been found practicable to go, in procuring and supporting a foreign missionary force in any one field; as there has been in the support of an English army in India: nor are nations conquered by one simultaneous, universal onset, but by successive victories. It has been found, too, that a less number of foreign missionaries is needful for the work in a heathen country, than was once supposed. There must be room for the free growth and action of a numerous native ministry, and for devolving upon that ministry the heaviest responsibility it will bear.

The popular sentiment at home is believed to have required too much of the missions. A standard has been prescribed for their ultimate success, which renders their satisfactory termination quite impossible, or at best throws it into the far, uncertain future. The Christian religion has been identified, in the popular conception of it, with a general diffusion of education, industry, civil liberty, family government, and social order, and with the means of a respectable livelihood and a well-ordered community. Hence our idea of piety in native converts has generally involved the acquisition and possession, to a great extent, of these blessings; and our idea of the propagation of the gospel by means of missions is, to an equal extent, the creation among heathen tribes and nations of a state of society such as we enjoy. And for this vast intellectual, moral, social transformation we allow but a short time.

We have expected the first generation of converts, even among savages, to come pretty fully into our fundamental ideas of morals, manners, political economy, social organization, justice, equity, — although many of these are ideas which old Christian communities have been ages in acquiring. If we have discovered that converts under the torrid zone go half clothed, are idle on a soil where a small amount of labor supplies their wants, sometimes forget the apostle's cautions to his converts, "not to lie one to another," and "to steal no more," in communities where the grossest vice scarcely affects the reputation, and are slow to adopt our ideas of the rights of man, we at once doubt the genuineness of their conversion, and the faithfulness of their missionary instructors.

It is an important and encouraging consideration, in the effort to bring missions to a successful issue, that an increasing outlay is not always necessary to meet the demands of a growing and prosperous mission. This results from an increase of intelligence, experience, and piety in missionaries, thus augmenting their superintending and executive power; from a similar growth in the native ministry; from substituting the less expensive native agency for the missionary, thus multiplying stations without increasing the foreign force; from developing the native churches; from new discoveries in the relations and powers of the missionary enterprise, increasing the simplicity and economy of its spiritual machinery; and from new arrangements and combinations, to meet the constantly increasing expenditure in some parts of the system, by a constantly diminishing outlay in others.

The work of the missionary has been performed mainly at central points; and when this work shall have been completed at all these points, and there is no more need of new stations, — when it is possible for gospel institutions to exist, through divine grace, without the longer presence of the missionary, — then the work of the mission in that community is obviously completed. The missionary, having "no more place in those parts," should go and preach the gospel elsewhere. It is a great point to know when to do this. After a native church is formed, it should have, as soon as possible, a native pastor and the needed church officers; and the native pastor should have ample scope for preaching, and for all his ministerial and pastoral abilities and duties. The local church is the divinely appointed illuminating power for its district. It is the great power in missions. It is a leaven, which may be expected in time to leaven the whole lump. With a somewhat reserved and discreet superintendence on the part of the nearest missionary, it will thrive best, after a proper organization, by being left to itself. Thus station after station may be finished, and new conquests be continually made, with almost no enlargement in the number of the foreign force, and also without any material increase of expenditure; provided the native pastors have not been rendered too expensive by an injudicious education, doing less to fit them for their work than to make them dissatisfied in it, and provided the duty of self-support has been properly urged upon the native churches.

CHAPTER IV.

PROGRESS OF THE WORK.

Communities that have been Christianized. — SANDWICH ISLANDS. Missionaries and their Children. — Solution of the Problem. — Present Dangers. — The Founders and Fathers of the Mission to remain. — CHEROKEES. The Mission discontinued. — CHOCTAWS. Dr. Kingsbury's Testimony. — Hinderances to Progress. — The Missions successful. — Discontinued. — TUSCARORAS. Long since Christianized. — Why the Mission was not sooner discontinued. — STATIONS. What is meant by a Christianized Station. — Illustrations. — Pastors of Station Churches. — The Centralizing Policy, and its Effect on Village Stations. — When it should be changed. — Education for Native Preachers of the First Generation. — Historical Catalogue of the Missions.

THE Board can not be said to have completed the work of any one of its missions, if this involve the idea of a native Christian community able to stand alone. Yet several of the heathen communities in which it has labored have been Christianized, in the popular acceptation of that term.

The SANDWICH ISLANDS have been thus Christianized. In the year 1853, at Cincinnati, Ohio, the Prudential Committee made the following statement to the Board: —

The mission to the Sandwich Islands left the United States October 23, 1819, and first saw the Islands early in the following April. God prepared their way; one of the strangest of revolutions having occurred just before their arrival. The national idols had been destroyed, the temples burned, the priesthood, tabus, and human sacrifices abolished. All this, however, was only a removal of obstacles. It really did nothing to improve the character of the people, nor could it alone have ameliorated their condition.

The horrid rites of idolatry had ceased; but the moral, intellectual, social desolation was none the less profound and universal. Society was in ruins, and could not exist at a much lower point; and it was there the mission commenced its work. What desolation was there in the native mind, as regards all useful knowledge! The language was unwritten, and of course there were neither books, schools, nor education. The nation was composed of thieves, drunkards, and debauchees. The land was owned by the king and his chiefs, and the people were slaves. Constitutions, laws, courts of justice there were none, and no conception of such things in the native mind. Property, life, every thing was in the hands of arbitrary, irresponsible chiefs, who filled the land with discord and oppression.

But that people has become a Christian nation; not civilized, in the modern acceptation of the term; not able, perhaps, to sustain itself unaided in any one great department of national existence. Laws, institutions, civilization, the great compact of social and political life, are of slower growth than Christianity. A nation may be Christian, while its intellect is but partially developed, and its municipal and civil institutions are in their infancy. In this sense, the Hawaiian nation is a Christian nation, and will abide the severest scrutiny by every appropriate test. All the religion they now have claims the Christian name. A fourth part of the inhabitants are members in regular standing of Protestant Christian churches. The nation recognizes the obligations of the Sabbath. Houses for Christian worship are built by the people, and frequented as among ourselves. So much, indeed, was the blood of the nation polluted by an impure commerce with the world, before our Christian mission, that the people have a strong remaining tendency to licentiousness, which the gospel will scarcely remove till a more general necessity exists for industry and remaining at home. The weakness of the nation is here. But Christian marriage is enjoined and regulated by the laws, and the number of marriage licenses taken out, in the year 1852, exceeded two thousand. The language is reduced to writing, and is read by nearly a third part of the people. The schools contain the great body of the children and youth.

The annual outlay for education, chiefly by the government, exceeds fifty thousand dollars. The Bible, translated by the labors of eight missionaries, was in the hands of the people before the year 1840; and there are elementary books in theology, practical religion, geography, arithmetic, astronomy, and history, — making together a respectable library for a people in the early stages of civilization. Since the press first put forth its efforts in the language on the 7th of January, 1822, there have been issued nearly two hundred millions of pages. Through the blessing of God on these instrumentalities, a beneficent change has occurred in all the departments of the government, in the face of fierce outrages from seamen and traders, and deadly hostility from not a few foreign residents. The very first article in the Constitution, promulgated by the king and chiefs in the year 1840, declares "that no law shall be enacted which is at variance with the word of the Lord Jehovah, or with the general spirit of his word;" and that "all the laws of the Islands shall be in consistency with God's law." What was this but a public, solemn, national profession of the Christian religion, on the high Puritan basis? And the laws and administration of the government since that time, have been as consistent with this profession, to say the least, as those of any other Christian government in the world. The statute laws organizing the general government and courts of justice, the criminal code, and reported trials in the courts, printed in the English language, make five octavo volumes in the library of the Board. Court houses, prisons, roads, bridges, surveys of lands, and their distribution, with secure titles, among the people, are in constant progress.

Here, then, let us, as a Board of Foreign Missions, in the name of the community for which we act, proclaim with shoutings of grace, grace! that the people of the Sandwich Islands are a Christian nation, and may rightfully claim a place among the Protestant Christian nations of the earth!

While there could be no question that the Hawaiian nation was at that time a Christian nation, in every sense in which the term is applicable to the nations of Christendom, yet it was certain that the missionaries could not then be spared from the field; nor was there any institution, save the American Board, to sustain them in that remote position. The problem to be solved was one of great difficulty. There were no precedents. The Prudential Committee had to feel their way step by step. The missionaries, with but few exceptions, were fearful and backward to loose their hold upon the Board. A new and peculiar arrangement was therefore entered upon to meet the new and peculiar emergency. The plan was to substitute the home missionary system for the foreign; the Board occupying the place of a Home Missionary Society. This change was brought about gradually. The plan was first proposed in the year 1848, and received its form from the manner in which the case first came before the Committee.

There were then about one hundred and thirty children of missionaries at the Sandwich Islands, nearly fifty of whom were ten years old and upward. An application was received from five families, containing twenty-five children, for permission to come to this country, and provide for the support and education of the older children; and there were then sixteen other families which would soon be similarly situated. The bearing of this upon the welfare, and even the existence, of the mission was at once perceived. It resulted from the modern method of conducting missions to the heathen mainly by married missionaries, in connection with the extraordinary healthfulness of the Islands, favoring the enlargement of families. But this very oceanic climate, along with the growing commercial relations of the Sandwich Islands, and the Christianized state of the people, gave occasion for a method of retaining the families there. The missionaries were encouraged to take a qualified release from their connection with the Board, and become Hawaiian citizens; and if they should declare their intention of remaining at the Islands in the gospel ministry, they were to receive their proportional part of the property held by the Board at their respective stations; and the government also engaged, on this condition, to insure them an absolute right in the lands thus held.

Through the divine blessing, this arrangement was successful. The five families referred to are still at the Islands, and so, with but a single exception, are the others. The missionaries have passed the ordeal with far less damage than was feared. The Board is advancing prosperously in the second stage of its work, except that there is yet no definite prospect of a time when it may safely withdraw its expenditure. During this critical period, Providence has made it for the interest of the great commercial nations to restrain each other from any considerable interference with the native government. The obstacles arising from a wicked and lawless foreign commerce, once so formidable, have been coming under the restraints of law and public opinion, somewhat as in older Christian lands. The reckless zeal of Roman Catholic missionaries has been one of the chief influences requiring the presence of a strong Protestant force. This hostile influence is not, however, without its advantages to the missionaries and to the native Christians; and perhaps the most effectual barrier against Papal inroads will be the multiplication of native churches with a native ministry — those spiritual fortresses which our Lord requires to be erected all over the world, and which he engages to defend. But in the way of securing a competent native ministry, there are all those inherent difficulties in the nature of man, which so impede and impair the graces of the churches in our own land, and they are enhanced and aggravated by the long reign of heathenism. Churches with such a ministry, and so situated, would seem to need the continued presence and guardianship of the founders and fathers of the new Christian community.

The CHEROKEES may be regarded as, in the popular sense, a Christian nation. At the Fiftieth Anniversary of the Board, the following announcement respecting the mission to the Cherokees was made by the Prudential Committee: —

This mission, one of the oldest under the care of the Board, has been in operation about forty-three years, and has employed eighteen clerical missionaries, twenty-nine laymen of different occupations, and sixty-six female assistant missionaries, or one hundred and thirteen in all; and three hundred and fifty-six thousand four hundred and twenty-one dollars have been expended in it from the treasury of the Board. As the result of these and other kindred efforts, the Cherokees have been elevated from the savage state to their present degree of civilization. Doubtless, among the ignorant portions of the people, there are remains of superstitious notions and habits greater than are found in older Christian communities; but however low may be the standard of their Christianity, it is their only religion. The people are generally, as with us, ranked in one of the evangelical denominations. And they are accessible to Christian preachers, and listen to them with the same deference as do their white brethren in the adjoining States. They inhabit chiefly the eastern section of their territory, which borders on the State of Arkansas, extending north and south about one hundred miles, and east and west about seventy-five miles, and their number is reckoned at twenty-one thousand. Our three missionary brethren residing among them, concur in the opinion that they reckon themselves, and are to be acknowledged, a Christian people. Mr. Torrey says, "Christianity is recognized among them, as much as in any portion of the United States. Their constitution provides that no person who denies the being of a God, or a future state of reward and punishment, shall hold any office in the civil department of this nation." Mr. Ranney says, "The nation, as such, I presume, would claim to be called a Christian nation. Some laws have been passed by the Cherokee Council which have recognized Christianity as the religion of the nation. This has been done incidentally, rather than directly and positively. I suppose that almost universally they would desire to be called Christians." And Mr. Willey bears a similar testimony. "I think," he says, "that the Cherokees, as a nation, may justly be called a nominally Christian nation. The Cherokee Constitution recognizes the Christian religion, and requires a belief in it by all who hold office under the government. All teachers in the public schools are required by law to have the Bible read in their schools daily; and when they are prepared for it, they are requested to pray daily in their schools."

It is our privilege to make the like record concerning the CHOCTAWS. Of their title to the Christian name we have the high testimony of the pioneer in both the Choctaw and Cherokee missions — the Rev. Cyrus Kingsbury, D. D., already mentioned. Writing from Pine Ridge, in the Choctaw nation, March 11, 1861, in reply to inquiries, Dr. Kingsbury says, —

"I unhesitatingly answer, that the Choctaws are a Christian nation, in the popular acceptance of that term.

"1. There is no other religion known among this people but the Christian religion. All who make any pretensions to religion receive the Christian Scriptures, as containing those doctrines which they are to believe and those duties which they are to practice.

"2. As large a proportion of the Choctaws, it is believed, are professors of the Christian religion as are to be found in any other portion of our country. The numbers connected with the different churches I am not able to give; probably it amounts to between one fifth and one fourth of the whole population. A large proportion of those who are not members of the churches are believers in the Christian Scriptures, in the popular acceptation of that phrase.

"3. In the transaction of all public business, the Christian Sabbath is observed as a divine institution; no public business is transacted on that consecrated day.

"4. The sessions of the General Council are, I believe, uniformly opened and closed with prayer.

"5. All public officers and jurymen are required to take the oath usually administered in the United States, and in the usual form.

"6. No man is considered competent to be a witness who denies the existence of a Supreme Being.

"The progress of the Choctaws in agriculture and general improvement," Dr. Kingsbury adds, "has suffered much from the want of that necessary stimulus, a good market. This, together with their natural indolence, has kept the larger portion of the nation in very humble circumstances. For the last three or four years there have been short crops, and in the past year almost an entire failure. This has greatly reduced their means of support, and put it out of the power of most of our church members to do more than to provide for their own most pressing wants. And, indeed, this could not have been done without very considerable aid from abroad.

"In the peculiar and trying circumstances," he continues, "in which the Choctaws have been, and still are, placed, they have felt the necessity of reliable, intelligent men, to give influence and direction to their public councils. This has led the Choctaws to press into the service of the nation all our [native] ordained, and most of our licensed, preachers. This has had a tendency to divert the preachers more or less from the great work of the gospel ministry. Party feelings having been strong, they have, as a thing in course, lost influence with those on the opposite side. The necessity there has been for intelligence and integrity in the public service of the nation, and the better remuneration for those services, have probably induced some to turn attention to those pursuits, who otherwise might have entered the ministry. These and other circumstances have much retarded our progress in bringing forward a native ministry."

The Board began its labors among this people as early as 1818, and prosecuted them forty years, receiving into the church of Christ during that time, and mainly in the latter half of the period, some twenty-seven hundred members. It found the Choctaws a nation of pagans; it left them as really a Christian nation, in the year 1859, as can be truthfully affirmed of the other nations of Christendom. The appropriate work of the Board, under its charter as a foreign missionary institution, had then been accomplished. The twelve churches connected with it, containing thirteen hundred and sixty-two members, had long been in connection with the Presbyterian Church, (old school;) and, upon the withdrawal of the Board, it was a thing of course for that body to assume the responsibility of rendering the aid that might yet be needful for sustaining the gospel institutions among that Christianized people, upon the home missionary or some other plan. There are now fifteen hundred church members, who were all admitted upon the strict principle, and chiefly by missionaries in connection with the American Board.

The TUSCARORAS, a remnant of one of the "Six Nations" of Indians, are a Christian people. For nearly sixty years, indeed, they have enjoyed the fostering care of different missionary organizations. The New York Missionary Society directed its attention to these Indians early in the present century. A church of eight members was organized prior to 1813. On the 3d of July, 1826, the mission was transferred to the Board. These people appear to have been Christianized long ago; for the United Foreign Missionary Society, which received them from the New York Society, made the following statement concerning them, in the year 1821: "The whole nation, now residing at Tuscarora, have taken a decided stand in favor of the Christian religion. They have already made considerable progress in acquiring the arts and habits of civilized life. Having in a great measure abandoned the chase as the means of subsistence, they now depend for their support principally upon the produce of the soil. They occupy comfortable dwellings; and in passing through their villages, you behold wagons, plows, and other implements of husbandry, arranged around their doors. Some of their youth have made considerable proficiency in the elementary branches of an English education."

That the Tuscarora people should have been continued under the pupilage of a foreign missionary institution for forty years after such a testimony, is to be accounted for by the fact, that the proper responsibilities of such institutions had not a clear definition in the public mind. The Prudential Committee declared to the Board their belief, in 1860, that such a people were not the proper objects of a foreign mission; that they had the ability to sustain in great measure the preaching of the gospel; and that some home missionary organization would be ready to meet any reasonable deficiency.

It is by finishing the work at STATIONS, in the influential centers of population, that missions are to be brought to a successful close. Such a result at a station implies indeed a great deal, as all, who are practically conversant with missions, know full well. It implies not only the greater light of the central church at the station, but also lesser lights in adjacent villages. In an extended territory, there may be many a dark intervening space between these constellations, —as there was in the Roman empire for ages after history recognizes it as Christian; and it may even be desirable for missionary societies to leave these dark spaces for the native churches to illuminate with the gospel, and thus to exercise and strengthen their graces.

The progress yet made by the Board in establishing the institutions of the gospel in other countries than those just named, admits of only a brief illustration.

One of the first stations occupied by the mission to the Armenians of the Turkish empire, was at Pera, the portion of Constantinople where the missionaries first had their residence. Pera has now a self-supporting church, composed of evangelical Armenians, with a native pastor—the whole independent of the missionaries, who reside elsewhere. The pastor of this church, Mr. Eutujian, attended the Jubilee Meeting, and made an address in the Armenian language, which was interpreted by Dr. Hamlin. Difficulties have indeed arisen in this church, perhaps as a consequence of this very independence, just as they arose in the churches at Corinth and Galatia; and such are of course to be expected.

At Aintab, in the interior of Asia Minor, the regions of Cilicia, where a station was commenced in 1848, there is now a self-supporting church of near three hundred members, with a native pastor, a Sabbath congregation of nine hundred, and schools of six hundred youths and almost four hundred adults, and a Sabbath school of sixteen hundred members.

At Brûsa, near Mount Olympus, in the ancient Bithynia, two missionaries were residing in 1844. The last of these was removed in 1852, and a native pastor took charge of the church. Nothing more has since been needed there, except an occasional missionary visit, and some pecuniary aid.

Trebizond, on the south-western shore of the Black Sea, had two missionaries, and afterward one; but since 1857 it has had none: the whole being left, as at Brûsa, to the native church and pastor, with some pecuniary aid and spiritual care. From the nature of the case, like the churches of Macedonia, most mission churches are, for a time, in "deep poverty."

The station at Marash, fifty or sixty miles from Aintab, dating only from the year 1854, has a church of two hundred and twenty-seven members, a congregation of near a thousand, a numerous Sabbath school, and a native pastor.*

* Dr. H. G. O. Dwight, from Constantinople, visited Aintab and Marash in the spring of 1861. He arrived at the former place on Saturday. "The next day was the Sabbath," he writes, "and it was to me a most delightful day. I had the privilege of preaching to more than a thousand people, and of addressing a Sabbath school, all assembled in one room, of sixteen hundred and sixty-eight members, including the teachers. In the evening of the same day, I attended the monthly concert, at which probably seven hundred were present."

Speaking of Marash, he says, "This place is indeed a wonder. Twelve years ago, there was not a Protestant here, and the people were proverbially ignorant, barbarous, and fanatical. Six years ago, the Evangelical Armenian Church was organized, with sixteen members. The congregation at that time consisted of one hundred and twenty.

"On the last Sabbath, I preached in the morning to a congregation of over a thousand; and in the afternoon, at the communion, I addressed nearly or quite fifteen hundred people, when forty new members were admitted to the church, making the whole present number two hundred and twenty-seven. Nearly one hundred of these have been added since Mr. White came here, two years ago. Previous to the late communion, one hundred and sixteen persons were examined, but only forty were admitted to the church. It is confidently believed by our brethren that many of those who were told to wait are truly converted persons; but, as the cases are recent, prudence seemed to dictate that they should be put on a longer trial. One entire half of the body of the church was filled with females, packed closely together on the floor. The other half, and the broad galleries around three sides of the house, were completely crowded with men. A new church, in the other end of the town, is needed immediately."

The cases thus far instanced are among the benighted, but still nominally Christian, people of Western Asia, and the tendency is more or less strongly to similar results at the thirty other stations, and even at very many of the hundred outstations belonging to the several missions in that great and interesting field.

When we speak of a Christianized station, however, we ought not to be understood as implying all that is meant when speaking of a Christianized people. At neither of the places named above has evangelical Christianity yet become the predominant religion among the people. We mean only that the Christian church has acquired an actual, influential footing there, somewhat analogous to that of churches in the young cities and towns of our new western settlements.

This is more or less true at many of the local stations in the missions among pagan nations. The church at Chavagacherry, in Ceylon, where a missionary once resided, is now consigned, together with its district, to a native pastor, and the same is true of the churches and districts of Karadive and Valaney; and none of the other native churches are more flourishing than these. The church at Bombay — the first gathered by missionaries of the Board — has now a native pastor, though he is not supported by the church; so have the first and second churches in Ahmednuggur; so has the church at Seroor. These are all churches at stations, and the pastoral relation has been well sustained. The Madura mission has native pastors for six of its twenty-eight churches, and one of these is a station church.

The opinions of the executive officers of the Board, and of the Prudential Committee, have inclined toward the ordaining of native pastors at all the station churches, as fast as the suitable men can be found; but, excepting the Mahratta mission, it can hardly be said that the missions of the Board in pagan nations are yet prepared to come fully into the practice. It seems to be gaining ground in the missions of Western Asia; and, as far as is known, the experiment there has been generally successful.

It has been found hard to overcome the difficulties in the way of raising up self-sustaining churches, whether at stations or outstations, whether in nominally Christian or pagan lands. These difficulties are so various as to allow of only the most comprehensive notice, if indeed the time has come for treating the subject very positively.

Preaching, congregations, churches, schools, native helpers, every thing, of course centers at first at the station, clustering around the resident missionary. But there is danger of continuing the centralizing policy too long, and it is believed that this has frequently been done. This tendency in the working of missions is natural and strong, both in the missionary and his converts, as was singularly manifested, a few years since, in one of the India missions. The ground inclosed around the mission house is there called a "compound," and being of some extent, and vested with certain privileges, it had an attractive power on the minds of village converts throughout the region. These converts, being chiefly from a caste not attached to the soil as cultivators, were able to leave their villages, and many were drawn, with their families, to the mission compounds at the central stations, thus forming small Christian villages, built up, and in part sustained, by the Board, and invested, to some extent, with European protection and privilege. It was thus an asylum for the poor, oppressed converts. But though it brought them around the missionary, where, besides being easily cared for, they made up a numerous station church, its nature as an asylum fostered the feeling of dependence in the native mind, gave to the centers an appearance of prosperity and strength which they had not in fact, and discouraged the forming of rural stations and churches, and the extension of the mission. Self-sustaining native Christian churches could not thus be formed, and the villages might be as long in coming to the Christian light, as in the Roman empire of the first Christian centuries. The thing had grown up insensibly, and upon discovering the evil, it was speedily corrected. The villagers were generally sent home, village stations and village churches were formed, and dispersion and diffusion became the order of the day.

The natural reluctance of missionary brethren to diminish the number of members in the station churches by forming churches in the villages, and the number of hearers at the station by forming congregations in the villages, and the array of Christian life about them by pushing it off to the outposts, will be understood and appreciated by pastors. It is an evil hard to overcome, seeing that the missionary's family state obliges him to have a fixed habitation, where he must needs be much at home.*

* The Rev. Henry Ballantine thus refers to this change of missionary policy, writing from Ahmednuggur, February 7, 1861: —

"A glance at the following table, showing the gradual increase in the number of members of the churches belonging to the mission since its establishment in 1831, is instructive and encouraging. The whole period has been divided into terms of five years, that the progress of the mission may be more easily seen.

Members received from 1831 to 1835, inclusive, . . .	9
" " " 1836 to 1840, " . . .	7
" " " 1841 to 1845, " . . .	75
" " " 1846 to 1850, " . . .	63
" " " 1851 to 1855, " . . .	78
" " " 1856 to 1860, " . . .	363
Total, ...	595

"The members received into the churches during the last five years are as follows: In 1856, 30; 1857, 56; 1858, 86; 1859, 64; 1860, 127: total, 363.

"From this it will be seen that the average for each term of five years from 1840 to 1855 was just 72, exactly nine times the average of the first two terms of five years; while the number received during the last term of five years was five times as great as the average for five years from 1840 to 1855, and forty-five times as great as the average for five years from 1831 to 1840. Again, it appears that the number received during each year of the last five years was, on an average, 72 — the same as the average number received during each period of five years from 1841 to 1855.

"Should it be asked how the sudden increase in the number of converts in the last term of five years can be accounted for, I would say, there is no doubt that the new policy inaugurated in the mission in 1855, putting missionaries out in the districts to labor among the people, has been the means, in the hands of God, of greatly extending the knowledge of the truth, and of bringing many more converts into our churches. Some members of the mission desired to see this policy pursued ten years before it was adopted; but at length the Deputation, coming to India in 1854, decided the matter which had been discussed in the mission so long, and the plan was at once put in execution."

No doubt the delays consequent upon this slow development of the lessons of experience, have greatly enhanced the obstacles to self-sustaining church organizations in the fields occupied by the Board. There is a time for all things. As, in delicate processes of crystallization, complete success depends on allowing the crystals to form at the right time, so, in missions, there is a time for reversing the centralizing policy, when the native elements will crystallize most perfectly under their own proper laws of social life, and not under those of the foreign countries from whence the missionaries came. In some such manner, converts have too often been disqualified in a measure for a patient attendance on the ministry of even the best educated native preachers, and the native preachers have thus been disqualified for living on the proper native salary, if they have not been also for the retirement and obscurity of rural life. The secular education of adults, though exceedingly below the common standard in old Christian countries, has still been too much in advance of the religious; and our native preachers have been educated more for the demands of the future, than for those of churches in their earliest possible existence; while both churches and pastors were, and must needs be, in leading-strings held by the missionaries. The opinion is now becoming general in the missions of the Board, that the study of the English language, except in special instances, has not facilitated the rearing up of self-relying native churches. It was at least premature. Perhaps, too, there has been a higher standard than was expedient for the mere intellectual culture of native preachers and pastors, in the first generation.

Historical Catalogue of the Missions.

The following missions are now, or have been, connected with the Board: —

1. *Mahratta Mission*, in Western India; instituted in 1813; in two missions from 1842 to 1852; in four, from 1852 to 1858; one discontinued, 1858; the three others reunited in one, 1860.

2. *Ceylon Mission*, 1816.

3. *Cherokee*, (N. A. Indians,) 1816; discontinued, 1860.

4. *Choctaws*, (N. A. Indians,) 1818; discontinued, 1859.

5. *Sandwich Islands*, 1820; discontinued on the foreign missionary basis, and continued on the home missionary basis, 1853.

6. *Palestine*, 1821; merged in the Syria mission, 1845.

7. *Malta*, 1822, — for the press, which was removed to Smyrna in 1833.

8. *Syria*, 1823.

9. *South America*, (exploring,) 1823–1826.

10. *Turkey*, 1826; North and South, 1856–1860; Western, Eastern, and Central, 1860.

11. *Osages*, (N. A. Indians,) commenced by United Foreign Missionary Society, 1820; transferred to the Board, 1826; discontinued, 1837.

12. *Maumee*, (N. A. Indians,) commenced by Western Missionary Society, 1822; transferred to United Foreign Missionary Society, 1822, and to the Board, 1826; discontinued, 1835.

13. *New York Indians*, commenced by New York Missionary Society, 1801; transferred to United Foreign Missionary Society, 1821, and to the Board, 1826; Tuscarora Branch discontinued, 1860.

14. *Mackinaw*, (N. A. Indians,) commenced by the United Foreign Missionary Society, 1823; transferred to the Board, 1826; discontinued, 1836.

15. *Chickasaws*, (N. A. Indians,) commenced by Synod of South Carolina and Georgia, 1821; transferred to the Board, 1827; discontinued, 1835.

16. *Stockbridge Indians*, 1828; discontinued, 1848.

17. *Greece*, 1830; discontinued, except the station at Athens, 1841.

18. *China*, 1830; — at *Canton*, 1830; at *Amoy*, 1842, transferred to Board of Foreign Missions of the Reformed Dutch Church, 1858; at *Fuhchau*, 1847; at *Shanghai*, 1853; at *Tientsin*, 1860.

19. *Ojibwas*, (N. A. Indians,) 1830.

20. *Siam*, 1831; missionaries in part transferred to Fuhchau, 1847; discontinued, 1850.

21. *Creeks*, (N. A. Indians,) 1832; discontinued, 1837.

22. *Sumatra*, (exploring,) 1833.

23. *Patagonia*, (exploring,) 1833 and 1834.

24. *Madura*, 1834.

25. *Nestorians*, 1834.

26. *Singapore*, 1834 ; discontinued, 1843.
27. *Pawnees*, (N. A. Indians,) 1834 ; discontinued, 1844.
28. *Sioux*, or *Dakotas*, (N. A. Indians,) 1834.
29. *Western Africa*, at *Cape Palmas*, 1834–1843 ; removed to the *Gaboon*, 1843.
30. *Cyprus*, 1834 ; discontinued, 1840.
31. *Oregon*, 1835 ; broken up by the massacre of 1847.
32. *Southern Africa*, 1835 ; — one mission at *Mosika*, 1836, broken up by war, 1837 ; the other at *Port Natal*, 1836.
33. *Abenaquis*, (N. A. Indians,) 1835 ; discontinued, 1858.
34. *Madras*, 1836.
35. *Borneo*, (exploring,) 1836 and 1837.
36. *Persian Mohammedans*, 1838 ; discontinued, 1841.
37. *Borneo*, 1838 ; in part transferred to Amoy, in China, 1844 ; discontinued, 1852.
38. *To the Jews in Turkey*, 1844 ; discontinued, 1856.
39. *Arcot*, in India, 1851 ; transferred to Board of Foreign Missions of the Reformed Dutch Church, 1857.
40. *Micronesia*, in the N. Pacific Ocean, 1852.

CHAPTER V.

THE MISSIONARIES.

The Missionary described. — The Principle underlying his Engagement. — Makes the First Advance. — Appointment, Designation, and Support. — Age, Constitution, Habits. — Ordination. — Marriage. — The Number of Missionaries. — Whence they came. — Education. — Length of Service. — Protective Care of Providence. — Missionary Physicians. — Unmarried Females. — Farmers and Mechanics. — Salaries. — Disabled Missionaries. — Children of Missionaries. — Schools, Asylums, Permanent Funds. — The Present System found to work well.

A MISSIONARY is described in the by-laws of the Board, as one who has been ordained a minister of the gospel, and has actually come under its direction. All others — licensed preachers, physicians, schoolmasters, printers, etc. — are assistant missionaries; but, in the reports of the Board, they are to be designated by their specific occupations.

Underlying the theory of missions, as prosecuted by the American Board, is the principle that the missionary goes forth in the discharge of his own personal responsibility to Christ. The Board, the churches, are helpers, co-workers in his mission. There is an implied covenant, and he is one of the parties. The enlistment is voluntary; and so are the contributions of the donor. Both are alike servants of Christ. Christians at home are indebted to the missionary only as the missionary is to them. The missionary is doing their work no more than they are doing his. The Board declared this principle many years ago, as best comporting with the happiest and most successful prosecution of missions, during a prolonged period, and on an extended scale.

The missionary candidate has therefore been expected to make the first advance, and to offer himself for the service. The Secretaries, when visiting theological seminaries, have been accustomed to inquire for the students whose minds were known to be exercised on this subject, and to confer with such. It has devolved on the Prudential Committee, when the candidate presented himself, to be satisfied as to the reality of his call of God to the work of missions. That was to be determined by the proper evidence, and on the presumption that whom the Lord calls to this work he will endow with the requisite physical, mental, and spiritual abilities, and allow no insuperable providential barriers to stand in the way. The engagement is not for a specified term of years, but for life, "if the Lord will."

The appointment and the designation of missionaries are not always decided at the same time. By accepting an appointment, the missionary accepts also the rules and regulations of the Board, the nature of which he is supposed to understand. The Board pays no expenses of missionary candidates in their preparation for the ministry, and no debts contracted after appointment, unless expressly authorized; nor does it assume the expenses of appointed missionaries before the time arrives to prepare for their departure. On the principle stated at the opening of this chapter, the missionary's claim upon the Board for support, when in the field, has always been understood as for no more than an equitable proportion of the funds placed at its disposal; the Board being able to divide only what it receives. Missionaries have gone forth trusting in God that there will always be enough for their wants, incurring whatever risk there may be; which past experience shows to be very small, since no missionary of the Board has ever yet been compelled to retire from the field or to remain at home for want of funds.

The reply made by a convention of delegates from the three Tamil missions, in 1839, to an inquiry as to the age, constitution, and habits most suitable for a missionary to India, has been found applicable to the missions generally. It was this: "A missionary to an old mission should be young, that he may easily get the language, and that his habits may more easily be shaped to the climate. If he goes to form a new mission, more age may be an advantage; but generally a missionary should not be above thirty, where he is expected to acquire the language, unless he have a peculiar turn for it. As to habits, they should be rather active than sedentary, but he should be capable of study; if not learned, he should be able to learn, and ready to teach. His constitution should be good, but the most sanguine and robust need not expect the best health. There may be a proper distinction between pliancy of constitution and weakness. A bilious habit is undesirable, but too much may be feared from it, as too much may be hoped in favor of pulmonary tendencies; though the climate is friendly to the latter, and unfriendly to the former. The advice of a skillful and candid physician should have much weight." The average of the ages of seventy-five ordained missionaries at the time of their appointment since the year 1851, is twenty-seven years.

For a number of the first years, the Prudential Committee was accustomed to invite the ordaining council for the missionary, (if he belonged to the Congregational body;) and when the ordination was over, they passed votes of thanks to those who had performed the services. But for a long time past, the missionary has been left, after receiving official notice of his appointment, to arrange for his ordination with his friends, or his church, or some other ecclesiastical body. Where the judgments and hearts of the people have been with the candidates, the ordination services have proved a blessing. Hence the missionary is usually advised to seek ordination among his own people.

The experience of the Board favors the marriage of missionaries, as a general rule, and always when they are going to a barbarous people. Wives are a protection among savages, and men can not there long make a tolerable home without them. When well selected in respect to health, education, and piety, wives endure "hardness" quite as well as their husbands, and sometimes with more faith and patience.

The number of missionaries and assistant missionaries sent forth from the beginning, is indicated in the following table:—

MISSIONS.	Ordained.	Phys'ns who received Ordination.	[illegible]ns not Ordained.	[illegible] Assistant Missionaries.	Female Assistant Missionaries.	Total.
Dr. and Mrs. Judson and Mr. Rice,	2				1	3
West Africa, ...	16	1	1	1	18	36
South Africa, ...	21	2	0	1	23	45
Greece, ...	3	0	0	0	3	6
Armenians, ...	62	4	1	2	73	138
Syria, including Cyprus, ...	27	1	2	1	36	66
Assyria, ...	6	1	2	0	9	17
Nestorians, ...	19	1	2	1	26	48
Mahrattas, ...	28	0	0	4	39	71
Ceylon, ...	24	2	1	1	30	56
Madura, ...	24	0	2	0	30	56
Madras, ...	5	2	0	1	9	15
Arcot, ...	3	0	0	0	4	7
Canton, ...	10	2	1	1	9	21
Amoy, ...	4	0	0	0	5	9
Fuhchau, ...	8	0	0	0	11	19
Shanghai, ...	2	0	0	0	1	3
Siam, ...	7	0	1	0	9	17
Singapore, ...	4	1	0	1	4	9
Indian Archipelago, ...	3	1	0	0	3	6
Borneo, ...	7	0	0	0	6	13
Sandwich Islands, ...	46	3	6	21	80	153
Micronesia, ...	7	2	0	0	7	14
South America, ...	2	0	0	0	0	2
Choctaw Indians, ...	18	1	1	34	90	143
Cherokee Indians, ...	16	1	2	26	66	110
Dakotas, ...	9	1	0	3	15	27
Ojibwas, ...	4	0	0	7	14	25
Chickasaws, ...	4	0	0	0	6	10
Creeks, ...	1	0	0	0	1	2
Osages, ...	5	0	0	6	15	26
Pawnees, ...	1	0	1	2	4	8
Oregon Indians, ...	3	0	1	2	5	11
Mackinaw, ...	1	0	0	7	9	17
Stockbridge Indians, ...	2	0	0	2	4	8
Maumee Indians, ...	1	0	0	1	4	6
New York Indians, ...	9	0	0	3	22	34
Abenaquis Indians, ...	1	0	0	0	0	1
Total, ...	415	26	24	128	691	1258

GENERAL SUMMARY.

MISSIONS.	Ordained Missionaries.	Phys'ns not Ordained.	Assistants.	Males.	Females.	Total.
Africa, ...	37	1	43	40	41	81
W. Asia, European Turkey, Greece,	117	7	151	128	147	275
Western India, ...	28	0	43	32	39	71
Southern India and Ceylon, . . .	56	3	75	61	73	134
Eastern Asia and the Islands, . .	45	2	50	49	48	97
North Pacific Ocean, ...	53	6	108	80	87	167
South America, ...	2			2	0	2
North American Indians, ...	75	5	348	173	255	428
Dr. and Mrs. Judson and Mr. Rice,	2		1	2	1	3
Total, ...	415	24	819	567	691	1258

It thus appears, that the five ordained missionaries sent forth into the heathen world in the year 1812, have been followed by others to the number of four hundred and ten. The eight males and females, composing the first company, now stand associated, on the historic page, in a company of twelve hundred and fifty-eight.

Whence came these missionaries? It would cost too much labor to ascertain the colleges where the greater part of the ordained missionaries were graduated. The seminaries in which they obtained their theological education, so far as their history is known, may be chronologically arranged in the following order: The first class at the Andover Seminary completed its course in the year 1809; at Princeton, in 1812; at Bangor, in 1820; at Auburn, in 1825; at New Haven, in 1826; at the Western Reserve, in 1832; at Lane, in 1833; at East Windsor, in 1836; at Union, in 1838. The number of the missionaries derived from each of these institutions is indicated in the following table: —

SEMINARIES.	Whole number.	Now in the field.	SEMINARIES.	Whole number.	Now in the field.
Andover, Mass., ...	130	66	New Brunswick, N. J., . . .	14	5
Bangor, Me., ...	15	10	Western Reserve, Ohio, . .	9	6
East Windsor, Conn., . . .	13	6	Lane, Ohio, ...	16	7
New Haven, Conn., ...	20	4	Quincy, Ill., ...	2	1
Union, New York City, . . .	41	29	Union, Va., ...	7	1
Auburn, N. Y., ...	28	9	Southern, S. C., ...	2	0
Princeton, N. J., ...	31	7			
			Total from Seminaries, . .	328	151
Unknown, but the greater part supposed not to have been connected with theological seminaries, — the larger portion of these being in missions to North American Indians, ...				87	15
			Grand total, ...	415	166

It will be seen, that nearly all the missionaries who went to countries beyond sea, enjoyed the advantages both of the four years in college, and of the additional years (generally three) in the theological seminaries.

The average length of missionary service performed by one hundred and thirty-four brethren, who went from the Andover

Seminary up to the year 1858, will doubtless admit of a general application. The sum total of these one hundred and thirty-four missionary lives was eighteen hundred and seventy-three years, (reckoning from their departure, and, when they returned home, to the time of their arrival,) so that the average for each is fourteen years. The average length of service of the thirty-four who died in the field, was eleven years. The sixty-six then living and prosecuting their missionary work, had seen an average of seventeen years and a half, and the period was of course growing longer. Two, who died on the islands of the Pacific, averaged seventeen years and six months; and twelve then living there, averaged eighteen years and four months. Five, who died in Southern India and Ceylon, attained to the average of thirteen years and nine months, (which is larger than any where else, save the Pacific,) and the average period of nine then living in India, was twenty-one years and nine months. Dr. Mullens, a highly intelligent English missionary at Calcutta, states, from a careful induction of the lives of two hundred and fifty missionaries in India, that he found the average duration of missionary labor in that country was sixteen years and three quarters.

It should be added, that fifteen of the Andover brethren were in the field from thirty and a half years to forty-two and three fourths. Two saw forty-two years of foreign service; and the highest average among the older men was in India.*

There should be grateful acknowledgment made of the protective care of Providence over the missionaries and their families, when going to and returning from their respective fields, and in their numerous explorations, their long and perilous voyages and journeys, in all manner of conveyances, over all continents and seas, and in all climates; and so too of the travels of officers and agents of the Board. The length of these travels is not much short of a million of miles. One

* Memorial of the Semi-centennial Celebration of the Founding of the Theological Seminary at Andover, pp. 55, 56.

of the Secretaries has traveled considerably over fifty thousand. Of the nearly fifteen hundred persons, only two suffered the loss of life by shipwreck — Dr. Armstrong, one of the Secretaries, and Mr. Pohlman, a missionary in China. Messrs. Munson and Lyman and Dr. Satterlee died by the hands of savages, while on tours of exploration. Mr. Benham, of the Siam mission, was drowned while crossing a river near his own dwelling; and the massacre of Dr. Whitman and others by the Oregon Indians, in 1848, was in their own houses.

The fifty physicians, ordained and unordained, were all expected to be missionary physicians, that is, to make their medical practice subservient to the grand object of the missions. The employing of missionary physicians grows mainly out of the practice of employing married missionaries. Their first care is of the mission families; but they are expected to exert a conciliating influence among the natives by the kindly offices of their profession. Missionary physicians have not been sent where the needful medical attendance was believed to be otherwise attainable.

The tables show an excess of one hundred and twenty-four females above the number of males. The greater part of these unmarried women were in missions to the American Indians. The practice of sending unmarried females beyond sea, has obtained only to a very limited extent. It has been so difficult to secure for them permanent and agreeable homes, and well-defined and appropriate spheres of labor in no danger of failing, that the appointments are now in great measure restricted to female boarding schools at the central points of the larger missions. Every considerable mission needs one such school, and one or two competent female teachers for its instruction. It is the correlative institution with the school for training a native ministry.

In the year 1825, there were sixteen farmers and mechanics in the missions among the Cherokee and Choctaw Indians. The expectations connected with this class of agents not having been realized, it has gradually been withdrawn. The civilizing agencies, as they may be called, have been found the most expensive, the most troublesome, and the least productive. The first company sent to the Sandwich Islands contained a farmer; but it soon appeared that he, though a worthy Christian man, had no vocation there, and he returned home. Mere civilization, coming in contact with savages, is an unhealthful influence: it must come to them through the gospel.

The support of the missionaries and their families has been provided for in various ways, and the manner is doubtless still open to improvement. In the North American Indian and the Sandwich Islands missions, it was for a long time on the principle of common stock; and at the Islands there was a secular agent, and a depository of such goods as the missionaries needed. Salaries have taken the place of this system, as being every way more economical. There was much difficulty, after the year 1848, in bringing the depository at the Islands to a satisfactory close. The missionaries obtained their goods there at cost, and even without charge for duties: what would they do when thrown upon the market and merchants of Honolulu? But the matter was at length adjusted; and, through the skill and faithfulness of the agents, a considerable sum was realized out of the settlement of the depository toward the expenses of the mission. In India, the salaries were originally based on the usage of English missionary societies, giving a certain sum to each married couple, and additional sums for each child, house rent, etc. The Board also adopted their plan of outfit. The English manner of determining the salaries not proving altogether satisfactory, the missionaries in Western Asia were induced to receive their support nearly as pastors do in the United States — the salaries covering every thing, and varying with the circumstances of the individual.

The Board allows no pensions, and has no permanent funds for disabled or superannuated missionaries, or for the widows or children of missionaries. It provides for them in a different way. Its rules in respect to the former classes of persons are as follows: —

When superannuated or disabled missionaries or assistant

missionaries, or the widows of missionaries or assistant missionaries, return to this country with the approbation of the Prudential Committee, it shall be the duty of the Committee to make such grants toward their support as the circumstances of each case shall require, and as shall best comport with the missionary character and the interests of the missionary cause; it being understood,—

1. That no pensions or annuities are to be settled on any person, and that no grant is to be made, except in extraordinary cases, for any other than the current year.

2. That, except in extraordinary cases, after the lapse of a year from their return, no grant is to be made to returned missionaries or assistant missionaries, who are neither superannuated nor disabled by sickness, and yet are not expected to resume their missionary labors.

3. That missionaries and assistant missionaries, who return on account of sickness, and recover their health, and remain in this country, are no longer to be regarded as having claims upon the Board for pecuniary assistance.

4. That missionaries and assistant missionaries, who return on account of sickness, and partially recover their health, so as to attend to the ordinary business of life for a number of years, are not to be regarded, when they again lose their health, as having the same claims upon the Board as they had when they first arrived.

The rules concerning the return of the children of the missionaries to the United States, and their subsequent support, are the following: —

1. When missionaries or assistant missionaries desire to send their children to this country for education, and when it is decided, in a manner conformable to the rules and usages of the Board, that the children may come, the arrangements for the passage, so far as they involve expense, shall have the concurrence of the mission, and the allowance, extraordinary cases excepted, shall be only for a passage direct to this country.

2. When the children arrive in this country, the Prudential

Committee will see that they have a suitable conveyance to the places where they are to be educated or to reside; and the Committee may make grants, on application from the parents or guardians, to an amount not exceeding sixty dollars a year for a boy, and fifty dollars for a girl, until the children are eighteen years old.

3. Children who are left orphans, and without a suitable home in the mission, or responsible guardian, will receive the immediate and kind consideration of the Prudential Committee, who will make an arrangement for their return home, and provide for them the best guardianship in their power.

4. The allowances made on account of the children of living missionaries or assistant missionaries, wherever the children may be educated, shall be charged to the mission to which the parents belong; and the allowances made on account of orphan children shall, in ordinary cases, be charged to the mission to which the parents belonged at the time of their decease.

5. Such are the multiplied cares and duties of the Prudential Committee, and the Treasurer and Secretaries, that it is not regarded as practicable or expedient for them to undertake the guardianship of the children sent to this country.

The sixty dollars given to a boy, and the fifty to a girl, annually, until eighteen years of age, when applied for by the parent or guardian, — admitting of exceptions in extraordinary cases, — were not designed to be sums so large as to interfere with outgoings from the natural fountains, which exist in blood relationships, early friendships for the parents, etc., but rather to stimulate and facilitate their flow. These sums have been found neither too large, nor too small, but the happy medium. The somewhat peculiar circumstances of this country have of course been considered — the assimilating, absorbing power of society; the constant intermingling of the great social currents; the ease of obtaining employment and self-support; and the almost unhealthful stimulus to activity in all the departments of life, often rendering it difficult to retain children long enough under parental guardianship and control; the whole inseparable from the rapidly developing resources of a vast, new country. The leading object is to bring returned missionary children into the great social currents; and this is best secured by giving free scope for the operation of blood relationships and friendships, and for the freest intermixture with native-born children in the schools and employments of the parental home and country.

Every human system has its hardships, but the results to the returned children of missionaries — now a considerable number — have been at least as favorable as with the children of pastors.

To facilitate the working of the entire system, books are kept by the Secretaries, in which a page is devoted to each returned missionary, widow, and child, with such entries of facts and grants as secure a prompt action on every request.

Schools and asylums for missionary children have sometimes been urged upon the Board. It is believed that the missionaries would now generally object to them, for the reasons above stated. Some of the best friends of the cause have also been in favor of instituting a permanent fund for superannuated and disabled missionaries, and for the children of missionaries. But it is the opinion of the Board, that the existing mode of providing for disabled missionaries and the children of missionaries, is preferable to one which should have a permanent fund for its basis — more simple, more humane, more effective, more in accordance with the social condition and institutions of our country; no more a charity; much less like a pension; less liable to perversion; with better effect on missionaries and their children; more accordant with the natural laws under which God places his children; and less likely to interfere with the ordinary receipts of the Board.

CHAPTER VI.

THE CHURCHES.

Relation of Missionaries to Native Churches and Pastors. — Organization of Churches among the Armenians. — In Syria. — Among the Nestorians. — Among the Mahrattas. — In the Arcot Mission. — At Madras. — In the Madura District. — Corporate Powers of the Missions. — Churches in Ceylon. — Caste and Polygamy. — Churches in the Sandwich Islands. — Among the Cherokees. — Among the Choctaws. — Slavery. — Tabular View of the Churches.

It will be a convenient and suitable introduction to this chapter, to quote the response made by the Prudential Committee, in the year 1856, to the request of the Committee of Thirteen on the Deputation to India, for their views on the relation of missionaries to the native churches and pastors.

Organization of Churches.

In general, a missionary will gather his first church at his station. But he will find, sooner or later, that God has given him seals of his ministry in other places; and the question will be forced upon him, Ought I to form these scattered sheep into a separate flock? It may be difficult at times to answer this inquiry. The proper solution will not depend solely on the number of candidates for membership in the new church, for ten in one case may be worth more than twenty in another; or on the number of men who are to join it, as five may be enough in one case, while more would hardly suffice in another; or on the materials for office-bearers, as it may sometimes be expedient to organize a church without any officers; or on the installation of a native pastor at an early day, for this is by no means indispensable. It would seem, however, that the missionary should be able to answer the following questions in the affirmative: Can I provide a competent guide and teacher, ordained or unordained, for the proposed church? Will the gospel have a freer entrance to the unevangelized masses by reason of such a step?

As soon as possible, every church should have its own native pastor, the members, on their part, contributing for his support according to their ability, and he, on his part, adapting himself in a reasonable degree thereto. Such aid as the mission may render should be considered as supplemental and temporary. And not only should the pecuniary burden be thrown upon the church as fast as possible; the responsibility of government should also be assumed at the proper time.

In the first instance, missionaries are obliged to form churches and ordain pastors. They have the requisite power, because it is essential to their work. What they are to do beyond this early stage of ecclesiastical development, it is not for us to say. The subject is not within our sphere. It is wholly in the hands of the missionaries; and on no account should it be interfered with. They have the right to decline forming any ecclesiastical organization for themselves, retaining their connection with presbyteries, classes, associations, etc., in this country; or, to assume one that shall embrace the native churches and pastors. In the contingency first supposed, they will give to the native churches and ministry such an organization as they may think best, to be afterward modified by the latter or not, according to their own free choice. In the second contingency, it is presumed, they will not feel at liberty to go outside of the principles of ecclesiastical order which are recognized by the denominations represented in the Board.

And in no case should there be any ecclesiastical control exercised by missionaries over the native churches and ministers, save that which may grow out of the action of bodies composed of both elements. A wise disbursement of funds will provide all the checks which are necessary or proper.

And this leads us to speak of a fundamental principle of great importance. The expenditure of money should always be the act of a mission. It can never be intrusted to an ecclesiastical body, however constituted; because, in such an event, there can be no just accountability. By our present system the Prudential Committee are responsible to the Board for all the moneys received into the treasury; and the missions are responsible to the Committee for all the moneys sent to their respective fields. The Board, therefore, know where to look; and the Committee know where to look. Every dollar can be followed to its place of disbursement. Any other plan would be fatally defective.

We are expected to state our convictions in regard to the expediency of forming ecclesiastical bodies that shall combine the missionary and the native elements. This is a question of peculiar delicacy. Still, as we have disclaimed all right of interference in such matters, and shall be understood to express an opinion merely, we will venture to say that we consider such a union undesirable.

At this point it will be necessary to inquire more particularly into the exact position which a missionary occupies.

He is a foreigner. No matter how closely he may have identified himself with his calling; in his relations to the people among whom he dwells, he is only a stranger. He remains a citizen of the United States. If laid aside from his labors, he returns here. If he dies, his family return here. On the other hand, the natives will always regard him as one from a distant land. His speech, his dress, his food, each bewrayeth him. They may honor him greatly, and love him much; but one of themselves he can never be.

His work is temporary. It may, indeed, outlast his life; still, it is destined, with God's blessing, to have an end. When the churches shall have reached a certain point, he expects to move forward. He is like the general who penetrates the enemy's country just as fast as he can secure the key-points.

His duties are peculiar. He is an evangelist. When he gathers churches, it is not to be their pastor; he raises up others to take this charge and burden. True, he may act as a pastor for a time; but it is simply from necessity. His sphere is aggression, conquest.

He is also a disbursing agent. He must have money, not only for his own support, but for other objects. He must sustain schools, employ assistants, and scatter abroad the word of life. To this end a weighty trust is committed to him.

Is it expedient that such men should form ecclesiastical relations with the native churches and pastors? We think not. It seems to us that simplicity of arrangement is against it. The true and abiding elements in the ecclesiastical body are the native churches and the native ministry. Why, therefore, should the missionary element be introduced, when there is no necessity for it? And congruity is against it. The missionary and the native pastors can never sustain precisely the same relations to their common work. There is a radical, insurmountable diversity.

Separate action will be for the advantage of all parties. The independence of the native element will be more sure. If missionaries are in the ecclesiastical body, they will exert, almost of necessity, a predominating influence. The power of self-government will be best developed in this way. The native churches and ministers must have responsibilities to bear before they can learn how to bear them. By this plan there will be less danger of embarrassment and disorder when the missionaries leave for "regions beyond."

On the other hand, the mission will do its work with the greatest freedom if it act only as a mission. United with the native element, it will often be obliged to consider questions in a twofold capacity. This may be very undesirable. Suppose, for example, the missionaries to be outvoted by the native churches and pastors, in a matter which involves the expenditure of money. When they take up the subject as a mission, they will find themselves in a position of special difficulty. As members of the ecclesiastical body, though in a minority, they are bound to yield to its decision; as members of the mission, in view of their pecuniary accountableness, they may feel constrained to nullify the act.

It may be said that the native body will need the wisdom and experience of the missionaries. But all the assistance which is desirable, it would seem, may be obtained in the form of counsel. The advisory influence which may be exerted according to some natural arrangement, and the regulating power which necessarily grows out of the disbursement of money, will probably suffice for the happiest development of the churches that may be formed in any part of the world.

The actual proceedings of the missionaries will appear in the concise statement which follows, concerning native churches and other ecclesiastical bodies in the several missions.

Western Asia.

The mission to the Armenians was the first to give a regular organization to its native churches. This it did at its annual meeting in June, 1846, at the request of native brethren after they had been expelled from their national church for not conforming to its idolatrous practices. Three forms of church government were represented at the meeting of the missionaries, but there was a perfect agreement among them.*

The first three articles of the plan of organization were these: —

1. The officers of the Evangelical Armenian Church shall consist of elders or bishops, (called also pastors, etc.,) and deacons, to be chosen by the male members of the church, and set apart by prayer and the imposition of hands.

2. In the first Evangelical Armenian church in Constantinople there shall be, for the present, one elder or bishop, and two deacons; it being understood that the number of either may hereafter be increased, as circumstances demand.

3. Inasmuch as discipline, according to the Scriptures, (1 Cor. v. 4 and 2 Cor. ii. 6,) belongs not to the clergy alone, but with them to the people, and inasmuch as it is not always convenient nor expedient for the whole church to come together

* For a full statement of the Plan of Organization, Confession of Faith, Covenant, Rules of Discipline, etc., see Appendix to the Annual Report for 1846, pp. 238-244, and Missionary Herald for 1846, pp. 317-320.

for this purpose, they shall choose three or more brethren as "helps," "governments," (1 Cor. xii. 28,) to form, with the pastor and deacons, a church session or standing committee, for the examination of candidates for admission into the church and the administration of discipline.

The fourth provides that one half of the session or committee be elected annually. The next article is quoted entire: —

5. The first bishops or pastors and deacons, chosen by the church, shall be set apart to their office by prayer and the imposition of hands, in the presence of the church, by missionaries of the American Board, and such other ministers of Christ as may be invited to assist; it being understood that this is merely a rule of present expediency and convenience; and also, that it belongs to the Evangelical Armenian church to provide, thereafter, for the ordination of its own officers, according to the apostolic example.

Candidates for admission to the church, who give satisfactory evidence of piety to the standing committee or church session, are to be proposed by the pastor at a regular meeting of the church, two weeks previous to the communion: the male members vote on the question of their admission; and they are received on assenting to the confession of faith and the covenant, which is done in the presence of the church.

The rules of discipline provide for the trial of offenders as follows: "The trial of persons for offenses shall be conducted by the standing committee or church session, who, after a thorough and impartial investigation of the case, shall report their decision to the male members of the church, with the written evidence for and against the accused, the final sentence being passed by vote of the church."

Obstinate cases of disagreement between the church and the standing committee are to be referred to a meeting of the pastors and delegates of the associated churches. And members aggrieved by the decision of the standing committee or session and church, may, in like manner, appeal to the same body, whose decision, in all cases, is to be final. To this body it belongs, also, to try an accused minister, with power to suspend or depose him from the ministry.* After being thus deposed, he is to be "subject to the discipline of the church to which he belongs, in the same way as other private members."

The first church was organized July 1, 1846, at Pera, the suburb of Constantinople, in which the foreign embassadors reside, and where the missionaries commenced operations. It soon afterward elected a pastor, two deacons, and three helpers. The ordination was on the 8th of July, by an ecclesiastical council invited by the church, consisting of missionaries of the Board, and one from the mission of the Free Church of Scotland to the Jews. The services were in the Turkish and Armenian languages. This church is now self-supporting, and its pastor, the Rev. K. H. S. Eutujian, addressed the Board at its Jubilee Meeting.

Churches on this ecclesiastical basis were soon after formed in Nicomedia, Ada Bazar, and Trebizond. At the present time there are forty churches among the Armenians, and twelve hundred and seventy-seven members. The number received the past year exceeded two hundred, and the number from the

* In a volume called The Evangelical Church Member's Guide, published by the mission in Armenian, this body is spoken of under the name of the Presbyterial Assembly, or Presbytery. Dr. Wood, one of the Secretaries of the Board, was formerly connected with the Armenian mission, and has translated from this Guide as follows: —

The ecclesiastical assemblies, commonly defined, are of four kinds or grades: —

1. The gathering of all the members of a particular church, with its pastors and officers. This is called the Assembly (or meeting) of the Church.

2. The pastor of the church, with the helpers and deacon or deacons. This is the Assembly of the Care-takers, (session, consistory, standing committee.)

3. The pastors and representatives of all the churches in a particular district. This is the Presbyterial Assembly, (presbytery, classis, consociation.)

4. A general ecclesiastical convocation, composed of representatives of all the churches of every district. This is designated the General Assembly.

The words in parentheses were supplied by the translator as explanatory; and he says, "The office of these several bodies is defined in accordance with the plan adopted in 1846 — the General Assembly being declared a bond of union merely, without legislative or judicial functions."

beginning is fourteen hundred and fifty. There are seven native pastors, and somewhat more than thirty licensed native preachers.

The native Protestants in Syria were probably induced to move for an ecclesiastical organization among themselves by the action of their Armenian brethren. On the 9th of February, 1848, they presented a petition and a plan for organization to the mission, then assembled at Beirût. Certain modifications were suggested by the mission to the native brethren, in view of the Constitution and Discipline of the Evangelical Armenian Church, "in order that their organization might not materially differ from that already recognized in other parts of the empire." * The only important divergence is in the following article: "When the evangelical churches in Syria become three or more in number, the cases of disagreement in the particular churches shall be referred to a regular council of the elders and delegates of the other sister churches, each church choosing one delegate; and the decision of such council shall be final."

Three churches have been formed within the bounds of the Syria mission, containing an aggregate of one hundred and nineteen members, of whom nineteen were added the past year. As yet there are no native pastors.

The reason for organizing distinct evangelical churches in Turkey has been stated. The converts were subjected to excommunication, and even outlawry, by their ecclesiastical authorities. Matters have not gone to such an extreme among the Nestorians of Persia. Though the Patriarch, lately deceased, has been hostile to the reformation, he has ventured to excommunicate no one, not even the Bishop Mar Yohanan, who had violated the usage of the bishops of his church by marrying, after the example of Luther and the apostles. A brother of the Patriarch has been one of the most efficient

* For the Petition, Constitution, and Discipline in full, see Missionary Herald for 1848, pp. 266–270.

fellow-laborers of the mission. The good old bishop, Mar Elia, "dispensing with the usual mummeries and readings in a dead language," lately united with the missionaries in the ordination of a promising young mountain Nestorian, "according to apostolic forms," as an evangelist. The mission has believed that the cause of Christ would not be promoted among that people, thus far, by the organizing of distinct local churches. But a separation of the true church from the world has been deemed needful, and about the year 1855, the mission adopted the practice of inviting the hopeful converts to communion with the mission church, after there had been a careful personal examination into the experience and life of each individual. A communion season in January, 1858, is thus described: "The whole day was given up to religious services. An early morning prayer meeting was held, and soon after breakfast the people assembled again for the same purpose, and continued together till near noon, when there was a recess for refreshments. This might not inaptly be termed a love-feast, where large companies sat down to a plain repast, and ate bread together 'with gladness and singleness of heart, praising God.' Previous to the administration of the Lord's Supper, a translation of the covenant of the mission church was read, and the communicants all rose with us and gave their assent to it. It was a scene of solemn and thrilling interest to the Nestorians, and we have reason to believe its effect was most happy. The great severity of the season prevented many females at a distance, most of them mothers of little children, from coming. Some incidents will show how the ordinance, administered in the primitive simplicity of apostolic usage, is prized as a means of grace. One poor woman came about sixty miles, through deep snow, in piercing cold, crossing a bleak mountain, to enjoy the hallowed occasion. Two individuals came a greater distance, from another direction. These seasons are growing in interest, and are eminently a means of advancement in the divine life, and of spiritual edification to Christ's chosen ones here." *

* Missionary Herald for 1858, p. 155.

Four hundred persons had been thus recognized by the mission, at the close of the year 1860, of whom three hundred and eighty-five were then in full communion. The native communicants have become so numerous, that the ordinance is now administered in different places. Lights thus kindled without the pale of the Nestorian Church, (yet, in another sense, within,) are working a gradual but sure separation between the precious and the vile, and exerting a strong reforming influence.*

INDIA.

In the oldest mission of the Board — that among the Mahrattas of Western India — churches existed in 1854 at Bombay, Ahmednuggur, Seroor, and Satara, with an aggregate of about one hundred and sixty members, with no native office-bearers at that time, and with the most primitive simplicity of form. A Presbyterian church had been formed at Ahmednuggur in March, 1833, consisting of fourteen members, ten of them Hindoos, with a native elder and a native deacon; but the denominational character of the church was not long preserved. We have no information as to the time when it ceased, or of the reasons for the change. The church at Ahmednuggur was divided into two churches in 1854, a native pastor was ordained over each, deacons were appointed, and arrangements made for forming village churches. Eight such churches now exist in the region about Ahmednuggur; and the number of members in the thirteen churches of the whole mission is three hundred and ninety-six. Nearly seventy new members were received in the year 1859. There are at present four native pastors.

In June, 1856, before the reunion of the several missions, the Ahmednuggur mission drew up the following plan for the native churches, on which it is supposed those churches will manage their ecclesiastical affairs: —

* Annual Report of the Board, 1860, p. 85.

The native churches under the care of the Ahmednuggur mission shall each have a deacon, or deacons, and a pastor when one can be obtained. When a pastor can not be obtained, the missionary in charge of the field in which the church is situated shall act as pastor of the church.

In the introduction of members to the church, in the discipline of the church, in the election of a pastor and deacons, and in all other business which may come before the church, the male members of the church in good standing shall be regarded as the fountain of authority, and the majority of votes of these members, assembled in a meeting regularly called, shall decide every question.

At the meetings of the church, the missionary acting as pastor shall have no vote, though he may express his opinions when he thinks best.

It shall be competent for any church to choose a committee, or appoint elders, who, with the pastor, shall be empowered to perform the business of the church, and decide all those questions which are mentioned above as to be decided by the majority of votes of male members of the church.

The native pastors shall be formed into a Presbytery, (if they approve this plan,) the duties and forms of which are hereafter explained.

The Presbytery shall consist of the pastors of churches under its care, and of a delegate from each church.

Three pastors shall form a quorum competent to perform the regular business of the Presbytery.

The missionaries shall form no part of the Presbytery; but the mission may appoint some one or more of its members to attend the meetings of the Presbytery, to give advice in matters of difficulty; but no one shall be allowed to vote on any question of business except the regular members of the Presbytery.

The Presbytery shall have power to license men to preach the gospel, and to withdraw the license; to ordain pastors and evangelists, and to depose ministers who, after a regular trial, are found unworthy to remain in that office; and to do all other acts connected with the discipline of ministers usually devolving upon the Presbytery — thus relieving the mission entirely of those ecclesiastical duties which from necessity it has temporarily been called upon to perform.

The Presbytery shall also receive appeals from churches under its care in reference to difficulties which the church can not settle, and shall adjudicate the same according to the teachings of the word of God, and the principles laid down in the Book of Discipline of the Presbyterian Churches of Scotland and America.

The Arcot mission had five churches in 1857, with one hundred and twenty-six members. These churches are formed on the doctrines and rules of the Reformed Dutch Church, with which the members of the mission are connected. Native pastors are to be united with the missionaries in a classis.

The two churches in the Madras mission contain seventy-four members. They are assimilated to the Scotch churches of that city, and perhaps form a part of the Presbytery of Madras.

The ten churches in the Madura mission numbered five hundred and seventy-one members in 1855. The number in the following year was six hundred and seventy-seven. The present number is ten hundred and twelve; and there are now twenty-eight churches — eleven being at the stations, and seventeen formed elsewhere. The Mandahasalie district has nine churches; Periaculum, seven; and Madura city, Dindigul, and Tirumungalum, two each. There are six native pastors. A seventh, ordained in 1855, and the first in the series, has removed to Madras, and is acting pastor of the church at Royapûrum.

The mission wrote as follows in 1851: "When the Holy Spirit blesses the truth, and converts a portion of the people, we are to receive all who give evidence of piety into the visible catholic church, and afterward to form them into associations resembling, so far as circumstances admit, the churches planted by the apostles. We are then to watch over and teach these

Christians to act for themselves, and in due time ordain over them suitable native pastors." A constitution of the Ecclesiastical Association of the American Madura Mission, as revised in 1851, lies before us. There is no account of its formation, and the deputation heard no mention made of it during their sojourn with the mission in 1855. It was composed of the members of the mission *de facto*. While the churches were in their infancy, every ordained missionary was recognized as having the right, in his own proper district, to organize churches, judge of the qualifications necessary for church membership, receive members, and excommunicate for immoral conduct. As the native helpers sustained a general relation to the mission, they could not be disciplined without the consent of the Association. Licensure to preach the gospel belonged to the Association, as also the discipline of its own members; and it was made its duty, as soon as practicable, to prepare and recommend to the mission churches a system of church and ecclesiastical polity best adapted to promote their purity and increase. Except, perhaps, in a single church, no native office-bearers were appointed previous to 1855.

The district of Mandahasalie was, and still is, under the care of the Rev. H. S. Taylor. On the 25th of May, 1857, Mr. Taylor met the two native pastors, with delegates from six of the seven native churches within the bounds of his district. Certain rules for an ecclesiastical union had been previously sent to the several churches for their consideration, and these were now adopted. The Mandahasalie Christian Sungkum, or Society, was thus formed, composed of the native pastors and delegates of the churches in the Mandahasalie district. The missionary was enrolled merely as an adviser. Village congregations where no churches had been formed were allowed to send delegates, who might speak in the meetings, but not vote. Churches must hold the common confession of faith in order to come into the union. The object of the Sungkum was to seek the good of the churches. The churches could ask its advice, or it could give advice unasked, if it thought proper. Respecting the organization of new churches, and the ordination of pastors, the Sungkum could do these things, or seek to have them performed by the mission.*

The Madura mission denied the right of this body to ordain native pastors with an understanding or implied pledge, that those pastors should be aided in their support by the mission funds, unless the previous consent of the mission had been obtained. The matter was referred to the Prudential Committee, and it will be seen, from their reply, that they fully sustained the judgment of the mission. They wrote as follows: —

Having no ecclesiastical authority, the Board can confer none. Its principle is "entire non-intervention, on the part of the Board and its officers, on the whole subject of ecclesiastical relations and organizations." And the province of the missions, in all that they do in virtue of authority derived from the Board, is, in the language of the Board, "to decide upon the places where labor shall be performed, and the persons and instrumentalities to be employed, and the distribution of funds." In respect to all matters such as these, the brethren assemble and act under the authority of the Board, and appeals may be taken, on all such matters, to the Prudential Committee. These, indeed, are among the positive duties of the mission, as an agency constituted by the Board, which it may not delegate to any other bodies.

But, as indicated above, ministers and missionaries of Christ, however brought together, have other relations besides those sustained to the Board, and other responsibilities and duties besides those for which the Board holds them directly accountable to itself. It is from another and higher source they derive their authority to organize churches, and ordain preachers and pastors. It is not for us to say how *these* duties can best be performed, except that all can see, since one part of the work — namely, the financial — is necessarily managed by the entire body of missionaries, how desirable it is that there be unity of action in the management of the other part.

* Missionary Herald for 1857, p. 306.

There is nothing in the rules or proceedings of the Board to prevent the brethren acting together for these objects, under Christ's commission, as a mission, if they choose so to do. Only it should be distinctly understood by every one, that they are then acting as a body of ministers, in their ecclesiastical relations and capacity; and it will be found useful, and it is recommended, that there be a record of these proceedings, distinct and separate from that of the other class of proceedings.

What is said of the ecclesiastical organizations in connection with the Ceylon mission, rests chiefly on the very competent authority of the Rev. Benjamin C. Meigs, one of the first company of missionaries sent by the Board to that island. The missionaries formed themselves into a church on their first arrival in 1816. Being all from the Congregational body, the church of course assumed that form. Native converts were received into this church until 1831, when, for greater convenience in exercising necessary discipline, separate churches were formed, one at each station; the missionaries, at the same time, constituting themselves into an association "for mutual aid in regulating the concerns of the different churches." This body was called the "Consociation or Presbytery." There being no elders in the local churches, there were of course none in this body, nor was there ever a lay representation from the churches. At the quarterly communions, when the churches all met in one place, some of the native preachers were requested to distribute the bread and wine. Deacons do not appear to have been appointed in more than one of the station churches: they certainly were in the village churches, when they received native pastors. "In the government of the church," says the venerable missionary, "the native members seemed disposed to put the laboring oar into the hands of the missionaries. This, however, we resisted. It was our constant object to train all the male members of the church to feel their responsibility; and that they had an important part to perform, both in the examination of candidates for communion, and in the discipline of the church. We very rarely took any step without their approbation, or at least the concurrence of a majority of the male members." From 1835 or 1836 to 1840, the word Consociation was dropped from the name of the mission when acting as a general ecclesiastical body, and then it was resumed; but there were no other changes. The body was made up of the ordained missionaries, the unordained missionary physician, and the missionary printer, who was a layman. It obviously had more authority than an Association, and less than a Presbytery, but differed in its constitution from an Association, Consociation, or Presbytery. Cases of discipline in the mission families, should such arise, were to be attended to in this body, and not in the native churches. In 1855, the mission began the organization of village churches separate from those which had their centers at the residence of the missionaries, and the ordination of native pastors over those churches; and about the same time they discontinued the somewhat indefinite ecclesiastical name, acting simply as a body of missionaries. There are now three village churches and pastors. In what manner these are to be ecclesiastically united, seems not yet decided. It was thought best to reorganize the missionaries and their families in a church, as on their first arrival; but this was a private matter, for the benefit of those families, with no direct bearing on the natives.

Caste is one of the greatest social evils in India, and is thoroughly discountenanced by all the missions under the care of the Board. It is an evil, like intemperance in our own country, that requires a perpetual watch and perpetual effort; and thus it will be for a long time to come. It connects itself with notions of family rank and consequence, and of the value of dowry; and many native Christians seem too desirous of retaining their connections with their heathen relatives, and too fearful of the consequences that would follow from breaking wholly with the world. The following pledge was signed by about ninety of the leading members of the church, in connection with the Ceylon mission, in 1855, namely: "We, the undersigned, do solemnly pledge ourselves and affirm, that we will wholly renounce in ourselves, and discountenance in others, all caste and other distinctions and usages in society, which tend to foster pride, impair the affections, and hinder the kindly offices of Christian love, and that we will not object to eating any kind of food, on account of the caste of the person or persons by whom it was cooked or offered to us." And the mission declared its intention of carrying out this declaration, both in the spirit and letter. "In the formation of future village churches," they say, "in the appointment of officers, and in the ordination of pastors over them, every precaution will be taken to proceed upon correct principles in reference to caste."

The action of the India missions during the visit of the deputation, with regard to polygamy, was explicit and satisfactory. The Mahratta mission came to the following result: "When a legal divorce can be effected, it should always be required before an individual be admitted to the church. The only cases of real difficulty which present themselves to our minds are when a legal divorce can not be effected. We believe, however, that it is not expedient to admit any one to the church, even in such cases, without his giving a written pledge to the church that he will no longer cohabit with more than one wife, and that he will also, if necessary, support the wife thus put away so long as she shall lead a virtuous life. Such a man, though unable to free himself from the legal relation of husband to the person thus put away, we believe to be free from the guilt of polygamy, and hence a proper candidate for admission to the church."

The Madura mission laid down this principle: "That as polygamy is contrary to the original design of the Deity in the institution of the marriage relation, and opposed to all the teachings of Christ, and as there is no positive evidence that the apostles ever admitted polygamists into the churches established by them, no polygamist, however well fitted he may be in other respects, should be admitted to any of our churches until he has entered into covenant with the church that he will henceforth be the husband of only one wife."

No polygamists have ever been received into the church in the Ceylon mission, nor, indeed, into those of any other of our India missions; and it was the expectation of the missions that none ever would be received. The brethren in Arcot say, "Polygamy has not existed, and will not be allowed to exist, in any of our churches."

Among the Zulus, polygamy prevails in its most revolting and debasing form, and constitutes one of the greatest obstacles to the introduction of the gospel. A high English ecclesiastic having declared his intention not to interfere with the married life of the Zulus, and having reflected on the practice of his American brethren, a public discussion was the consequence. "The discussion," they state, "has resulted in confirming us more and more in the conviction, that our rule," excluding polygamists from the mission churches, "is good—is right—just what God and the interests of his kingdom demand of us, and demand of the people among whom we labor."

Sandwich Islands.

The first missionary company for the Sandwich Islands was constituted a church in Boston, October 15, 1819, just before embarkation. The mission church consisted of seventeen members, viz.: the two missionaries and the five assistants, with their wives, and three natives of the Sandwich Islands, all of whom had previously belonged to other churches, and were in regular standing. The covenant and articles of faith were drawn up with great care and solemnity The religious services were in the vestry of Park-street Church, by Drs. Morse and Worcester, and by Rev. Sereno E. Dwight, pastor of the church. The articles and covenant were assented to and subscribed by the members, in the presence of many Christian friends.* For several years the new missionaries appear to

* Missionary Herald for 1819, p. 263.

have joined this church on arriving at the Islands. The first mention that has been found of the formation of native churches was in 1829. In 1834, there were seven churches, and the number of members up to that time was seven hundred and ninety-five. The years 1837 and 1838 were distinguished for one of the most remarkable outpourings of the Spirit on record. About five thousand converts were received in one year, from June, 1837, into the seventeen churches then existing.* The admissions in the following year were ten thousand seven hundred and twenty-five; and there were then fifteen thousand nine hundred and fifteen members in regular standing. This number was increased, the next year, to eighteen thousand four hundred and fifty-one. The average number of persons admitted, annually, to the churches, in the eighteen years subsequent to 1841, (1842–1859,) was one thousand four hundred and twenty-three. At the latest date there were twenty-three churches, and fourteen thousand four hundred and thirteen members. The number from the beginning is forty-three thousand seven hundred and fifty-eight; and sixteen thousand three hundred and fifty-two have died.

The mission has been accustomed to hold a general meeting, in the month of May, for Christian fellowship and the transaction of business. But it having been virtually discontinued, some eight or ten years since, as an organized body, the Hawaiian Evangelical Association took its place, holding its annual meeting at the same time, and transacting the customary business of the missionary body. This association was formed as early as 1823, "for mutual improvement and aid in laying the foundation, maintaining the order, and building up the house of the Lord in these islands of the sea." In 1830, the original missionary church — composed then, it would seem, only of persons who were or had been members of the mission — was converted, by the Association, into a superintending body for the native churches. In the following year, the missionary pastors at the several stations were requested to prepare some

* Report of the Board, 1839, p. 128.

of the more promising church members to be set apart as elders. In 1835, the Association adopted the Presbyterian rules of discipline as their general guide. The act of 1830, respecting the mission church, was set aside by the Association in 1839, which then recommended, that the several pastors and churches elect ruling elders, and that the pastor and elders of each church constitute a session, or committee, for the government of that church. It was also recommended "that those churches which may prefer the Congregational form of government, be at liberty to adopt it at their discretion; providing always, that the doings of such churches be subject to the review and control of the Presbytery, and also that they be represented in the Presbytery by their pastor and a delegate from each church." It entered into this plan of organization, that there be a Presbytery on each of the four large islands, to be composed of ministers and ruling elders, or delegates, which should "unite in one General Council, to meet at such times and places as shall be agreed upon from time to time, and exercise a general review and control over all the individual Presbyteries." Appeals were to be "from the church session, or congregation, to the Presbytery, and from thence to the General Council."

It afterward appeared that there were brethren who dissented from this action; though Presbyteries are said to have been formed on the Islands of Kauai, Maui, and Hawaii, prior to 1841. Neither of them was permanent, and it may be they were premature. They could hardly have been in operation in 1846, for we find the Association then adopting the following resolution: "That the brethren, clerical and lay, of each island, or a number of clergymen not less than three, be appointed a committee of this body, to examine and license such native church members as they shall judge suitable candidates for the ministry."

In 1854, the mission, as has been intimated, voted to transact their annual business in the sessions of the Hawaiian Evangelical Association, having first revised and enlarged its constitution. The Association was now empowered, 1. To examine, license, and ordain candidates for the gospel ministry, install and dismiss pastors, and perform all proper ecclesiastical business that might come before them; 2. To entertain references from pastors, churches, or any other ecclesiastical bodies, and labor by its counsels to promote the purity and unity of the churches; 3. To exercise the functions of an ecclesiastical court, in respect to any of its members who might be cited before it on charges of criminal or disorderly conduct, or for heretical opinions.

A Presbytery was formed for the Islands of Maui and Molokai in July, 1860. At its first meeting it licensed two young natives as preachers, and ordained a native pastor as assistant of Mr. Alexander, at Wailuku. In October following, an Evangelical Association was formed at Hilo for the Island of Hawaii, consisting of all the missionaries on the island, with an equal number of lay delegates from the native churches. About a hundred honorary delegates were admitted to sit and deliberate with the Association, but not to vote. There are as yet no native pastors on Hawaii. Two preachers received license. The exercises, continued through a week, were all in the Hawaiian tongue, and greatly interested the native members and spectators.* These organizations, and other similar ones to be formed on the other islands, will have an auspicious bearing on the native pastorate, and on the perpetuity of the native churches.†

North American Indians.

The first church among the Cherokees was organized at Brainerd, during the visit of Mr. Cornelius, on the last Sabbath in September, 1817. Churches were subsequently formed at Carmel, High Tower, Willstown, Candy's Creek, and Creek Path. The churches of the mission were con-

* Missionary Herald, 1861, pp. 65, 67.

† "We are glad to inform you that an Association or Presbytery has been formed in each of the four large islands — that of Maui including the church in Molokai." — *Letter of June* 1, 1861.

nected with the Union Presbytery of East Tennessee and the Presbytery of North Alabama. The breaking up of the stations within the chartered limits of the States of Georgia, Tennessee, and Alabama, in 1838, and the removal of the Cherokees beyond the Mississippi, of course broke up these churches. The missionaries, in reorganizing churches at Dwight, Honey Creek, and elsewhere, after the removal, adopted the Congregational rule, which continues to this day. John Huss, who was ordained as an evangelist in 1833, took the pastoral charge of the church at Honey Creek in 1840, where he remained till his death, in 1858. He could speak only his own language, but showed what excellent preachers and pastors, through the grace of God, we once hoped to find among the Cherokees. For thirty-five years he adorned his Christian profession, "walking in all the commandments and ordinances of the Lord blameless." The only other ordained Cherokee preacher was Stephen Foreman, who studied theology at the Union and Princeton Seminaries, and was licensed by the Union Presbytery in 1833, and by the same ordained to the work of the ministry in 1835. He still lives, but has been chiefly employed as a translator under the late Dr. Worcester. The five churches connected with the mission in 1859, contained two hundred and forty-eight members.

The first church among the Choctaws was organized at Elliot, March 28, 1819, in the Indian territory east of the Mississippi. It consisted at first of only the ten missionary brethren and sisters. The mission has since, through the divine blessing, taken a strong religious hold upon the Choctaws. After the lapse of forty years, in the year 1859, there were twelve Choctaw churches connected with the mission, with thirteen hundred and sixty-two members; and the accessions to the church in that year were one hundred and thirty-two. The churches were under Presbyterian rules, and have long been united in a presbytery. Their geographical position, both east and west of the Mississippi, naturally connected them with the Presbyterian Church; and after the division of that Church, the Choctaw churches preferred to be in connection with the Old School body.

The relation of the mission churches to slavery, where that has existed, has been the same as that sustained to caste, polygamy, and other evils and sins. The qualification required for admission to the ordinances of the gospel, has been common to all the churches in the missions, and also to the churches in this country supporting them; namely, a credible profession of faith in Christ, in the judgment of those whose duty it is to act in the case. With that principle the Board, not being an ecclesiastical body, has had no power to interfere. The churches among the Cherokees and Choctaws, acting on that principle, have admitted holders of slaves to their communion; but the statistics show that this class of church members has been decreasing for some years.

TABULAR VIEW OF THE CHURCHES.

Missions.	Churches.	Received the last year.	Present number.	Number from the begin'ng.
Gaboon Mission,	1	6	15	38
Zulu Mission,	7		186	
Armenians,	40	226	1,277	1,450
Syria Mission,	3	19	119	157
Mosul,	1		19	
Nestorian Mission,		51	385	401
Mahratta Mission,	13	69	396	466
Madras Mission,	2	11	74	
Arcot Mission, (1857,)	5		126	
Madura Mission,	28	78	1,012	1,278
Ceylon Mission,	9	46	457	
Three China Missions,	3	13	28	35
Amoy Mission, (1857,)	5		126	130
Sandwich Islands,	23	573	14,413	43,758
Micronesia Mission,	1		4	4
Cherokees, (1859,)	5		248	
Choctaws, (1859,)	12	132	1,362	
Dakotas and Ojibwas,	2	5	91	
Senecas and Tuscaroras,	3	27	283	
Total,	163	1,256	20,621	

CHAPTER VII.

SCHOOLS.

Schools in Early Stages of the Missions. — COMMON SCHOOLS. Largest Numerical Development. — Sandwich Islands. — India Missions. — Whole Number of Pupils. — Value of the Schools. — With Heathen Masters. — With Christian Masters. — China. — North American Indians. — Western Asia. — General View. — HIGHER SCHOOLS. India. — Before and after the Introductory Stages. — Tamil People. — Batticotta Seminary. — Oodooville Female School. — Pasumalie Seminary. — Madura Female School. — English Language. — Higher Vernacular Education. — Schools for Small Boys. — Schools at Ahmednuggur. — At Bombay. — The American Mission Institution. — In Syria. — Armenians. — Nestorians. — Choctaws and Cherokees. — The Past and Present. — Use of the English Language. — General Results. — The Board preëminently concerned in Education. — The Oahu College. — Foreign Youth in this Country. — School at Cornwall. — Great Interest awakened. — The Disappointment. — Discontinuance. — Greek and Armenian Youth. — Result. — Foreign Youth to be educated in their own Countries.

THE American Board has gone largely into education as a means of propagating the gospel, especially in the former part of the half-century. It results from the nature of the foreign missionary enterprise, that schools will be more prominent at the outset, than in the more advanced stages of progress. They form a part of the machinery most readily put in motion, and most appreciated by the heathen. And where heathen teachers are employed, it is possible to institute schools at once, and with little danger of opposition.

COMMON SCHOOLS.

The common schools, — or free schools, as they are often called, — regarded as a part of the missionary organization and action, are subject to considerable variety and fluctuation. Their largest numerical development has generally been in the earlier stages of the mission. This was remarkably the case at the Sandwich Islands. In 1830 and the two following years, the number of pupils on these Islands was reported for those years respectively, in round numbers, at thirty-nine thousand, forty-five thousand, and fifty-three thousand. This was before the great religious awakening, which commenced in 1837 Learning to read was easy, with their simple alphabet, and it seemed to form a part of the great national revolution. By far the largest portion of the pupils were adults, who attended as their ordinary occupations would permit. The teachers were from among the people, and gained their knowledge by spending a few months at the station schools, under the immediate supervision of the missionaries. The number of these teachers in 1831 was nine hundred. Their qualifications were extremely moderate, and after 1832 the schools declined rapidly for want of teachers able to instruct beyond the mere rudiments. Yet more than a fourth part of the eighty-five thousand Hawaiians had learned to read the word of God; some in every place had learned to write, and some to use the elementary principles of arithmetic. The cheapness of this instruction was wonderful. Not a dozen of the teachers were paid any thing by the mission. The supply of books was almost the only expense, and even these were not distributed gratuitously; though, for want of a circulating medium, the people could pay for them only with the products of the Islands, or by their labor. A reorganization of the schools became at length indispensable, and a school was commenced for the education of teachers. The number of pupils reported in the common schools in 1837 was little more than two thousand, the greater part of whom were probably children. The number had risen in 1843 to eighteen thousand seven hundred, which is larger than any number since reported. Four years later, the Hawaiian government assumed the entire support of the common schools, including the wages of the teachers, and have continued to expend some thirty thousand dollars annually for the free schools, the high school at Lahainaluna, (which was made over to the government by the Board in 1849,*) and the high school at Honolulu for the children

* Report of the Board for 1849, pp. 198, 239.

of chiefs. The Island government has also given ten thousand dollars toward the endowment of the Oahu College, now an independent institution, which the Board had commenced at Punahou, near Honolulu. Aside from a portion of the expenses of the college until it shall have completed its endowment, the only charge for education at the Islands now resting on the American Board is for a select school on Hawaii, and for another on Kauai. An effort by the government to introduce the study of the English language into some of its schools, did not prove successful.

Next to the Sandwich Islands, the most remarkable development of common schools, in connection with the missions of the Board, has been in India. This class of schools had reached the numerical meridian in the Mahratta and Ceylon missions, just as the Madura mission was commencing its career. In 1831, the number of pupils was one thousand nine hundred and forty in the Mahratta mission, and in 1836 it was six thousand and thirty-five in the Ceylon mission. The great financial crisis of 1837 obliged the latter mission to send away some five thousand pupils; and would have brought a similar catastrophe upon the Mahratta mission, but for the interposition of English residents, who generously contributed two thousand five hundred dollars for the schools. The largest numbers in the Mahratta schools, since that time, were between the years 1844 and 1851; in the Ceylon schools, between 1841 and 1854; and in the Madura schools, between 1838 and 1849. The pupils in the Mahratta schools were but half as many in 1842 as they were sixteen years before. The number in the Madura schools had been reduced one half in 1850, as compared with the year 1841; but it is as large at the present time as it was ten years ago. The Ceylon schools, though containing fewer pupils, in 1854, by some thousands, than eighteen years before, had numbered four thousand for the ten preceding years, and have as many now as the missionaries, with all their other cares and labors, are able to superintend efficiently.

The whole number of pupils taught in the free schools of these three missions from the beginning until 1860, is estimated at seventy thousand; namely, twelve thousand in the Mahratta mission, thirty-three thousand in the Ceylon, and twenty-five thousand in the Madura. The character and value of the schools are best known to the members of the several missions. The Mahratta missions, in a report on education in common schools, adopted in 1854, gave the following testimony: "We can not point to a single case of conversion from among all this number. A few instances of conversion have occurred among the superintendents and teachers of these schools, and these men are among our most valuable helpers at the present time. While preaching in the villages, we occasionally meet with those who were formerly pupils in these schools. Often such persons are interested and attentive hearers, and often they are among the abusers of us and our work. The result seems to show, that these schools have failed of accomplishing, except to a very slight extent, what was hoped from their establishment, in the way of influencing the people, and gaining them over to the truth. From this result follows, as a general rule, the inexpediency of employing heathen teachers in common schools. The main ground upon which such schools are urged at present is, that they are a means of communicating with the people, of forming some kind of connection with them, of getting a congregation. It is probable, however, that in most cases the missionary can secure a hearing for his message without the aid of such schools."

The Ceylon mission stated, in their report on the subject in 1855, that about thirty cases were recollected of hopeful conversion in the common schools; but that the children usually left the school at so early an age as not to justify the expectation of any considerable number of conversions. Of heathen schoolmasters, — employed because so few Christian masters could be had, — eighty had joined the church, and twenty-five of these had shown by their subsequent conduct that they were unworthy members. People assembled in considerable number, and with some regularity, in many of the school bungalows; but it was not certainly owing to the children's being taught there, for the people often assembled readily in many other places. Moreover, the schools had depreciated in value, because the parents were less willing to spare the children from their gardens and fields. "Hence," it is said, "we have a succession of little children in our schools, who can not, from the nature of the case, be expected to receive as much benefit as those who are older." *

Similar causes have operated in the Madura mission. "When there are several children in a family," says the report of the mission in 1855, "one will be sent to tend cattle, another sheep; others, who are able to labor, will accompany the parents into the field, while those who are too young for this will be left at the house to watch the infant. Our people are not all so poor as this, but many are. In these facts we see a sufficient reason why our schools have declined. When first commenced, nearly all the children attended; but the parents soon discovered that they had undertaken more than they were able to perform, and withdrew them."

The practice of employing heathen schoolmasters had nearly ceased previous to the year 1855. At the outset of the missions, if none such had been employed, there could have been no mission common schools. The value of their service was doubtless over-estimated at the time. The schools thus taught were in a degree delusive both to the missionary and his supporters. It was not unlike employing infidel schoolmasters in Christian lands. The religious value of the education thus received, or of the influence of these masters on the whole, admits of considerable doubt. The large houses of worship in Jaffna, and in certain parts of the Madura district, once filled every Sabbath by the pupils of those congregated schools, are monuments of the power of that system to create congregations for the time being, and of the unreasonableness of trusting to it for stated congregations after the pay of the teachers was withdrawn. Yet the experience thus gained was

* Mission Report, 1855.

worth what it cost. Were it not for that experience, schools under the instruction of heathen masters would perhaps be thought even now a deserving branch of the missionary work. Nor should we forget that in the early stages of modern missions, when the good seed of the word had not begun to yield its harvests of converts, such schools exerted an important influence among the churches at home. The teaching of so many thousands of heathen youth to read the Scriptures, and to repeat the leading facts in the gospel history, was itself a result; it was a success; and being highly valued, it did much to sustain and extend the missionary spirit in the churches. And though more excellent ways of employing funds can now be pursued, it is presumed that those schools will hereafter appear to have been a labor by no means lost upon the native mind of India.

Common schools taught by Christians must needs be useful every where, and are to be employed to the extent of the available funds for that purpose, and of the available superintendence; first, for the children of native Christians, and then for heathen children. Considering, however, the other increasing demands on the missionary treasury, the Board has of late years found itself much restricted in the educational department.

The ability to read among the males in China is extensive, and there is not yet much access to the females. There is little to be said, therefore, concerning missionary schools among the Chinese. An inquiry into the history of the common schools in the missions of Western Asia, would show, that the number of pupils has there steadily increased to the present time — from six hundred in 1837 to sixteen hundred and ninety-five in 1852, and five thousand five hundred and thirty-seven in 1860. Perhaps the reason of this is, that the schools among the Armenians have been mainly restricted to the children of Protestants and of those who were inclined to the Protestant faith, and so have grown continuously with the progress of the reformation. Schools have been prominent among the efforts to reclaim the Indian tribes in North Amer ica. For a long course of years, the pupils in the schools among the aborigines numbered from six to eight hundred; but with a decline after 1856.

Taking a general view of common-school education in the missions, it appears that the highest number of pupils was in the year 1832, when it was sixty thousand; of whom fifty-three thousand were at the Sandwich Islands, and five thousand five hundred in the Ceylon and Mahratta missions. The smallest number since that time was in 1837, when it was twelve thousand. The largest subsequent number was twenty-nine thousand eight hundred and thirty; and this was in 1846. The present number is eighteen thousand, including the free schools supported by the government of the Sandwich Islands. The whole number of pupils in the common schools from the beginning, is believed to have exceeded two hundred thousand.

The Higher Schools.

The higher schools, for the most part, have been boarding schools. Most of the earlier pupils in the Ceylon boarding schools (which were in operation a long time before those of any other missions of the Board beyond sea) were heathen youth. The object of these schools, as well as of the similar early boarding schools in the Mahratta and Madura missions, was twofold: first, the conversion of the pupils, and secondly, the procuring of native helpers. As the missions passed beyond their introductory stages, there was an increase in the demand for native Christian helpers, and the higher schools were progressively modified, becoming more and more of the nature of *training* institutions — for schoolmasters, catechists, preachers, and pastors. The exigencies of the work and the state of the funds both required this. The change, however, was gradual, rendering the schools more and more directly and effectively missionary institutions.

The earlier boarding schools were composed of small boys,

isolated from heathen friends and from idolatrous festivals. The average number of the pupils in the Ceylon schools was eighty-five. These schools were superseded in 1831, or soon after, by the English Preparatory Schools, which had no boarding pupils. The main design of these schools was to prepare pupils for the Batticotta Seminary, and the instruction was therefore both in English and Tamil, and for the most part by Christian teachers. The English schools, with an average of two hundred and seventy-six pupils, were continued twenty-five years, and ceased to be sustained by the mission only when the Batticotta Seminary was made more exclusively a Training and Theological School, with its studies in the vernacular language.

The Batticotta Seminary was instituted in the year 1823, and continued in operation thirty-one years. The Rev. Daniel Poor was its principal during the first thirteen years. Being familiar with the Tamil language, his instructions, especially those of a religious nature, were mostly in that language. During Mr. Poor's connection with the institution, great prominence was given to religious instruction in the vernacular, and the number hopefully converted and gathered into the church was greater than during any other period of equal length in the history of the mission. Great efforts were made by him to bring mathematical and astronomical studies into conflict with the fallacies of Hindoo science. The Rev. H. R. Hoisington was principal from 1836 to 1841, and again from 1844 to 1849. Though in delicate health during much of the time, he was eminently devoted to his profession, and labored earnestly to make the Seminary subsidiary to the great purposes of the mission. The study and use of the English language had now become so prevalent and absorbing as to retard the acquisition of the Tamil by new missionaries; and those who had the care of the institution after Dr. Poor, are said not to have been able to communicate readily with the students, except in the English language.*

* Report of the Mission, 1855.

In the year 1844, the instruction in the biblical department was assigned to the Rev. Samuel S. Whittelsey; who, it was hoped, from his knowledge of the vernacular, would be able to give greater prominence to biblical instruction, and to create an enthusiasm in that direction which would check the tendencies in favor of English and science. These fond hopes were disappointed in the early removal of Mr. Whittelsey by death. Others, who were afterward connected with the institution, did what they could to bring the truth to bear upon the minds and hearts of the students, and, by the blessing of God, their labors were not in vain.*

The whole expense of the pupils was for a long time borne by the mission; but subsequent to the year 1843, all who were able were required to pay for their board. An unforeseen result of this requirement was the introduction of a class of students from wealthy families, whose sole object was to fit themselves for government service, or some lucrative post in agriculture or commerce. It was the prevalent opinion in the mission, before the visit of the deputation in 1855, that it was time to cease any longer cultivating the excessive passion among the natives for the English language; and it was also the general opinion at that time, that there was not sufficient numerical force in the mission to make the Seminary what it needed to be, either on the existing basis or on any other. The mission therefore made certain important changes in the institution. They excluded the English language from the regular course of instruction; reduced the number of students to the demands for mission service; made the board and instruction gratuitous; shortened the period of residence; and decided to receive none under fourteen years of age, and none but Christians or the sons of Christians. After a brief suspension, the institution resumed operations as a Theological and Training School, and nearly on the basis above described. As had been expected, the natives continued to prosecute their studies of the English language, at their own cost, with a view

* Report of the Mission, 1855.

to secular advantages, and with no apparent diminution in numbers — an English high school having been formed at Batticótta under competent native instruction, with English preparatory schools in the villages. This was an important step in the direction of self-sustaining institutions; and it is a striking evidence of the hold Christianity had obtained in Jaffna, that all these were, and still are, decidedly Christian schools.

The number of graduates and students on the catalogue of the Batticotta Seminary, in the year 1855, was six hundred and seventy, of whom four hundred and fifty-four were then living. At that time the mission had eighty-one of these in its employ, and thirty-one were in the employ of other missionary societies. Of the rest, one hundred and fifty-eight were in government service in Ceylon and India; one hundred and eleven in different kinds of secular business on the island and continent; and seventy-three were not reported. In the religious statistics of the institution, three hundred and fifty-two are recorded as having been church members. Deducting ninety-two excommunicated persons, and sixty-four who had died, there were one hundred and ninety-six still living in full membership of the Christian church. The present helpers of the mission and native pastors were nearly all educated at the Batticotta Seminary.

Correlative with the Batticotta Seminary was the Oodooville Female Boarding School, established in 1824. It was designed to impart a careful Christian education to a select number of females, under circumstances that would exclude them from heathenish influences, and be most hopeful for their moral and intellectual improvement. By this means more suitable and acceptable companions would be provided for the young men educated in the Mission Seminary.* The school was alternately under the care of Mr. and Mrs. Miron Winslow and Mr. and Mrs. Levi Spaulding until 1833, when it came permanently under the care of the latter, who still sustain a parental relation to the members and graduates of the school.

* Report of the Mission, 1855.

The influence of the Oodooville school has been excellent. Many Christian families, scattered over the province, the island, and the continent, exerting a silent but important influence, testify to its usefulness. Tokens of God's special blessing have been granted in frequent revivals, and in the uniform prosperity of the institution.* More than two hundred had left the school prior to the year 1855, of whom one hundred and seventy-five were members of the church. The studies were in the English and Tamil languages.

In 1855, changes were made in the school corresponding with those in the Batticotta Seminary. The age for admission was raised; the length of residence was reduced; the studies were restricted to the vernacular language; and the pupils, somewhat less in number, were to be either Christians themselves, or from families at least nominally Christian; with such occasional exceptions as should be deemed advisable by the mission. With these modifications, the Oodooville Female Boarding School is now in successful operation, with thirty-nine pupils.†

The boarding schools in Ceylon illustrate those of the Madura and Mahratta missions in their earlier stages. The English language, as well as the vernacular, entered into their course of instruction. This was true of the Pasumalie Seminary, near the city of Madura, established in 1842, and of the Female Boarding School at Madura, formed in 1846 by the union of two that had been only a short time in existence. Some decisive action of the Madura mission adverse to caste, in 1847, greatly reduced these schools for a time, but exerted a permanently healthful influence upon them. It was soon after determined by the mission, that the exclusive object of the Seminary is to raise up a native ministry, and that the course of instruction ought to be mainly in Tamil, the English language being studied as a classic but two hours a day.

In the year 1855, the Madura mission resolved to exclude

* Report of the Mission, 1855. † Annual Report, 1860, p. 110.

the English language from the Female Boarding School, and also from the Pasumalie Seminary, as a medium of instruction, in all cases where proper text-books in Tamil could be obtained. Catechists of approved talent and piety were admitted for a short course of study preparatory to the pastoral office. Experience has since proved the advantages of a purely vernacular training in a mission sent to people in the lowest walks of life. The boarding schools for small boys in this mission were brought to a close in 1858.

The Rev. Henry Ballantine, in a review of the twenty-five years of his missionary life at Ahmednuggur and its surrounding country, speaks as follows: —

"In 1836, a boarding school for heathen boys was put in operation, and soon after a boarding school for heathen girls. They continued several years, but not much fruit was realized from these labors. In 1852, our educational efforts took a different direction. The number of Christian children had become quite large, and it became necessary for us to provide means for their education. We were anxious also to provide Christian teachers for schools in the villages, and to prepare catechists for the work of reading the Scriptures and explaining them to their countrymen. We determined to devote our attention principally to the education of Christian children, and to preparing them for the work for which there appeared to be such a loud call. We now have in Ahmednuggur a school containing twenty-five boys, mostly professed Christians, drawn from all the churches in the mission, who are preparing to be teachers and catechists; and a school containing more than forty girls, many of whom are members of the church, who, we trust, will be fitted to become wives of teachers and catechists. We have also schools in different places, taught by young men and young women, who have been trained in these schools at Ahmednuggur; and in them are collected the children, not only of Christians, but also of all who are favorable to Christianity, and of any who will send their children to be taught Christian truth. The teachers of these schools are all Christians. This is a great advance upon the system put in operation twenty-five years ago, when we had no Christian teachers. We have also, now, a class of ten young men studying for the ministry. These are engaged, during several months of the year, in giving religious instruction in the villages." * The boarding school for heathen boys, mentioned above, was closed in 1851.

A boarding school for females, collected and superintended by Mrs. Hume, at Bombay, was discontinued at the close of 1854, in consequence of her return to the United States. The average number of pupils, for the last eight years, was from twenty to twenty-five, all born in the country, but not exclusively Hindoos; and the school was in part sustained by donations received in India. Eleven of the pupils were received into the church during ten years, and several are now in stations of usefulness.

Earnest representations were received by the Prudential Committee, at the close of 1853 and early in 1854, from their brethren in Western India, in favor of establishing an expensive school at Bombay, like those of the Scotch and English Societies already existing, in that and other large cities of India, in which the English language should be taught, and made the chief medium of instruction. The Committee did not see their way then clear to go into precisely this class of institutions; but they authorized the Bombay mission to commence a high school, in which the vernacular language should be the chief medium of instruction, especially in the inculcation of religious truth, the annual expense not to exceed fifteen hundred dollars. These resolutions were passed May 2, 1854; but the brethren at Bombay felt unable to wait for the action of the Committee, and opened the school on their proposed plan in June, 1854. It was called the American Mission Institution, and the number of pupils rose to one hundred and seventy-five. The annual expense, not including the support of the principal, was eighteen hundred and eighty-

* Missionary Herald for June, 1861.

two dollars. The deputation were authorized by the Prudential Committee to sanction such an institution, should they be satisfied that there were conclusive reasons for it. Such reasons not appearing, the school was not adopted among the institutions of the Board.

As the brethren in the Mahratta missions had before recommended the establishment of such a school at Bombay, it is proper that they should state the reasons which afterward induced them, upon a broader view of the subject, to advise its discontinuance. They were as follows: —

Such an institution, when founded, must be modeled with reference not only to its results on the mission with which it is immediately connected, but also with reference to the general policy and plans of the Board, of whose system of operations it forms a part. What would be expedient and highly desirable, viewed only in reference to a particular station, may be inexpedient on the whole. The following considerations seem to us to weigh against the present high school at Bombay, and to render it undesirable that it should be continued on its present basis.

1. The English language is made, to too great an extent, the medium of communicating instruction. Experience has seemed to show that such schools are not the most efficient instruments in forwarding the great work of missions — that of making known the gospel to the heathen, and saving souls. The vernacular of any people is believed to be the most suitable language in which to communicate truth, and through which to affect the heart. Schools in which the vernacular is the grand medium of instruction, and the English, if introduced, is only taught as a classic, seem to be founded on the best basis, and to promise and produce the best results.

2. The expense of such a school as that at Bombay is an objection to continuing it. It must be able to compete with other schools of a similar character at Bombay, or it can not be successfully maintained. To do this, it must have those advantages and appurtenances which money alone can procure. It does not appear that the present expense can be essentially

reduced, consistently with making the school what it should be in order to answer the ends for which it was established. The funds of the Board are limited; they are not sufficient to carry forward all operations that would seem desirable or highly useful. There must, consequently, be a choice of fields, and in each field a choice of means. If there are two kinds of labor which promise equally well in all other respects, the selection must be made with reference to economy. It is known that such high schools are among the most expensive operations undertaken by the mission Boards; and with the present amount of funds, and a choice of the means to be employed, it does not appear that a due regard to economy would warrant the necessary expenditure for sustaining such a school at Bombay.

3. The influence of such schools on other mission fields is undesirable. If the High School at Bombay is continued, there are other missions of the Board which will feel that they have equal claims to be allowed such an institution. It will be impossible to convince them that there are good reasons for allowing such a school in one large city, and not in another. Thus the decision in respect to the institution involves, practically, a decision in respect to several other places where the same want exists. It becomes, in fact, a question of mission policy. Shall a large part of the funds be appropriated to maintain these expensive English schools in the different fields occupied by the Board? The question is not one on which there is no experience to guide us. The experiment has been tried elsewhere, under the most favorable auspices, and the results, if not actually disastrous, have at least proved unsatisfactory. The system seems to be a forced, artificial one, and produces artificial fruits. In view of these facts, it does not seem desirable to make it a part of our mission policy; and we think the institution at Bombay should not be made an exception to the general policy of the mission.*

The mission in Syria commenced a high school for training

* Report of the Missions, 1854.

native helpers in the year 1836, and closed it in 1842. The English language was taught in the school, and when the war with Mohammed Ali brought the English forces to the Syrian shore, the officers needed dragomans, and the pupils were drawn away, and to a great extent demoralized. When the present Seminary was opened, in 1846, at Abeih on Lebanon, it was on the basis of almost wholly excluding the English language, and of preserving, as far as possible, the Oriental manners and customs among the students. And it was on the same principle that the Female Boarding School has been lately revived, and placed at the Sûk el Ghûrb on the mountain, under the care of two ladies from this country. The former school was at Beirût, and excellent in its kind.

The mission for the Armenians has had two processes for training its native ministry. The first is thus described in a report adopted at Constantinople in 1855: "There is one class that will enter the work without any extended course of preparatory study. But they should be men of earnest piety, and good judgment, and well instructed in Bible doctrines. Almost every missionary station will produce some such men, and no missionary can do a better work than to prepare them, to the extent of his ability, for the ministry of the word. This preparation, however, will be partial. They will remain in their own community, will maintain their native habits of living, and need have no connection with the family of the missionary. It will be somewhat like taking the strong artisan, and preparing him, by a few days' training, for the exigencies of a great campaign. Too great reliance must not be placed upon these. They will be like the elders ordained by the apostles in every city, but probably far inferior in spiritual and intellectual attainments. They will often make mistakes, will sometimes be found incompetent; but still Christ will be preached, and his truth, though committed to such imperfect instruments, will triumph, that the excellency of the power may be of God, and not of man."

The other process is exemplified in the Bebek Seminary, commenced in 1840; in the Theological School commenced at Tocat a few years since, and, in consequence of the burning of the mission premises, removed from thence to Kharpût in 1859; and in the Theological School recently commenced in the Central mission to Turkey. The Bebek Seminary is at the metropolis, in the center of Mohammedan civilization, and embraces a liberal course of study, including the English language and its sources of knowledge. The plan of the school at Kharpût embraces four years of study, with a long winter vacation for evangelical labors in the villages. A female boarding school has been for some years in operation in Constantinople, and there is also one of recent date at Aintab; both taught by females from the United States.

Nowhere have the higher schools been more signally blessed with hopeful conversions, than among the Nestorians. That for males was commenced in 1836, and the one for females in 1838. Two thirds of those who have been educated in the male seminary give hopeful evidence of piety. The same may be said of an equal portion educated at the female seminary. A large portion of the educated young men are preachers of the gospel, or teachers in the schools; and the greater part of the pious graduates of the female seminary have become wives of those missionary helpers. Both of these institutions have been signally favored with revivals of religion. The instruction has been almost wholly in the native tongue.

The boarding schools among the American Indians have all had a peculiar nature from the beginning, owing to the circumstances and character of the people for whom they were designed.

The first schools among the Cherokee and Choctaw Indians were for boarding pupils. While the Choctaws were east of the Mississippi, there were among them four large schools of this description. After their removal westward, four female boarding schools were instituted. One of these, at Good Water, was transferred, in 1854, to the Board of Foreign Missions of the Presbyterian Church. The pupils east of the

Mississippi were about one hundred and seventy, one third being females. West of the river, nearly all were females, numbering one hundred and thirty. The boarding pupils in the Choctaw schools, from the beginning, may have been two thousand; there were not so many among the Cherokees.

The remarks that follow upon the character and value of the schools, are founded substantially upon the testimony of one of the oldest missionaries, and relate to the recent Choctaw schools. As schools for the cultivation of truth and piety, the hopes of their founders have not been fully realized. The schools deriving nearly five sixths of their support from the national annuities, the missionaries had but little influence in the selection of pupils, and were often obliged to continue those in school who were an injury to the others. The object, with most of the parents, was not the spiritual good of their children, but their social and material elevation; and it was a remark of Mr. Evarts, that the patrons of the missions were impatient for the civilization of the Indians, and would not give them time. The missions were constrained to adopt a kind of hot-bed process. Large annuities, always disastrous in their effect upon Indians, had been settled upon them by the United States in return for lands which had been ceded; and as ample reserves from these funds had been made for schools, it seemed desirable that they should be under the control of religious men. This was the inducement to missionaries and missionary Boards to take charge of them; and the schools, under such auspices, and with such means at command, were led to aim at a literary character too high for the actual civilization of the Indians. Had the Choctaws, for instance, been sufficiently isolated to have retained the use of their own language, and to have used none but the vernacular in the schools, it would have been better for their moral and religious interests. With few exceptions, those who acquired most knowledge of the English language were furthest from embracing the gospel. The tendency was to elevate them so far above their parents, and the mass of their people, that "they became vain in their imaginations, and their foolish heart was darkened." Intelligence and civilization were advanced, and the schools were productive of much general improvement; but it was found, with some happy exceptions, that those who remained longest at them were most headstrong and ungovernable. Could the schools have been strictly missionary, with a few select youth of both sexes training with special reference to their becoming teachers and preachers, the result might have been more favorable as regards these objects, and the labor and expense would have been far less. Yet, as it was, quite a number of Choctaw men, who for years have had a leading influence in the nation, were indebted to these schools, wholly or in part, for their education. This is true of four persons, who, at different times, have held the highest national offices; of the three candidates for the office of principal chief in a late election; of the two native pastors, and three of the four licentiates in the churches connected with the mission; and of two of the supreme judges among the Choctaws, the national attorney, and two district attorneys. It should be added, that the Methodists, the Presbyterian Board, and the Cumberland Presbyterians, have boarding schools among the Choctaws, from which some good preachers have issued. But few educated in the boarding schools west of the Mississippi have as yet given evidence of piety.

In a general view of the boarding schools it may be said, that where youth have been taken into them at a very early age, and where the isolation has been complete, the proportion of hopeful conversions has been considerable. But the converts, in such cases, have generally been found less practical, less devoted and self-denying, than was expected. Hence some of the changes that were made in the boarding-school system, as recorded in this chapter; such as requiring more age for admission, a shorter residence, a Christian parentage, (if not actual piety,) and a more purely religious course of study, thus making the high schools more exclusively and effectively missionary institutions.

The following quotation from the Report of the Deputation to the India Missions, made to the Board at its special meeting in 1856, will serve to show the present state of opinion on the use of the English language in the higher schools: —

The Board will kindly bear in mind the distinction we have made between the means to be used in the large cities and in the rural districts of India, and that our remarks are not designed to have a special bearing upon the former. We make a distinction also between teaching English as a study, and using it as a medium of instruction. The Prudential Committee and the Secretaries have said little heretofore on the use to be made of the English language, because they did not know what were the proper metes and bounds to its use. It is a question to be settled by experience, and there has not yet been experience enough to harmonize the views even of missionaries. The Mahratta missions have recorded it as their opinion, that "there is no reason for the study of English in their schools for catechists and teachers, at least in the Deccan. They should be strictly vernacular schools. Our ordinary catechists and teachers," they say, "are to be employed in laboring for their countrymen in the Mahratta language. It is important that their training should be vernacular. The vernacular of any people," they add, "is believed to be the most suitable language in which to communicate truth, and through which to affect the heart. Schools [for the higher education] in which the vernacular is the grand medium of instruction, and the English, if introduced, is only taught as a classic, seem to be founded on the best basis, and to promise and produce the best results."

The Madura mission decided, that the class of young men of promise and piety between the ages of fifteen and twenty-five, preparing for schoolmasters, catechists, and eventually, in some cases, pastors, should be restricted to purely Tamil studies. But they say that a part of the higher class should, in their opinion, "study the English language, both for mental discipline, and that they may have access to English literature. But as a medium of instruction, the English should be excluded where proper text-books in Tamil can be obtained." The Ceylon mission declared it to be their opinion that it was not expedient to continue the study of English in the Female Boarding School. They affirm their ability to show by many facts, "that efforts to evangelize a people through a foreign tongue, have not proved successful." They also state that the system of instruction pursued in the Batticotta Seminary "has tended to give a prominence to instruction in the English language and the sciences, which has led many of the students to neglect their own language. Though great efforts have been made on the part of the missionaries in charge to give special prominence to biblical instruction in the vernacular, and bring in science to illustrate and impress the truth, the current in favor of English and the sciences has steadily advanced, with little interruption. A class of men, too," they affirm, "has been raised up, who, though well educated, and in some respects well qualified for service among the people, are not in the best manner fitted by their course of training for that kind of humble and persevering labor which is most needed in making known the gospel, and giving it a footing permanently in the villages, on a self-sustaining basis." And they add, that the "missionaries connected with the institution have been hindered in the acquisition of the colloquial language of the country. They have not been compelled by circumstances to speak in Tamil, and the temptation to use their own mother tongue has too often prevailed. The same may be true to some extent of other missionaries, who have catechists under their care that can speak the English language."

The mission accordingly gave it as their conviction, "that no instruction in English should be given in the regular course;" and that "the course of study, being wholly in the vernacular, should be eminently biblical, such as will, by the blessing of God, prepare the pupils to wield the sword of the Spirit, which is the word of God. Sacred history, geography, and science, should be brought in to aid in this work, and all should center in the Bible, and be made to explain its truths."

It has been already stated, that we suggested the expediency of teaching the English language to a select advanced class in theology, but that the mission did not deem it expedient at that time to make a formal provision for such an arrangement.

After so extensive a use of the English language in their school system, none can be more competent than our brethren of the Ceylon mission to judge and speak of its real value as a missionary instrument. How far the mission has had an agency in creating the passion for it, which seemed to pervade the district at the time of our visit, we do not know. It seemed to us that the mission acted on the very best reasons in excluding the English language from their schools, and from the course of study in the Seminary. The English language, as acquired by the Tamil young man, found no market in his native village, nor within the territory occupied by the mission, except as the mission became the purchaser by giving him a salary that would meet his own views. The consequence was, that it was needful to give larger salaries than the village churches would be able to pay; and too often the graduate went into the more lucrative service of the government, or of some merchant or planter, and thus his labors and influence were lost to the mission and to his native village. Were our object merely to educate and civilize the people, this might do; but the churches can not afford to prosecute their work in this manner.*

Such is the relation which the Board now sustains, and has sustained, to education and missionary schools.

1. In the present advanced state of most of its missions, it finds a more profitable use for its funds than in the support of heathen schoolmasters. Nor does past experience encourage any great outlay for common schools, composed of very young heathen children, even with Christian masters; nor for boarding schools, that are chiefly made up of such children. Christian children should of course receive a Christian education; but, even here, it is not wise to be forward to relieve

* Report of the Deputation to the Board, 1856, p. 44.

parents of one of their most obvious and sacred duties. Into these schools as many heathen children should have admission as can find room; and there should be schools also expressly for such, if there be reliable teachers for their instruction, and funds for their support.

2. The Board has been obliged, in the progress of its work, to decline connection with expensive educational institutions for general education, to prepare young men for secular and worldly pursuits. Its higher schools, whether for males or females, have been more strictly training institutions, with express and direct reference to carrying out the great purposes of the missions. Moreover, it has been found necessary to exclude the English language, in great measure, from the training schools for educating village teachers, preachers, and pastors.

3. The education in the missions under the care of the Board, regarded as a whole, was never so effective, in a missionary point of view, never so valuable, as at the present moment. Perhaps there are as many common schools as the missionaries can well superintend. What these schools most need is better teachers, and to derive more of their support from the parents of the pupils. The self-supporting principle among native Christians, in all its applications, needs an unsleeping guardianship and culture. It is here that the grand practical difficulty lies in the working of specific charities. Where a man can support himself, it would be cruel to support him.

4. The following is a summary of the educational department as it was at the close of the year 1859: —

Number of Seminaries,		11
Number of other Boarding Schools,		13
Number of Free Schools, (omitting those at the Sandwich Islands,)		345
Number of Pupils in Free Schools, (omitting those at S. I.,)	9,744	
Number of Pupils in Seminaries,	530	
Number of Pupils in Boarding Schools,	341	
Whole Number of Pupils in Seminaries and Schools,		10,615

Dr. Wood, one of the Secretaries, has furnished a view of the educational work of the American Board at the close of 1859, as compared with that of other foreign missionary institutions of this country.

	Pupils.	Whole Yearly Expenditure.
Board of the Presbyterian General Assembly,	4,524	$234,037
Baptist Missionary Union,	2,678	96,214
Board of the Episcopal Church,	1,018	89,738
Total,	8,220	$419,989
American Board, exclusive of Sandwich Islands,	10,615	$361,959

If to the three societies named above are added the Board of the Reformed Protestant Dutch Church, the foreign department of the American Missionary Association, and the Indian, African, Bulgarian, India, and China missions of the Methodist Episcopal Society, the aggregate of pupils is about nine thousand eight hundred, while that of the expenditure is about six hundred thousand dollars.

It thus appears that the American Board now has, in proportion to its expenditure, a larger number of pupils in its missionary schools, than any other foreign missionary organization in this country, and seventy-nine per cent. more than the average of those six societies. The reports of some of these societies do not enable us to determine the comparative number of pupils in the different grades of schools. It is ascertained, however, that in the missions of the Episcopal Board, a somewhat larger part are in boarding schools than are found in the similar institutions of the American Board. The same is true of the General Assembly's Board, including schools in the Indian missions for which aid is obtained from the United States government; but, in the other missions of that Board, the proportion falls a little below that in the corresponding missions of the American Board. The proportion is presumed to be still smaller in other societies. The American Board is thus seen to be doing more, proportionally, in the educational department, than other American Missionary Societies have been led to undertake in missions beyond sea.

The Oahu College.

The Oahu College at Honolulu, Sandwich Islands, is not numbered among the institutions of the Board, though growing out of its operations, and hitherto partly supported from its funds. It was commenced in 1841, as a school for the children of missionaries. In 1851 it was opened also to other children; and two years later it received an act of incorporation as a College from the Hawaiian government. The charter declares that "no course of instruction shall be deemed lawful in said institution, which is not accordant with the principles of Protestant Evangelical Christianity, as held by that body of Protestant Christians in the United States of America, which originated the Christian mission to the Islands, and to whose labors and benevolent contributions the people of these Islands are so greatly indebted." There is an additional security for the institution in the following article, namely: "Whenever a vacancy shall occur in said corporation, it shall be the duty of the trustees to fill the same with all reasonable and convenient dispatch. And every new election shall be immediately made known to the Prudential Committee of the American Board of Commissioners for Foreign Missions, and be subject to their approval or rejection, and this power of revision shall be continued to the American Board for twenty years from the date of this charter." The property of the College, in buildings, land, etc., in 1856, was valued at twenty-seven thousand dollars, which was derived chiefly from the Board. To this the Hawaiian government have added ten thousand dollars toward an endowment of fifty thousand dollars, and subscriptions were obtained in this country to the amount of six thousand dollars. The effort was arrested by the great commercial crisis of 1857.

FOREIGN YOUTH IN THIS COUNTRY.

In its earlier years, the Board expected much from the education of foreign youth in this country. Though the effort was unsuccessful, it was not fruitless, so much did it add to the stock of useful missionary experience. The first efforts in behalf of this class would seem to have been called forth by the interest awakened in Henry Obookiah, and other Sandwich Islands youth, whom commerce with the Pacific had thrown upon our shores.

A Foreign Mission School was instituted for such in 1816, in a pleasant part of Cornwall, Conn. A small farm was purchased, with two dwelling houses. The people of Cornwall gave, in consideration of the school being established there, a convenient academical building, with woodland, etc., to the value of about thirteen hundred dollars.

The object of the school was the education, in this country, of heathen youth, so that they might be qualified to become useful missionaries, physicians, surgeons, schoolmasters, or interpreters, and to communicate to the heathen nations such knowledge in agriculture and the arts, as might prove the means of promoting Christianity and civilization. Mr. Edwin W. Dwight, the friend of Obookiah, was the first principal. He was succeeded, after a year, by Rev. Herman Daggett; and he, in 1824, by Amos Bassett, D. D. There were ten pupils from heathen lands the first year, chiefly from the Sandwich Islands; two were young natives of Connecticut, who afterward spent several years as teachers at the Sandwich Islands. "The raised hopes, founded, under Providence, on the unquestioned piety, the distinguished talents, and the excellent character of Obookiah, terminated in his triumphant departure from these earthly scenes before the first year of the school had expired."* In 1820, the number of pupils was twenty-nine; four from the Sandwich Islands, one from Tahiti, one from the Marquesas, one Malay, eight Cherokees, two Choc-

* Report of the Board for 1820, p. 307.

taws, three of the Stockbridge tribe, two Oneidas, one Tuscarora, two Caughnewagas, one Indian youth from Pennsylvania, and three youth of our own country. The report for that year — the last drawn up by Dr. Worcester — speaks thus of the school: "Besides being taught in various branches of learning, and made practically acquainted with the useful arts of civilized life, the pupils are instructed constantly and with especial care in the doctrines and duties of Christianity. Nor has this instruction been communicated in vain. Of the thirty-one heathen youth, — including, with the twenty-six now at school, the deceased Obookiah, and the four who have gone with the mission to their native Islands, — seventeen are thought to have given evidence of a living faith in the gospel, and several others are very seriously thoughtful on religious concerns." At the end of five years, the number of pupils was thirty-four — chiefly from the isles of the Pacific, and from the Indian tribes. Five were youth of our own country. Nineteen were then members of the church. The school was very popular. We learn from the Report of the Board for 1822, that it was becoming a subject of conversation among intelligent Christians, and of serious inquiry, whether more extensive measures could be adopted to educate young foreign ers cast upon our shores. In 1823, two lads from the Greek Islands were placed in the school, but this class was not found to mingle happily with the other pupils.

In the year 1825, a considerable number of the youth educated at the Cornwall School had been returned, where there were missions, to their native lands, and the theories of the past were corrected by experience. This experience is stated in the Report of that year. "It is now nine years," says the Report, "since this seminary was founded. The favor of God has been extended to it, and much good has been effected by its instrumentality. Still, every human institution has its defects, and is exposed to evils which can not always be foreseen. Difficulties have been experienced, in regard to the youth who have returned to their native lands, which were not fully anticipated. It was always supposed that steadfast religious principle was necessary to their support against the numerous temptations by which they would be assailed. This is indeed the case. But even those who continue to sustain a character of undoubted piety, are under some disadvantages with respect to missionary service. The abundant provision which was made for them while in this country, added to the paternal attention which they every where received, but ill prepared them for the privations which they must bear among their uncivilized brethren. The expense of maintaining them in any tolerable state of comfort, is much greater than it would be if they had never become habituated to the modes of life in an improved state of society. There is great reason to believe that youth in a heathen country can be so instructed at missionary stations as to be very useful to their countrymen at an early period; and, while they are greatly raised in their manner of living, and in their whole character, they may yet preserve a large share of their original hardihood, and be able to associate with their uninstructed countrymen more freely and acceptably, than if they had spent several years in a strange land. The indications of Providence seem to teach, that the best education of youth born heathen, having reference to their success as teachers of their brethren, must be given through the instrumentality of missionary institutions in their respective countries. Some individuals may derive great benefit from a residence in a Christian land; but, judging from the experience of missionary societies in Great Britain, and from what has come to the immediate knowledge of this Committee, and considering the dangers of climate, the exposures to immorality at sea, the temptations presented on returning to places where previous restraints are withdrawn, it is questionable whether young men of the class here referred to, may not almost universally be better prepared for efficient labor under the paternal care of missionaries, than in any other way. In regard to this subject, the Board eminently need the guidance of divine wisdom. If it should seem best that the Foreign Mission School be discontinued, there should be no regret that it was founded. It has answered valuable purposes, which, so far as man can discern, could not have been answered without it."

The reasons for discontinuing the school are fully stated in the Report of the Board for 1826. They are an amplification of the above statement. It was closed in the following year; but not without some manifestations of divided opinion as to the expediency of the measure, and some dissatisfied feeling.

The experiment was continued in another form, for a time, by placing several Greek and Armenian youth in academies and colleges. The experience proved so unsatisfactory in the end, that all thought of educating foreign youth in this country, whether from heathen lands or from the Oriental churches, was abandoned; and it became a settled policy of the Board to do all its educational work in the countries where it has its missions. The cost of the Foreign Mission School, in the ten years of its existence, was thirty-four thousand five hundred and ninety-eight dollars.

CHAPTER VIII.

PREACHING AND THE PRESS.

PREACHING. What the Preacher needs. — What is meant by Preaching. — Prerequisites for Success. — Gathering of Congregations. — Their Nucleus a Church. — Christian Congregations in the Madura Mission. — Signs of Progress. — The School and the Congregation. — Successful Preaching. — Street and Itinerant Preaching. — Preaching Houses. — Cost of Village Churches. — Houses of Worship at the Sandwich Islands — Wise Suggestions on Church Building. — THE PRESS. Number of Languages reduced to Writing. — Cherokee Alphabet. — Choctaw and Hawaiian Alphabets. – Arabic Type. — Syriac Type. — Number of Languages employed. — Number of Printing Establishments. — Amount of Printing in the Missions.

PREACHING.

THE missionary preacher needs an idiomatic and free use of the native language, and he needs hearers. It is not easy to say how far the four hundred and fifteen ordained missionaries sent forth by the American Board have been able to preach idiomatically and fluently in the vernaculars. We speak of preaching in the popular sense, by those who have been specially and solemnly set apart for it, "with the laying on of the hands of the presbytery." There have been signal instances of success in preaching, where the missionary entered the field beyond the age of thirty; but it is apprehended there have been a considerable number of failures. For such languages as the Arabic, the Tamil, and the Chinese with its intonations, the organs are then becoming too rigid, and the power of ceaseless attention to sounds difficult to acquire. Most of those who became masters of the language went under that age. Yet it would not be easy to lay down a positive rule. A burning desire to save souls, wisely applied to the appropriate means, will make itself understood and felt by the people of any language.

The gathering of a congregation is, in most unevangelized countries, a work of time and faith, requiring patience and perseverance. It seems to need the presence of a working body of believers; and their efficacy is much increased by becoming an organized church. The church is the proper nucleus of a congregation. The "Christian congregations" of the Madura mission are not Christian churches, and frequently exist without them; they are a sort of Christian association, a peculiar institution, bound together by some sort of agreement with the local missionary, growing out of peculiarities in the social condition. They are an outer court, and will probably lose their present form as the local churches acquire influence under native pastors. A small congregation in unchristianized countries is a much stronger proof of religious interest, than a large one is in countries where attendance involves no personal hazard. Much more is this true of a small church, where every earthly interest is periled by a Christian profession. Large stated congregations — as at the Sandwich Islands, and at Kessab and Aintab in Northern Syria—imply a preponderating Christian influence where they exist, repressing persecution. Where, too, serious hearers are readily found in every direction, though in small numbers, — as in Asiatic Turkey, among the Nestorians, and in regions around Ahmednuggur, — it is certain that the gospel has gained headway, and that the time of harvest is near.

Experience has shown that neither the common school nor the boarding school forms a good nucleus for the congregation. However useful, and even necessary, in other respects, the schools have failed in this. They furnish an audience, but seldom a congregation that survives them. The insufficiency of both classes of schools for this purpose was exemplified in one of the oldest of the India missions. The five older stations of the mission enjoyed, for nearly forty years, the labors of some of the ablest of missionaries, familiar with the language, good and faithful preachers, with every facility, during all this time, which popular schools of varied form could give. Yet, as was ascertained by a careful analysis, when the pupils in the mission schools, and persons in the employ of the mission and depending on it for their support, were separated from the congregations, there remained only about one hundred adults who were not members of the church, for the whole of these five older congregations. This did not prove the impracticability of the field, but the insufficiency of the schools as a means of securing permanent congregations. We have elsewhere spoken of their utility and importance in other respects as a part of the missionary enterprise. The schools just adverted to, besides contributing materially to the stock of missionary experience, did much to prepare the way for the spread of the gospel. In another of the India missions, where there had been a similar experience, the missionaries, enlightened by the past, very forcibly insist on direct efforts for gathering local churches, as the only effectual method of filling a country with Christian congregations. The subject is so important that we copy their very intelligent remarks upon it: —

The course of the missionary in regard to preaching, — they say, — must be different in the same place, according to the different stages of the work. When he first enters upon his labors at a new station, his great effort will be to draw people around him, and interest them in the presentation of gospel truth. In doing this, it will not probably be found necessary to make use of schools in order to collect a congregation, as has been hitherto deemed important in most of our missions. The missionary who declines to establish schools for this purpose, must go forth to one place and another, preaching in the streets to small companies, or gathering larger companies around him at chaudis, or in the chapel. When conversions occur, he must instruct his converts in the Christian faith. He must have his regular congregations on the Sabbath, for which he must exert himself in preparing religious instruction, feeding the flock of God, over which the Holy Ghost hath made him an overseer. But he must not be satisfied with this. He must look beyond the mere pastorate of a church. He must endeavor to collect native churches in different places, and he must train up some of his converts to be the pastors of these churches. He should be prepared to commit the truths of the gospel to faithful men, that they may teach them to others also. As they increase in knowledge of the distinctive doctrines of the gospel, and in adaptation to the work of making them known to others, he must give them the opportunity of exercising their talents, standing out of the way when necessary, that they may gradually be prepared to come forward and perform the duties of faithful ministers of Jesus Christ. He should ever himself be aiming at further extension, seeking how he may collect new churches, and prepare pastors for them, thus making all his plans subserve the one object of fully planting the gospel of Christ in the country where he resides, by the establishment of churches with their appropriate pastors and other officers. The missionary should feel it to be his business to go forward and find out where new churches can be established, collect the nucleus, and then furnish the native laborer who shall carry on the work. Dr. Judson said, when he had succeeded in collecting a church of one hundred members in Birmah, that he was satisfied; his anticipations of success were fully realized. The days of the pioneers of Christian missions are now past. Henceforth let it be the aim of the missionary to collect, not one church of a hundred members, but twenty, fifty, or a hundred churches, over which native pastors shall be placed. With such an object in view, the minor plans of a missionary will all be arranged more wisely, than if he makes his arrangements to remain an indefinite time in one spot. And not only so, the views of the churches which he gathers will be more correct, than if he settles down in one place, feeling little interest in the regions beyond. If he labors to extend the gospel with its privileges to the whole country round, his churches and their pastors will be churches and pastors of the right kind, possessed of a missionary spirit, and laboring with one heart for the spread of the gospel among their countrymen. On the contrary, if the missionary becomes absorbed in teaching, or in home labor, there is great danger, as we all have had opportunity to observe, that his young men will also be absorbed in study, or teaching, or some other local occupation, and their views will thus become very much confined; and instead of being good soldiers of Jesus Christ, there is great reason to fear they will become effeminate, delicate, worldly, and unfit to do the work of an evangelist, or to labor efficiently in the cause of their Master.*

These wise suggestions have been since carried into practice by the missionaries on the ground where, six years ago, they were written. They had then only two churches, and now they have fifteen. The average annual accession of members has risen from twenty-eight to seventy-two, and the last year it was one hundred and twenty-seven. These churches are effective nuclei for stated congregations, with a steady and remarkable increase of power for accelerating the spread of the gospel and the multiplication of new churches and congregations.†

Street preaching, where crowds are collected, requires a peculiar combination of talents, as well as great readiness in the language, and a quick and accurate perception of the manners and prejudices of the people. It is now practiced in a more quiet way than formerly, avoiding what would bring together a crowd or excite a tumult, and aiming to present the truths of the gospel in a conciliatory manner.

Much time and labor have been expended by the India missions in preaching tours to villages and towns in the rural districts. The missionary sometimes carries a tent, and, pitching it at some central place, holds daily religious services there and in the neighboring villages; then passes on to another convenient center. It is desirable that the missionary stay long enough in a place to see if an interest is awakened in any mind; and if there is, to follow it up with further instruction. It is important, also, that there be repeated visits to places where the Holy Spirit seems to be operating on the

* Report of the Mahratta Missions, 1854.

† See p. 266.

minds of men. "By thus coöperating with God, following where he leads, and laboring where his providence directs, we may expect the most satisfactory results. And wherever several individuals are converted to God, there a native catechist should be placed, and the interest be extended as far as possible. New centers of light being thus established one after another, we may hope for the more rapid diffusion of the knowledge of the gospel through the country." *

There has been no small amount of needless expense in preaching houses, in the early stages of the missions. These houses should obviously be such as the heathen will be most disposed to frequent. It is the recorded judgment of the Ceylon mission, after ample experience, that buildings for worship there should be open bungalows, with an ola roof, supported by plain wooden posts, costing only from twenty-five to seventy-five dollars. When the people desire something more costly, they should build for themselves.†

The Madura mission recommend, for churches at the stations, a plain structure, costing from one hundred and fifty to two hundred and fifty dollars, according to different circumstances. For the village churches they recommend a plain mud building, with a thatched roof, the cost of which might vary from twelve to twenty-five dollars.† The cost of village churches in the Mahratta mission was estimated at from twenty-five to one hundred and fifty dollars, all of the plainest description, and no larger than necessity demands — "reference being had to the time when the congregations will bear the whole expense of erecting their places for worship."

Missionaries, assembled at Constantinople in 1855, declared it not to be desirable to erect a church edifice in any place, whether city or village, at the very commencement of an evangelical work. They thought the spiritual building should precede the material; that a church should first be formed, and a congregation gathered. When a church, congregation, and preacher exist, then a suitable house of worship would be

* Report of Mahratta Missions, 1854. † Mission Report, 1855.

important. The building should be adapted to the existing prospects of the congregation, not for the distant future. "While it should allow some room for growth, it should never be such a structure as to appear naked or empty when the usual congregation is gathered into it. In most cases, therefore, it will be advisable, that the first buildings should be churches and school houses in one. If the building be simple, neat, and somewhat churchly in its appearance, and have good light and air, every reasonable aim will be attained." *

The Sandwich Islands people have built their own churches, and have generally furnished them with bells; so that the traveler is often agreeably reminded that he is in a Christian country. Their churches, built of stone, have cost much labor, but no great amount of money.

It takes a long time to correct the views of ministerial education, and of church building, which we carry with us into the heathen world. The saving in church building, which grew out of the discussions in the Eastern missions, in the years 1854 and 1855, is already very considerable, and will ultimately become a large sum; with a decided advance, at the same time, toward meeting the tastes and habits of the people, and securing the construction of the buildings at the cost of those for whom they are intended. Expensive church edifices at the mission stations have resulted more from the taste or convenience of the resident missionary, than from forethought of their effect on the natives after the spread of the gospel and the organization of native churches shall have required the erection of preaching houses in the rural districts; and they often prevent the forming of new congregations in neighboring villages.

The Press.

The missionaries connected with the Board have found it necessary to reduce twenty languages to writing, preliminary

* Report of the Missionaries, 1855.

to the preparation of books. These were the Greybo, Mpongwe, Dikĕlĕ, Zulu-Kaffir, Modern Syriac or Nestorian, Dyak, Hawaiian, Micronesian, Cherokee, Choctaw, Creek, Osage, Ottawa, Ojibwa, Abenaquis, Sioux or Dakota, Pawnee, and three languages of the Oregon Indians. The Roman character was employed, with some modifications, in all these languages, excepting the Syriac and Cherokee. In the former, the Syriac character was used; and in the latter, the syllabic alphabet invented by Guess, or Sequoyah, a Cherokee, past the middle age, who knew only his native tongue. "Having become acquainted with the principle of the alphabet, — that marks can be made the symbols of sound, — this uninstructed man conceived the notion that he could express all the syllables in the Cherokee language by separate marks, or characters. On collecting all the syllables, which, after long study and trial, he could recall to his memory, he found the number to be eighty-two. In order to express these, he took the letters of our alphabet for a part of them, and various modifications of our letters, with some characters of his own invention, for the rest. With these symbols he set about writing letters; and very soon a correspondence was actually maintained between the Cherokees in Wills Valley and their countrymen beyond the Mississippi, five hundred miles apart. This was done by individuals who could not speak English, and who had never learned any alphabet, except this syllabic one, which Guess had invented, taught to others, and introduced into practice."* Either Guess, or some one else, discovered four other syllables, making the syllables of the Cherokee language eighty-six. This is a singular fact, considering that the language is very copious in some directions, a single verb undergoing some thousands of inflections. The late Dr. Samuel A. Worcester, of the Cherokee mission, thus speaks of this invention: —

"A few hours of instruction are sufficient for a Cherokee to learn to read his own language intelligibly. He will not,

* Report of the Board for 1825, p. 51.

indeed, so soon be able to read fluently; but when he has learned to read and understand, fluency will be acquired by practice. The extent of my information will not enable me to form a probable estimate of the number in the nation who can thus read; but I am assured, by those who had the best opportunity of knowing, that there is no part of the nation where the new alphabet is not understood. That it will prevail over every other method of writing the language, there is no doubt. If a book were printed in that character, there are those in every part of the nation who could read it at once, and many others would only have to obtain a few hours' instruction from some friend, to enable them to do so. They have but to learn their alphabet, and they can read at once."* Dr. Worcester subsequently spent many years, until his death in 1859, in translating the Scriptures and preparing other books in the Cherokee language, using only the syllabic alphabet, as the public sentiment required that to be used exclusively in Cherokee books and schools.

Every sound in the Cherokee language has a vowel termination. Such not being the case in the Choctaw, the sounds of that language were too numerous to admit of a separate character for each. Every sound has a vowel termination, also, in the Hawaiian language, and five vowels and seven consonants suffice to express all the sounds. A few diphthongal combinations are needed, but each letter retains its original sound. A syllabic alphabet was of course possible for the Hawaiian, but it is said that ninety-five characters would have been required. With the few characters now in use, each having but one sound, the native very easily learns to read, spell, and write. Nine additional consonants are employed to preserve the identity of foreign and Scripture names, and these are imparted to the pupil after he has learned to read pure native words.

This curious specimen of Cherokee literature will be found on the following page, with the sounds of the letters, and the Lord's Prayer in the Cherokee language.

* Missionary Herald for 1826, p. 48.

CHEROKEE ALPHABET.

Ꭰ a	Ꭱ e	Ꭲ i	Ꭳ o	Ꭴ u	Ꭵ v
Ꭶ ga Ꭷ ka	Ꭸ ge	Ꭹ gi	Ꭺ go	Ꭻ gu	Ꭼ gv
Ꭽ ha	Ꭾ he	Ꭿ hi	Ꮀ ho	Ꮁ hu	Ꮂ hv
Ꮃ la	Ꮄ le	Ꮅ li	Ꮆ lo	Ꮇ lu	Ꮈ lv
Ꮉ ma	Ꮊ me	Ꮋ mi	Ꮌ mo	Ꮍ mu	
Ꮎ na Ꮏ hna	Ꮑ ne	Ꮒ ni	Ꮓ no	Ꮔ nu	Ꮕ nv
Ꮖ gwa	Ꮗ gwe	Ꮘ gwi	Ꮙ gwo	Ꮚ gwu	Ꮛ gwv
Ꮜ sa Ꮝ s	Ꮞ se	Ꮟ si	Ꮠ so	Ꮡ su	Ꮢ sv
Ꮣ da Ꮤ ta	Ꮥ do Ꮦ te	Ꮧ di Ꮨ ti	Ꮩ do	Ꮪ du	Ꮫ dv
Ꮬ dla Ꮭ tla	Ꮮ dle	Ꮯ dli	Ꮰ dlo	Ꮱ dlu	Ꮲ dlv
Ꮳ dsa	Ꮴ dse	Ꮵ dsi	Ꮶ dso	Ꮷ dsu	Ꮸ dsv
Ꮹ wa	Ꮺ we	Ꮻ wi	Ꮼ wo	Ꮽ wu	Ꮾ wv
Ꮿ ya	Ᏸ ye	Ᏹ yi	Ᏺ yo	Ᏻ yu	Ᏼ yv

Sounds represented by Vowels.

a as *a* in *father*, or short as *a* in *rival*,
e as *a* in *hate*, or short as *e* in *met*,
i as *i* in *pique*, or short as *i* in *pit*,
o as *aw* in *law*, or short as *o* in *not*, nearly,
u as *oo* in *moon*, or short as *u* in *pull*,
v as *u* in *but*, nasalized.

Consonant Sounds.

The sound of g is nearly as hard g in English, but approaching to k. That of d nearly as in English, but approaching to t. Other consonants as in English.

In some words g, l, n, d, w, and y are aspirated, as if preceded by h. Aspiration gives to g the power of k, and to d the power of t.

THE LORD'S PRAYER IN CHEROKEE.

ᎣᎩᏙᏓ ᎦᎸᎳᏗ ᎮᎯ, ᎦᎸᏉᏗᏳ ᎨᏎᏍᏗ ᏕᏣᏙᎥᎢ. ᏣᎬᏫᏳᎯ ᎨᏒ ᏫᎦᎾᏄᎪᎢ. ᎠᏂ ᎡᎶᎯ ᏫᏥᎦᎵᏍᏓ ᎭᏓᏅᏖᏍᎬᎢ, ᎾᏍᎩᏯ ᎦᎸᎳᏗ ᏥᏂᎦᎵᏍᏗᎭ. ᏂᏓᏙᏓᏘᏒ ᎣᎦᎵᏍᏓᏴᏗ ᏍᎩᎥᏏ ᎪᎯ ᎢᎦ. ᏗᎨᏍᎩᎥᏏᏉᏃ ᏕᏍᎩᏚᎬᎢ, ᎾᏍᎩᏯ ᏥᏗᎦᏲᏥᎾᎰ ᏦᏥᏚᎩ. ᎠᎴ ᏝᏍᏗ ᎤᏓᎪᎴᏰᏗᏱ ᎨᏒ ᏫᏗᏍᎩᏯᏘᏅᏍᏔᏅᎩ, ᏍᎩᏳᏓᎴᏍᎨᏍᏗᏉᏍᎩᏂ ᎤᏲ ᎨᏒᎢ. ᏣᏤᎵᎦᏰᏃ ᏣᎬᏫᏳᎯ ᎨᏒᎢ, ᎠᎴ ᏣᎵᏂᎩᏗᏱ ᎨᏒᎢ, ᎠᎴ ᎡᏣᎸᏉᏗᏳ ᎨᏒ ᏂᎪᎯᎸᎢ. ᎡᎺᏅ.

INTERPRETATION, WITH PRONUNCIATION ACCORDING TO THE ALPHABET.

aw gi daw da | ga *lv* la di ehi | ga *lv* quo di yu | ge se sdi | de tsa daw *v* i | dsa *gv* wi yu hi ge *sv* | wi ga na nu gaw i | a ni e law hi | wi dsi ga li sda | ha da *nv* ste *gv* i | na sgi ya | ga *lv* la di | tsi ni ga li sdi ha | ni da daw da qui *sv* | aw ga li sda *yv* di | sgi *v* si | gaw hi i ga | di ge sgi *v* si quo naw | de sgi du *gv* i | na sgi ya | tsi di ga yaw tsi na haw | tsaw tsi du gi | a le tla sdi | oo da gaw le ye di yi ge *sv* | wi di sgi ya ti *nv* sta *nv* gi | sgi yu da le sge sdi quo sgi ni | oo yaw ge *sv* i | tsa tse li ga ye naw | tsa *gv*, wi yu hi | ge *sv* i | a le | dsa li ni gi di yi | ge *sv* i | a le | e dsa *lv* quo di yu | ge *sv* | ni gaw hi *lv* i | e me n

Our Father | heaven dweller, | Hallowed | be | thy name. | Thy kingdom | let it make its appearance. | Here upon earth | take place | Thy will, | the same as | in heaven | [it] is done. | Daily [adj.] | our food give to us | this day. | Forgive us | our debts, | the same as | we forgive | our debtors. | And do not | temptation being | lead us into [it]. | Deliver us from | evil existing. | For thine | the kingdom | is, | and | the power | is, | and | the glory | is, | forever | amen.

The late Dr. Eli Smith, of the Syria mission, with the aid of Mr. Homan Hallock, formerly in charge of the press at Malta and Smyrna, introduced a new and beautiful form of Arabic type into the books printed at the mission press in Syria, based on the perfect calligraphy of the smaller Koranic manuscripts. The printed page, thus resembling the manuscript, falls in with the Arab prejudice, and all the printing has since been in this type, which is thus described by the mission after it had been three years in use: "It is vastly superior in respect to the form of the letters. Such is the uniform and decided testimony of intelligent natives every where. Our books are incomparably more acceptable than those which were printed with the old type; more acceptable, we may safely say, in respect to typography, than any that were ever printed in the language. And not only are the letters more beautiful than the old, but, bearing a closer resemblance to the best calligraphy, they are, of course, far preferable for the use of schools, and especially for all who are learning to write."*

Mr. Edward Breath, who has long had the management of the press and foundery at Ooroomiah, has satisfied the Nestorian taste by his success in cutting a type in exact imitation of the plain, heavy letter of the Syriac manuscripts.

The number of languages in which books have been printed at the presses owned by the Board is forty-three; namely, the Modern Greek, Hebrew, Spanish, Armenian, Turkish,† Bulgarian, Arabic, Syriac, Mahratta, Gujarate, Sanscrit, Hindoostanee, Portuguese, Persian, Tamil, Telugu, Siamese, Malay, Bugis, Dyak, Chinese, Japanese, Hawaiian, Marquesas, Micronesian, Greybo, Mpongwe, Dikĕlĕ, Zulu-Kaffir, Cherokee, Choctaw, Creek, Osage, Ojibwa, Ottawa, Seneca, Abenaquis, Sioux or Dakota, Pawnee, three in Oregon, and the English. The fact is worth recording, that no less than twenty of these languages were spoken by missionaries assembled at the house of the

* Report of the Board, 1844, p. 135.

† Armeno-Turkish and Greco-Turkish do not denote languages so much as the manner of writing the Turkish language.

writer of these pages, on the evening following the fiftieth anniversary of the Board.

A tabular view will show the number of printing establishments that have been owned and employed at different times by the missions under the care of the Board; when they we instituted and discontinued; the number of presses, fonts, founderies, and binderies; the number of languages, and the amount of printing.

MISSIONS.	Printing Establishments.	Instituted.	Presses.	Fonts.	Founderies.	Binderies.	Languages employed.	Discontinued.	Pages printed from the beginning.
West Africa, . . .	1	1837	1	1			3		2,500,000
South Africa, . . .	1	1836	1	1			1		2,000,000
Turkey, ...	1	1822*	2	10	1	1	6	1852†	191,805,860
Syria, ...	1	1835	3	4	1	1	1		28,472,800
Nestorians, . . .	1	1841	1	5	1	1	1		15,263,720
Mahrattas, ...	1	1816	9	15	1	1	6	1859	130,000,000
Madras, ...	1	1839	12	16	1	1	3		357,969,621
Ceylon, ...	1	1821	4	3	1	1	1	1855	171,747,198
Siam, ...	1	1835	2	3	1	1	1	1848	11,600,813
Singapore, ...	1	1834	2	8	1	1	5	1842	14,071,168
China, ...	1	1833	2	4			1	1857‡	25,000,000
Sandwich Islands, .	1	1820	2	4	1	1	2	1859	200,000,000
Cherokees,§ . . .	1	1835	1	2			1	1861	13,918,800
Choctaws, ...		1825					1	1848	3,788,300
Sioux or Dakotas, .							1		991,000
Creeks, ...							1		68,000
Ojibwas, ...							1		1,841,000
Osages, ...							1		63,000
New York Indians, .	1		1	1			1		459,676
Pawnees, ...							1		4,907,100
Oregon, ...	1		1	1			3	1848	300,000
Abenaquis, ...							1		63,000
Total, . . .	15		44	78	9	9	43‖		1,176,831,056

There have been fifteen printing establishments. At Constantinople, the Board now owns only the Armenian types. In

* Commenced in Malta, afterward at Smyrna and Constantinople.

† Types owned from this time, but not the presses.

‡ Destroyed by fire in the war of that year.

§ The Cherokee printing was begun at New Echota, at a press owned by the tribe, in 1829. The Choctaw printing began in 1825, and, with that in the greater part of the Indian languages, was executed out of the nation.

‖ The number of languages, not including the English, is really forty-two. The Ceylon and Madras presses both made use of the Tamil.

Ceylon, the establishment was sold to native Christian printers in 1855. Those at Bombay and the Sandwich Islands were sold because the needful printing could be executed at other presses. The Siamese and Singapore presses were transferred to Canton; and the Cherokee and Oregon establishments ceased with the missions. The printing establishment at Canton was burned by the Chinese in their war with England, but they have since refunded the value of it. The Armenian, Arabic, and Syriac types were cast from matrices prepared at the expense of the Board. The number of pages printed in the forty-two foreign languages employed by the missionaries of the Board, exceeds the number mentioned in the table; which is eleven hundred and seventy-six million eight hundred and thirty-one thousand and fifty-six.

Several of the printing establishments have at times been sources of income, especially where they went into job-printing in the English language. The Bombay press earned forty-six thousand seven hundred and forty-three dollars in the eight years ending with 1853. The presses at Madras, Canton, and elsewhere, have been productive in this way. But it has not been deemed expedient, on the whole, to continue job-printing in the English language; nor, indeed, to keep up the establishments on a scale for any great amount of remunerative job-printing even in the vernaculars, with the single exception of the one at Madras; it being found that there was necessarily too great a tax upon the time of the missionary superintendent.

CHAPTER IX.

DEPUTATIONS.

Visits to Missions necessary. — Mr. Evarts to the Indian Missions, 1818. — Dr. Worcester, 1821. — Mr. Evarts, 1822 and 1824. — Changes required by Experience. — Mr. Greene, 1827, 1833, and 1842. — Changes. — Mr. Anderson to the Mediterranean, 1828, 9. — Messrs. Anderson and Hawes, 1843, 4. — Results. — Mr. Treat to the Cherokee and Choctaw Missions, 1847. — Objects of the Visit. — Christian Fellowship. — Mr. Treat to Cattaraugus, 1849, and to Dakotas and Ojibwas, 1854. — Dr. Wood to Cherokee and Choctaw Missions, 1855. — Messrs. Anderson and Thompson to the India Missions, 1854, 5. — Dr. Anderson to the Mediterranean, 1855. — Proceedings in the India Missions. — Reports and Letters. — Main Object of the Discussions. — Course of the Deputation arraigned at Utica, 1855. — Special Meeting of the Board in Albany, 1856. — Report of the Deputation. — Case referred to a Special Committee. — Correspondence with the Missionaries. — Report of the Special Committee, and Resolutions of the Board. — Resolutions of the Prudential Committee. — Results of these Occurrences.

THEY whose posts of duty are at the centers of great missionary systems, are more favorably situated than the members of any one mission can be, for obtaining comprehensive, practical views of missionary principles and measures. All the rays of missionary experience converge to the center; and a wise disbursement of the funds requires a constant application of principles to missions in their ever-varying circumstances and relations. Generally, sufficient information for this purpose is gained from correspondence, and from personal intercourse with returned missionaries. But sometimes it is needful for some one of the executive officers — generally the Secretary in charge of the correspondence with the mission — to go and confer with the brethren face to face. The larger English and European Missionary Societies have been in this practice from an early period. This has not been with the expectation of obtaining information which the brethren in the field can not embody in their correspondence, but to secure the advantages of the freest possible interchange of opinions.

To go, when it can be done, is better than to write. A correspondence across a thousand or ten thousand miles is a slow process; and when much is pending, and there is a consequent liability to excited feelings, misunderstandings are apt to arise, and to retard, if they do not prevent or impair, the proper results; while a few days or weeks of familiar conference would suffice for their easy and perfect attainment.

The earliest deputation sent by the Board was in the spring of 1818, when Mr. Evarts, the Treasurer, visited the Cherokee mission, then just entering its untried and complicated labors. He was met there by the Rev. Elias Cornelius, who commenced his career of usefulness as an agent of the Board. The visit was alike satisfactory to the mission and to the Prudential Committee.

In the spring of 1821, Dr. Worcester, the Corresponding Secretary, principally with the hope of restoring his failing health, undertook a visit to the missions among the Choctaws and Cherokees. On his arrival in the Choctaw country, going up from New Orleans, he had become so much enfeebled that he could only make brief visits to some of the stations, speaking words of Christian sympathy and encouragement to the mission families. He proceeded to Brainerd, among the Cherokees, and there, sinking under the weight of disease and the fatigue of the journey, he closed his earthly labors. His heavenly spirit and his prayers were a source of strength and comfort to all who were favored with his presence.

Mr. Evarts, as Corresponding Secretary, made a second visit to the Cherokee mission in 1822, having, as on the former occasion, a partial reference to his impaired health. He was accompanied by the Rev. William Goodell, now of the mission to Turkey, then an agent of the Board, and under appointment as a missionary. The Rev. Cyrus Kingsbury, who had gone from the Cherokee mission to commence one among the Choctaws, met him at Brainerd for a free conference on the affairs of both missions.

Mr. Evarts made a third visit to the Cherokee mission in the early part of 1824, and extended his official tour to the stations of the Choctaw mission. The Indian missions had then a complicated system of labors, including missionaries, schoolmasters, farmers, and mechanics of several kinds. This may have arisen partly from the coöperation of the United States government in the support of the schools and secular operations of the missions; but the religious sentiment of those times was in favor of this mixed operation, to civilize the savage while aiming at his conversion and the institution of Christian communities. The difficult question was, how to keep this complicated machinery in easy, constant, vigorous motion.

Dr. Worcester was too ill, when he reached the Cherokee mission, to do any thing there. But in his brief address to the Choctaw mission, he said, "The mission among the Choctaws is one. It is designed to occupy different stations, and to be in different divisions; all to be under a general superintendence. Each primary establishment is to have a head, or rector, who is to be also an ordained minister. The work, besides, is to be divided into several parts, and to be assigned to different persons, according to their respective qualifications. You are all indeed brethren, and are always to regard yourselves as such. Nevertheless, there are, and must be, distinctions of a very important kind. So it is in the church. It has its distinctions of office, — of labor and service, order and subordination, — distinctions according to the will of God. Besides the general principles of the Bible, which imply order and subordination, there are several chapters in the Epistles on the subject. This order is of no less importance on missionary ground than elsewhere."

The evils naturally attendant on this system had become developed at the time of Mr. Evarts's third visit. The plan proposed by Dr. Worcester for the Indian missions was upon the supposition that when a considerable number of individuals are laboring together, they may be saved the inconvenience of joint consultations by explicit directions from the Committee, or by a delegated power of superintendence to some one of their number. Mr. Evarts found, that whatever explicit directions the Committee had given, had been promptly followed; but that it was impossible for persons at a distance to enter into the details of different operations, carried on simultaneously at the same place, and changing daily. He was more than ever impressed with the fact, that the system of missionary operations must be a system of mutual confidence, and that the services to be rendered by those who devote themselves to the work, must be in the largest sense voluntary and free. It was a delicate matter to establish any system of subordination that should even seem to encroach upon this freedom, or to have the effect of placing one class of laborers under the direction of another. Those to whom authority might be intrusted, would feel a hesitation in using it, so that it would in fact avail but little; and those who were placed under their brethren would be apt to feel a constraint and unwillingness which might grow into a settled disaffection to the work. "It is well known," Mr. Evarts said, "that where a considerable number of persons are to act together, though they all possess the best intentions, the same economy can not be practiced as would be practiced by the same persons individually. This state of things arises from a commendable disposition to yield to each other, as far as possible; from different habits of economy; from a divided responsibility; and from a constant tendency to relax in exertions which are shared by many. It has been supposed, that a division of labor, which should render each individual accountable for a particular department, would answer the end of securing individual responsibility, and prevent interference with each other's duties. This course has been repeatedly attempted; but so numerous are the interruptions of any regular plan at a missionary station, from the visits of natives and travelers, from sickness, from a failure of supplies, and from a great variety of unexpected events, that very soon the arrangement has been broken up, one person after another has been called from his assigned sphere to meet exigencies in some other part of the system, and affairs have relapsed into their original state."

These difficulties would never have been thoroughly understood except by experience; but being understood, the Committee came thus early to the following conclusions, which subsequent experience has fully sustained: "That the instruction of the heathen in Christian knowledge and true piety is the great object of missions, and should never be merged in a mass of secular cares; that mission schools are principally to be valued as a means of communicating divine truth; that the main reliance should be on the plain doctrines of the gospel for any permanent melioration of the character and condition of any heathen people; that the secular labors in a mission should be as few and as simple as possible; and that but few missionaries and assistants ought to reside at one station." The changes now brought about in the internal arrangements of the Cherokee mission, were based upon these principles.

At the meeting of the Board in 1826, an arrangement was concluded with the United Foreign Missionary Society, by which the missions of that society among the Osages, the Ottawas, and the Indians at Mackinaw, and in Western New York, were transferred to the Board. Preliminary steps were also taken for receiving the Chickasaw mission, instituted by the Synod of South Carolina and Georgia. In view of this prospective enlargement of the Board's operations, and in order to become personally acquainted with the new missions, a plan was formed for an extended visitation, by Mr. Evarts, of all the stations among the south-western Indians, accompanied by the Rev. David Greene, who had been appointed an Assistant Secretary, and to whom the correspondence with the Indian missions was to be specially confided. Events prevented Mr. Evarts from making this tour, and Mr. Greene, in the autumn of 1827, entered upon it alone. After meeting the Synod of South Carolina and Georgia in Charleston, and consummating the transfer of the Chickasaw mission, he proceeded to the country of the Cherokees, and visited all the stations, aiding the mission families in arrangements for the more efficient prosecution of the labors in the several departments of their work. During this visit, the font of Cherokee type in the peculiar alphabetical character of Guess, and the printing-press which had been purchased at the expense of the tribe, were put in operation. It was the first press ever owned by an Indian tribe, or devoted exclusively to their use; and it employed the only new alphabetic character that had been invented for many centuries.

Having finished his work among the Cherokees, Mr. Greene proceeded to the Chickasaw country, and visited all the stations, aiding the missionaries in adjusting their affairs to their new relations. Passing on to the Choctaw mission, he spent several weeks in labors similar to those performed among the Cherokees.

In company with Mr. Kingsbury, whom the Prudential Committee had associated with him for the stations beyond the Mississippi, he proceeded to the Arkansas Cherokees. The affairs of the several stations were carefully inspected, and such changes brought about as promised to render the operations of the missions more harmonious and efficient.

The deputation then visited the mission among the Osages, where, in consequence of its unsettled state during the process of transition from the United Foreign Missionary Society to the Board, their arrival seemed most opportune. This mission presented some new features and difficulties, in consequence of its being among a migratory and untutored tribe. As the result of consultation, the mission was placed on a new and more satisfactory footing.

Having finished their work in the Osage mission, Mr. Kingsbury returned by way of St. Louis, and Mr. Greene pursued his way to the Ottawas, in the north-west part of Ohio, and then to the Tuscaroras and Senecas, in Western New York. With these missions the tour was concluded, having extended through eight months, and required about five thousand miles of travel.

In the summer of 1829, Mr. Greene visited the mission at Mackinaw, and the one near Green Bay — the only missions among the Indians which he had not previously seen. The former was among those transferred from the United Foreign

Missionary Society, and the latter had been recently established by the Board. Important necessary changes were effected. Mr. Greene made a second visit to Mackinaw in 1833. In 1842, the Indians in Western New York having disposed of one of their reservations on which was a missionary station, it was deemed expedient for the same Secretary to repeat his visit to that mission.

These official visits had the effect to diminish the expenditures of the missions to an amount far greater than their cost. They also threw much light on the path of the Prudential Committee, and were an important means of increasing the harmony and efficiency of the several missions. The changes resulted for the most part, at least in later years, from the free action of the missions. Still, to a very great extent, they could not have been as well effected, if at all, without a visit of this sort. The presence of a deputation of course created a necessity for the mission's reviewing its entire system of action, and subjecting every important part of it to a deliberate conclusion of some sort; and all under the advantage of the presence of one intimately conversant with the views of the Prudential Committee, and with the general operations of the Board.

In the year 1828, the members of the Syria mission, compelled by war to leave Beirût, were all on the Island of Malta. They were the only missionaries of the Board then in the countries of the Mediterranean. There had been a temporary occupation of Smyrna on two occasions, and a short sojourn of a missionary at Constantinople. The mission to Greece was of later origin, and so was that to the Armenians; while the Nestorians were as yet unknown to the Protestant Christian world. The battle of Navarino had liberated Greece, after nearly the whole of the Morea had been ravaged and burned by Ibrahim Pasha; and our countrymen were sending shiploads of supplies to the destitute and famishing inhabitants.

A variety of circumstances conspired to make it seem important to the Prudential Committee, that some one conversant with their views and proceedings should visit Malta for an extended conference with the missionaries assembled there; and it was decided to send Mr. Anderson, then Assistant Secretary in the foreign department. He was instructed, after having completed his business at Malta, to visit Greece, which was then supposed to present a very promising field for missionary enterprise. It was among the reasons for this agency, — as in the similar mission of Mr. Greene to the Indian stations, — that it would add materially to the ability of the Secretary for the future discharge of his official duties. He reached Malta on the 1st of January, 1829; and near the close of February, in company with the Rev. Eli Smith, one of the missionaries, — afterward extensively known by his explorations in Armenia and the Nestorian country, and by his labors in the Arabic translation of the Scriptures, — he visited the Ionian Islands, the Morea, several of the Greek Islands, and Smyrna. From thence they returned to Malta. While at Ægina, the seat of the Greek government, Mr. Anderson, in conformity with his Instructions, sought an interview with Count Capodistrias, the President of Greece, who gave written replies to his inquiries. Perhaps the most important thing in these replies was the declaration, which there is good reason to believe was sincere, that the Holy Scriptures in Modern Greek should be among the books for use in the common schools. The Rev. Jonas King, who was then in Greece in charge of one of the cargoes of provisions sent to the impoverished people, assisted in some part of this intercourse. Mr. King soon afterward renewed his connection with the Board, — having for several years subsequent to 1823 been the associate of the Rev. Pliny Fisk in Syria, — and has continued his useful labors in Greece down to this day, residing first on the Island of Tenos, and then in Athens, which he was one of the first to reoccupy subsequent to the war of revolution. It was mainly through an influence exerted at that time, and continued by Dr. King, that the Modern Greek Scriptures, or at least the New Testament, became, and has ever been, a school book in Greece. Mr. Anderson returned to Boston near the close of 1829.*

The Greek mission, during thirteen years from the time of its institution, went through a process of growth and decline, till the Prudential Committee were at a loss what to do with it. The Armenian mission was then having a prosperous development in the populous suburbs of Constantinople, and in some of the northern sections of Asia Minor; and, both there and in Syria, fundamental questions in missionary policy had ripened for discussion, which was needful both for the missions and for the Committee. It was therefore decided, in 1844, to send Dr. Anderson, who had long been Secretary for the foreign department, once more to the Mediterranean. Happily, the Rev. Joel Hawes, D. D., of Hartford, Conn., had resolved to visit the East at that time, in company with his only daughter, Mrs. Van Lennep, going, with her husband, to join the Armenian mission, and he was requested to render such aid to the Secretary as his plans and convenience might allow. In point of fact, the two brethren were associated in every journey and in every meeting while on mission ground; and the service rendered by Dr. Hawes was highly appreciated by the missions, and of much value to the cause. The more important places visited were Athens, Smyrna, Constantinople, Brûsa, Trebizond, Beirût, and Jerusalem; and somewhat more than sixty meetings were held with the brethren of the missions. The results can not here be enumerated. Those in Syria — on the best manner of cultivating the field — will serve as a specimen. "It was agreed, that the grand aim of our mission is of course the

* Some are yet living, who may remember how much the interest of the United Monthly Concert in Park-street Church was increased, on the first Monday evening of January, 1830, by the choir under the direction of Dr. Lowell Mason, when, at the close of a statement by Mr. Anderson, they sang the hymn, —

'Watchman, tell us of the night,
What its signs of promise are,"—

in the well-known strains, then recently composed by Dr. Mason, and for the first time heard in public.

converting of men to God; that the preaching of the gospel is the great, divinely-appointed means to this end; that whenever and wherever there are small companies of natives ready to make a credible profession of piety, they are to be recognized as churches, entitled to the ordinances of baptism and the Lord's Supper, and to such a ministry as can be given them; that the reformed churches are to have no reference to any of the degenerate Oriental churches, and may be expected to combine persons from several, and perhaps all, the various sects existing in the mountains; and that the method of church organization and administration should involve the principle of throwing such responsibility on every individual member, as will develop his talents and Christian graces to the utmost possible extent."

As the closing of the Greek mission — except so far as it could be prosecuted by Dr. King alone at Athens — was one of the more important results of the inquiries and consultations in Greece, Asia Minor, and Constantinople, the dark picture of the religious state of the Greek mind, at that time, given by the Secretary in his report, will interest the thoughtful reader. "To me," he says, "the condition of the Greek mind, in relation to evangelical efforts for the benefit of the Greek people, appears altogether extraordinary. We are not mistaken in the material facts in the case. The Greeks have retired from us. To a most affecting extent they have become inaccessible to our preaching, our books, and our influence. They will no longer hear us; and there is reason to believe it is now true, that few of them read when we address them through the press on the subjects of vital godliness. I do not see where or in what way the Greek mind is, to any considerable extent, approachable, just now, to a spiritual influence from Protestant ministers of the gospel. The political state of the Greek mind — grasping after the recovery of Constantinople and the restoration of the Eastern empire, and relying on the unity of the Greek Church as a means to this end — has a wonderful influence on the thoughts and feelings of the whole community, especially the higher classes. I am reluctant to mention also the national pride of the Greeks, which has been much increased since the revolution, and their strong aversion to strangers, and certain other traits in their character, all combining to render it difficult for foreigners to gain their confidence or awaken their gratitude by acts of kindness and benevolence. And then there are the high, arrogant assumptions of the Greek Church, which is more exclusive than the Roman; claiming for her clergy the only apostolical succession, and for her trine immersion, performed by her clergy, the only baptism; and regarding that baptism as having a regenerative power, and all who are not thus baptized as beyond the pale of the Christian church and the hope of salvation. Of course all Protestant preachers of every name, episcopal and non-episcopal, are looked upon as unbaptized heretics. There is, moreover, the tyranny of the Greek Church, and the dreadful terror of excommunication on the part of the people, requiring the deepest convictions of the truth to sustain the inquirer against the threats of his spiritual guides; and, connected with this, there is the almost universal and decided hostility of the Greek clergy to every Protestant movement. The patriarch and synod at Constantinople are believed to be not less opposed to the circulation of the Scriptures in the vernacular tongue, than the pope and cardinals at Rome. And it is time for us to consider the disproportion that exists between the means that have been employed and the results. Twenty-seven ordained missionaries of different denominations have labored more or less in this field. A million copies of books and tracts have been printed by different missionary societies, and scattered broadcast over the Greek community. Two hundred thousand copies of the New Testament, and parts of the Old, have been put in circulation in the Modern Greek language. Not a small number of Greek young men have been educated in America and England, by benevolent individuals and societies; and more than ten thousand Greek youth have been more or less educated in Greece and Turkey at the schools of the various missions. And yet, not ten persons are known, who are confidently believed to have been truly converted to God by these means! How unlike these results to those we find among the Armenians!"

In 1847, the Prudential Committee thought it desirable that a visit should be made to the Cherokee and Choctaw missions. Mr. Greene was designated for this service, in the first instance; but, after the Annual Meeting at Buffalo, it was found that his health would be unequal to such a journey. It became necessary, therefore, that Mr. Treat, one of the Corresponding Secretaries, should take his place.

The object of the Committee was twofold. They wished to become thoroughly acquainted with the state and prospects of the missions, and with their relations, and those of the churches under their care, to the subject of slavery.

Mr. Treat left Boston on the 30th of November. His route was by New York, Philadelphia, and Baltimore, to Pittsburg; thence by the Ohio, Mississippi, and Arkansas Rivers to Little Rock. The rest of the way to the Cherokee Nation he traveled on horseback, arriving at Dwight, January 4, 1848. It has been practicable, quite recently, to reach the same point in one week. Among the Cherokees, he visited every station of the Board, in company with Mr. Willey, as also the stations of the Baptists and Moravians, and conferred freely with such persons as were most competent to impart the information which he needed, wherever they might be found. Mr. Butrick, who had identified himself with the interests of the red man for thirty years, and Messrs. Butler and Worcester, who had suffered imprisonment for the maintenance of his rights, were then among the living. To sit down with these brethren, and hear them speak of their labors, their trials, the changes which had passed over the Indians, the triumphs which the gospel had achieved in the transformation of individuals, and their confident belief that nothing but the gospel could save the aboriginal race, was no ordinary privilege.

A meeting of the Cherokee mission was held at Dwight, after the different stations had been visited. Various questions were discussed, the subject of slavery in its relations to the work of Indian evangelization receiving its due share of attention. The time spent in devotional exercises threw a hallowed influence around the deliberations of each successive day. The fourth Sabbath in January was a memorable occasion. The mission families, the Indian communicants, and the colored communicants, in the afternoon, sat together around the table of their common Lord, with the feeling that "Christ is all and in all."

Owing to an unexpected rise of the Choctaw rivers, an entire week was required for the journey from Dwight to Pine Ridge, the station occupied by Mr. Kingsbury. On his way thither, the Secretary visited the boarding schools at Fort Coffee and Mount Hope, in charge of the Methodist brethren; also the academy at Spencer, under the direction of the Presbyterian Board. The institution last named has exerted a greater influence upon the intellectual progress of the Choctaws than any other.

Mr. Treat proceeded at once to visit the mission families, in doing which he became acquainted with many intelligent men, church members and others, with more or less of aboriginal blood in their veins; and, as four Sabbaths were spent in the Choctaw country, he had considerable opportunity to become acquainted with the churches.

The mission assembled at Pine Ridge near the close of the month; but in view of what is already known to the public, there is no occasion to speak of its deliberations. The condition and prospects of the missionary work, at that time, were fully set forth in the Annual Report for 1848. Various documents, growing out of the relation of the Indian churches to slavery, were submitted to the Board at its meeting in Boston, and published in the Report for the same year.

Mr. Treat arrived at the Missionary House after an absence of seventeen weeks, having journeyed (including eleven hundred miles on horseback) more than six thousand miles.

Several visits have also been made by Mr. Treat to the missions in Western New York. The first of these, and the only one that will be mentioned here, occurred in 1849, when he repaired to Cattaraugus by direction of the Prudential

Committee, in consequence of certain complaints which had been preferred against the brethren stationed on that Reservation. The year 1848, it will be recollected, was memorable for its revolutions. The last of these was inaugurated among the Senecas; the government, which had been in the hands of the chiefs from time immemorial, having been suddenly transferred to the people. Those who lost place and power so unexpectedly, as was very natural, felt aggrieved by the change; and they could not be persuaded that the missionaries had done all in their interest which they had a right to expect; on the contrary, they affirmed that the influence of these brethren had been employed adversely to them. Mr. Treat soon discovered that no attempt at conciliation was likely to succeed; hence he permitted the complainants to prefer their charges in a formal manner, and support them with such evidence as they could adduce, the missionaries being at liberty to introduce rebutting testimony. Two days were devoted to an investigation which certainly could shelter itself behind no precedent, ancient or modern. The allegations were peculiar, both in form and substance; and the witnesses could not be dissuaded from taking the widest range in submitting their statements. There was a profusion of Indian oratory, moreover; and the "summing up" threatened at one time to become an indefinite debate. The result was favorable to the missionaries; and the Indian character appeared well throughout the investigation. With a large share of persistency, there was mingled a good degree of shrewdness and intellectual power. Though some of the witnesses exhibited the deepest interest in the issue of the question, all appeared to be honest.

In July, 1851, treaties were entered into by the United States government and four bands of Dakota Indians, whereby the latter agreed to surrender to the former, at the end of two years, the immense territory lying east of Lake Traverse and the Sioux River, with the exception of a tract about one hundred and fifty miles long and twenty miles wide, including the valley of the Minnesota River from Lake Traverse to the mouth of Little Rock River. The Senate of the United States, however, refused to confirm the reservation above described, but substituted a provision which allowed the Indians to occupy the same during the pleasure of the President. To this change the Dakotas subsequently assented. As the labors of the missionaries had been chiefly upon the ceded territory, a modification of the plans of the Committee became indispensable. Mr. Treat was therefore directed to visit the brethren who remained in connection with the Board (two having already taken their release) in the spring of 1854. He left Boston on the 10th of May, and was absent till the 30th of June. Having reached Traverse des Sioux by steamboat, he proceeded on horseback from that point (then the western limit of civilization) to Lac-qui-parle, distant one hundred and thirty miles. Thence he returned with Mr. Riggs to Yellow Medicine, the station of Dr. Williamson, where the annual meeting of the mission commenced its sessions on the 2d of June. The results of the conference which followed, are stated in the Annual Report for 1854, p. 173, and need not be repeated here.

Having returned to St. Paul, Mr. Treat proceeded northward to Crow Wing, where Rev. S. Hall, with others, was commencing a new station. Here the Secretary was obliged to contemplate the obstacles which the feud between the Dakotas and Ojibwas, so formidable and so relentless, had suddenly interposed. There were other hinderances, moreover, which made it a grave question whether the Board could be justified in continuing its labors in that locality. When the facts were reported to the Committee, they concluded to abandon a field which seemed to promise so much of trial and so little of success. In consequence of this step, Mr. Hall became a home missionary at Sauk Rapids, Minnesota.

In 1856, Mr. Treat visited Odanah, the station which Mr. Wheeler occupies among the Ojibwas. He was able to take a hopeful view of a field that was comparatively new, and measures were considered with reference to a more vigorous prosecution of the missionary work, which in due time received the sanction of the Prudential Committee.

In the spring of 1855, Dr. Wood, the Corresponding Secretary resident in New York, was commissioned to visit the Choctaw and Cherokee missions, to make further efforts for removing the difficulties growing out of the question of slavery. He spent a part of the months of April and May in the two missions, in the most free and fraternal conference with the brethren. His subsequent report to the Prudential Committee was approved by the Board assembled at Utica, and was published in the minutes of that meeting. Dr. Wood's object was fully attained in the Cherokee mission; and though, in the final result with the Choctaw mission, he was disappointed, his visit prepared the way for the Board to retire from that field in 1859.

The third official visit of Dr. Anderson to the foreign field, was to the missions in India, in the years 1854, 5, in company with the Rev. Augustus C. Thompson, a member of the Prudential Committee. These brethren sailed from Boston in August, 1854. The time of departure, and the times for visiting the several missions, were adjusted to the varied seasons as they occur in India, with the expectation of reaching home before the meeting of the Board in 1855. They arrived at Bombay in November, just after the rains; visited the Deccan in the cool of winter; finished their work in the Madura mission before the hot season; reached Ceylon when the dry southwest monsoon had begun to send its healthful breezes across the district of Jaffna; and so were at Madras and in Arcot when the hot season was nearly over. The time allotted to this tour having more than expired, Mr. Thompson's pastoral duties called him home; and the visit to Calcutta, the political, intellectual, and religious center of India, which then seemed important and useful in various respects, was performed by the senior member of the deputation alone. This was in midsummer, which is the rainy season in Bengal; and the visit, after so long a course of severe labor, was not without risk of health and life. On his way home, the Secretary visited the Syria mission, and Kessab, Antioch, Aleppo, Aintab, and Constantinople. More than seven months were spent among the India missions, near a month at Calcutta, and two months in the Syria and Armenian missions.

On reaching a mission, the first business of the deputation was to visit the several stations, that they might gain an accurate acquaintance with them by a free, personal intercourse with the brethren. The object of this visit was not to discuss questions of missionary policy, but to perfect their knowledge of facts, and to ascertain the individual impressions of the missionaries as to the proper method of dealing with the facts. In this, which was the most toilsome part of their duty, they were generally successful; and this was an essential preparation for the protracted meetings of the missions which followed. The number of stations thus visited was thirty-seven. There were formal conferences with the Mahratta, Madura, Ceylon, Madras, Arcot, and Syria missions, and with such members of the Armenian mission as could assemble at Aintab and Constantinople. The aggregate number of missionary brethren present at these meetings was fifty-eight; the number of sessions was one hundred and six, occupying the business hours of seventy-eight days; and the number of written reports discussed and adopted in these sessions was eighty-seven. The reports — upon the basis of which the several missions have been since acting successfully — were drawn up after the discussions, as a fair embodiment of the opinions of the meeting, and were printed, together with letters from the deputation commenting upon them, for the use of the missions and of the Prudential Committee.*

* These Reports and Letters, bound up with the Report of the Deputation to the Board, and that of the Special Committee on their case, make a considerable octavo volume. The documents written in India were printed there; and the mode of proceeding at these meetings was followed by several Conferences of Missionaries in other parts of India; as, also, by a Conference on Missions held in Liverpool in the year 1860. The Rev. Joseph Mullens, D. D., one of the London Society's missionaries in Calcutta, to whom missions in India and all missionary bodies are under great obligation, was one of the secretaries of the last-named Conference. It is gratifying to be able to

The missions of the Board in India being chiefly in rural districts, the main drift of the discussions, and of the reports, was in favor of carrying the gospel into the villages in such a way, that gospel institutions might speedily take root in them.

At a meeting of the Board in Utica, in September, 1855, the committee on that part of the Prudential Committee's Report relating to the Tamil missions, stated to the Board, that, from other sources than the Report, they had derived information of changes brought about by the deputation, which involved "the abandonment of the English language, the relinquishment of schools for the heathen, a total change in the ecclesiastical constitution of the [Ceylon] mission, and, in a word, a new basis of missionary effort;" and they recommended the appointment of a special committee to examine into the case. The Board could not know how far such statements were founded in misapprehension, as neither member of the deputation had then returned to the country. The report was, therefore, after a discussion of some length, laid upon the table; and the Prudential Committee was requested to call a special meeting of the Board, whenever the matters

quote the following opinion of these documents from Dr. Mullens's Historical Account of previous Missionary Conferences, in the very instructive volume issued by the Liverpool Conference, of which twenty-five thousand copies were circulated the first year. "They are contained," he says, "in a volume of six hundred pages, printed privately for the use of the Board and its friends; and it is not too much to say, that no volume of equal size, published during the era of our modern missions, contains so much valuable information on all the details of missionary experience, on several most important fields of labor, as that volume of missionary papers. It might be published with great advantage to the friends of all missionary societies; and deserves the careful study of all missionaries, and the managers of all missionary agencies, especially in the countries and provinces of Asia." Referring to similar documents issued by Conferences of English Baptist Missionaries in India, and E. B. Underhill, Esq., Secretary of the Baptist Missionary Society, then in India as a deputation, Dr. Mullens says, "A range of topics was discussed similar to that of the American brethren; and the result, as in their case, was embodied in reports by the missionaries, and letters by the deputation. They are also equally valuable. To the missionary in India, no works will give a more complete insight into the worth and working of all sorts of plans, than the nine sets of Papers and Letters contained in these volumes of the two Societies."

connected with the visit of the deputation to India should be ready for its consideration. Mr. Thompson arrived home in the following month, and Dr. Anderson in January. A special meeting of the Board was held in Albany, in March, 1856, as related in a previous chapter, to which the deputation presented a printed report in a pamphlet of about sixty pages, the leading object of which is thus described in the conclusion: —

A main object of this report, fathers and brethren, has been briefly to describe the more important adaptations of means, by our respected brethren in India, to the progressive demands of the work in the three older missions. You have seen the Ahmednuggur, Madura, and Ceylon missions successively in that more advanced stage of progress, when they were enabled to form centers of operation distinct from the stations, with that best of all spiritual germs — the church. Such churches you have seen organized, for the first time, in each of those missions, and furnished, also for the first time, with native pastors. As an important means to the same end, you have seen the way opened for commencing village stations in the Deccan of Western India, with resident missionaries, remote from the cities, thus providing for successive constellations of light and influence in that most interesting region. Next you have seen the schools subjected to modifications, to adapt them to this new position of the work. Men may be converted by preaching, without schools; but how, without them, can we build up and perpetuate churches and congregations? You have seen that one of the main inquiries in the Madura mission was, how to strengthen the large system of vernacular schools connected with the village congregations. It was to invigorate them, and through them the congregations, and thus to lead on to the gathering of village churches, that the boarding schools at four of the stations in that mission were to be progressively relinquished, and that more variety was to be imparted to the studies of the Seminary at Pasumalie. So in Ceylon, where the work of preparation had been elaborately performed, and had been much longer in progress, where were scores of native Christians ready to be formed into village churches, and educated natives for pastors, the Board has seen that the time had fully come for entering at once and earnestly into the only method of planting gospel institutions effectually in all parts of the Jaffna district. Going, then, as the mission did, for the establishment of village churches, it perceived the need of having Christian schools, to be under the especial care of those churches, and to look mainly to them for support. Without such, the churches could not live and grow. The Board will remember, that twenty Christian schools were instituted in Jaffna; while the heathen were not overlooked, an equal number having been provided for their children, besides the privilege of attending the Christian schools. Nor will it be forgotten that, among the reasons for discontinuing the English station schools, was their evident incompatibility with the success of the vernacular village schools. And it must have been seen, that the Batticotta Seminary could not meet the high spiritual demands upon it, in this new order of things, without some such thorough reconstruction as it received from the mission, even at the expense of a temporary suspension of its functions in order more effectually to secure that result; and also, that the Female Boarding School at Oodooville must needs be adapted in form and character to its correlative institution. Simplicity, order, economy, spirituality, are essential to the high prosperity of these and all other missions; and to the attainment of each of these great excellences the missions aimed in their late discussions, and not without success.

After a protracted discussion,—in which the deputation took little part, preferring to have the matter go to a committee, which should take time for correspondence with the missionaries,—a committee was appointed, consisting of thirteen members, to whom the whole case was referred; and they were to report at the next annual meeting of the Board. This committee was composed of the following persons:

Nathan S. S. Beman, D. D., Mark Hopkins, D. D., Leonard Bacon, D. D., David H. Riddle, D. D., Hon. Erastus Fairbanks, Hon. Linus Child, Benjamin C. Taylor, D. D., Horace Holden, Esq., Asa D. Smith, D. D., Hon. William Jessup, Richard T. Haines, Esq., Ray Palmer, D. D., and Philemon H. Fowler, D. D. In accordance not less with the wishes of the deputation than with the evident proprieties of the case, the Special Committee addressed a series of questions to each member of the missions that had been visited; and the same was also sent to the returned missionaries in this country, several of whom came before the committee. The annual meeting was delayed until the 28th of October, that the Special Committee might receive answers from all the missionaries before making up their report. This report, as printed, makes a pamphlet of fifty-nine pages. The following is their result, as regards the proceedings and influence of the deputation: —

"In regard to the late visit of the Deputation to the Eastern Missions, the Special Committee believe they have performed a great and needful work; that they have discharged their high trust as faithful, devoted men; that they ought to receive the cordial thanks of this Board; and that we may confidently hope, that a new spirit may pervade and animate our missions abroad, and a strong missionary impulse be given to our churches by this labor of love. It is true, some diversity of opinion exists in relation to missionary policy; but it is not a diversity which respects the *kind* of agencies to be employed in order to save the soul and evangelize the world, but such as respects the specific *forms* and relative *proportions* in which these agencies are to be used. And in looking over the whole missionary field, there is great unanimity even on this latter point."

The report has the names of all the committee appended, and was accepted by the Board at Newark, with no debate on any part relating to the proceedings of the deputation. It was, also,

"*Resolved*, That the Deputation to the Eastern Missions have performed a great and needful work; that they have discharged their high trust as faithful, devoted men; that they receive the cordial thanks of the Board; and that we may confidently hope, that a new spirit may pervade and animate our missions abroad, and a strong missionary impulse be given to our churches by this labor of love."

On the 2d of December following, the Chairman of the Prudential Committee, by direction of the Committee, reported the following Minute, which was unanimously adopted, viz.:—

In view of the proceedings of the Board at Utica, the Prudential Committee deemed it inexpedient to take any action on the doings of the deputation to India, or of the missions during their visit, until after the subject should have been acted upon by the Board, at their special meeting to be called for that purpose. After the appointment of the Special Committee by the Board at Albany, though the Prudential Committee early took occasion to satisfy their own minds as to the general correctness of those proceedings, and had an informal interchange of opinions on the subject, they abstained from all formal action upon the same; waiting the final action of the Board on the report of the Special Committee. But now that the Special Committee have made their report, and that the Board has passed upon it, sustaining the deputation and the missions, there is no reason why the Prudential Committee should longer abstain from the action, which, under ordinary circumstances, it would have been their duty to take, in the first instance, on the doings of the deputation and the missions. Now, therefore, in order to give a proper effect and influence to the reports which were adopted by the several missions in India and Turkey, during the visit of the deputation, it is

Resolved, 1. That, in the several instances where the deputation gave a formal sanction to the proceedings of the missions embodied in these reports, the Prudential Committee confirm their action.

2. That the Secretaries be instructed to report hereafter, as they shall find it convenient, the cases, in the proceedings of the India missions, which were reserved by the deputation for

the consideration of the Prudential Committee after their return home.

3. That the Prudential Committee approve of the proceedings of the Syria mission, embodied in the reports adopted during the visit of Dr. Anderson in the autumn of 1855.

4. That the reports adopted by a meeting at Constantinople of such missionaries as could conveniently assemble there during Dr. Anderson's visit, though not viewed as the action of the Armenian mission, and of course not binding on the mission, are regarded by the Prudential Committee as of much value, and are in general accordance with the views entertained by the Committee on the subjects discussed in the reports.

These occurrences resulted in much good. Attention was awakened to a subject but little understood, namely, the true policy of foreign missions. The Board, and still more the Special Committee, added largely to their stock of valuable information in respect to the working of missions, and to the principles underlying the whole enterprise. And by means of the religious newspapers, which were discussing the matter for a whole year, and by the report of the Special Committee, of which a large number of copies were circulated, a great amount of practical knowledge was widely diffused through the Christian community.

CHAPTER X.

LITERATURE OF THE BOARD AND OF ITS MISSIONS.

Missionary Literature a Necessity. — AT HOME. Sermons. — Periodicals. — Reports. — Missionary Tracts. — ABROAD. School Books. — Versions of the Scriptures. — Helps for understanding the Scriptures and their Application. — RESULTANT LITERATURE. Biographies. — Exploring Tours. — Works Historical, Descriptive, and on the Results of Missionary Experience.

A RELIGION must have a literature. Dealing with the deepest problems of philosophy, — existence, its ground and laws; good and evil, their nature, tendencies and results; with the principles, rules and motives which should govern all human action of body or of mind, — it must, in order to be a religion, have certain ideas, and must have forms of expression, more or less settled and uniform, for conveying them from one mind to another. The character of a religion must depend on the character of those ideas; and the best expression of them is indispensable to its most successful propagation.

The American Board, laboring to procure the intelligent, hearty and practical reception of truth on these great subjects by heathen minds, and calling the friends of truth and of human welfare to its aid, must of necessity produce a various and valuable literature in many languages. It must furnish to vast multitudes of intelligent Christians, the means of understanding and appreciating its labors; it must furnish to those for whose good it labors, the means of understanding and appreciating the truths to be taught; and, in prosecuting these labors, it could not fail incidentally to cause the development of many thoughts and the collection of much information which the civilized world would desire to possess.

Home Literature.

In commending its labors to those whose aid it might expect, the Board has resorted, from the first and extensively, to the literature of the pulpit. Forty-seven sermons before the Board at its annual meetings, twenty-six before auxiliary societies, thirteen at ordinations of missionaries, fourteen funeral sermons, and thirteen others on various subjects connected with the work, have been printed by the Board and others, and are in the library of the Board. Most of these are by men selected for their eminent fitness for the work. They present the work of missions, or parts of it, in more than a hundred different aspects—setting forth the scriptural authority for this form of Christian effort; the scriptural encouragement for engaging in it; the wretchedness of the heathen for the want of it; the spirit and modes in which it should be prosecuted; the traits of character developed in its prosecution; the indications of God's favor attending it; the value of results already secured; the certainty of its ultimate triumph; and numerous other topics, which sanctified genius has been able to seize upon and illustrate. They exhibit more than a hundred different styles of thought and of eloquence, and, in almost every case, of a high order, as may be seen by a single glance at the names of the preachers. Taken together, they form almost a complete encyclopedia of argument on subduing the world to Christian civilization and to its glorious Author.

Next to these discussions of principles, based on divine revelation, and of binding force prior to any teaching of experience, comes the record of facts, proving that the divine will is understood and successfully obeyed. These facts are spread out, mainly, in several periodicals.

The oldest and most important of these is the Missionary Herald, commenced in January, 1818, in connection with the Panoplist, and published by itself since January, 1819, in a monthly pamphlet of thirty-two pages, making, in its separate form, thirty-nine octavo volumes of three hundred and eighty-four pages. Its leading contents are, selections and compilations from the correspondence of missionaries; in other words, the accounts given by some hundreds of educated men, during about forty years, of their travels, labors, and observations in many countries, from Eastern Canada to Oregon; in Northern, Western, Southern and Eastern Africa; from Paris and Malta to the Caspian Sea and Ispahan; in India, the Malayan Archipelago, China, and the Islands of the Pacific; describing countries and climates, routes, means and modes of travel and transportation; tribes, races and nations; their characteristics, physical, mental and moral; their social condition and habits; their institutions of religion, education and government; their industrial pursuits, and the means of subsisting and preserving health among them. These and many other like things must be observed and described, not fully, but so far as they afford facilities or oppose obstacles to the great work, or modify the manner of its prosecution.

But all this is merely preliminary to the history of the work itself—the history of Christian civilization, its beginning and progress, in many nations, of a great diversity of character, and in a great variety of circumstances; not compiled by theorists, a thousand years afterward, from fragmentary notices that accident has preserved and time has spared, but carefully and minutely recorded at the time, by the very men who commenced and guided the upward movement. The details show by what efforts men of diverse characters and genius succeeded or failed in first gaining the confidence of communities as diverse as themselves; in awakening the desire for improvement, and securing interested attention to new ideas of human life and destiny; the multifarious workings of mind when imbruted by heathenism, and when misled by corrupt Christianity, both in seeking and in resisting Christian truth; the action of hierarchies and governments, half civilized and uncivilized, when disturbed by the advance of light into their dominions; how schools, where schools were wanting or worthless, have been started, conducted, modified according to circumstances, multiplied, made to grow into systems of popular education, leading on to the establishment of higher institutions, literary, scientific and professional; the Christian experience of individual converts, showing the inward struggles through which a multitude of minds, of various character and condition, have attained to the intelligent and cordial reception of Christian truth, and the resulting transformations of character; the planting and training of churches, in forms varying as the exigencies of each required, and their various degrees of success; the influence of advancing Christian light and morality on the action of governments, even to the extent of their peaceful reconstruction in better forms and on better principles; the transformation of society by the gradual adoption of the industry, the commerce, the arts, the comforts and the decencies of civilized Christian life. The men and women by whose labors all these things have been done, have described them from day to day as they occurred, that the Christian world might understand, appreciate and sustain their labors, and that minds competent to the task might suggest every possible improvement in the modes of conducting them. These accounts, either in the words of their authors, or carefully and skillfully condensed, fill the greater part of these thirty-nine octavo volumes; forming a library which has been and is studied with intense interest, not only by the prince of geographers, and other literary and scientific men, but by statesmen of the highest order of intellect, who have no sympathy with its religious spirit.

Parts of the same information, and other similar matter, but adapted to the use of those who have little leisure for reading, and of youth, have filled the volumes of the Day Spring and the Journal of Missions since January, 1842.

Annually, the Secretaries of the Board, under the direction of its Prudential Committee, prepare a careful summary of all the doings of the Board, foreign and domestic, of the labors of its missionaries and their results, and of the progress and condition of their work. This is laid before the Board at its annual meeting. The several parts are referred to appropriate committees, and after a rigid scrutiny by them, and, if need be, discussion and amendment by the Board itself, the whole is adopted and published as the Annual Report of the Board. The fifty Annual Reports, of perhaps two hundred octavo pages each on an average, contain therefore, in the form of annals, a carefully-prepared history of the operations of the Board and its missions, and of their results.

Copious as have been these regular periodical issues, they have been found insufficient to meet all exigencies. New questions, new situations of affairs, new subjects for discussion and appeal, spring up unexpectedly, or present themselves to the industrious observer of the missionary work, and demand attention. To meet these demands, missionary tracts have been issued from time to time, during the whole history of the Board, till the number of copies amounts to one million five hundred and eighty-two thousand eight hundred and seventy.

Such is the home literature of the Board, preliminary, preparatory, and subservient to its foreign labors.

Foreign Literature.

The foreign work of the Board consists, in a great measure, of the creation of a literature, or rather of many literatures, for the use and benefit of many peoples and tongues and nations, each adapted to the peculiar character and wants of those for whom it is designed.

Next to the oral proclamation of the gospel, the great work of a mission is, to enable and induce a people to read and understand, that they may believe and obey, the sacred Scriptures. In order to this, the people must have those Scriptures in their own language, and must be able to read; and in order to any thing more than very imperfect success, they must be furnished with the literary helps and mental cultivation necessary to an intelligent study of the Scriptures, and application of their doctrines to the conduct of their lives.

The literature created by a mission, then, must include provisions for elementary education, the Scriptures in the vernacular, and helps in understanding and applying them.

First in the order of time, after oral preaching, is providing the means of elementary education, and this, often, in languages that have no alphabet. In such case, the words of the language must first be learned by conversation with those who speak it. The words must then be analyzed into the simple sounds of which they are composed, and then a character must be selected or invented to represent each of those simple sounds. As almost every language has some sounds peculiar to itself, and as every person has peculiarities of utterance, and as an unlettered people has no recognized standard of correct pronunciation, the formation or adaptation of an alphabet is sometimes a very laborious task. It has, however, been done in four African languages, the Grebo, Mpongwe, Dikĕlĕ, and Zulu-Kaffir; in thirteen American, the Cherokee, Choctaw, Creek, Osage, Pawnee, Dakota, Ojibwa, Ottawa, Seneca, Abernaquis, and three in Oregon; in the Hawaiian, Marquesas, and one or two of the Micronesian languages; and in the Modern Nestorian and Dyak in Asia.

In all these languages, of course, the books necessary to teach the art of reading must be prepared and published. And in several other languages, having alphabets, some of them ancient, it has been found necessary to prepare or adopt, — commonly to prepare, — and to publish, books for instruction in spelling and reading; for example, the Seneca, in America; the Grebo, in Africa; the Modern Armenian, Armeno-Turkish, Hebrew-Spanish and Modern Greek, in Europe; the Arabic, Mahratta, Tamil, Siamese and Chinese, in Asia; making, with the former, some thirty or forty languages, in which it was necessary to furnish children and youth with proper means of learning to read. Where some of these languages were spoken, there were indeed schools, as in Greece, in which children were taught to read the words of the ancient language, without understanding it; but for years, primary schools in Modern

Greek depended on the "Alphabeterion," a primary school book of one hundred and thirty-two pages, of which the press at Malta and at Smyrna had furnished forty-two thousand copies before 1837. It has also been found necessary to the best progress of the work to publish grammars of the Modern Greek, Armenian, Arabic, Ancient and Modern Syriac, Hebrew, Tamil, Hawaiian, Dakota, Grebo, Mpongwe, and Zulu, and dictionaries, more or less complete, of the Armenian, Hebrew, Tamil, Chinese, Hawaiian, Grebo, Mpongwe, Zulu, and Dakota. A dictionary of the Modern Syriac, of about ten thousand words, has been prepared, but is not yet published. In nine of these languages, schools have been furnished with works on arithmetic; in three, on algebra; in three, on astronomy; in ten, on geography; and in six, on history; and others, doubtless, have escaped notice in this brief enumeration. In the higher studies, in some countries, much use has been made of books in the English language, some of which it has been necessary to prepare and publish.

This immense contribution to the school literature of the world has cost a great amount of labor; but it has been found indispensable to the raising up of intelligent Christian populations, capable of maintaining themselves permanently at the elevation to which missionary labors had raised them. The aid thus rendered to the sciences of comparative philology and ethnography, though merely one of the incidental results of these labors, has a value which only scholars in those departments can fully appreciate.

But all this is merely preparatory to the reading of the sacred Scriptures, that they may be understood, believed, and obeyed. That it may be of any religious use, these nations must be furnished with the Scriptures, each in its own spoken language. In some of these languages, as the Modern Greek, the Arabic, the Chinese, and some of the languages of India, versions already existed, of such character that they might be usefully circulated, but still needing careful revision. In others, new translations were indispensable.

In this latter class may be placed all those languages in which the creation of an alphabet was necessary. In some of these, the Scriptures have been published entire. In others, portions have been published, sufficient to guide the honest inquirer into the way of eternal life.

Of new translations into languages already having alphabets and versions of the Scriptures, perhaps the most important is the Arabic. As the Arabic is the language of the Koran, and therefore the sacred language of the whole Mohammedan world, it seemed a duty to furnish the millions who read that language with the Scriptures in a form that would command their respect, for both its literary and its mechanical execution. There had been for centuries two Arabic versions, both esteemed respectably good, and they had long been in print; but they failed to commend themselves to the taste of native Arabic scholars, and it was commonly supposed in Europe and America that the Mohammedans regarded the printing of sacred books as a profanation, and would never allow the Koran to be printed. This was found, on more perfect acquaintance with native readers of Arabic, to be a misapprehension. Their objection to printed books arose from the bad, unscholarly appearance of the letters, and not from the manner in which they were produced. With great labor and patient research, numerous specimens of approved Arabic calligraphy were collected, the letters in the best of them were taken as models, and types were made, and books were printed, acceptable to the critical taste of literary Arabs. The new type was not only used by the mission at Beirût, but was immediately adopted by the most respectable publishers in Europe. By this achievement, the art of printing was first made practically available, to any considerable extent, to the nations whose native or sacred language is the Arabic.

It was also found that the old Arabic versions of the Scriptures were far from being satisfactory, either in idiomatic elegance of style or accuracy of rendering, and that a new translation was indispensable. This, in a language having such an extensive and cultivated literature as the Arabic, was no ordinary task; but it must be accomplished. Besides the best dictionaries, grammars and other philological helps known in Europe, others, some of them very extensive, the work of Arab scholars, still in manuscript, were collected. Native linguists, competent and cordially interested in the work, were engaged as assistants. After years of intense labor, the New Testament has been translated, printed, and put in circulation, and the publication of the Old Testament is far advanced. This gives the New Testament now, and will give the whole Bible soon, in a suitable and acceptable form, to all who read the Arabic language, and through them to all who speak it, and in an important sense to the whole Moslem population, among whom the language of the Koran is sacred and understood by their literary men — a population extending from Morocco and Timbuctû on the west, beyond Calcutta on the east, and numbering at least one hundred and twenty millions.

An examination of the proper tables will show to what peoples, and nations, and languages, in various regions of the earth, the Board has furnished the Holy Scriptures, what have been furnished with parts of them, and in what abundance each has been supplied.

It will be noticed that a work very similar to that done for the readers of Arabic, has been done in the Modern Syriac, spoken by the Nestorians. For the Armenians, acceptable printing could be done at an Armeno-Catholic convent near Venice; but the convent kept the type for its own exclusive use. Type equally good, from the foundery of the Board at Smyrna, broke up that monopoly, and naturalized good printing among the Armenians.

The helps which the Board has furnished for understanding and applying the Scriptures, besides what it has furnished in school books, are mostly such books and tracts as are used in the more enlightened parts of Protestant Christendom, to impart doctrinal knowledge and promote practical piety and Christian morality. A large part of them are translations of well-approved English works. Others are English works translated and modified, or works originally written to meet some peculiar wants of the people for whom they are published. The Pilgrim's Progress and the Saints' Everlasting Rest speak the language of universal Christianity, and are appropriate every where. Tracts on opium-smoking are needed in China and Siam. Where practical and devotional works have their proper effect, the mind is put on the right road to the understanding of the Scriptures, and of all literature and science. From minds thus moved flow living waters. David Malo writes Hawaiian Tracts. Leang Afa utters, in Chinese, "Good Words, to admonish the Age." Meshakah discusses skepticism in Arabic, in a style worthy to be printed and circulated in Mount Lebanon, and translated and published in the Bibliotheca Sacra.

In attempting to speak particularly of the extent and value of this department of the literature of the Board, time and space would fail. They must be estimated from a consideration of the appropriate tables.

Resultant Literature.

There is, also, what may be called the resultant literature of the Board, consisting of works for which its operations have afforded materials, inducements and facilities. Among these, the first place seems due to Missionary Biography.

Memoirs have been published of all the deceased Secretaries of the Board — of Worcester, Evarts, Cornelius and Armstrong in volumes, and of Wisner in the Herald. The first and second, taken together, give, perhaps, the most complete account any where to be found of the religious condition and history of New England during the period in which the Board was formed — of the influences which led to its formation, and of the struggles by which, and the difficulties through which, it grew to its maturity. Besides Samuel J. Mills, whose close connection with the origin of the Board renders it proper to include him, and besides numerous biographical sketches in the Herald and Journal, biographies have been published, nearly all in separate volumes, of seventeen male and eleven female missionaries, all of them persons of good education, and several of them of superior mental power, giving accounts of their labors, travels and observations in the Islands of the Pacific, in China, Siam, the Malayan Archipelago, India, Persia, Eastern and Western Turkey, Syria, Palestine, Egypt and Greece, besides what they did and witnessed in lands more civilized and Christian.

To these should be added several memoirs of children of missionaries, born and educated on missionary ground, and of native converts — among the most important of which, for the knowledge they incidentally afford of the countries and peoples to which they relate, are those of Catharine Brown, the Cherokee, of Obookiah and "Blind Bartimeus," the Sandwich Islanders, and of Babajee, the converted Brahmin.

Of the many exploring tours preparatory to the establishment of missions, the accounts, for the most part, have been published only in the Missionary Herald; but three have resulted in the publication of volumes which demand particular notice.

In 1829, Grecian independence having just been achieved, the Morea and Greek Islands were explored by the Rev. Rufus Anderson, Assistant Secretary of the Board, and the Rev. Eli Smith, one of its missionaries. Mr. Anderson, on his return, published a volume, which received honorable notice from the Royal Geographical Society in London as a valuable and much needed contribution to geographical science.

The "Researches of the Rev. Eli Smith and Rev. H. G. O. Dwight in Armenia, including a Journey through Asia Minor and into Georgia and Persia, with a Visit to the Nestorian and Chaldean Christians of Oroomiah and Salmas," was published, in two volumes, in 1833. It was soon reprinted in London, and highly commended in some of the leading English reviews.

Rev. Samuel Parker's "Exploring Tour beyond the Rocky Mountains," made, under the direction of the Board, in 1835,

1836 and 1837, brought to light no field for a great and successful mission; but it added much to the science of geography, and is remarkable as having first made known a practicable route for a railroad from the Mississippi to the Pacific.

Kindred to these are about twenty works giving general information collected by their authors during their missionary labors. Among the more important of these is the Rev. Hiram Bingham's "Residence of Twenty-one Years in the Sandwich Islands," which gives "the civil, religious and political history of those Islands," in six hundred and sixteen octavo pages. The Rev. Justin Perkins has given an account of his "Residence of Eight Years in Persia," among the Nestorians and Mohammedans, in five hundred and twelve octavo pages. Both of these include particular accounts of the missions with which their authors were connected. The Rev. J. L. Wilson has condensed into a small duodecimo volume, the well-matured results of his observations and inquiries during eighteen years of missionary labor in Western Africa. Williams's "Middle Kingdom," in twelve hundred and four pages, is probably the best account ever published of the Chinese Empire as it had been and was in 1848. "India, Ancient and Modern," has been described, in six hundred and eighteen octavo pages, by Rev. D. O. Allen, who had been twenty-five years a missionary. For the same number of years the Rev. W. M. Thompson had been a missionary in Syria and Palestine when he published, in two volumes, — eleven hundred and seventy-one pages, — "The Land and the Book; or, Biblical Illustrations, drawn from the Manners and Customs, the Scenes and Scenery, of the Holy Land."

And here it is not improper to claim, as belonging, in an important degree, to this department of the literature of the Board, the great modern authority on the geography of Palestine, Robinson's "Biblical Researches." Without the preparations made by the mission at Beirût, and especially by the Rev. Eli Smith, who accompanied Dr. Robinson in his explorations, such a work would have been impossible.

To a great extent, the present Arabic names of places mentioned in the Bible are the old Hebrew names, modified according to certain rules which Mr. Smith perfectly understood. With the assistance of well-informed natives, he had prepared a complete list of all the small districts into which Palestine is divided, with their several locations, and lists, nearly perfect, of all the names of places in each of these districts. By means of these lists, every day's work could be planned to the best advantage, as the travelers knew what they could search for with any hope of success, and very nearly where to search for it. Nor was it a slight advantage, that Mr. Smith was perfectly familiar with the language, character, and habits of the people among whom these explorations were to be made, whose aid they often needed, and whose acquiescence in their proceedings was always necessary; and that he was personally known and esteemed by many of them, and especially by those whose friendly influence was most important. Dr. Robinson, in his published "Researches," has fully acknowledged the value of this assistance; but it requires a better understanding of the circumstances than many readers possess, fully to appreciate the amount of his acknowledgment.

The "History of the American Board of Commissioners for Foreign Missions, compiled chiefly from published and unpublished Documents of the Board,"* was published in four hundred and fifty-two octavo pages in 1842, and brought down the history of the Board and its missions to the previous year.

In prosecuting the missionary work for so many years, in so many countries, so distant and diverse, and by the labors of so many educated, thinking men, a great amount of experience must be accumulated; modes of operation, the best that could be devised at first, will be found capable of improvement, or the progress of the work will have made them inappropriate; differences of opinion as to the best mode of

* By the writer of this chapter.

proceeding will show themselves, and there must be, occasionally, reconsiderations and revisions of system and method, in the light of all that experience. So it has been in respect to several missions of the Board; especially in the Sandwich Islands, in the Turkish Empire, and in India. The results of such revisions, when published, are of special value to Missionaries and the conductors of missionary societies. Of this class of publications, the Report of the Deputation to the Missions in India, in 1856, and the documents connected with it, are the most important in the history of the Board, and perhaps in the whole history of modern missions.

A glance at the lists of publications, in the appropriate tables, will show, and a careful examination will show more clearly, in proportion to its carefulness, that an appreciative review of the literature of the Board and of its missions, doing justice to each of the numerous works which it comprises, would fill volumes, and require years of labor. Nothing of that kind, therefore, has been attempted here. Perhaps, however, this brief and imperfect classification may aid the thoughtful in forming some estimate of its extent, its variety, and its value.

CHAPTER XI.

THE FIELD AND THE WORK AT THE CLOSE OF THE HALF-CENTURY.

Fifty Years ago. — The Field and Work at the Present Time. — Knowledge of the World and its Inhabitants. — Political Ascendency of Protestant Christianity. — General Acknowledgment of Missions as a Duty. — Extent of Missionary Organizations. — Success of Missions. — Islands of the Pacific. — Africa. — West Indies. — Eastern Asia. — Madagascar. — Tahiti. — Sandwich Islands. — Turkey. — Nestorians. — India. — Distribution of the Holy Scriptures. — Estimated Pecuniary Value of the Missionary Enterprise. — The existing Missions will fill the Earth by their Growth. — The Call to the People of God.

"SOME effort of attention is necessary," says Dr. Leonard Bacon, "to any just view of what the condition of the world was, and what, on any merely human calculation of probabilities, were the prospects of the Christian religion in this world, fifty years ago. The great wars, which had begun in the first French revolution, nearly twenty years before, were still agitating all European Christendom; and, only two years later, the United States were drawn into that vortex. Political liberty was almost annihilated on the continent of Europe, the despotism of the first Napoleon being then at its hight. In France, in Switzerland, in every country on that continent, evangelical religion was, to human view, almost extinct; no general or effective reaction having taken place against the tendencies to mere formalism, and to unbelief, which had so widely characterized the preceding century. Our own country had hardly begun to be recognized as a power among the nations; the present form of our federal government had been in existence only twenty-one years, and only twenty-seven years had passed since the close of our revolutionary war. Outside of Christendom there was no recognized preparation, and hardly a visible opening, for the spread of the gospel.

The great Mohammedan empire of Turkey had only ceased to be terrible to Christian nations; it had not begun to fall, or to be dismembered; nor had any change taken place, either in the spirit and policy of its rulers, or in the character of its people. The East Indian empire, which a corporation of British traders had established, with its center at Calcutta, was a recent thing, and was, in fact, as completely an anti-Christian power, and as jealous of all Christian propagandism, as that of the Mogul emperors had been, when they reigned in absolute dominion at Delhi. China, like Japan, was closed and guarded against Christianity in every form. Africa, except along its ravaged and pestilential coast, was a continent of mystery, hardly visited, save by the traders in slaves; for even in the United States, whose government was earlier than that of any other country in prohibiting the slave trade, the importation of slaves from Africa had been unlawful only two years. On our own frontier, the pagan savage, who had learned nothing from civilization but its vices, and had been enriched by it only with new implements and means of destruction, was still encamped in Ohio, was hunting the buffalo on all the prairies, and his canoe had not begun to be displaced by the raft and the flat-boat on the waters of the Upper Mississippi. What is now our western coast was hardly known to commerce; California was one of the remotest and least valued possessions of Spain, and no eye of avarice had caught the sparkle of its golden sand. The first overland journey up to the sources of the Mississippi, and down along the leaping waters of the Columbia to the Pacific, had just been accomplished at the expense of our national government. At that time, the entire census of the United States included less than one fourth of the population which will be counted in the census of the present year, and the capability of the wealth which has now been realized on this continent had never been estimated. To draw out a full comparison of the civilized world as it then was, with the civilized world as it now is, both in itself and in its relations to what lies beyond the realm of civilization, would require a volume; but it may help us to conceive the difference, if we remember that then the scientific law or principle, on which the electric telegraph depends, had not been discovered or conjectured; that the idea of railways was, at the most, no more than a vague and visionary thought; and that all the steamboats that had ever been successfully constructed — two or three in number — were creeping on the Hudson and the Delaware at the rate of perhaps five miles an hour.

"The spirit that prays for the coming of God's kingdom in all the earth," continues this writer, "and that longs to preach the gospel to every creature, has never wholly slumbered in any Christian land; for it is inseparable from a living Christianity every where. From the days of the apostolic Eliot, who was at once the pastor of the church at Roxbury and the laborious missionary to Indians within ten miles of his own door, the saintly succession of evangelists among the heathen has never failed from the churches of New England. But prior to 1810, the spirit of evangelism in the American churches had 'lacked opportunity' for full manifestation and development. In Connecticut, there was a missionary society, which was the organ of all the Congregational churches in the State, and which, though first and chiefly occupied with missions to the new settlements, had once, for a short time, attempted a mission among the Indians of the far north-west. A Connecticut Bible Society was instituted in 1809, to promote the distribution of the Scriptures. In Massachusetts, and in two or three other States, similar institutions existed for missions, especially to the new settlements, and for aiding in the supply of Bibles; but, as lately as fifty years ago, the idea of a widely-extended coöperation for spreading the knowledge of Christ, either abroad or at home, had never been shaped into a plan. In some other countries, and especially in free and Protestant Great Britain, the missionary spirit was waking up, and was organizing institutions of various names and forms for sending the gospel through the world. For more than a century there had been in the Church of England a Society for Propagating the Gospel in Foreign Parts, which employed its resources chiefly in sending missionaries into the British colonies; among which the New England colonies, and especially Connecticut, though better provided with the means of religious instruction than England itself had ever been, were liberally cared for, till they were separated from the mother country. The Moravians, few and feeble, but full of Christian zeal, had been at work for almost eighty years — a silent but constant rebuke to the Christian world. The English Wesleyans, at an early day in their history, had begun to do something for the conversion of the slaves in the West Indies. In 1792, Carey and others had brought about the formation of a Missionary Society for the Baptists in England. Three years later, the London Missionary Society came into being on a liberal basis of coöperation, though chiefly sustained by Congregationalists, or, as they were then called in England, Independents. The Church Missionary Society, sustained and controlled by the evangelical party in the Church of England, was instituted under the name of the Society for Missions to Africa and the East, in 1801 — nine years before our Board of Missions offered itself to the American churches as their almoner and servant in the foreign missionary work. In 1810, there were a few English and Scotch missionaries in India; a few were laboring in the British African colony of Sierra Leone, and a larger number in Southern Africa. The London Society had its missions in Tahiti and the Society Islands; and Morrison, in their service, had set himself down before the gates of China, patiently striving to master the language of that great empire, that it might learn to tell the story of redemption. There were missionaries among the slaves in various West Indian colonies. The Moravians had their stations in Greenland and Labrador, a few among the North American Indians, and a few elsewhere — few when compared with the vastness of the field, but many when compared with the weakness and the poverty of the body by which they were sustained. Nothing was done or attempted by the American churches; a little more than a beginning had been made by our British kindred in the work of spreading the gospel through the world.

"We may say, then, that fifty years ago, when the foreign missionary work of the American churches had not been begun, the entire movement of these modern times for the evangelization and conversion of the world was only in its earliest stage of progress. Every where that was the day of small things, in comparison with what we see to-day." *

It should be added to this well-drawn statement, that the foreign missionary was scarcely recognized as entitled, when abroad in his distant field, to that protection which the merchant and traveler might lawfully demand; nor was his vocation then recognized as among the legally authorized pursuits of life. Even in the Christian Church, notwithstanding the parting injunction of its ascending Lord, to PREACH THE GOSPEL TO EVERY CREATURE, the work of missions was but partially acknowledged as among the standing Christian duties. It may be that those who shall look back to the present time from the close of the second half-century, will regard the period we are now commemorating as itself comparatively a day of small things. May they have reason so to do. But contrasting the present with our own past, we are constrained to say, What hath God wrought! A brief survey will now be taken of the field, and of the work, as they are at the present time.

Many things, besides the sending forth of heralds of the cross, and the publication of the gospel, are indispensable to the conversion of the world. Though merely preparatory to it, they are nevertheless essential, and therefore a part of the work, and of God's plan and providence for its accomplishment. Among them may be mentioned, —

1. *A Knowledge of the Geography of the Earth.* — How little our fathers knew of Africa, of Central Asia, India, and China, and of the islands of the sea! But the entire world, with the exception of some few portions, and those hastening

* New Englander, 1860, p. 712.

to the light, is now well known. So far as the world's conversion involves a knowledge of its surface, that part of the enterprise is far advanced toward completion.

2. *A Knowledge of the Social and Religious Condition of Mankind.*—What more needs to be learned concerning the governments, manners, customs, habits, and religions of our race? What more needs to be done in collecting and recording facts for awakening the sympathies and enterprise of the Christian Church? This part of the work has been substantially accomplished. When the Board sent forth its first missionaries, it was impossible to say what particular field they should occupy. The Prudential Committee could now easily assign definite locations to many scores of new missionaries.

3. *The Political Ascendency of Protestant Christianity.*—India, with its hundred and fifty millions, bows to Protestant rule; and that has created a political necessity for throwing a protecting shield over evangelical missionaries in Birmah, China, Persia, and Turkey. Every war in Asia, for the past half-century, has been fulfilling the prophecy, that the valleys shall be exalted, and the mountains and hills made low, the crooked made straight, and the rough places plain. The apocalyptic angel has hold upon "the dragon, that old serpent, which is the Devil and Satan." The great anti-Christian powers are acting under mighty restraints. We see it in the Pacific, in China, in India, and in Turkey. And these providential influences are more and more evidently preparing the way for Christ's progress, with his gospel, through the unevangelized nations. Just at the close of the half-century, we saw the representatives of the four great powers of Christendom assembled in China, and uniting in the declaration that the Christian missionary ought to receive the respect, confidence, and protection of all governments, and treating upon this basis with a third part of the heathen world for the toleration and safety of these gospel messengers and of their converts.*

4. *A General Acknowledgment by Evangelical Protestant*

* Missionary Herald for 1858, p. 364.

Churches of the Duty to propagate the Gospel among all Nations. — This appears, indeed, in many Christians, and in many churches, to be little more than the result of an intellectual conviction, and so is yet but feebly operative. Though it be really as much a duty to propagate the gospel, as it is to attend on public worship, or at the Lord's table, yet comparatively few Christians take this view; nor do pastors often press the duty thus upon their people. But the diffusion of even a mere intellectual conviction of the claims of foreign missions, is a great point gained; and this part of the work is in a good measure accomplished.

5. *The Extent of Organization for performing the Work.* — What are called voluntary associations for religious purposes, in distinction from local churches, are not a new thing. They have existed from an early period. Through them the gospel has ever been propagated by the Church beyond the influence of its own immediate pastors. Monasteries were voluntary societies; and so were the different orders of monks. It was by means of such associations that Christianity was propagated among our ancestors, and over Europe. These are the Papal forms of missionary societies and missions.

The Protestant form is what we see in Missionary, Bible, Tract, and other kindred societies; not restricted to ecclesiastics, nor to any one profession; combining all classes; embracing the masses of the people; free, open, responsible. They are associations formed by the contributors of the funds; not so much the American Board, not so much the Board of the General Assembly, as individuals, churches, congregations, freely acting together, through such agencies, for a common object.

This free, open, responsible, Protestant form of association, embracing both sexes, and all classes and ages, — the masses of the people, — is peculiar to modern times. It could not have been worked, could not have existed, even, with sufficient energy for the conversion of the world, without facilities for intercommunication among the nations, civil and religious liberty, extended habits of reading, and a wide-spread intelligence.

The success which has attended the missions, is all that is needful to animate to greater zeal in this good work. Dr. Joseph Mullens, of Calcutta, who has given great attention to this subject, spoke thus at the closing session of the late Liverpool Missionary Conference: —

"What a glorious position do we occupy, compared with that in which the fathers and founders of our missionary societies stood when they commenced the work, only a few years ago! Our modern missions are only sixty years old, and already we see the face of the wide world rapidly changing under their mighty influence. I doubt if a single convert had been made through those labors before the year 1800. Dr. Carey had gone to India; his few brethren had joined him, and they had settled at Serampore as the center of their labors. A few of our brethren had sailed for the South Sea Islands. There were one or two missionaries in Africa, one or two in the West Indies, and the rest of the world was an awful blank. But now we look abroad upon the earth, and, without reckoning the work carried on in our English colonies, we see at this moment sixteen hundred foreign missionaries from Europe and America, laboring in heathen countries, and in many languages. As one result of our work, we have already gathered two hundred thousand communicants, in many thousands of native churches, now sitting beneath the banner of the gospel, rejoicing in Sabbath ordinances, and all the blessed privileges that cluster round the gospel of Christ. Our work began amidst the apathy of friends, and the loudest obloquy on the part of our enemies. Society in England was thoroughly devoted to worldliness, and steeped in the most shameless wickedness and vice. French infidelity, the great product of the revolution, was all the rage among the so-called thinkers of the day, an infidelity which found its way to our colonies, and to the English settlements in India, and which there, as elsewhere, brought forth its bitter fruit. But just when the enemy had come in like a flood, the Spirit of the Lord lifted up a standard against him; and now, thanks be to God, that glorious standard has been lifted high, and all branches of the Christian Church, throwing aside their doubts and casting away their apathy, are delighted to enlist in its service, and to go forth under the great Captain of our salvation, conquering and to conquer in his name.

"We go to Africa; and where, at the beginning of this century, the Hottentot, and Fingoe, and Kaffir were shot down without mercy, there we find a people, one hundred thousand in number, saved from destruction, brought to Christ, and adorning the doctrine of the Saviour, whom their fathers never knew. We go to the negro settlements in the West Indies. How many thousands there have become Christians, redeemed not only from the slavery of earth, but from the slavery of sin! They who, only thirty years ago, were sold in the open market, have proved the most liberal supporters of gospel schemes that the modern Church has known, and were the first converts to maintain ministers of their own. Only seventeen years ago, the various ports of China were open to gospel teaching for the first time; and now we see in those ports no less than eighty Protestant missionaries, of many Churches, working for Christ. Already, in the course of those seventeen years, they have been permitted to gather into their churches some fourteen hundred communicants. We pass on to Birmah; and there we find, rejoicing in the light and liberty of the truth, many thousands of Karens; every one of whom, thirty years ago, was entirely ignorant of its very existence. There they are, meeting like ourselves on the Sabbath; working like ourselves for their ignorant brethren; supporting their pastors with the most active and self-denying zeal; contemplating the destitution of their heathen countrymen with compassion; and sending forth one and another of their brethren, with their lives in their hands, to preach Christ among the barbarous tribes still living in the mountains and the dense jungles of their own wild land. We pass on to India; and again we see, in several provinces of that extended empire, churches and Christians gathered, and the foundations of a great work in the future, laid by the hand of missionaries, who have been working there for many years. Obstacles to our entrance, to our permanent residence, to our safety in the country, have all passed away; and, blessed be God, after the appalling history of the recent mutiny, we rejoice to know that India has found not only order and peace, not only the services of faithful missionaries within her own borders, but has at last found a place, deep and firmly fixed, in the hearts of our brethren at home; and we feel sure that, when the claims of that mighty continent are faithfully pressed upon them, our voice will be heard, and a hearty response given to our appeal. And let us not forget the successful toil of our brethren in Turkey, to revive the decayed Churches, and to grapple with Mohammedan error at its very heart.

"Not only may we rejoice in these great successes, but, with all my missionary brethren here present, I cheerfully acknowledge, that in securing them, we have been largely indebted to our native brethren, working side by side with us in these fields of labor. We were told in very affecting terms, by Dr. Tidman, the other day, to look at the poor Island of Madagascar. More than twenty years ago the English missionaries were driven from that island by the unrighteous queen, and scarcely fifty native Christians were left behind. They possessed but very small portions of the word of God, some little tracts, and a few hymns. They have been bitterly and unrelentingly persecuted, with satanic cunning and satanic hate. They have been fined, imprisoned, degraded, and made slaves; they have been poisoned by the tangena water; they have been speared to death; they have been cast over lofty precipices; they have been burned at the stake, while the glorious rainbow arched the heavens and inspired them with more than mortal joy. They have given more than a hundred martyrs to the Church of Christ; but are far from being rooted out of the land. While, twenty years ago, when the persecution began, there were not fifty Christians on the island, it is believed that there are now at least five thousand; all of whom have been raised up by the special blessing of the divine Spirit upon the teachings of native agents and the secret study of God's holy word.

"We pass away to the Island of Tahiti; and there we see that, whilst French Popery has endeavored to exert its influence, and to present its blandishments to those who were despised as the poor and ignorant natives of the country, they have adhered most faithfully to their Protestant religion. We find that when the missionaries were compelled to leave the country, their own native pastors came forward; received from heaven all the grace ever promised to Christ's children in the time of need; and at this hour, in spite of French Popery, and in spite of French brandy, the members of the Tahitian churches are more numerous than when the missionaries were compelled to leave them." *

Richard H. Dana, Esq., a respected member of the Episcopal Church, and of the Boston bar, after being two months at the Sandwich Islands in the year 1860, thus speaks of the value of the missionary work on those Islands: —

"It is no small thing to say of the missionaries of the American Board, that in less than forty years they have taught this whole people to read and to write, to cipher and to sew. They have given them an alphabet, grammar, and dictionary; preserved their language from extinction; given it a literature, and translated into it the Bible and works of devotion, science, and entertainment, etc., etc. They have established schools, reared up native teachers, and so pressed their work that now the proportion of inhabitants who can read is greater than in New England. And whereas they found these islanders a nation of half-naked savages, living in the surf and on the sand, eating raw fish, fighting among themselves, tyrannized over by feudal chiefs, and abandoned to sensuality, they now see them decently clothed, recognizing the law of marriage, knowing something of accounts, going to school and public worship with more regularity than the people do at home, and the more elevated of them taking part in conducting the affairs of the constitutional monarchy under which they live,

* Missionary Conference at Liverpool, p. 331.

holding seats on the judicial bench and in the legislative chambers, and filling posts in the local magistracies."

The missions of the American Board in Turkey require a more particular notice than they have yet received in our survey of the field and the work at the close of our half-century; and here we can not do better than to quote again from Dr. Bacon.

"Still more important in respect to the progress of civilization," says Dr. Bacon, "are the results which are beginning to be developed in Turkey. Thirty years ago, all the Protestantism within the limits of the Turkish empire was in the souls of not more than ten earnest inquirers after truth and duty, who had rejected the superstitious doctrines and practices of the nominally Christian communities in which they were born, and from which they had not seceded. To-day the Protestantism of Turkey, profoundly interesting in a religious view, and regarded with wondering thankfulness by evangelical Christians every where, has already become a political fact of great significance. Not only is it recognized by alarmed and jealous ecclesiastics, Armenian, Greek, and Papal, combining to maintain their several hierarchies, — it has long been known as a stubborn fact in the deliberations of the Sublime Porte; it is already an element in the international diplomacy of Europe. There are now in Turkey more than forty evangelical churches, including nearly thirteen hundred communicants. The Protestant population connected with these churches, attending upon their worship, and professing to acknowledge theirs as the true Christianity, is counted by thousands, and is continually increasing. These Protestant churches, formed and guided by our missionaries, have obtained from the government, not merely a promise that their existence shall be winked at, but a legal standing and a recognized place among the distinct communities that constitute the empire. Turkish Protestantism has its charter of incorporation as a civil community, its own internal government, its civil chief and representative at the imperial metropolis. In an empire which consists of many distinct nations, dispersed and interspersed through various provinces,—religious and ecclesiastical connection, rather than country or community of origin or of speech, being the essence of nationality,—the native Protestantism, that had no existence till within the last few years, has become a nation. And among those nationalities, it is distinguished by two characteristics equally American and Christian. First, in that internal self-government which is its chartered privilege, it is purely republican. Its local officers are chosen by popular election, each local community being (like the inhabitants of a New England town, though with far less of personal liberty) a municipal democracy. Its civil chief and his official council at Constantinople are chosen by the united suffrages of all the local communities throughout the empire. Thus Protestantism in Turkey is an organized and chartered republic, with limited powers, under the sovereignty of the Sultan; while in all that empire there is no other rudiment or germ of republicanism. The second characteristic is, that by the Protestants in Turkey, the distinction between church and state is clearly drawn and persistently maintained. Every other nationality is recognized and governed simply as a national church, through its ecclesiastical officers, its patriarch or metropolitan bishop being the organ of communication between the community and the imperial government.

"These two peculiarities of the Protestant organization are not without a marked effect on the character and position of the Protestants as a body, and the influence of the unique institution is beginning to be felt in other communities. This Protestantism,—or, as we might say, this Americanism,—with its internal democracy, civil and religious, and with its careful and palpable separation of secular offices from ecclesiastical functions, is the most vital and growing thing in Turkey. To its converts from the old Monophysite communion of the Armenian nation, from the Jacobite Syrian Church, from the Greek Church, and from the various Papal sects, it is now adding converts from Islamism. The spirit of inquiry concerning

52

this reformed Christianity, that abhors idolatry, and that rests on no other authority than the Holy Scriptures, is manifesting itself in every direction. Nothing but the embarrassment of the Board, with its limited resources, and with its burden of indebtedness caused by the successes in that field, seems to prevent an almost indefinite expansion of the work. The missions in Turkey have become in some respects without a parallel among the missionary enterprises of the age. No other mission opens such prospects. In none is the crisis so imminent. In none are such results dependent on the question of seizing or neglecting the present opportunity. More than one third of all the annual expenditure of the Board has been concentrated there, and twice as much might be expended there to advantage. If those who make the Board their almoner fail not in the exigency, there is good reason for the confidence that in a few years more, unless some great catastrophe shall intervene, the Protestantism of Turkey will be able to provide for itself." *

The Nestorians are partly in Turkey, partly in Persia. A spiritual reformation is in progress among them; though it has been retarded by the extreme ignorance and poverty of the people, by an unprincipled hierarchy, an oppressive government, and the wiles of Popery. So many Nestorian priests have become "obedient to the faith," that the missionaries have felt encouraged to labor for a spiritual reform, without radical ecclesiastical changes. The truly pious Nestorians are being gradually drawn together, under the force of circumstances, for the simple observance of the Lord's Supper, for Christian fellowship, for mutual watch and care, for securing an edifying ministry and pastoral oversight. Thus a reformed church seems to be actually growing up, with an appropriate ministry, ritual, and worship. Among a people so few in number, so poor and oppressed as the Nestorians, surrounded by enemies, in the heart of Asia, it remains to be seen whether

* New Englander, 1860, p. 721.

this evangelical community can live and flourish. If it prove indeed a part of the true Church, though it be but a small flock in the wilderness, the Good Shepherd may go before it, and guard it from every danger. Perhaps it really is in no more need of his grace and power, than is every other portion of the Church in this depraved and hostile world. Certainly the Nestorians have an imperishable missionary history. The fruits of their missions in Central and Eastern Asia, existed for more than a thousand years. From the fifth to the ninth centuries, they had schools at Edessa, Nisibis, Seleucia, Dorkena, Bagdad, and elsewhere in Assyria and Persia. They occupied the region which forms the modern kingdom of Persia, in all parts of which they had churches. They were numerous in Armenia, Mesopotamia, and Arabia. They had churches in Syria, in the Island of Cyprus, and among the mountains of Malabar in India. They had numerous churches in the vast regions of Tartary, from the Caspian Sea to Mount Imaus, and beyond, through the greater part of what is now known as Chinese Tartary, and even in China itself. It would seem that such a people, now revisited and revived by a purer gospel than they once propagated with so much zeal and success, had yet an evangelical work to perform in the vast and benighted regions of Central Asia. It will be for those, on whom it shall devolve to investigate and record the missionary developments of the next half-century, to state the results, as yet imperfectly unfolded, of this mission of the American Board to the Nestorians.

Of the fields that are occupied by the Board still further east, — the Mahratta and Tamil, — it may suffice to say, that they are among the best in India. The people are accessible; the government is tolerant, and reasonably protective; there is freedom to sow, and security in reaping, and promise of an ample harvest in due season.

Auxiliary to these great movements of the age for the universal propagation of the gospel, are the efforts for multiplying versions and copies of the sacred Scriptures, and for distributing them, in the different languages of the world. In the first fifty years of the British and Foreign Bible Society, from 1804 to 1854, nearly twenty-eight millions of copies of the Scriptures were distributed, in whole or in integral portions, in connection with the labors of that Society; and above twenty millions more were distributed by kindred institutions in different parts of the world; making a total of nearly fifty millions. These were in more than one hundred and fifty different languages or dialects, in one hundred and twenty-five of which no portion of the sacred volume had previously appeared in print.*

It is not known that an attempt has ever been made to affix a pecuniary valuation to this mighty system of means for the spiritual renovation of the heathen world. It is clear, indeed, that some of its results will not submit to human valuation. Such are the many thousand converts, who have been received into the Christian Church. Such are the ideas imparted to the understanding; the impressions made upon the conscience and heart; the intellectual and religious influences exerted upon the heathen. The precious metals of all the mines of the world would not express their value; for the world itself is of no account in comparison with a single soul. But there is an aspect, in which a specific value may be assigned to the work. Regarding it as an enterprise, a business, a system of means and agencies, there is no more impropriety in an inquiry as to its value, than there is as to the value of any other enterprise of man. What, we may ask, is the value of these organized agencies, at home and abroad? Were there a mart for the sale and purchase of such commodities, what might be the estimate put upon this vast system of means and agencies? In other words, what would it cost to reproduce the system, with all its means for direct action and reaction in the Christian and heathen world?

* History of the British and Foreign Bible Society, by Rev. George Brown, 1859, vol. ii. p. 487.

We shall venture to suggest a conjectural answer in respect to the system under the care of the American Board. The aggregate expenditure for these missions has exceeded eight and a half millions of dollars. The most valuable results of this expenditure, through the grace of God,—namely, the salvation of souls,—must, for the reasons already mentioned, be left entirely out of the account. But the system of agencies is a thing distinct from its results. It involves property, in the common sense — buildings in different parts of the world, printing establishments, libraries, apparatus, etc. And there are the home organizations: the Board, with its thousands of members; the Prudential Committee and executive officers, with a large and valuable experience; the agencies; a vast organism of auxiliaries, associations, collectors, annual sermons and reports; widely-circulated periodicals; a multifarious acquaintance with ministers, churches, and people; and a financial credit, the growth of half a century, now extended through the commercial world. There is a vast organism abroad, the growth also of fifty years: missions, many of them established long ago, in different and widely-distant parts of the unevangelized world, after much suffering and disappointment, at great expense of money, labor, health, and even life; numerous missionaries, liberally educated, conversant with the people and their languages, able to preach the gospel, and to do all the work of an embassador of Christ to the heathen; acclimated, experienced, and of tried character; the result of a large expenditure in the case of each individual. There are churches, congregations, schools of every grade; native helpers, not a few with the training of many years; and a large acquaintance, a widely-extended, long-established influence in the several countries; a name, a prestige, a character, a moral power, not easily nor soon acquired in any country, and least of all in heathen lands.

What would it cost to reproduce the means and agencies, the results and influences, which stand connected with the American Board?

Such has been the progress of facilities for access to distant parts of the world, and for sustaining missions in them, and also the growth of experience as to the mode of conducting missions, that the reproducing of the system would cost less time, money and labor, now, than it did originally. But would it not require thirty years, and an expenditure of six millions? Then, the money expended upon it has not been thrown away. It has been a good investment — more productive, more secure, than it would be in any banking institution of the world. Much of the gain is already deposited in heaven; but the trading, working capital has a visible, tangible existence, in an array of means, instrumentalities, facilities, opportunities for bringing the gospel to bear broadly upon peoples and nations, upon myriads of immortal beings.

Extending our view, and embracing the foreign missions of all the Protestant Churches, and all the organizations, agencies, and influences which keep them in vigorous and successful operation, the value of the whole is at once seen to be immense. Is it thirty — is it forty — is it fifty millions? Who is able to make out the valuation? It is a property, that is built upon faith in the command, promise, power, and truthfulness of Him, who is Head over all things to the Church. Who ever made a wiser, more profitable investment of money, labor, health, and even life, than was made by the partners, living and dead, in this glorious enterprise for the salvation of the heathen world?

It was evidently the design of Providence to develop more fully the evil nature of sin, before the gospel should be made the common inheritance of mankind. That has been accomplished. The "Mystery of Iniquity," the "Man of Sin," the "False Prophet," were to be revealed; and they have been. The False Prophet has appeared, and uttered his lies; the Man of Sin has come, and done as wickedly as was predicted; the Mystery of Iniquity has been unfolded, until there is no longer room for doubt as to the evil and destructive nature of sin. And now the set time would seem to have come for the great remedial influences. These are to be applied by means of Christian missions; and, few as these yet are, they have been so diffused, under the leadings of Providence, that they have only to grow, in order to cover the earth with leaves which are to be for the healing of the nations. Every man and woman may now operate upon the most distant nations. The frequent and urgent calls upon the benevolent, result from the character impressed upon our age, and from our own multiplied, far-extending relations. The pall of death has been lifted from the nations; they have been brought near; and our eyes are filled with the sight, and our ears with the cry, of their distress. God has leveled mountains, bridged oceans, and made highways into every land; and now he speaks to us with an emphasis such as he never used in addressing his people of former times.

APPENDIX.

53

APPENDIX.

I. ACT OF INCORPORATION.

COMMONWEALTH OF MASSACHUSETTS.

In the year of our Lord One Thousand Eight Hundred and Twelve: An Act to Incorporate the American Board of Commissioners for Foreign Missions.

Whereas William Bartlet and others have been associated under the name of the American Board of Commissioners for Foreign Missions, for the purpose of propagating the gospel in heathen lands, by supporting missionaries and diffusing a knowledge of the Holy Scriptures, and have prayed to be incorporated in order more effectually to promote the laudable object of their association, —

Sec. 1. *Be it enacted by the Senate and House of Representatives in General Court assembled, and by the authority of the same,* That William Bartlet, Esq., and Samuel Spring, D. D., both of Newburyport, Joseph Lyman, D. D., of Hatfield, Jedediah Morse, D. D., of Charlestown, Samuel Worcester, D. D., of Salem, the Hon. William Phillips, Esq., of Boston, and the Hon. John Hooker, Esq., of Springfield, and their associates, be, and they hereby are incorporated and made a body politic by the name of the AMERICAN BOARD OF COMMISSIONERS FOR FOREIGN MISSIONS, and by that name may sue and be sued, plead and be impleaded, appear, prosecute, and defend, to final judgment and execution; and in their said corporate capacity, they, and their successors forever, may take, receive, have, and hold in fee-simple or otherwise, lands, tenements, and hereditaments, by gift, grant, devise, or otherwise, not exceeding the yearly value of four thousand dollars; and may also take and hold, by donation, bequest, or otherwise, personal estate to an amount the yearly income of which shall not exceed eight thousand dollars; so that the estate aforesaid shall be faithfully appropriated to the purpose and object aforesaid, and not otherwise. And the said corporation shall have power to sell, convey, exchange, or lease all or any part of their lands, tenements, or other property for the benefit of their funds, and may have a common seal, which they may alter or renew at pleasure. *Provided*, however, that nothing herein contained shall enable the said corporation, or any person or persons, as trustees for or for the use of said corporation, to receive and hold any gift, grant, legacy, or bequest, heretofore given or bequeathed to any person in trust for said Board, unless such person or persons could by law have taken and holden the same if this act had not passed.

SEC. 2. *Be it further enacted*, That the said Board may annually choose from among themselves, by ballot, a President, a Vice President, and a Prudential Committee; and also, from among themselves or others, a Corresponding Secretary, a Recording Secretary, a Treasurer, an Auditor, and such other officers as they may deem expedient; all of whom shall hold their offices until others are chosen to succeed them, and shall have such powers and perform such duties as the said Board may order and direct; and in case of vacancy by death, resignation, or otherwise, the vacancy may in like manner be filled at any legal meeting of the said Board. And the said Treasurer shall give bond, with sufficient surety or sureties, in the judgment of the Board, or the Prudential Committee, for the faithful discharge of the duties of his office.

SEC. 3. *Be it further enacted*, That all contracts and deeds, which the said Board may lawfully make and execute, signed by the chairman of the said Prudential Committee, and countersigned by their clerk, (whom they are hereby authorized to appoint,) and sealed with the common seal of said corporation, shall be valid in law to all intents and purposes.

SEC. 4. *Be it further enacted*, That the first annual meeting of the said Board shall be on the third Wednesday of September next, at such place as the said William Bartlet may appoint, and the present officers of said Board shall continue in office until others are elected.

SEC. 5. *Be it further enacted*, That the said Board, at the first annual meeting aforesaid, and at any subsequent annual meeting, may elect, by ballot, any suitable persons to be members of said Board, either to supply vacancies, or in addition to their present number.

SEC. 6. *Be it further enacted*, That the said Board shall have power to make such by-laws, rules, and regulations, for calling future meetings of said Board, and for the management of their concerns, as they shall deem expedient; *provided* the same are not repugnant to the laws of this Commonwealth.

SEC. 7. *Be it further enacted*, That one quarter part of the annual income from the funds of said Board shall be faithfully appropriated to defray the expense of imparting the Holy Scriptures to unevangelized nations in their own languages: *Provided*, that nothing herein contained shall be so construed as to defeat the express intentions of any testator or donor, who shall give or bequeath money to promote the great purposes of the Board. *Provided*, also, that nothing herein contained shall be so construed as to restrict said Board from appropriating more than one quarter of said income to translating and distributing the Scriptures whenever they shall deem it advisable.

SEC. 8. *Be it further enacted*, That not less than one third of said Board shall at all times be composed of respectable laymen ; and that not less than one third of said Board shall be composed of respectable clergymen; the remaining third to be composed of characters of the same description, whether clergymen or laymen.

SEC. 9. *Be it further enacted*, That the legislature of this Commonwealth shall at any time have the right to inspect, by a committee of their own body, the doings, funds, and proceedings of the said Corporation, and may at their pleasure alter or annul any or all of the powers herein granted.

In the House of Representatives, June 19, 1812. This bill, having had three several readings, passed to be enacted.

TIMOTHY BIGELOW, *Speaker*.

In the Senate, June 20th, 1812. This bill, having had two readings, passed to be enacted.

SAMUEL DANA, *President*.

June 20, 1812. By the Governor, Approved.

CALEB STRONG.

Copy — Attest,

ALDEN BRADFORD,

Secretary of the Commonwealth.

N. B. The *Associates*, alluded to in the foregoing act, were the Hon. JOHN TREADWELL, LL. D., the Rev. TIMOTHY DWIGHT, D. D., LL. D., President of Yale College, Gen. JEDIDIAH HUNTINGTON, and the Rev. CALVIN CHAPIN, all of Connecticut.

II. CORPORATE MEMBERS OF THE BOARD.

MAINE.

Election.
1832. Enoch Pond, D. D., Bangor.
1838. Benjamin Tappan, D. D., Augusta.
1842. William T. Dwight, D. D., Portland.
1843. Swan Lyman Pomroy, D. D., Portland.
1851. George F. Patten, Esq., Bath.
1854. John W. Chickering, D. D., Portland.
1856. George E. Adams, D. D., Brunswick.
1856. William W. Thomas, Esq., Portland.
1857. Amos D. Lockwood, Esq., Lewiston.

NEW HAMPSHIRE.

1832. Nathan Lord, D. D., Hanover.
1840. Zedekiah S. Barstow, D. D., Keene.
1842. Rev. John Woods, Fitzwilliam.
1842. John K. Young, D. D., Laconia.
1857. Nathaniel Bouton, D. D., Concord.
1859. Hon. William Haile, Hinsdale.
1860. Hon. George W. Nesmith, Franklin.

VERMONT.

1838. John Wheeler, D. D., Burlington.
1838. Charles Walker, D. D., Pittsford.
1839. Silas Aiken, D. D., Rutland.
1840. Willard Child, D. D., Castleton.
1840. Edward W. Hooker, D. D., Fairhaven.
1842. Hon. Erastus Fairbanks, St. Johnsbury.
1842. Benjamin Labaree, D. D., Middlebury.
1842. Rev. Joseph Steele, Middlebury.
1859. Lewis H. Delano, Esq., Hardwick.

MASSACHUSETTS.

1820. William Allen, D. D., Northampton.
1823. Heman Humphrey, D. D., Pittsfield.
1827. John Tappan, Esq., Boston.
1828. Henry Hill, Esq., Boston.
1832. Rufus Anderson, D. D., Boston.
1832. Rev. David Greene, Westboro'.
1832. Charles Stoddard, Esq., Boston.
1834. Rev. Sylvester Holmes, New Bedford.
1837. Nehemiah Adams, D. D., Boston.
1838. Thomas Snell, D. D., North Brookfield.
1838. Aaron Warner, D. D., Amherst.
1838. Mark Hopkins, D. D., LL. D., Williamstown.
1840. William Jenks, D. D., Boston.
1840. Alfred Ely, D. D., Monson.
1840. Horatio Bardwell, D. D., Oxford.
1840. Ebenezer Alden, M. D., Randolph.

Election.
1842. Richard S. Storrs, D. D., Braintree.
1842. Ebenezer Burgess, D. D., Dedham.
1842. John Nelson, D. D., Leicester.
1842. Hon. Samuel Williston, Easthampton.
1843. Rev. Selah B. Treat, Boston.
1845. Hon. William J. Hubbard, Boston.
1845. Henry B. Hooker, D. D., Boston.
1845. Hon. Linus Child, Lowell.
1845. Calvin E. Stowe, D. D., Andover.
1847. Samuel M. Worcester, D. D., Salem.
1848. Andrew W. Porter, Esq., Monson.
1848. Hon. Samuel H. Walley, Boston.
1849. Augustus C. Thompson, D. D., Roxbury.
1850. Hon. William T. Eustis, Boston.
1850. Hon. John Aiken, Andover.
1852. William Ropes, Esq., Boston.
1853. John Todd, D. D., Pittsfield.
1854. Seth Sweetser, D. D., Worcester.
1854. James M. Gordon, Esq., Boston.
1855. Amos Blanchard, D. D., Lowell.
1857. Hon. Alpheus Hardy, Boston.
1860. Hon. Reuben A. Chapman, Springfield.
1860. William S. Southworth, Esq., Lowell.

RHODE ISLAND.

1846. Rev. Thomas Shepard, D. D., Bristol.
1850. John Kingsbury, LL. D., Providence.

CONNECTICUT.

1817. Jeremiah Day, D. D., LL. D., New Haven.
1832. Noah Porter, D. D., Farmington.
1836. Thomas S. Williams, LL. D., Hartford.
1838. Joel Hawes, D. D., Hartford.
1838. Mark Tucker, D. D., Vernon.
1838. Hon. Thomas W. Williams, New London.
1838. Hon. Joseph Russell, Ellington.
1840. Hon. Seth Terry, Hartford.
1840. John T. Norton, Esq., Farmington.
1842. Alvan Bond, D. D., Norwich.
1842. Leonard Bacon, D. D., New Haven.
1842. Henry White, Esq., New Haven.
1843. Joel H. Linsley, D. D., Greenwich.
1843. Rev. David L. Ogden, New Haven.
1852. Gen. William Williams, Norwich.
1854. Samuel W. S. Dutton, D. D., New Haven.
1855. George Kellogg, Esq., Rockville.

Election.
1859. Theodore D. Woolsey, D. D., LL. D., New Haven.
1859. Hon. Wm. A. Buckingham, Norwich.
1860. Lucius Barbour, Esq., Hartford.
1860. Elisha L. Cleaveland, D. D., New Haven.
1860. John A. Davenport, Esq., New Haven.

NEW YORK.

1812. Eliphalet Nott, D. D., Schenectady.
1823. Lyman Beecher, D. D., Brooklyn.
1824. Gardiner Spring, D. D., New York.
1826. Thomas DeWitt, D. D., New York.
1826. Nathan S. S. Beman, D. D., Troy.
1826. Thomas McAuley, D. D., LL. D., New York.
1834. James M. Mathews, D. D., New York.
1838. Isaac Ferris, D. D., New York.
1838. Thomas H. Skinner, D. D., New York.
1838. William W. Chester, Esq., New York.
1838. Pelatiah Perit, Esq., New York.
1839. William B. Sprague, D. D., Albany.
1840. Reuben H. Walworth, LL. D., Saratoga Springs.
1840. Diedrich Willers, D. D., Fayette, Seneca County.
1840. Hon. Charles W. Rockwell, New York.
1840. David H. Little, Esq., Cherry Valley.
1840. Charles Mills, Esq., Kingsborough.
1842. Samuel H. Cox, D. D., Leroy.
1842. Aristarchus Champion, Esq., Rochester.
1842. Hon. William L. F. Warren, Saratoga Springs.
1842. Horace Holden, Esq., New York.
1842. William Adams, D. D., New York.
1842. Jōel Parker, D. D., New York.
1843. William Wisner, D. D., Ithaca.
1843. Edward Robinson, D. D., New York.
1843. William Patton, D. D., New York.
1843. William W. Stone, Esq., New York.
1845. John Forsyth, D. D., Newburgh.
1846. Hon. Henry W. Taylor, Canandaigua.
1846. James Crocker, Esq., Buffalo.
1846. Calvin T. Hulburd, Esq., Brasher Falls.
1848. David Wesson, Esq., Brooklyn.
1848. Laurens P. Hickok, D. D., Schenectady.
1848. William M. Halsted, Esq., New York.
1848. Simeon Benjamin, Esq., Elmira.
1850. Robert W. Condit, D. D., Oswego.
1851. Rev. Simeon North, LL. D., Clinton.
1851. Samuel W. Fisher, D. D., Clinton.
1852. Walter S. Griffith, Esq., Brooklyn.
1852. Isaac N. Wyckoff, D. D., Albany.

Election.
1852. Hon. William F. Allen, Oswego.
1852. George W. Wood, D. D., New York.
1853. Asa D. Smith, D. D., New York.
1853. Oliver E. Wood, Esq., New York.
1853. Rev. Montgomery S. Goodale, Amsterdam.
1853. Rev. William S. Curtis, Clinton.
1854. Walter Clarke, D. D., New York.
1854. Ray Palmer, D. D., Albany.
1855. Philemon H. Fowler, D. D., Utica.
1855. George B. Cheever, D. D., New York.
1855. Samuel T. Spear, D. D., Brooklyn.
1855. Jacob M. Schermerhorn, Esq., Homer.
1857. William E. Dodge, Esq., New York.
1860. Jonathan B. Condit, D. D., Auburn.
1860. James W. McLane, D. D., Brooklyn.
1860. William A. Booth, Esq., New York.
1860. Simeon B. Chittenden, Esq., Brooklyn.

NEW JERSEY.

1823. S. V. S. Wilder, Esq., Elizabethtown.
1826. Theodore Frelinghuysen, LL. D., New Brunswick.
1832. Hon. Peter D. Vroom, Trenton.
1838. David Magie, D. D., Elizabethtown.
1838. Richard T. Haines, Esq., Elizabethtown.
1840. Hon. Joseph C. Hornblower, Newark.
1840. David H. Riddle, D. D., Jersey City.
1842. J. Marshal Paul, M. D., Belvidere.
1843. Benjamin C. Taylor, D. D., Hudson.
1848. Abraham B. Hasbrouck, LL. D., New Brunswick.
1848. Hon. Daniel Haines, Hamburg.
1853. Jonathan F. Stearns, D. D., Newark.
1855. Rev. Thornton A. Mills, Newark.
1856. Lyndon A. Smith, M. D., Newark.
1860. Hon. William Pennington, Newark.

PENNSYLVANIA.

1832. John McDowell, D. D., Philadelphia.
1838. William R. DeWitt, D. D., Harrisburg.
1838. Ambrose White, Esq., Philadelphia.
1840. Hon. William Darling, Philadelphia.
1840. William Jessup, LL. D., Montrose.
1840. Bernard C. Wolf, D. D., Easton.
1840. Rev. Albert Barnes, Philadelphia.
1840. J. W. Nevin, D. D., Mercersburg
1842. Harvey Ely, Esq., Erie.
1843. Samuel H. Perkins, Esq., Philadelphia.
1855. John A. Brown, Esq., Philadelphia.
1855. Hon. William Strong, Philadelphia.
1855. George A. Lyon, D. D., Erie.
1857. Matthias W. Baldwin, Esq., Philadelphia.

Election.
1859. Thomas Brainerd, D. D., Philadelphia.
1859. James W. Weir, Esq., Harrisburg.

MARYLAND.

1838. James G. Hamner, D. D., Baltimore.

DISTRICT OF COLUMBIA.

1842. Rev. John Cross Smith, Washington.

VIRGINIA.

1826. Gen. John H. Cocke, Fluvanna County.

MISSOURI.

1851. Henry A. Nelson, D. D., St. Louis.
1857. Truman M. Post, D. D., St. Louis.
1860. John B. Johnson, M. D., St. Louis.

TENNESSEE.

1842. Samuel Rhea, Esq., Blountsville.

OHIO.

1838. George E. Pierce, D. D., Hudson.
1843. Samuel C. Aiken, D. D., Cleveland.
1851. D. Howe Allen, D. D., Walnut Hills.
1851. Henry Smith, D. D., Walnut Hills.
1853. Douglass Putnam, Esq., Harmar.
1853. Robert W. Steele, Esq., Dayton.
1853. Henry L. Hitchcock, D. D., Hudson.
1855. M. LaRue P. Thompson, D. D., Cincinnati.
1857. T. P. Handy, Esq., Cleveland.

MICHIGAN.

Election.
1838. Eurotas P. Hastings, Esq., Detroit.
1851. Harvey D. Kitchell, D. D., Detroit.
1851. Hon Charles Noble, Monroe.

INDIANA.

1842. Charles White, D. D., Crawfordsville.
1851. Hon. Jeremiah Sullivan, Madison.
1853. Rev. John W. Cunningham, Laporte.

ILLINOIS.

1812. Ansel D. Eddy, D. D., Wilmington.
1845. Baxter Dickinson, D. D., Chicago.
1851. Julian M. Sturtevant, D. D., Jacksonville.
1851. Rev. Aratas Kent, Galena.
1851. Robert W. Patterson, D. D., Chicago.
1851. William H. Brown, Esq., Chicago.
1853. Rev. Augustus T. Norton, Alton.
1853. David A. Smith, Esq., Jacksonville.
1853. Rev. William Carter, Pittsfield.
1860. Prof. Samuel C. Bartlett, Chicago.

IOWA.

1851. Rev. John C. Holbrook, Dubuque.
1857. Rev. W. Henry Williams, Keokuk.

WISCONSIN.

1840. Rev. Chauncey Eddy, Beloit.
1851. Aaron L. Chapin, D. D., Beloit.
1851. Eliphalet Cramer, Esq., Milwaukie.
1860. Rev. Enos J. Montague, Summit.

III. OFFICERS OF THE BOARD.

PRESIDENTS.

Election.		Death or Resignation.
1810.	John Treadwell, LL. D.,	1823.
1823.	Joseph Lyman, D. D.,	1826.
1826.	John Cotton Smith, LL. D.,	1841.
1841.	Theodore Frelinghuysen, LL. D.,	1857.
1857.	Mark Hopkins, D. D., LL. D.	

VICE PRESIDENTS.

Election.		Death or Resignation.
1810.	Samuel Spring, D. D.,	1819.
1819.	Joseph Lyman, D. D.,	1823.
1823.	John Cotton Smith, LL. D.,	1826.
1826.	Stephen Van Rensselaer, LL. D.,	1839.
1839.	Theodore Frelinghuysen, LL. D.,	1841.
1841.	Thomas S. Williams, LL. D.,	1857.
1857.	William Jessup, LL. D.	

PRUDENTIAL COMMITTEE.

Election.		Death or Resignation.
1810.	William Bartlet, Esq.,	1814.
1810.	Samuel Spring, D. D.,	1819.
1810.	Samuel Worcester, D. D.,	1821.
1812.	Jeremiah Evarts, Esq.,	1830.
1815.	Jedediah Morse, D. D.,	1821.
1818.	Hon. William Reed,	1834.
1819.	Leonard Woods, D. D.,	1834.
1821.	Samuel Hubbard, LL. D.,	1843.
1821.	Warren Fay, D. D.,	1839.
1828.	Benjamin B. Wisner, D. D.,	1835.
1831.	Elias Cornelius, D. D.,	1832.
1832.	Hon. Samuel T. Armstrong,	1850.
1832.	Charles Stoddard, Esq.	
1834.	John Tappan, Esq.	
1835.	Daniel Noyes, Esq.,	1845.
1837.	Nehemiah Adams, D. D.	
1839.	Silas Aiken, D. D.,	1849.
1843.	William W. Stone, Esq.,	1850.
1845.	Hon. William J. Hubbard,	1859.
1849.	Augustus C. Thompson, D. D.	
1850.	Hon. William T. Eustis.	
1850.	Hon. John Aiken.	
1851.	Hon. Daniel Safford,	1856.
1854.	Henry Hill, Esq.	
1856.	Isaac Ferris, D. D.,	1857.
1856.	Asa D. Smith, D. D.	
1856.	Walter S. Griffith, Esq.	
1857.	Alpheus Hardy, Esq.	
1859.	Hon. Linus Child.	
1860.	William S. Southworth, Esq.	

CORRESPONDING SECRETARIES.

Election.		Death or Resignation.
1810.	Samuel Worcester, D. D.,	1821.
1821.	Jeremiah Evarts, Esq.,	1831.
1831.	Elias Cornelius, D. D.,	1832.
1832.	Benjamin B. Wisner, D. D.,	1835.
1832.	Rufus Anderson, D. D.	
1832.	Rev. David Greene,	1848.
1835.	William J. Armstrong, D. D.,	1847.
1847.	Rev. Selah B. Treat.	
1848.	Swan L. Pomroy, D. D.,	1859.
1852.	George W. Wood, D. D.	

ASSISTANT CORRESPONDING SECRETARIES.

Election.		Death or Resignation.
1824.	Rev. Rufus Anderson,	1832.
1828.	Rev. David Greene,	1832.

RECORDING SECRETARIES.

Election.		Death or Resignation.
1810.	Calvin Chapin, D. D.,	1843.
1843.	Rev. Selah B. Treat,	1847.
1847.	Samuel M. Worcester, D. D.	

ASSISTANT RECORDING SECRETARIES.

Election.		Death or Resignation.
1836.	Charles Stoddard, Esq.,	1839.
1839.	Bela B. Edwards, D. D.,	1842.
1842.	Rev. Daniel Crosby,	1843.

TREASURERS.

Election.		Death or Resignation.
1810.	Samuel H. Walley, Esq.,	1811.
1811.	Jeremiah Evarts, Esq.,	1822.
1822.	Henry Hill, Esq.,	1854.
1854.	James M. Gordon, Esq.	

AUDITORS.

Election.		Death or Resignation.
1810.	Joshua Goodale, Esq.,	1812.
1812.	Samuel H. Walley, Esq.,	1813.
1813.	Charles Walley, Esq.,	1814.
1814.	Chester Adams, Esq.,	1817.
1817.	Ashur Adams, Esq.,	1822.
1822.	Chester Adams, Esq.,	1827.
1827.	William Ropes, Esq.,	1829.
1829.	John Tappan, Esq.,	1834.
1829.	Charles Stoddard, Esq.,	1832.
1832.	Hon. William J. Hubbard,	1842.
1834.	Daniel Noyes, Esq.,	1835.
1835.	Charles Scudder, Esq.,	1847.
1842.	Moses L. Hale, Esq.	
1847.	Hon. Samuel H. Walley.	

IV. CORPORATE MEMBERS DECEASED OR RESIGNED.

[The names under each State are arranged according to the time of decease or resignation. The year is that ending with the annual meetings in September or October.]

MAINE.

Election.		*Death or Resignation.*
1813.	Jesse Appleton, D. D.,	1820.
1826.	Edward Payson, D. D.,	1828.
1842.	David Dunlap,	1843.
1813.	Gen. Henry Sewall,	1845.
1842.	William Richardson,	1847.
1842.	Eliphalet Gillett, D. D.,	1849.
1836.	Levi Cutter,	1856.
1845.	Asa Cummings, D. D.,	1856.
1838.	John W. Ellingwood, D. D.,	1860.

NEW HAMPSHIRE.

1812.	John Langdon, LL. D.,	1820.
1812.	Seth Payson, D. D.,	1820.
1820.	Hon. Thomas W. Thompson,	1822.
1830.	Hon. George Sullivan,	1838.
1820.	John Hubbard Church, D. D.,	1840.
1842.	Hon. Mills Olcott,	1845.
1842.	Rev. Archibald Burgess,	1850.
1840.	Hon. Edmund Parker,	1856.
1838.	Samuel Fletcher,	1859.

VERMONT.

1818.	Hon. Charles Marsh,	1849.
1840.	William Page, Esq.,	1850.

MASSACHUSETTS.

1810.	Samuel H. Walley, *r.*,	1811.
1810.	Samuel Spring, D. D.,	1819.
1810.	Samuel Worcester, D. D.,	1821.
1818.	Zephaniah Swift Moore, D. D.,	1823.
1811.	Jedediah Morse, D. D.,	1826.
1812.	Hon. William Phillips,	1827.
1810.	Joseph Lyman, D. D.,	1828.
1823.	Edward A. Newton, *r.*,	1828.
1812.	Hon. John Hooker,	1829.
1812.	Jeremiah Evarts,	1831.
1822.	Samuel Austin, D. D.,	1831.
1831.	Elias Cornelius, D. D.,	1832.
1828.	Benjamin B. Wisner, D. D.,	1835.
1818.	Hon. William Reed,	1837.
1821.	Warren Fay, D. D., *r.*,	1839.
1810.	William Bartlet,	1841.
1842.	Rev. Daniel Crosby,	1843.
1821.	Samuel Hubbard, LL. D.,	1847.
1826.	John Codman, D. D.,	1848.
1832.	Hon. Samuel T. Armstrong,	1850.
1826.	Hon. Lewis Strong, *r.*,	1852.
1835.	Daniel Noyes,	1852.
1839.	Bela B. Edwards, D. D.,	1852.
1842.	Hon. Alfred D. Foster,	1852.
1826.	Justin Edwards, D. D.,	1853.
1819.	Leonard Woods, D. D.,	1854.
1821.	Joshua Bates, D. D.,	1854.
1840.	Hon. David Mack,	1854.
1851.	Hon. Daniel Safford,	1856.
1840.	Daniel Dana, D. D.,	1859.

RHODE ISLAND.

1812.	William Jones, Esq.	

CONNECTICUT.

1810.	Timothy Dwight, D. D., LL. D.,	1817.
1810.	Gen. Jedidiah Huntington,	1819.
1810.	John Treadwell, LL. D.,	1823.
1836.	Henry Hudson,	1843.
1819.	John Cotton Smith, LL. D.,	1846.
1842.	Rev. Thomas Punderson,	1848.
1840.	Daniel Dow, D. D.,	1849.
1810.	Calvin Chapin, D. D.,	1851.
1848.	Nathaniel O. Kellogg,	1854.
1823.	Bennet Tyler, D. D.,	1858.
1851.	Charles J. Stedman,	1859.
1830.	Roger Minot Sherman, *r.*,	1830.
1842.	Chauncey A. Goodrich, D. D.,	1860.
1852.	Abel McEwen, D. D.,	1860.

NEW YORK.

1818.	Col. Henry Linclean,	1822.
1819.	Divie Bethune,	1825.
1812.	John Jay, LL. D.,	1829.
1824.	Col. Henry Rutgers,	1830.
1826.	Col. Richard Varick,	1831.
1812.	Egbert Benson, LL. D.,	1833.
1822.	Jonas Platt, LL. D.,	1834.
1826.	William McMurray, D. D.	1836.
1826.	John Nitchie,	1838.
1816.	Stephen Van Rensselaer, LL. D.,	1839.
1824.	Eleazar Lord, *r.*,	1841.

Election.		*Death or Resignation.*
1832.	Zechariah Lewis,	1841.
1840.	Gerrit Wendell,	1841.
1812.	James Richards, D. D.,	1843.
1813.	Alexander Proudfit, D. D.,	1843.
1832.	Orrin Day,	1847.
1835.	William J. Armstrong, D. D.,	1847.
1843.	Walter Hubbell,	1848.
1843.	Asa T. Hopkins, D. D.,	1848.
1838.	Henry White, D. D.,	1850.
1842.	John W. Adams, D. D.,	1850.
1824.	David Porter, D D.,	1851.
1838.	D. W. C. Olyphant, *r.*,	1851.
1839.	Eliphalet Wickes,	1851.
1848.	Erskine Mason, D. D.,	1851.
1812.	Henry Davis, D. D.,	1852.
1826.	Nathaniel W. Howell, LL. D.,	1852.
1824.	Philip Milledoler, D. D.,	1853.
1838.	Elisha Yale, D. D.,	1853.
1840.	Anson G. Phelps,	1854.
1840.	Hiram H. Seelye,	1855.
1836.	Rev. Henry Dwight,	1857.
1842.	Charles M. Lee, LL. D.,	1857.
1854.	Anson G. Phelps, Jr.,	1858.

NEW JERSEY.

1812.	Elias Boudinot, LL. D.,	1822.
1823.	Edward Dorr Griffin, D. D.,	1838.
1812.	Samuel Miller, D. D., *r.*,	1839.
1826.	James Carnahan, D. D., *r.*,	1849.
1826.	Archibald Alexander, D. D., *r.*,	1850.
1855.	F. T. Frelinghuysen, *r.*,	1859.

PENNSYLVANIA.

1812.	Robert Ralston,	1836.
1812.	Ashbel Green, D. D., *r.*,	1840.
1834.	Alexander Henry,	1847.
1826.	Samuel Agnew, M. D.,	1850.
1832.	Cornelius C. Cuyler, D. D.,	1850.
1826.	Thomas Bradford,	1852.
1838.	Matthew Brown, D. D.,	1853.
1842.	Eliphalet W. Gilbert, D. D.,	1853.
1838.	Thomas Fleming,	1855.
1826.	John Ludlow, D. D.,	1857.
1848.	Charles S. Wurts, *r.*,	1858.
1835.	William S. Plumer, D. D., *r.*,	1859.
1826.	William Neill, D. D.,	1860.

MARYLAND.

1834.	William Nevins, D. D.,	1836.

Election.		*Death or Resignation.*

DISTRICT OF COLUMBIA.

1819.	Elias Boudinot Caldwell,	1825.
1826.	Joseph Nourse,	1841.

VIRGINIA.

1823.	John H. Rice, D. D.,	1831.
1832.	George A. Baxter, D D.,	1841.
1826.	William Maxwell,	1857.
1834.	Thomas P. Atkinson, *r.*,	1859.

NORTH CAROLINA.

1834.	Joseph Caldwell, D. D.,	1835.
1834.	W. McPheters, D. D.,	1843.

SOUTH CAROLINA.

1826.	Moses Waddell, D. D.,	1840.
1826.	Benjamin M. Palmer, D. D.,	1848.
1839.	Reuben Post, D. D , *r.*,	1855.

GEORGIA.

1826.	John Cummings, M. D.,	1838.
1834.	Thomas Golding, D. D.,	1848.
1834.	Hon. Joseph H. Lumpkin.	

TENNESSEE.

1826.	Charles Coffin, D. D.	
1834.	Isaac Anderson, D. D.	

ILLINOIS.

1821.	Gideon Blackburn, D. D.,	1839.

INDIANA.

1838.	Elihu W. Baldwin, D. D.,	1841.
1853.	Samuel Merrill,	1855.

OHIO.

1832.	James Hoge, D. D., *r.*,	1847.
1826.	Robert G. Wilson, D. D.,	1856.
1834.	Robert H. Bishop, D. D.,	1855.
1851.	Gabriel Tichenor,	1855.
1845.	Rev. Harvey Coe,	1860.

MISSOURI.

1840.	Artemas Bullard, D. D.,	1856.

V. MISSIONARIES AND ASSISTANT MISSIONARIES SENT FORTH BY THE AMERICAN BOARD OF COMMISSIONERS FOR FOREIGN MISSIONS.

[Pages 268 and 273.]

NOT a few of those mentioned in the following list, have been connected with two or more of the missions, and their names are of course repeated. Hence an enumeration from this catalogue would not correspond with the table referred to in the body of the work. The true number is there indicated. The star (*) denotes the decease of the missionary. The letter *r.* means that the individual is not now in connection with the Board. The occasion of these discharges, in the missions beyond sea, has generally been a failure of health in the wife or husband. In the missions among the North American Indians, — those missions being peculiar in their nature, and near home, — the connection of laymen, as farmers, mechanics, or teachers, has been less permanent than in the remoter missions, and not unfrequently has been entered upon for a specified time. This was specially true in respect to unmarried females, a great number of whom have been employed in the Indian missions. The list is intended to contain all such, and only such, as actually received from the Prudential Committee the appointment as assistant missionary; but perfect accuracy here is a matter of some difficulty.

Among those connected with the missions beyond sea, where death has occurred since their connection with the Board was dissolved, the fact, when known, is denoted by *r.** A considerable number of deaths among those formerly connected with the Indian missions, may have escaped notice.

WESTERN AFRICA.

CAPE PALMAS, AFTERWARD GABOON, MISSION.

r. J. Leighton Wilson,	*r.* Mrs. Jane E. Wilson.
* David White,	* Mrs. Helen M. White.
* Alexander E. Wilson, M. D., — from the Zulu Mission,	* Mrs. Mary H. Wilson, — afterward Mrs. Griswold.
William Walker,	* Mrs. Prudence R. Walker.
	* Mrs. Zerviah L. Walker.
	Mrs. Catharine H. Walker.
* Benjamin Griswold,	* Mrs. Mary H. Griswold.
* John M. Campbell.	
Albert Bushnell,	* Mrs. Lydia A. Bushnell.
	Mrs. Lucina J. Bushnell.
Ira M. Preston,	Mrs. Jane S. Preston.
r. William T. Wheeler.	
Jacob Best,	Mrs. Gertrude Best.

* Rollin Porter,	* Mrs. Nancy A. Porter.
Epaminondas J. Pierce,	* Mrs. Susan Pierce.
* Hubert P. Herrick,	r. Mrs. Julia Herrick.
* Henry M. Adams.	
r. Andrew D. Jack,	r. Mrs. Mercy E. Jack.
r. Morris L. St. John, M. D.,	r. Mrs. Sarah A. St. John.
r Walter H. Clark.	

Missionary Physician.

* Henry A. Ford, M. D.,	r. Mrs. Olivia Ford.

Assistant Missionaries.

r. Benjamin V. James, — now at Liberia.	r. Mrs. Margaret E. James.
	r. Miss Olivia Smith, — afterward Mrs. Ford.
	Miss Jane A. Van Allen.

SOUTH AFRICA.

ZULU MISSION.

* George Champion,	* Mrs. Susan Champion.
Aldin Grout,	* Mrs. Hannah Grout.
	Mrs. Charlotte Grout.
Daniel Lindley,	Mrs. Lucy Lindley.
r. Henry I. Venable,	r. Mrs. Martha A. Venable.
* Alexander E. Wilson, — see West Africa,	* Mrs. Mary J. Wilson.
* Newton Adams, M. D.,	r. Mrs. Sarah C. Adams.
* James C. Bryant,	r. Mrs. Dolly F. Bryant.
Lewis Grout,	Mrs. Lydia Grout.
Silas McKinney,	Mrs. Fanny M. McKinney.
* Samuel D. Marsh,	r Mrs. Mary S. Marsh.
David Rood,	Mrs. Alzina V. Rood.
William Ireland,	Mrs. Jane Ireland.
Andrew Abraham,	Mrs. Sarah L. Abraham.
Hyman A. Wilder,	Mrs. Abby T. Wilder.
Josiah Tyler,	Mrs. Susan W. Tyler.
r. Jacob L. Döhne,	r. Mrs. Caroline Döhne.
Seth B. Stone,	Mrs. Catharine M. Stone.
William Mellen,	Mrs. Laurana W. Mellen.
Stephen C. Pixley,	Mrs. Louisa Pixley.
Elijah Robbins,	Mrs. Adaline Robbins.
Henry M. Bridgman,	Mrs. Laura B. Bridgman.

Assistant Missionaries.

r. J. Q. A. Butler,	r. Mrs. Anna S. Butler.

EUROPE.

MISSION TO GREECE.

Jonas King, D. D.,	Mrs. Anna A. King.
Elias Riggs, — see N. Arm. Miss.,	Mrs. Martha J. Riggs.
r. Samuel R. Houston,	r. Mrs. Mary R. Houston.
* Nathan Benjamin, — see N. Arm. Miss.,	r. Mrs. Mary G. Benjamin.
r. George W. Leyburn,	r. Mrs. Elizabeth W. Leyburn.

WESTERN ASIA.

MISSION TO CYPRUS.

* Lorenzo W. Pease,	r. Mrs. Lucinda Pease.
r. James L. Thompson.	
Daniel Ladd, — see N. Arm. Miss.,	Mrs. Charlotte H. Ladd.

MISSION TO THE JEWS.

* Eliphal Maynard,	r. Mrs. Celestia A. Maynard.
Wm. G. Schauffler, — see N. Arm. Miss.,	Mrs. Mary R. Schauffler.
Edward M. Dodd, — see N. Arm. Miss.,	Mrs. Lydia H. Dodd.
Justin W. Parsons, — see N. Arm. Miss.,	Mrs. Catharine Parsons.
Homer B. Morgan, — see S. Arm. Miss.,	* Mrs. Harriett G. Morgan.

NORTHERN ARMENIAN MISSION.†

* Daniel Temple,	* Mrs. Rachel B. Temple.
	r.* Mrs. Martha Temple.
William Goodell, D. D.,	Mrs. Abigail P. Goodell.
r. Josiah Brewer.	
* Elnathan Gridley.	
Harrison G. O. Dwight, D. D.,	* Mrs. Elizabeth Dwight.
	* Mrs. Mary Dwight.
William G. Schauffler, D. D.,	Mrs. Mary R. Schauffler.
Elias Riggs, D. D.,	Mrs. Martha J. Riggs.
r. Thomas P. Johnston,	r. Mrs. Marianne C. Johnston.
r. John B. Adger,	r. Mrs. Elizabeth K. Adger.
r. Henry A. Homes,	r. Mrs. Anna W. Homes.
* Nathan Benjamin,	r. Mrs. Mary G. Benjamin.
Daniel Ladd,	Mrs. Charlotte H. Ladd.
r. William C. Jackson,	r. Mrs. Mary A. Jackson.
r. Cyrus Hamlin, D. D., — at Constantinople,	* Mrs. Henrietta A. L. Hamlin.
	* Mrs. Harriet M. Hamlin.
	r. Mrs. Mary E. Hamlin.
Henry J. Van Lennep,	* Mrs. Emma L. Van Lennep.
	* Mrs. Mary Van Lennep.
	Mrs. Emily A. Van Lennep.
Geo. W. Wood, D. D., — now Cor. Sec.,	* Mrs. Martha B. Wood.
Edwin E. Bliss,	Mrs. Isabella H. Bliss.
* Joel S. Everett,	* Mrs. Seraphina Everett.
Josiah Peabody,	Mrs. Mary L. Peabody.
r. Isaac G. Bliss, — at Constantinople,	r. Mrs. Eunice B. Bliss.
Edward M. Dodd,	Mrs. Lydia H. Dodd.
Justin W. Parsons,	Mrs. Catharine Parsons.
Oliver Crane,	Mrs. Marion D. Crane.
r. George W. Dunmore,	r. Mrs. Susan Dunmore.
* Joseph W. Sutphen,	Mrs. Susan H. Sutphen, — now Mrs. Morgan.
Wilson A. Farnsworth,	Mrs. Caroline E. Farnsworth.
r. William Clark,	r. Mrs. Elizabeth W. Clark.
Jasper N. Ball,	Mrs. Caroline W. Ball.

† The former division of the missions is retained, as more convenient in this catalogue of the missionaries.

	Sanford Richardson,		Mrs. Rhoda A. Richardson.
r.	Edwin Goodell,	r.	Mrs. Catharine J. Goodell.
r.	Benjamin Parsons,	r.	Mrs. Sarah W. Parsons.
r.	Alexander R. Plumer,	r.	Mrs. Elizabeth B. Plumer.
	Ira F. Pettibone.		
	Orson P. Allen,		Mrs. Caroline R. Allen.
	George A. Pollard,		Mrs. Mary H. Pollard.
	Tillman C. Trowbridge,		Mrs. Margaret Trowbridge.
	Crosby H. Wheeler,		Mrs. Susan A. Wheeler.
	Charles F. Morse,		Mrs. Eliza D. Morse.
	Oliver W. Winchester,		Mrs. Janette S. Winchester.
	Julius Y. Leonard,		Mrs. Amelia Leonard.
	Theodore L. Byington,		Mrs. Esther Byington.
r.	William Hutchison,	r.	Mrs. Foresta G. Hutchison.
	William W. Meriam,		Mrs. Susan Meriam.
	Joseph K. Greene,		Mrs. Elizabeth A. Greene.
	James F. Clarke,		Mrs. Isabella G. Clarke.
	Herman N. Barnum,		Mrs. Mary Barnum.
	George F. Herrick.		
	William F. Arms,	*	Mrs. Emily Arms.
	William W. Livingston,		Mrs. Martha E. Livingston.

Missionary Physicians.

r.	Fayette Jewett, M. D.,	r.	Mrs. Mary Ann Jewett.
	Henry S. West, M. D.,		Mrs. Lottie M. West.

Treasurer of the Mission.

	George Washburn,		Mrs. Henrietta Washburn.

Assistant Missionaries.

r.	Homan Hallock,	r.	Mrs. Elizabeth Hallock.
		*	Miss Harriet M. Lovell, — afterward Mrs. Hamlin.
			Miss Maria A. West.
		r.	Miss Melvina Haynes.
		r.	Miss Mary E. Tenney, — now Mrs. Hamlin.
			Miss Sarah E. West.

SOUTHERN ARMENIAN MISSION.

	Benjamin Schneider, D. D.,	*	Mrs. Eliza C. Schneider.
			Mrs. Susan M. Schneider.
	Philander O. Powers,	*	Mrs. Harriet Powers.
			Mrs. Sarah L. Powers.
*	Azariah Smith, M. D.,	r.	Mrs. Corinth J. Smith.
	Homer B. Morgan,		Mrs. Susan H. Morgan.
	Andrew T. Pratt, M. D.,		Mrs. Sarah F. Pratt.
	George B. Nutting,	*	Mrs. Sarah E. Nutting.
			Mrs. Susan A. Nutting.
r.	Alfred G. Beebe,	*	Mrs. Sarah J. Beebe.
r.	George A. Perkins, — at Constantinople,	r.	Mrs. Sarah E. Perkins.
	Jackson G. Coffing,		Mrs. Josephine Coffing.
	George H. White,		Mrs. Joanna White.
	Alvin B. Goodale, M. D.,		Mrs. Mary E. Goodale.
	Zenas Goss.		

Assistant Missionary.

Miss Myra A. Proctor.

SYRIA MISSION.

* Pliny Fisk.
* Levi Parsons.
Jonas King, — see Mission to Greece.
r. Isaac Bird, ... r. Mrs. Ann Bird.
William Goodell, — see N. Arm. Miss., . Mrs. Abigail P. Goodell.
* Eli Smith, D. D., ... * Mrs. Sarah L. Smith.
* Mrs. Maria W. Smith.
r. Mrs. Hetty S. B. Smith.
* George B. Whiting, ... r. Mrs. Matilda S. Whiting.
William M. Thomson, D. D., ... * Mrs. Eliza N. Thomson.
Mrs. Thomson.
* Story Hebard, ... * Mrs. Rebecca W. Hebard.
r. John F. Lanneau, ... r. Mrs. Julia H. Lanneau.
r. Elias R. Beadle, ... r.* Mrs. Hannah Beadle.
r. Charles S. Sherman, ... r. Mrs. Martha E. Sherman.
r. Samuel Wolcott, ... * Mrs. Catherine E. Wolcott.
r.* Nathaniel A. Keyes, ... r. Mrs. Mary Keyes.
r. Leander Thompson, ... r. Mrs. Anne E. Thompson.
Cornelius V. A. Van Dyck, M. D., . . . Mrs. Julia Van Dyck.
Simeon H. Calhoun, ... Mrs. Emily P. Calhoun.
r. William A. Benton, ... r. Mrs. Loanza Benton.
J. Edwards Ford, ... Mrs. Mary Ford.
r. David M. Wilson, ... r. Mrs. Emeline Wilson.
r. Horace Foote, ... * Mrs. Roxana Foote.
William W. Eddy, ... Mrs. Hannah M. Eddy.
William Bird, ... Mrs. Sarah F. Bird.
J. Lorenzo Lyons, ... Mrs. Catherine N. Lyons.
r. Edward Aiken, ... * Mrs. Susan D. Aiken.
r. Mrs. Sarah Aiken.
Daniel Bliss, ... Mrs. Abby M. Bliss.
Henry H. Jessup, ... Mrs. Caroline Jessup.

Missionary Physicians.

* Asa Dodge, M. D., ... r. Mrs. Martha W. Dodge.
* Henry A. DeForest, M. D., ... r. Mrs. Catharine T. DeForest.

Assistant Missionaries.

George C. Hurter, ... Mrs. Elizabeth Hurter.
* Miss Rebecca W. Williams, — afterward Mrs. Hebard.
r. Miss Betsey Tilden.
* Miss Anna L. Whittlesey.
r. Miss Sarah Cheney, — now Mrs. Aiken.
r. Miss Jane E. Johnson.
Miss Amelia C. Temple.
Miss Adelaide L. Mason.

ASSYRIAN MISSION.

William F. Williams, ... * Mrs. Sarah Williams.
* Mrs. Harriet B. Williams.
Dwight W. Marsh, ... * Mrs. Julia W. Marsh.
* Henry Lobdell, M. D., ... r. Mrs. Lucy C. Lobdell.
Augustus Walker, ... Mrs. Eliza M. Walker.
George C. Knapp, ... Mrs. Alzina M. Knapp.
Lysander T. Burbank, ... Mrs. Sarah S. Burbank.

Missionary Physicians.

	David H. Nutting, M. D.,		Mrs. Mary E. Nutting.
	Henri B. Haskell,		Mrs. Sarah J. Haskell.

NESTORIAN MISSION.

	Justin Perkins, D. D.,		Mrs. Charlotte Perkins.
r.*	Albert L. Holladay,	r.	Mrs. Anne Y. Holladay.
*	William R. Stocking,	r.	Mrs. Jerusha E. Stocking.
r.	Willard Jones,	r.	Mrs. Miriam Jones.
	Austin H. Wright, M. D.,		Mrs. Catherine A. Wright.
*	Abel K. Hinsdale,	r.*	Mrs. Sarah C. Hinsdale.
*	Colby C. Mitchell,	*	Mrs. Eliza A. Mitchell.
r.	Thomas Laurie,	*	Mrs. Martha F. Laurie.
*	David T. Stoddard,	*	Mrs. Harriet Stoddard.
		r.	Mrs. Sophia D. Stoddard.
	Joseph G. Cochran,		Mrs. Deborah W. Cochran.
	George W. Coan,		Mrs. Sarah Coan.
	Samuel A. Rhea,	*	Mrs. Martha A. Rhea.
			Mrs. Sarah J. Rhea.
*	Edwin H. Crane,	r.	Mrs. Ann E. Crane.
	Thomas L. Ambrose.		
	John H. Shedd,		Mrs. Sarah J. Shedd.
*	Amherst L. Thompson,		Mrs. Esther E. Thompson.
	Benjamin Labaree, Jr.,		Mrs. Elizabeth E. Labaree.
	Henry N. Cobb,		Mrs. Matilda E. Cobb.

Missionary Physicians.

*	Asahel Grant, M. D.,	*	Mrs. Judith S. Grant.
	Frank N. H. Young, M. D.		

Assistant Missionaries.

	Edward Breath,		Mrs. Sarah Ann Breath.
			Miss Fidelia Fisk.
			Miss Mary S. Rice.
			Miss Catherine A. Myers,—now Mrs. Wright.
		*	Miss Martha A. Harris,—afterward Mrs. Rhea.
			Miss Aura J. Beach.
			Miss Harriet N. Crawford.

MISSION TO PERSIA.

r.	James L. Merrick,	r.	Mrs. Emma Merrick.

SOUTHERN ASIA.

r.*	Adoniram Judson, D. D.,	r.*	Mrs. Ann H. Judson.
r.*	Luther Rice.		

MAHRATTA MISSION.

*	Gordon Hall,	r.	Mrs. Margaret Hall.
*	Samuel Newell,	*	Mrs. Harriet Newell.
		r.	Mrs. Philomela Newell,—afterward Mrs. Garrett.
r.	Samuel Nott,	r.	Mrs. Nott.

r. Horatio Bardwell,	r. Mrs. Rachel Bardwell.
* John Nichols,	r.* Mrs. Elizabeth Nichols,—afterward Mrs. Woodward, Ceylon.
* Allen Graves,	Mrs. Mary Graves.
* Edmund Frost,	* Mrs. Clarissa Frost,—afterward Mrs. Woodward, Ceylon, and Mrs. Todd, Madura.
r. David O. Allen, D. D.,	* Mrs. Myra Allen.
	* Mrs. Orpah Allen.
	* Mrs. Azuba C. Allen,—formerly Miss Condit, Borneo Mission.
r. Cyrus Stone,	* Mrs. Atossa Stone.
	r. Mrs. Abigail H. Stone.
* William Hervey,	* Mrs. Elizabeth H. Hervey.
r.* William Ramsey,	* Mrs. Mary Ramsey.
r. Hollis Read,	r. Mrs. Caroline Read.
r. George W. Boggs,	r. Mrs. Isabella W. Boggs.
Sendol B. Munger,	* Mrs. Maria L. Munger.
	* Mrs. Mary E. Munger.
Amos Abbott,	Mrs. Anstice Abbott.
Henry Ballantine,	Mrs. Elizabeth Ballantine.
r. Ebenezer Burgess,	* Mrs. Mary Burgess.
	* Mrs. Abigail Burgess.
r. Ozro French,	r. Mrs. Jane French.
* Robert W. Hume,	r. Mrs. Hannah D. Hume.
r. Royal G. Wilder,	r. Mrs. Eliza J. Wilder.
Samuel B. Fairbank,	* Mrs. Abbie Fairbank.
	Mrs. Mary Fairbank.
William Wood,	* Mrs. Lucy M. Wood.
	* Mrs. Eliza M. Wood.
r. George Bowen.	
Allen Hazen,	Mrs. Martha R. Hazen.
Lemuel Bissell,	Mrs. Mary E. Bissell.
William P. Barker,	Mrs. Lucelia U. Barker.
Samuel C. Dean,	Mrs. Elizabeth A. Dean.
Charles Harding,	Mrs. Julia M. Harding.

Assistant Missionaries.

* James Garrett,	r.* Mrs. Philomela Garrett,—formerly Mrs. Newell.
* William C. Sampson,	r. Mrs. Mary L. Sampson.
r. George W. Hubbard,	r. Mrs. Emma Hubbard.
r. Elijah A. Webster,	r. Mrs. Mariette Webster.
	Miss Cynthia Farrar.

CEYLON MISSION.

* James Richards,	r.* Mrs. Sarah Richards,—afterward Mrs. Knight, Church Mission.
* Edward Warren.	
Benjamin C. Meigs,	Mrs. Sarah M. Meigs.
* Daniel Poor, D. D.,	* Mrs. Susan Poor.
	r.* Mrs. Ann Poor.
Levi Spaulding,	Mrs. Mary Spaulding.
Myron Winslow,—see Madras,	* Mrs. Harriett W. Winslow.
* Henry Woodward,	* Mrs. Lydia Woodward.
	* Mrs. Clarissa Woodward.
* George H. Apthorp,	* Mrs. Mary Apthorp.

r.* Henry R. Hoisington,	r. Mrs. Nancy Hoisington.
r. Samuel Hutchings,	r. Mrs. Elizabeth C. Hutchings.
r. James R. Eckard,	r. Mrs. Margaret E. Eckard.
* Nathan Ward, M. D.,	Mrs. Hannah W. Ward.
* John M. S. Perry,	* Mrs. Harriet J. Perry.
* Samuel G. Whittlesey,	r. Mrs. Anna C. Whittlesey.
John C. Smith,	* Mrs. Eunice P. Smith.
	Mrs. Mary Smith, — formerly Mrs. Steele, Madura.
* Robert Wyman,	r. Mrs. Martha Wyman.
r. Adin H. Fletcher,	r. Mrs. Elizabeth W. Fletcher.
Wm. W. Howland,	Mrs. Susan Howland.
r. William W. Scudder,	* Mrs. Catherine E. Scudder.
Eurotas P. Hastings,	Mrs. Anna Hastings.
r. Cyrus T. Mills, — see Sandwich Islands,	r. Mrs. Susan L. Mills.
Marshall D. Sanders,	Mrs. Georgiana Sanders.
Nathan L. Lord, M. D.,	Mrs. Laura W. Lord.
r. Milan Hitchcock,	r. Mrs. Lucy A. Hitchcock.
James Quick,	Mrs. Maria E. Quick.
James A. Bates,	Mrs. Sarah A. Bates.

Missionary Physician.

Samuel F. Green, M. D.

Assistant Missionaries.

r. Eastman S. Minor,	* Mrs. Lucy Minor.
	r. Mrs. Judith M. Minor.
	Miss Eliza Agnew.
	r. Miss Sarah F. Brown.

MADURA MISSION.

r. William Todd,	* Mrs. Lucy Todd.
	* Mrs. Clarissa Todd.
r.* Alanson C. Hall,	* Mrs. Frances A. Hall.
* John J. Lawrence,	r. Mrs. Mary Lawrence.
* Robert O. Dwight,	* Mrs. Mary Dwight, — afterward Mrs. Winslow.
r. Henry Cherry,	* Mrs. Charlotte H. Cherry.
	* Mrs. Jane E. Cherry.
	r. Mrs. Henrietta Cherry.
r. Edward Cope,	r. Mrs. Emily Cope.
r.* Nathaniel M. Crane,	r. Mrs. Julia A. J. Crane.
Clarendon F. Muzzy,	* Mrs. Samantha B. Muzzy.
	Mrs. Mary Ann Muzzy.
William Tracy,	Mrs. Emily F. Tracy.
r. Ferdinand DeW. Ward,	r. Mrs. Jane Ward.
Horace S. Taylor,	Mrs. Martha E. Taylor.
James Herrick,	Mrs. Elizabeth H. Herrick.
Edward Webb,	Mrs. Nancy A. Webb.
John Rendall,	Mrs. Jane Rendall.
r. Geo. W. McMillan,	r. Mrs. Rebecca N. McMillan.
John E. Chandler,	Mrs. Charlotte M. Chandler.
r. George Ford,	r. Mrs. Ann J. Ford.
r. Charles Little,	* Mrs. Amelia Little.
	r. Mrs. Susan Little.
Joseph T. Noyes,	Mrs. Elizabeth A. Noyes.
Thomas S. Burnell,	Mrs. Martha Burnell.
William D. Capron,	Mrs. Sarah B. Capron.

	Charles T. White, ...		Mrs. Anna M. White.
	Edward Chester, ...		Mrs. Sophia Chester.
	George T. Washburn, ...		Mrs. Eliza E. Washburn.
	David C. Scudder, ...		Mrs. Harriet L. Scudder.

Missionary Physicians.

*	John Steele, M. D., ...		Mrs. Mary Steele.
r.	Charles S. Shelton, M. D., ...	r.	Mrs. Henrietta M. Shelton.

Assistant Missionaries.

r.	Alfred North, — from Singapore.	*	Mrs. Minerva North.
			Miss Sarah W. Ashley.

MADRAS MISSION.

	Myron Winslow, D. D., — see Ceylon, . .	*	Mrs. Catherine Winslow.
		*	Mrs. Ann Winslow.
		*	Mrs. Mary Winslow.
			Mrs. Ellen A. Winslow.
*	John Scudder, M. D., ...	*	Mrs. Harriet Scudder.
r.	Henry M. Scudder, M. D., ...	r.	Mrs. Fanny Scudder.
r.	John W. Dulles, ...	r.	Mrs. Harriet L. Dulles.
r.	Isaac N. Hurd, ...	*	Mrs. Mary C. Hurd.

Assistant Missionaries.

	Phinehas R. Hunt, ...		Mrs. Abigail Hunt.

ARCOT MISSION.

r.	Henry M. Scudder, M. D., — from Madras,	r.	Mrs. Fanny Scudder.
r.	William W. Scudder, — from Ceylon, . .	*	Mrs. Elizabeth O. Scudder.
r.	Joseph Scudder, ...	r.	Mrs. Sarah A. Scudder.
r.	Ezekiel C. Scudder, ...	r.	Mrs. Sarah R. Scudder.
r.	Jared W. Scudder, ...	r.	Mrs. Julia C. Scudder.

Assistant Missionary.

		r.	Miss Louisa Scudder.

EASTERN ASIA.

CANTON MISSION.

	Elijah C. Bridgman, D. D., — see Shanghai,		Mrs. Eliza J. Bridgman.
*	David Abeel, D. D., — see Amoy.		
*	Edwin Stevens.		
r.	Peter Parker, M. D., ...	r.	Mrs. Parker.
	Dyer Ball, M. D., — from Singapore, . .	*	Mrs. Lucy H. Ball.
			Mrs. Isabella Ball.
*	James G. Bridgman.		
	Samuel W. Bonney, ...		Mrs. Catherine Bonney.
*	William A. Macy, — see Shanghai.		
	Daniel Vrooman, ...	*	Mrs. Elizabeth C. Vrooman.
			Mrs. Maria W. Vrooman.
*	Frederick H. Brewster, ...	r.	Mrs. Mary G. Brewster.

Missionary Physician.

r.	William B. Diver, M. D.		

Assistant Missionaries.

r.	S. Wells Williams, LL. D., ...	r.	Mrs. Williams.

AMOY MISSION.

* David Abeel, D. D.
r. Elihu Doty, — from Borneo, ... * Mrs. Clarissa D. Doty.
r. Mrs. Eleanor A. Doty.
* William J. Pohlman, — from Borneo, . . * Mrs. Theodosia R. Pohlman.
r. John Van Nest Talmage, ... r. Mrs. Abby F. Talmage.
r. John S. Joralman, ... r. Mrs. Martha C. Joralman.

FUHCHAU MISSION.

r. Stephen Johnson, — from Siam, ... r. Mrs. Caroline M. Johnson.
Lyman B. Peet, — from Siam, ... * Mrs. Rebecca C. Peet.
Mrs. H. L. Peet.
* Seneca Cummings, ... r. Mrs. Abigail M. Cummings.
Caleb C. Baldwin, ... Mrs. Harriet Baldwin.
* William L. Richards.
Justus Doolittle, ... * Mrs. Sophia A. Doolittle.
Mrs. Lucy E. Doolittle.
Charles Hartwell, ... Mrs. Lucy E. Hartwell.
Simeon F. Woodin, ... Mrs. Sarah L. Woodin.

SHANGHAI MISSION.

Elijah C. Bridgman, D. D., — from Canton, Mrs. Eliza J. Bridgman.
Henry Blodget, ... Mrs. Sarah F. Blodget.
* William Aitchison.
* William A. Macy, — from Canton.

MISSION TO SIAM.

* David Abeel, D. D., — see Amoy.
* Charles Robinson, ... r. Mrs. Maria Robinson.
r. Stephen Johnson, — see Fuhchau, . . . * Mrs. Maria Johnson.
* Mrs. Mary Johnson.
r. Dan B. Bradley, M. D., ... * Mrs. Emilie Bradley.
r. Samuel P. Robbins, ... r. Mrs. Martha R. Robbins.
* Nathan S. Benham, ... r. Mrs. Maria N. Benham.
r.* Jesse Caswell, ... r. Mrs. Anna T. Caswell.
* Henry S. G. French, ... r. Mrs. Sarah C. French.
r. Asa Hemenway, ... r. Mrs. Lucia Hemenway.
L. B. Peet, — see Fuhchau, ... * Mrs. Rebecca C. Peet.

Missionary Physician.

r. Stephen Tracy, M. D., ... r. Mrs. Alice Tracy.

Assistant Missionary.

* Miss Mary E. Pierce.

SINGAPORE MISSION.

r. Ira Tracy, ... r.* Mrs. Adeline Tracy.
r. James T. Dickinson.
r.* Matthew B. Hope, M. D.
r. Joseph S. Travelli, ... r.* Mrs. Susan Travelli.
Dyer Ball, M. D., — see Canton, ... * Mrs. Lucy H. Ball.
George W. Wood, — see N. Armenian Miss., ... * Mrs. Martha M. Wood.

Assistant Missionaries.

r. Alfred North, — see Madura, ... * Mrs. Minerva North.

MISSION TO THE INDIAN ARCHIPELAGO.

* Samuel Munson, ... r. Mrs. Abigail Munson.
* Henry Lyman, ... r. Mrs. Eliza Lyman.
r. William Arms, ... * Mrs. Mary Arms.

MISSION TO BORNEO.

r. Elihu Doty, — see Amoy, ... * Mrs. Clarissa D. Doty.
r. Jacob Ennis, ... r. Mrs. Henrietta B. Ennis.
r. Elbert Nevins, ... r. Mrs. Maria L. Nevins.
r.* William Youngblood, ... r. Mrs. Josephine Youngblood.
* Frederick B. Thomson, ... * Mrs. Catharine Thomson.
* Mrs. Emma Thomson.
* William J. Pohlman, — see Amoy, . . . * Mrs. Theodosia R. Pohlman.
r. William T. Van Doren, ... r. Mrs. Jane A. Van Doren.
* Isaac P. Stryker.
r. William H. Steele.

Assistant Missionary.

* Miss Azuba C. Condit, — afterward Mrs Allen, Bombay.

NORTH PACIFIC OCEAN.

SANDWICH ISLANDS MISSION.

r. Hiram Bingham, ... * Mrs. Sybil Bingham.
r. Asa Thurston, — at the Islands, ... r. Mrs. Lucy Thurston.
* Samuel Whitney, ... r. Mrs. Mercy Whitney.
r. Artemas Bishop, — at the Islands, . . . * Mrs. Elizabeth Bishop.
r. Mrs. Delia Bishop.
r.* William Richards, — died at the Islands, r. Mrs. Clarissa Richards.
r. Charles S. Stewart, ... r.* Mrs. Harriet B. Stewart.
r. James Ely, ... r. Mrs. Louisa Ely.
r. Joseph Goodrich, ... r.* Mrs. Goodrich.
r. Lorrin Andrews, ... r. Mrs. Andrews.
r. Ephraim W. Clark, — at the Islands, . . * Mrs. Mary Clark.
Mrs. Sarah H. Clark.
r. Jonathan S. Green, — at the Islands, . . r.* Mrs. Theodosia Green.
r. Peter J. Gulick, — at the Islands, . . . Mrs. Fanny H. Gulick.
r. Dwight Baldwin, M. D., — at the Islands, Mrs. Charlotte Baldwin.
* Sheldon Dibble, ... * Mrs. Maria M. Dibble.
r. Mrs. Antoinette Dibble.
r.* Reuben Tinker, ... r. Mrs. Mary T. Tinker.
r. William P. Alexander, — at the Islands, r. Mrs. Mary Ann Alexander.
r.* Richard Armstrong, D. D., — died at the Islands, ... r. Mrs. Clarissa Armstrong, — at the Islands.
r. John S. Emerson, — at the Islands, . . . r. Mrs. Ursula S. Emerson.
r. Cochran Forbes, ... r. Mrs. Rebecca D. Forbes.
* Harvey R. Hitchcock, ... r. Mrs. Rebecca Hitchcock, — at the Islands.
r. David B. Lyman, — at the Islands, . . . r. Mrs. Sarah Lyman.
r. Lorenzo Lyons, — at the Islands, ... * Mrs. Betsey Lyons.
r. Mrs. Lucia G. Lyons.
* Ephraim Spaulding, ... r. Mrs. Julia Spaulding.
r. Benjamin W. Parker, — at the Islands, r. Mrs. Mary E. Parker.
r. Lowell Smith, — at the Islands, ... r. Mrs. Abba W. Smith.
r. Titus Coan, — at the Islands, ... r. Mrs. Fidelia Coan.
r. Isaac Bliss, ... r. Mrs. Emily Bliss.
r. Daniel T. Conde, ... * Mrs. Andelusia Conde.
r. Mark Ives, ... r. Mrs. Mary A. Ives.

r. Thomas Lafon, M. D., ...	*r.** Mrs. Sophia L. Lafon.
r. Edward Johnson, — at the Islands, . . .	*r.* Mrs. Lois S. Johnson.
r. Daniel Dole, — at the Islands, ...	* Mrs. Emily H. Dole.
	r. Mrs. Charlotte Dole, — formerly Mrs. Knapp.
r. Elias Bond, — at the Islands, ...	*r.* Mrs. Ellen M. Bond.
r. James W. Smith, M. D., — at the Islands,	*r.* Mrs. Mellicent K. Smith.
r. John D. Paris, — at the Islands, ...	* Mrs. Mary Paris.
	r. Mrs. Mary Paris.
r. George B. Rowell, — at the Islands, . .	*r.* Mrs. Malvina J. Rowell.
r. Asa B. Smith, ...	*r.* Mrs. Sarah G. Smith.
r. Eliphalet Whittlesey, ...	*r.* Mrs. Elizabeth K. Whittlesey.
r. T. Dwight Hunt, ...	*r.* Mrs. Mary Hunt.
r. John F. Pogue, — at the Islands, ...	*r.* Mrs. Maria K. Pogue.
r. Claudius B. Andrews, — at the Islands,	*r.* Mrs. Anna S. Andrews.
r. Samuel G. Dwight.	
* Henry Kinney, ...	*r.** Mrs. Maria L. Kinney.
r. William C. Shipman, — at the Islands,	*r.* Mrs. Jane Shipman.
r. William O. Baldwin, ...	*r.* Mrs. Mary Baldwin.
r. Anderson O. Forbes, — at the Islands,	*r.* Mrs. Forbes.
r. Cyrus T. Mills, — from Ceylon; at the Islands, ...	*r.* Mrs. Susan L. Mills.

Missionary Physicians.

*r.** Thomas Holman, M. D., ...	*r.* Mrs. Lucia Holman.
r. Abraham Blatchley, M. D., ...	*r.* Mrs. Jemima Blatchley.
r. Gerritt P. Judd, M. D., — at the Islands,	*r.* Mrs. Laura Judd.
r. Alonzo Chapin, M. D., ...	*r.* Mrs. Mary Ann Chapin.
r. Seth L. Andrews, M. D., ...	* Mrs. Parnelly Andrews.
r. Charles H. Wetmore, M. D., — at the Islands, ...	*r.* Mrs. Lucy S. Wetmore.

Assistant Missionaries.

*r.** Daniel Chamberlain, ...	*r.* Mrs. Chamberlain.
r. Samuel Ruggles, ...	*r.* Mrs. Nancy Ruggles.
*r.** Elisha Loomis, ...	*r.* Mrs. Maria T. Loomis.
* Levi Chamberlain, ...	*r.* Mrs. Maria Chamberlain, — at the Islands.
* Stephen Shepard, ...	*r.* Mrs. Margaret C. Shepard.
*r.** Andrew Johnstone, — died at the Islands,	*r.* Mrs. Johnstone.
* Edmund H. Rogers, ...	* Mrs. Mary Rogers.
	* Mrs. Elizabeth M. Rogers.
r. Lemuel Fuller.	
r. Henry Dimond, — at the Islands, ...	*r.* Mrs. Ann Maria Dimond.
r. Edwin O. Hall, — at the Islands, ...	*r.* Mrs. Sarah L. Hall.
r. Edward Bailey, — at the Islands, ...	*r.* Mrs. Caroline Bailey.
r. Samuel N. Castle, — at the Islands, . . .	* Mrs. Angeline L. Castle.
	r. Mrs. Mary Castle.
r. Amos S. Cooke, — at the Islands, ...	*r.* Mrs. Juliette Cooke.
* Horton O. Knapp, ...	*r.* Mrs. Charlotte Knapp, — now Mrs. Dole
* Edwin Locke, — at the Islands, ...	* Mrs. Martha L. Locke.
* Charles McDonald, — died at the Islands,	*r.* Mrs. Harriet T. McDonald.
r. Bethuel Munn, ...	* Mrs. Louisa Munn.
r. William S. Van Duzee, ...	*r.* Mrs. Oral Van Duzee.
r. Abner Wilcox, — at the Islands, ...	*r.* Mrs. Lucy E. Wilcox.
	r. Miss Maria Ogden, — at the Islands.
	r. Miss Lydia Brown, — at the Islands.
	r. Miss Marcia M. Smith.
r. William H. Rice, — at the Islands, . . .	*r.* Mrs. Mary S. Rice.
r. William A. Spooner, — at the Islands, . .	*r.* Mrs. Eliza A. Spooner.

MICRONESIA MISSION.

Benjamin G. Snow,	Mrs. Lydia V. Snow.
Luther H. Gulick, M. D.,	Mrs. Louisa Gulick.
Albert A. Sturges,	Mrs. Susan M. Sturges.
Edward T. Doane,	Mrs. Sarah W. Doane.
George Pierson, M. D.,	Mrs. Nancy A. Pierson.
Hiram Bingham, Jr.,	Mrs. Minerva C. Bingham.
Ephraim P. Roberts,	Mrs. Myra H. Roberts.

SOUTH AMERICA.

EXPLORING MISSIONS.

r. John C. Brigham.
r. Theophilus Parvin.
r. William Arms, — see Indian Archipelago. } Patagonia.
r. Titus Coan, — see Sandwich Islands. } Patagonia.

NORTH AMERICAN INDIANS.

CHEROKEE MISSION.

r. Cyrus Kingsbury, D. D., — see Choctaws,	* Mrs. Sarah B. Kingsbury.
r. Loring S. Williams, — see Choctaws,	r. Mrs. Matilda Williams.
* Daniel S. Buttrick,	* Mrs. Elizabeth Buttrick.
* Ard Hoyt,	r. Mrs. Esther Hoyt.
r. William Chamberlain,	r. Mrs. Flora Chamberlain.
* Alfred Finney,	* Mrs. Susanna Finney.
r.* Cephas Washburn,	r. Mrs. Abigail Washburn.
r.* Elizur Butler,	* Mrs. Esther Butler.
	r. Mrs. Lucy Butler.
r. William Potter,	r. Mrs. Laura Potter.
* Samuel A. Worcester, D. D.,	* Mrs. Ann Worcester.
	Mrs. Erminia Worcester.
r. Marcus Palmer, M. D.,	* Mrs. Clarissa Palmer.
	r. Mrs. Jerusha Palmer.
r. John Thompson,	r. Mrs. Ruth B. Thompson.
* Jesse Lockwood,	r. Mrs. Cassandra Lockwood.
Worcester Willey,	* Mrs. Mary Ann Willey.
	Mrs. Annie S. Willey.
Timothy E. Ranney,	Mrs. Charlotte Ranney.
r. Edwin Teele,	r. Mrs. Sarah E. Teele.
r. Horace A. Wentz.	
Charles C. Torrey,	Mrs. Adelaide L. Torrey.

Missionary Physicians.

r.* Roderick L. Dodge, M. D.,	r. Mrs. Emeline Dodge.
r. George L. Weed, M. D., — see Creeks.	

Assistant Missionaries.

r. Moody Hall,	r. Mrs. Isabella Hall.
r. Abijah Conger,	r. Mrs. Conger.
r. John Vail,	r. Mrs. Julia Vail.
r. John Talmage,	r. Mrs. Talmage.
r. James Orr,	* Mrs. Minerva Orr.
	r. Mrs. Julia F. Orr.
r. Jacob Hitchcock,	r. Mrs. Nancy Hitchcock.
* Daniel Hitchcock.	
r.* John C. Ellsworth,	r. Mrs. Eliza Ellsworth.

r. Henry Parker, ... r. Mrs. Philena Parker.
* Erastus Dean, ... * Mrs. Sarah Dean.
r. Sylvester Ellis, ... r. Mrs. Sarah Ellis.
r. Ainsworth E. Blunt, ... r. Mrs. Harriet Blunt.
r. Isaac Proctor, ... r. Mrs. Fanny Proctor.
r. Frederic Ellsworth, ... r. Mrs. Ellsworth.
r. William Holland, ... r. Mrs. Electa Holland.
r. Josiah Hemmingway.
r. Asa Hitchcock, ... * Mrs. Sophronia Hitchcock.
r. Mrs. Lucy Hitchcock.
r. Samuel Wisner, ... * Mrs. Judith Wisner.
r. Samuel Newton, ... * Mrs. Mary H. Newton.
r. Mrs. Newton, — formerly Mrs. Joslyn.
r. William H. Manwaring.
r. Fenner Bosworth, ... r. Mrs. Bosworth.
r. Luke Fernal, ... * Mrs. Joanna Fernal.
r. Kellogg Day, ... r. Mrs. Mary L. Day.
* Aaron Gray.
r. John F. Wheeler, ... r. Mrs. Wheeler.
r. Henry K. Copeland, — see Choctaws, . . r. Mrs. Abigail W. Copeland.
* Miss Ellen Stetson.
r. Miss Sophia Sawyer.
* Miss Cynthia Thrall.
r. Miss Lucy Hutchinson.
r. Miss Delight Sargent.
r. Miss Nancy Thompson.
r. Miss Hannah Kelly.
r. Miss Catharine Fuller.
r. Miss Flora Post.
r. Miss Esther Smith.
r. Miss Sarah A. Palmer.
r. Miss Theresa M. Bissell.
r.* Miss Mary A. Avery.
r. Miss Hannah Moore.
r. Miss Eliza Giddings.
r. Miss Julia S. Hitchcock.
r. Miss Jerusha E. Swain.
r. Miss Lois W. Hall.
r. Miss Julia F. Stone, — see Mrs. Orr.
r. Miss M. E. Denny.
r. Miss Lucina H. Lord.
r. Miss Harriet A. Sheldon.
r. Miss Elizabeth T. Hancock.
r. Miss Mary R. Spooner.
Miss S. Elizabeth Kenney.
Miss Sarah Dean.

CHOCTAW MISSION.

r. Cyrus Kingsbury, D.D., — in the Mission, * Mrs. Sarah B. Kingsbury.
r. Mrs. Electa Kingsbury.
r. Loring S. Williams, ... r. Mrs. Matilda Williams.
r. Joel Wood, ... r. Mrs. Clarissa H. Wood.
* Alfred Wright, ... r. Mrs. Harriet Wright.
r. Cyrus Byington, — in the Mission, . . . r. Mrs. Sophia Byington.
* Samuel Moseley, ... r. Mrs. Sarah Moseley.
* Harrison Allen, ... r. Mrs. Nancy Allen.
r. Henry R. Wilson, ... * Mrs. Sarah Wilson.

r. John R. Agnew.
r. Ebenezer Hotchkin, — in the Mission, . r. Mrs. Philena Hotchkin.
r. Charles C. Copeland, — in the Mission, . r. Mrs. Cornelia Copeland.
r. Joshua Potter, — see Senecas, ... r. Mrs. Jane Potter.
r. John C. Strong, ... r. Mrs. Celia S. Strong.
r. Oliver P. Stark, — in the Mission, . . . * Mrs. Margaret W. Stark.
r. Mrs. Harriet Stark.
r. John Edwards, — in the Mission, . . . r. Mrs. Rosanna H. Edwards.
r. George Pierson, M. D., — afterward at Micronesia, ... * Mrs. Salome Pierson.
r. Simon L. Hobbs, M. D., — in the Mission, r. Mrs. Mary C. Hobbs.
r. Elias L. Boing, ... r. Mrs. Anna M. Boing.

Missionary Physician.

r. William W. Pride, M. D., ... r. Mrs. Hannah Pride.

Assistant Missionaries.

* Aries V. Williams, ... * Mrs. Judith Williams.
r. Peter Kanouse.
r. Moses Jewell, ... r. Mrs. Jewell.
r. John G. Kanouse, ... r. Mrs. Kanouse.
* Isaac Fisk.
r. Anson Dyer, ... * Mrs. Dyer.
r. Zechariah Howes, ... r. Mrs. Lucy Howes.
r. John Smith, ... r. Mrs. Smith.
r. Calvin Cushman, ... r. Mrs. Laura Cushman.
r. Elijah Bardwell, ... r. Mrs. Lavina Bardwell.
* William Hooper, ... * Mrs. Vina Hooper.
r. Mrs. Eliza Hooper.
r. David Remington, ... r. Mrs. Esther Remington.
r. Philo P. Stewart, ... r. Mrs. Eliza Stewart.
r. Stephen B. Macomber, ... r. Mrs. Macomber.
r. Anson Gleason, — see Senecas, ... r. Mrs. Bethiah W. Gleason.
r. David Wright, ... * Mrs. Lucinda Wright.
r. Ebenezer Bliss.
r. David Gage, ... r. Mrs. Betsey Gage.
r. Samuel Moulton, ... r. Mrs. Lucinda Moulton.
r. Elijah S. Town, ... r. Mrs. Hannah E. Town.
r. John Dudley.
* Matthias Joslyn, ... r. Mrs. Sophia M. Joslyn, — afterward Mrs. Newton, of Cherokee Mission.
r. Abner D. Jones, ... r. Mrs. Eunice G. Jones.
* Jared Olmstead, ... r. Mrs. Julia S. Olmstead.
r. Peter Auten, ... r. Mrs. Lydia Auten.
r.* Miss Anna Burnham.
r. Miss Eliza R. Buer.
r. Miss Pamela Skinner.
r. Miss Nancy Foster.
r. Miss Eunice Clough.
r. Miss Louisa M. Williams.
r. Miss Elizabeth A. Merrill.
r. Henry K. Copeland, — from Cherokees, r. Mrs. Abigail H. Copeland.
* Mrs. Nancy Barnes.
r. Miss Sarah Kerr.
r. Miss Harriet Arms.
r. Miss Susan Tracy.
* Miss Harriet E. Crosby.
r.* David H. Winship, ... r. Mrs. Winship.

r. Lewis Bissell, ... * Mrs. Mary Bissell.
* Mrs. Mary J. Bissell.
r. Edwin Lathrop, ... r. Mrs. Cornelia F. C. Lathrop.
r. Miss Cornelia F. C. Dolbear,—see Mrs. Lathrop.
* Miss Catharine Belden.
* Miss Lucinda Downer.
r. Miss Lydia S. Hall.
r. Miss Laura E. Tilton.
r. Miss Harriet N. Keyes.
r. Miss Catharine A. Fay.
r. Miss Marcia Colton.
* Miss Harriet Goulding.
r. Miss Caroline Dickinson.
r. Miss Juliette Slate.
r. Miss Hannah Bennett.
r. Miss Mary A. Root.
r. David Breed, ... * Mrs. Sarah A. Breed.
r. Miss Jerusha Edwards.
r. Miss Caroline A. Fox.
r. Mrs. Ann B. Dana.
r. Miss Elizabeth J. Hough.
r. Miss Angelina Hosmer.
r. Miss Eunice Starr.
r. Horace D. Smith.
r. John A. Beals.
r. Miss Maria P. Arms.
r. Miss Harriet McCormick,—see Mrs. Stark.
r. Miss Chloe M. Bigelow.
r. Jason D. Chamberlain, ... r. Mrs. Elsey G. Chamberlain.
r. Abraham G. Lansing, ... r. Mrs. Sarah M. Lansing.
r. Samuel T. Libby,—in the Mission, . . r. Mrs. Hannah E. Libby.
r. Miss Priscilla G. Child,—in the Mission.
r. Miss Mercy Whitcomb.
r. Miss Elizabeth Backus.
r. Miss Mary M. Curtis.
* Miss Laura M. Aiken.
r. Harvey R. Schermerhorn.
r. Miss Frances W. Sawyer.
r. Miss Helen E. Woodward.
r. Miss Hannah E. Pruden,—see Mrs. Libby.
r. Miss Harriet A. Dada.
r. Miss Charity A. Gaston.
r. Miss Lucy E. Lovell,—in the Mission.
r. Miss Mary W. Lovell.
r. Miss Mary Ann Greenlee,—in the Miss.
r. Miss Mary J. Semple,—in the Mission.
r. Miss Eliza C. Kendall,—in the Mission.

DAKOTA MISSION.

Thomas S. Williamson, ... Mrs. Margaret Williamson.
r. Jedediah D. Stevens, ... r. Mrs. Julia Stevens.
Stephen R. Riggs, ... Mrs. Mary A. C. Riggs.
r. Samuel W. Pond, ... * Mrs. Cordelia Pond.
r. Mrs. Rebecca Pond.

r. Gideon H. Pond, ... * Mrs. Sarah Pond.
* Robert Hopkins, ... r. Mrs. Agnes C. Hopkins.
r. Moses N. Adams, ... r. Mrs. Nancy A. M. Adams.
r. John F. Aiton, ... r. Mrs. Nancy Aiton.
r. Joseph W. Hancock, ... * Mrs. Martha M. Hancock.
r. Mrs. Sarah Hancock.

Assistant Missionaries.

r. Alexander G. Huggins, ... r. Mrs. Lydia Huggins.
r. Miss Lucy C. Stevens.
r. Jonas Pettijohn, ... r. Mrs. Fanny Pettijohn.
Hugh D. Cunningham, ... Mrs. Mary B. Cunningham.
Miss Jane S. Williamson.
r. Miss Sarah Rankin, — afterward Mrs. Hancock.
r. Miss Lucy Spooner.
r. Miss Mary R. Spooner, — see Cherokees.
Mrs. Anna B. Ackley.

OJIBWA MISSION.

r. Sherman Hall, ... r. Mrs. Betsey Hall.
r. William T. Boutwell, ... r. Mrs. Hester Boutwell.
r. Frederick Ayer, ... r. Mrs. Elizabeth Ayer.
Leonard H. Wheeler, ... Mrs. Harriet Wheeler.

Assistant Missionaries.

r. Edmund F. Ely, ... r. Mrs. Catharine Ely.
r. Joseph Town, ... r. Mrs. Hannah Town.
r. John L. Seymour, ... r. Mrs. Jane B. Seymour.
r. Greenville T. Sproat, ... r. Mrs. Florantha Sproat.
r. Miss Delia Cooke.
r. Miss Sabrina Stevens.
r. Woodbridge L. James, ... r. Mrs. Phebe G. James.
r. Miss Abigail Spooner.
r.* Charles Pulsifer, ... r. Mrs. Hannah H. Pulsifer.
r. D. Irenæus Miner, ... r. Mrs. Lydia J. Miner.
David B. Spencer, ... Mrs. D. B. Spencer.
Miss Rhoda W. Spicer.

CHICKASAW MISSION.

r. Thomas C. Stuart, ... r. Mrs. Stuart.
r. William C. Blair, ... r. Mrs. Blair.
r. Hugh Wilson, ... r. Mrs. Ethalinda Wilson.
r. James Holmes, ... r. Mrs. Sarah A. Holmes.

Assistant Missionaries.

* Miss Prudence Wilson.
r. Miss Emeline H. Richmond.

MISSION TO THE CREEKS.

r. John Fleming, ... r. Mrs. Margaret Fleming.

Missionary Physicians.

r. Geo. L. Weed, M. D., — from Cherokees, r. Mrs. Eliza H. Weed.
r. Roderick L. Dodge, M. D., — from the Cherokees, ... r. Mrs. Emeline Dodge.

MISSION TO THE OSAGES.

r. William F. Vaill, ... r. Mrs. Asenath Vaill.
r. Nathaniel B. Dodge, ... r. Mrs. Sally Dodge.
r. Benton Pixley, ... r. Mrs. Lucia F. Pixley.
* William B. Montgomery, ... * Mrs. Harriet Montgomery.
r. Amasa Jones, ... r. Mrs. Roxanna Jones.

Assistant Missionaries.

r. William C. Requa, ... * Mrs. Susan Requa.
* Mrs. Jane Requa.
r. George Requa, ... * Mrs. Sarah S. Requa.
r. Mrs. Mary H. Requa.
r. Daniel H. Austin, ... r. Mrs. Lydia Austin.
r. Abraham Redfield, ... r. Mrs. Phebe Redfield.
r. Samuel B. Bright, ... r. Mrs. Charlotte Bright.
r. Richard Colby.
r. Miss Mary B. Choate.
r. Miss Mary Etris.
r. Miss Elvira G. Perkins.

MISSION TO THE PAWNEES.

r. John Dunbar, ... r. Mrs. Esther Dunbar.
Timothy E. Ranney, — see Cherokees, . Mrs. Charlotte Ranney.

Missionary Physician.

* Benedict Satterlee, ... * Mrs. Martha A. Satterlee.

Assistant Missionaries.

r. Samuel Allis, ... r. Mrs. Emeline Allis.
r. George B. Gaston, ... r. Mrs. Gaston.

MISSION TO OREGON INDIANS.

r. Henry H. Spalding, — in Oregon, . . . * Mrs. Eliza Spalding.
r. Cushing Eells, — in Oregon, ... r. Mrs. Myra Eells.
r. Asa B. Smith, — see Sandwich Islands, . r. Mrs. Sarah G. Smith.
r. Elkanah Walker, — in Oregon, ... r. Mrs. Mary Walker.

Missionary Physician.

* Marcus Whitman, M. D., ... * Mrs. Narcissa Whitman.

Assistant Missionaries.

r. William H. Gray, ... r. Mrs. Mary A. Gray.
r. Cornelius Rogers.

MACKINAW MISSION.

r. William M. Ferry, ... r. Mrs. Ferry.

Assistant Missionaries.

r. Martin Heydenburk, ... r. Mrs. Huldah W. Heydenburk.
r. John S. Hudson, ... r. Mrs. Hudson.
r. John Newland, ... r. Mrs. Newland.
r. Abel D. Newton.
r. Lucius Garey, ... r. Mrs. Frances M. Garey.
r. Mason Hearsey.
r. W. R. Campbell, ... r. Mrs. Dolly Campbell.

r. Miss Betsey McFarland.
r. Miss Hannah Goodale.
r. Miss Persis Skinner.

MISSION TO THE STOCKBRIDGE INDIANS.

* Jesse Miner, ... r. Mrs. Amanda Miner.
r. Cutting Marsh, ... r. Mrs. Eunice O. Marsh.

Assistant Missionaries.

* Augustus T. Ambler.
r. Chauncey Hall, ... r. Mrs. Matilda Hall.
r. Miss Sophia Mudgett.

MISSION AT MAUMEE.

r. Isaac Van Tassel, ... r. Mrs. Van Tassel.

Assistant Missionaries.

r. Sidney L. Brewster, ... r. Mrs. Sarah Brewster.
r. Miss Hannah Riggs.
r. Miss Rebecca Newell.

NEW YORK INDIANS.

r. Thompson S. Harris, ... r. Mrs. Marrianne Harris.
r.* Joseph Lane, ... r. Mrs. Rebecca Lane.
r. John Eliot, ... r. Mrs. Mary Eliot.
Asher Wright, ... * Mrs. Martha Wright.
Mrs. Laura M. Wright.
r. Asher Bliss, ... r. Mrs. Cassandra Bliss.
r. William Williams, ... r. Mrs. Mehetibel Williams.
r. William Hall, ... r. Mrs. Emeline Hall.
r. Gilbert Rockwood, ... r. Mrs. Avis Rockwood.
r. Joshua Potter, — from Choctaws, . . . r. Mrs. Jane Potter.
Anson Gleason, — from Choctaws, . . . Mrs. Bethiah W. Gleason.

Assistant Missionaries.

r. William A. Thayer, ... r. Mrs. Susan Thayer.
r. Hanover Bradley, ... r. Mrs. Catharine Bradley.
r. Miss Asenath Bishop.
r. Miss Nancy Henderson.
r. Miss Emily Root.
r. Miss Elizabeth Stone.
r. Miss Relief Thayer.
r. Miss Fidelia Adams.
r. Miss Hannah T. Whitcomb.
* Miss Margaret N. Hall.
Miss Mary L. Gleason.
Nathaniel H. Pierce, ... Mrs. Agnes D. Pierce.
r. Miss Sophia Mudgett.
r. Miss Mary Jane Thayer.
r. Miss Caroline A. Fox, — see Choctaws.
r. Miss Jerusha Edwards, — see Choctaws.
r. Miss Eunice Wise.
r. Miss Mary Kent.
r. Miss Harriet S. Clark.

VI. REGULATIONS FOR THE EXPENDITURE OF THE MISSIONS.

[Adopted October, 1860.—See p. 169.]

1. The annual appropriations to the several missions should cover every probable expenditure within the mission, including exchange on sale of bills by the treasurer of the mission.

2. The missions should keep rigidly within the amount appropriated, but should be allowed to transfer appropriations from one department of service to another, when considered necessary by the mission.

3. No mission should ask for a special grant during the year, except for very cogent reasons, nor unless it is willing the special grant should be charged to the appropriation for the next following year. In case the Prudential Committee make such grant, they should charge it to the next annual appropriation, unless the contingent fund for the year will bear it, or the state of the receipts indicate that it may safely be added to the annual appropriation without occasioning a debt. The mission should be informed whether it is charged to the contingent fund, or carried forward as a charge for the next year, or covered by a supplementary appropriation.

4. The appropriations, or reserved fund, for new missionaries, should embrace: 1. Estimated outfit of the missionaries to be sent during the year; 2. The cost of their outward passage; and, 3. Their expenses after reaching the field, until they can be put on salaries under the regular appropriations. If the expenses of a new missionary, after his arrival in the mission and before he is placed on a salary, are borne by the funds in the hands of the mission, the mission should charge the sum so expended to the Board, to be reimbursed by a supplementary appropriation chargeable to the fund reserved for new missionaries. After this fund has been exhausted, no more new missionaries should be sent out during that year, unless the receipts clearly indicate that it may be done without the hazard of thereby creating a debt.

5. The fund reserved for missionaries returning to their fields (whether by itself, or consolidated with that for new missionaries) should embrace the passage money, refit if any, and traveling and other expenses after their arrival, until they are put upon salaries. These last expenses, if paid by the mission from funds otherwise appropriated, should be charged to the Board, to be reimbursed and charged as in the case of new missionaries.

6. The reserved fund for homeward-bound missionaries should embrace the expenses of their return home. The homeward expenses should be borne by the mission, to the extent of the unexpended balance of the appropriation for the salary and other expenses of the returning missionary. If the mission pay more than this balance, the excess should be charged to the

Board, and should be reimbursed by the Committee, and charged to this reserved fund. — The appropriations for missionaries while in this country should be provided for by a distinct fund; and their expenses should be compensated for, as far as circumstances will permit, by the labors of those missionaries in behalf of the Board, under the direction of the Secretaries.

7. One of the Regulations of the Board is as follows, viz.: "When any missionary or assistant missionary of the Board shall desire, on account of ill health or any other cause, to return to the United States, he is required to obtain permission from the Prudential Committee so to do, when it is practicable, (always sending with his request the opinion of his mission,) and when impracticable to obtain such permission, he is required to obtain the consent of his mission; which consent shall always be subject to the revision of the Prudential Committee." If a mission, or its authorized committee, consent to the return of a missionary in disregard of this rule of the Board, the expense of the return should be charged to the mission, unless the return shall be approved by the Prudential Committee, after being informed of the facts. But, if the Committee shall subsequently approve of the return, the rights and liabilities of the parties are to stand as if there had been a previous consent.

8. The annual appropriation shall contain an item for contingencies; and this item shall be such percentage of the estimated receipts of the year, as experience shall show to be necessary. This appropriation is designed to cover such necessary expenditures as can not be foreseen when the annual appropriations are made. Balances remaining to the credit of either of these reserved funds, namely, for new missionaries, missionaries returning to their fields, missionaries in this country, or contingencies, may be transferred to either of the other reserved funds that shall most need them.

9. If, at the end of any year, there shall remain in the treasury of any mission an unexpended balance from previous appropriations, the treasurer of the mission shall certify the amount of such balance to the Treasurer of the Board, in order that he may take it into account in his remittances for the next following year.

VII. LITERATURE OF THE BOARD AND OF ITS MISSIONS.

[See pp. 190-194, 369-382.]

THE limits of this work do not admit of any thing like a full catalogue of the publications which come properly under the above heading. For general views, and for all that needs to be said concerning the Reports, Periodicals, and Tracts of the Board, the reader is referred to pages 190–194, 369–382. The titles of the Biographies, Histories, Travels, Sermons, and Miscellanies are necessarily very much abridged. Of the publications by the Missions, in various languages, some of the more important will be noted, with the number of titles in each language, so far as known.

MISSIONARY BIOGRAPHY.

Life and Labors of Samuel Worcester, D. D., Corresponding Secretary of the A. B. C. F. M. By his son, Samuel M. Worcester, D. D. 2 vols. Boston, Crocker & Brewster, 1852. pp. 468 and 488.

Memoir of Jeremiah Evarts, Esq., Corresponding Secretary of the A. B. C. F. M. By E. C. Tracy. Boston, 1845. pp. 448.

Memoir of Rev. Elias Cornelius. By B. B. Edwards. Boston, Perkins & Marvin, 1833. pp. 360.

Memoir and Sermons of W. J. Armstrong, D. D., Corresponding Secretary of the A. B. C. F. M. By Rev. Hollis Read. New York, 1853. pp. 411.

Memoir of Mrs. Harriet Newell, Missionary to India, who died at the Isle of France, Nov. 30, 1812, aged nineteen years. By Leonard Woods, D. D. Boston, Samuel T. Armstrong, 1818. pp. 258.

Memoirs of Samuel J. Mills. By Gardiner Spring, D. D. New York, 1820. pp. 247. Also, an Improved Edition, 1829, edited by E. C. Bridgman and C. W. Allen. pp. 259.

Memoir of Adoniram Judson, D. D. By Francis Wayland, D. D. Boston, 1853. 2 vols. pp. 544 and 521.

Memoir of Mrs. Ann H. Judson. By James D. Knowles. Boston, 1829 and 1856.

Memoir of Rev. Levi Parsons, Missionary to Palestine. By Rev. Daniel O. Morton. Smith & Shute, 1824. pp. 431.

Memoir of Rev. Pliny Fisk, Missionary to Palestine. By Alvan Bond. Boston, Crocker & Brewster, 1828. pp. 437.

Memoir of Rev. Gordon Hall, one of the First Missionaries of the A. B. C. F. M. By Horatio Bardwell. Andover, Flagg, Gould & Newman, 1834. pp. 260.

Life and Letters of Rev. Daniel Temple, Missionary in Western Asia. By his son, Rev. Daniel H. Temple. Congregational Board of Publication, 1855. pp. 492.

Memoirs of American Missionaries, formerly connected with the Society of Inquiry respecting Missions in the Andover Theological Seminary. Boston, Peirce & Parker, 1833. pp. 367.

Memoirs of Rev. Samuel Munson and Rev. Henry Lyman, Missionaries to the Indian Archipelago. By Rev. William Thompson. New York, 1839. pp. 196.

The Martyr of Sumatra: A Memoir of Henry Lyman. New York, 1856. pp. 437.

Memoir of Asahel Grant, M. D., Missionary to the Nestorians. By Rev. A. C. Lathrop. New York, M. W. Dodd, 1847. pp. 216.

Dr. Asahel Grant and the Mountain Nestorians. By Rev. Thomas Laurie, surviving Associate in that Mission. Boston, Gould & Lincoln, 1853 and 1856. pp. 418.

Memoir of David Abeel, D. D., Missionary to China. By Rev. G. R. Williamson. New York, Robert Carter, 1848. pp. 315.

Memoir of Rev. Henry Lobdell, M. D., Missionary at Mosul. By W. S. Tyler, D. D. Boston, American Tract Society, 1859. pp. 414.

Memoir of Rev. David Tappan Stoddard, Missionary to the Nestorians. By Joseph P. Thompson, D. D. New York, Sheldon, Blakeman & Co. pp. 422.

Memorial of Rev. Henry Martyn Adams, Missionary to Western Africa. By Rev. Albert Bushnell. Boston, Mass. Sabbath School Society, 1859. pp. 69.

American Missionary Memorial. By H. W. Pierson. New York, Harper & Brothers, 1853. pp. 504. [This volume contains sketches of Gordon Hall, James Richards, Adoniram Judson, Pliny Fisk, Levi Parsons, Daniel Temple, Azariah Smith, David Abeel, Frederic B. Thomson, Samuel Munson, and Henry Lyman; also of Harriet Newell, Ann H. Judson, Harriet L. Winslow, Catharine H. Scudder, and Sarah L. Smith.]

Sermons by Rev. Reuben Tinker, Missionary at the Sandwich Islands; with a Biographical Sketch. By M. L. P. Thompson, D. D. Buffalo, N. Y., 1856. pp. 421.

Memoir of Mrs. Myra W. Allen, Missionary in Bombay. By Cyrus Mann. Boston, Mass. Sab. School Society, 1834. pp. 256.

Memoir of Mrs. Harriet Wadsworth Winslow, of the Ceylon Mission. By Myron Winslow. New York, Leavitt, Lord & Co., 1835. pp. 408.

Remains of Mrs. Catharine Winslow, of the American Mission at Madras. By Rev. Jared B. Waterbury. Boston, Mass. Sabbath School Society, 1851. pp. 357.

Memoir of Mrs. Sarah Lanman Smith, of the Mission in Syria. By Edward W. Hooker, of Bennington, Vt. Boston, Perkins & Marvin, 1839. pp. 407.

Memoir of Mrs. Mary Elizabeth Van Lennep, Missionary in Turkey. By her Mother. New York, 1847 and 1860. pp. 382.

Memorial of Mrs. Henrietta A. L. Hamlin, Missionary in Turkey. By Margarette Woods Lawrence. Boston, Ticknor, Reed & Fields, 1854. pp. 321.

Memoir of Mary M. Ellis, Wife of the Rev. William Ellis, Missionary to the South Seas and the Sandwich Islands, and Foreign Secretary to the London Missionary Society. By William Ellis. London.

Memorial of Mrs. Seraphina Haynes Everett and Mrs. Harriet Martha Hamlin, Missionaries at Constantinople. By Mrs. Mary G. Benjamin. Boston, American Tract Society, 1860.

Bartimeus of the Sandwich Islands. By Rev. Hiram Bingham. New York, American Tract Society. pp. 58.

Memoir of Charles Lathrop Winslow. Boston, William Pierce, 1834. pp. 108.

Memoir of Lucy Goodale Thurston, of the Sandwich Islands. By Mrs. Cummings. New York, Dayton & Newman, 1842. pp. 233.

Memoir of Judith Grant Perkins, of Oroomiah, Persia. By her Father. Boston, John P. Jewett & Co., 1853. pp. 224.

Memoirs of Henry Obookiah, of Hawaii, a Member of the Foreign Mission School. Philadelphia, Am. S. S. Union, 1829. pp. 126.

Memoirs of the Converted Brahmin Babajee. By Rev. Hollis Read. 2 vols. New York, Leavitt, Lord & Co., 1836. pp. 264 and 275.

Sketches of Pious Nestorians who have died at Oroomiah, Persia. By Members of the Mission. Boston, Mass. S. S. Society, 1857. pp. 284.

Memoir of Catherine Brown, a Christian Indian of the Cherokee Nation. By Rufus Anderson. Boston, Crocker & Brewster, 1824. pp. 144.

Memoir of John Arch, a Cherokee Young Man. Mass. S. S. Union, 1832. pp. 33.

The Little Osage Captive. By Elias Cornelius. Mass. S. S. Society, 1832.

HISTORICAL WORKS BY MISSIONARIES.

A Sketch of Missions. By Myron Winslow, Missionary to Ceylon. Andover, Flagg & Gould, 1819. pp. 432.

India and its People, Ancient and Modern. By Rev. Hollis Read, Missionary to India. Columbus, Ohio, J. & H. Miller, 1859. pp. 384.

The Civil, Religious, and Political History of the Sandwich Islands. By Hiram Bingham, Twenty-one Years a Missionary at those Islands. Hartford, Hezekiah Huntington, 1847. pp. 616.

History of the Sandwich Islands Mission. By Rev. Sheldon Dibble, Missionary to those Islands. New York, Taylor & Dodd, 1839. pp. 268.

Western Africa, its History, Condition, and Prospects. By Rev. John Leighton Wilson, Eighteen Years a Missionary in Africa. New York, Harper & Brothers, 1856. pp. 527.

Residence of Eight Years among the Nestorians in Persia. By Rev. Justin Perkins. Andover, Allen, Morrill & Wardwell, 1843. pp. 512.

The Middle Kingdom; a Survey of the Geography, Government, Education, Social Life, Arts, Religion, etc., of the Chinese Empire and its Inhabitants. By S. Wells Williams, LL. D., Missionary to China. 2 vols. New York, Wiley & Putnam, 1848. pp. 590 and 614.

Christianity Revived in the East; or, A Narrative of the Work of God among the Armenians of Turkey. By Rev. H. G. O. Dwight, Missionary at Constantinople. New York, 1850. pp. 290.

Christianity in Turkey. The Protestant Reformation in the Armenian Church. By H. G. O. Dwight, D. D. London, 1854. pp. 360.

India, Ancient and Modern, Geographical, Historical, Political, Social, and Religious; with a Particular Account of the State and Prospects of Christianity. By David Oliver Allen, D. D., Missionary for Twenty-five Years in India. Boston, John P. Jewett & Co., 1856. pp. 618.

MISSIONARY TRAVELS.

Journal of a Residence in the Sandwich Islands during the Years 1823, 1824, and 1825. By Charles Samuel Stewart, Missionary at the Islands. London, Fisher & Jackson, 1828. pp. 407.

A Residence at Constantinople in the Year 1827. By Josiah Brewer, Missionary to the Mediterranean. New Haven, Durvie & Peck, 1830. pp. 372.

Observations upon the Peloponnesus and Greek Islands. By Rufus Anderson. Boston, Crocker & Brewster, 1830. pp. 334.

A Residence in the Sandwich Islands. By Charles Samuel Stewart, Missionary at the Islands. Boston, Weeks, Jordan & Co., 1839. pp. 348.

A Visit to the South Seas, in the United States Ship Vincennes. By Charles S. Stewart, Chaplain in the U. S. Navy. 2 vols. New York, John P. Haven, 1831. pp. 357 and 360.

Exploring Tour beyond the Rocky Mountains. By Rev. Samuel Parker. Ithaca, N. Y., 1838. pp. 371.

The Nestorians, or the Lost Tribes. By Asahel Grant, M. D. London, John Murray, 1841, and New York, 1841. pp. 338.

Researches of the Rev. E. Smith and Rev. H. G. O. Dwight, in Armenia. By Eli Smith. Boston, Crocker & Brewster, 1833. pp. 328 and 348. Republished in London.

The Land and the Book; or Biblical Illustrations drawn from the Manners, Customs, Scenes, and Scenery of the Holy Land. By William M. Thomson, D. D., Missionary in Syria and Palestine. 2 vols. New York, Harper & Brothers, 1859. pp. 557 and 614.

Life in India; or, Madras, the Neilgherries, and Calcutta. By Rev. John W. Dulles. Philadelphia, 1855. pp. 528.

Journal of a Residence in China and the Neighboring Countries, from 1829 to 1833. By David Abeel, D. D. New York, Leavitt, Lord & Co., [illegible]. pp. [illegible].

Journal of a Missionary Tour in India, performed by the Rev. Messrs. Read and Ramsey. By William Ramsey. Philadelphia, J. Wetham, 1836. pp. 367.

MISSIONARY SERMONS BEFORE THE BOARD.

Year.	*Place of Meeting.*	*Preacher.*	*Text.*
1813	Boston	* Timothy Dwight, D. D.	John 10 : 16.
1814	New Haven	* James Richards, D. D.	Ephes. 3 : 8.
1815	Salem	* Calvin Chapin, D. D.	Ps. 96 : 10.
1816	Hartford	* Henry Davis, D. D.	Ps. 119 : 96.
1817	Northampton	* Jesse Appleton, D. D.	1 Cor. 1 : 21.
1818	New Haven	* Samuel Spring, D. D.	Acts 8 : 30, 31.
1819	Boston	* Joseph Lyman, D. D.	Isaiah 58 : 12.
1820	Hartford	Eliphalet Nott, D. D.	Mark 16 : 15.
1821	Springfield	* Jedediah Morse, D. D.	Ps. 2 : 8.
1822	New Haven	* Alexander Proudfit, D. D.	Mal. 1 : 11.
1823	Boston	Jeremiah Day, D. D.	Neh. 6 : 3.
1824	Hartford	* Samuel Austin, D. D.	Gal. 1 : 15, 16.
1825	Northampton	* Joshua Bates, D. D.	John 8 : 32.
1826	Middletown	* Edward D. Griffin, D. D.	Matt. 28 : 18, 20.
1827	New York	Lyman Beecher, D. D.	Luke 11 : 21, Rev., &c.
1828	Philadelphia	* John H. Rice, D. D.	2 Cor. 10 : 4.
1829	Albany	* Archibald Alexander, D. D.	Acts 11 : 18.
1830	Boston	Thomas DeWitt, D. D.	Matt. 9 : 37, 38.
1831	New Haven	* Leonard Woods, D. D.	Isaiah 62 : 1, 2.
1832	New York	William Allen, D. D.	John 8 : 36.
1833	Philadelphia	* William Murray, D. D.	2 Cor. 10 : 4.
1834	Utica	Gardiner Spring, D. D.	Matt. 10 : 6.
1835	Baltimore	* Samuel Miller, D. D.	Numb. 14 : 21.
1836	Hartford	* John Codman, D. D.	Matt. 10 : 8.
1837	Newark	John McDowall, D. D.	Acts 4 : 12.
1838	Portland	Heman Humphrey, D. D.	Ps. 102 : 13–16.
1839	Troy	Thomas McAuley, D. D.	Isaiah 11 : 9.
1840	Providence	Nathan S. S. Beman, D. D.	Ps. 72 : 17.
1841	Philadelphia	* Justin Edwards, D. D.	Zech. 4 : 6.
1842	Norwich	William R. DeWitt, D. D.	2 Cor. 5 : 14.
1843	Rochester	Thomas H. Skinner, D. D.	Phil. 3 : 13.
1844	Worcester	Rev. Albert Barnes	Luke 14 : 28–32.
1845	Brooklyn	Mark Hopkins, D. D.	Ps. 55 : 22.
1846	New Haven	Joel Hawes, D. D.	1 Sam. 7 : 12.
1847	Buffalo	David Magie, D. D.	Isaiah 33 : 15.
1848	Boston	Isaac Ferris, D. D.	Matt. 6 : 10.
1849	Pittsfield	Samuel H. Cox, D. D.	Dan. 7 : 27.
1850	Oswego	Richard S. Storrs, D. D.	1 Cor. 15 : 58.
1851	Portland	David H. Riddle, D. D.	Isaiah 41 : 14, 15.
1852	Troy	Leonard Bacon, D. D.	2 Cor. 5 : 7.
1853	Cincinnati	William Adams, D. D.	Matt. 13 : 38.
1854	Hartford	Charles White, D. D.	Matt. 6 : 10.
1855	Utica	Nehemiah Adams, D. D.	Gal. 2 : 20.
1856	Newark	George W. Bethune, D. D.	1 Tim. 1 : 15.
1857	Providence	M. LaRue P. Thompson, D. D.	Matt. 28 : 20.
1858	Detroit	George Shepard, D. D.	Luke 11 : 41.
1859	Philadelphia	Robert W. Patterson, D. D.	Matt. 13 : 33.
1860	Boston	Samuel W. Fisher, D. D.	Isaiah 15 : 1-6, 43 : 21.

BEFORE AUXILIARY SOCIETIES.

The Kingdom of the Messiah. For. Miss. Soc. of Salem and Vicinity, 1813. By Samuel Worcester, D. D.

For. Miss. Soc. of Litchfield County, 1813. By Bennet Tyler.

The Enlargement of the Church of Christ. For. Miss. Soc. of Norwich and Vicinity, 1813. By Levi Nelson.

The Burden and Heat of the Day borne by the Jewish Church. At Shelburne, Mass., 1813. By Joshua Spaulding.

Soc. of For. Miss. of Boston and Vicinity, 1813. By Abiel Holmes, D. D.

Soc. of For. Miss. of Boston and Vicinity. By William Greenough.

Revelation necessary to Salvation. For. Miss. Soc. of Windham County, 1815. By Zebulon Ely.

Thy Kingdom come. For. Miss. Soc. of Boston and Vic., 1820. By Sereno E. Dwight.

The Relation of the Present State of Religion to the Millennium. For. Miss. Soc. of Boston and Vicinity, 1823. By James Sabine.

The Duty of Christians to the Jews. Palestine Miss. Soc. in Halifax, Mass., 1823. By Daniel Huntington.

The Moral Condition and Prospects of the Heathen. For. Miss. Soc. of Boston and Vicinity, 1824. By Benjamin B. Wisner.

Bible, For. Miss., and Education Societies of the County of Hampden, 1823. By William B. Sprague.

Palestine Miss. Soc., 1824. By Daniel Thomas.

Signs of the Times. Formation of an Aux. Miss. Soc., 1824. By Rev. Thomas Snell.

The Obligations of Christians to the Heathen World. Aux. For. Miss. Soc. of Boston and Vicinity, 1825. By Warren Fay.

Signs of the Times. For. Miss. Soc. of New York and Brooklyn, 1850. By Erskine Mason, D. D.

Christianity, its Destined Supremacy on the Earth. For. Miss. Soc. of New York and Brooklyn, 1851. By Richard S. Storrs, Jr.

Personal Piety, as related to the Missionary Work. For. Miss. Soc. of New York and Brooklyn, 1852. By Asa D. Smith, D. D.

For. Miss. Soc. of New York and Brooklyn, 1853. By M. S. Hutton, D. D.

Dr. George B. Cheever's Sermon, 1854. Same Society.

Dr. William Adams's Sermon, 1855. Same Society.

Rev. William Hogarth's Sermon, 1856. Same Society.

Rev. Samuel T. Spear's Sermon, 1857. Same Society.

Dr. Joel Parker's Sermon, 1858. Same Society.

Rev. Rufus W. Clark's Sermon, 1859. Same Society.

Dr. Walter Clarke's Sermon, 1860. Same Society.

Palestine Miss. Soc., 1857. By Rev. Ezekiel Russell.

ORDINATION SERMONS.

In the Tabernacle Church, Salem, Nov. 5, 1818, at the ordination of the Messrs. Pliny Fisk, Levi Spaulding, Myron Winslow, and Henry Woodward. By Moses Stuart.

The Promised Land. In Goshen, Conn., at the ordination of the Messrs. Hiram Bingham and Asa Thurston, as Missionaries to the Sandwich Islands, Sept. 29, 1819. By Heman Humphrey.

At North Bridgewater, Oct. 31, 1821, at the ordination of the Messrs. Daniel Temple and Isaac Bird, as Missionaries. By Rev. Richard S. Storrs.

At New Haven, Conn., Sept. 12, 1822, at the ordination of the Messrs. William Goodell, William Richards, and Artemas Bishop, as Missionaries. By Samuel Miller, D. D.

In the Tabernacle Church, Salem, Sept. 25, 1823, at the ordination of Rev. Edmund Frost, as a Missionary to the heathen; and the Rev. Messrs. Aaron Warner, Ansel D. Eddy, Nathan W. Fiske, Isaac Oakes, and George Sheldon, as Evangelists. By Elias Cornelius.

In Park-street Church, August 25, 1825, at the ordination of the Messrs. Elnathan Gridley and Samuel Austin Worcester, as Missionaries. By Leonard Worcester.

Rev. Joseph Tracy's Sermon at the ordination of Rev. Ira Tracy, Oct. 28, 1832.

Theory of Missions to the Heathen: a Sermon at the ordination of the Rev. Edward Webb, Oct. 23, 1845, as a Missionary. By Rufus Anderson.

The Moral Unity of the Human Race. At the ordination of Luther Halsey Gulick, M. D., as a Missionary to the Micronesia Islands, 1851. By Joseph P. Thompson, D. D.

In the North Church, New Haven, Nov. 9, 1856, at the ordination of Rev. Hiram Bingham, Jr. By Leonard Bacon, D. D.

FUNERAL SERMONS.

On the Death of Jeremiah Evarts. In Andover, July 31, 1831. By Leonard Woods, D. D.

At the Funeral of Benjamin B. Wisner, D. D., 1835. By Warren Fay, D. D.

The Christian Missionary desiring to be with Christ. At Westboro', Mass., June 30, 1840, at the Funeral of Rev. Ephraim Spaulding, Missionary. By Rufus Anderson, D. D.

Ministerial Fidelity exemplified. At the Funeral of the Rev. Daniel Crosby, Pastor of the Winthrop Church, Charlestown, March 3, 1843. By David Greene.

A Father's Memorial of an Only Daughter. In the First Church in Hartford, Dec. 9, 1844, on the death of Mrs. Mary E. Van Lennep, in Constantinople, Sept. 27, 1844. By Joel Hawes, D. D.

Occasioned by the Death of William J. Armstrong, D. D., 1846. By Nehemiah Adams.

In the North Dutch Church, Albany, May 6, 1849, on the death of Rev. William J. Pohlman, Missionary to China. By Duncan Kennedy, D. D.

The Rest of Heaven. At Reading, Mass., August 13, 1851, at the Funeral of the Rev. Daniel Temple. By William Goodell, Missionary at Constantinople.

At Oroomiah, Persia, July 9, 1854, occasioned by the death of Rev. William R. Stocking. By Justin Perkins.

At Seir, Persia, Sept. 17, 1854, occasioned by the death of Rev. Edwin H. Crane. By Rev. Samuel A. Rhea.

At Oroomiah, Oct. 11, 1857, occasioned by the death of Mrs. Martha Ann Rhea. By Rev. Austin H. Wright, M. D.

Occasioned by the death of Mrs. Harriet B. H. Williams, Missionary at Mosul; preached at Auburndale, Newton, Mass., Feb. 28, 1858. By Rev. Edward W. Clark.

OCCASIONAL SERMONS.

The Duty of the American Churches in respect to Foreign Missions. Preached in the Tabernacle, Philadelphia, Sabbath morning, Feb. 16, 1812; and in the First Presbyterian Church, on the afternoon of the same day. By Rev. Gordon Hall, a Missionary to the East: delivered the day but one before he sailed for India. Philadelphia, 1812; Andover, 1815.

At the Old South Church, Boston, June 7, 1819. By Myron Winslow.

The Dereliction and Restoration of the Jews. In Park-street Church, Boston, Sabbath, Oct. 31, 1819, just before the departure of the Palestine Mission. By Levi Parsons, Missionary to Palestine.

The Holy Land an Interesting Field of Missionary Enterprise. In the Old South Church, Sabbath evening, Oct. 31, 1819, just before the departure of the Palestine Mission. By Pliny Fisk, Missionary to Palestine.

A Sermon in the Old South Church, Boston, Dec. 16, 1821. By Rev. Daniel Temple, just before his departure as a Missionary to Western Asia.

In the First Church in Hartford, July 7, 1844, on occasion of the Author's Return from a Missionary Tour to the Countries east of the Mediterranean. By Joel Hawes, D. D.

Rev. Stephen Johnson's Thanksgiving Sermon, at Gouverneur, N. Y., Nov. 24, 1853.

Rev. Lewis Grout's Sermon at the Dedication of a Congregational House of Worship in Durban, South Africa, June 8, 1856.

Rev. Lewis Grout's Discourse on the Religion of Faith and that of Form. At Durban, 1857.

Rev. Lewis Grout's Discourse on the Christian Ministry. At Durban, 1857.

Rev. E. G. Beckwith's Discourse at Honolulu, Sandwich Islands, July 25, 1858, at the Funeral of Captain Richard Coady.

The Promise to Abraham. A Missionary Sermon. By Mark Hopkins, D. D.

MISCELLANEOUS WORKS.

Essays on the Present Crisis of the Condition of the American Indians; first published in the National Intelligencer, under the signature of William Penn. By Jeremiah Evarts, Secretary A. B. C. F. M. Boston, Perkins & Marvin, 1829. pp. 112.

Letters from the East. By John Scudder, M. D., Missionary in Ceylon. Boston, 1833.

Missionary Sermons and Addresses. By Eli Smith. Boston, 1833.

Letters to Children. By Rev. E. C. Bridgman, Missionary in China. Boston, 1834.

Meditations on the Last Days of Christ. By William G. Schauffler, Missionary of the A. B. C. F. M. Boston, William Pierce, 1837. pp. 380. Improved edition, 1858.

The Conquest of India by the Church. By Rev. Sendol B. Munger. Boston, 1845.

Letters from Broosa, Asia Minor. By Mrs. Eliza C. A. Schneider. Chambersburg, Pa., 1846. pp. 210.

Daughters of China; or, Sketches of Domestic Life in the Celestial Empire. By Eliza J. Gillett Bridgman. New York, Carter & Brothers, 1853. pp. 234.

Reports and Letters connected with Special Meetings of the Mahratta and Tamil Missions of the American Board of Commissioners for Foreign Missions. 1855. Also, Reports of the Syria Mission, and of a Conference at Constantinople; the above connected with the Visit of the Deputation. pp. 472.

Hints on Missions to India. By Myron Winslow, Missionary at Madras. New York, M. W. Dodd, 1856. pp. 236.

Thoughts on Missions. By Rev. Sheldon Dibble, Missionary in the Sandwich Islands. American Tract Society.

IN FOREIGN LANGUAGES.

The whole number of distinct publications in each language is stated, as far as known. As the aggregate of the titles in the lists that are at command approaches TWO THOUSAND, it will be seen that only a few of the larger and more obviously important works can be named. These will suffice to justify what is said with respect to the Literature of the Missions in the chapter on that subject. — It should be stated, that the Scriptures and religious Tracts were generally printed at the expense of Bible and Tract Societies.

ARABIC LANGUAGE.

Forty-four Titles.

Elements of Arabic Grammar, 12mo., pp. 168.
Arabic Syntax, 16mo., pp. 74.
Summary of Evangelical Doctrines, 12mo., pp. 60.
Office and Work of the Holy Spirit, 12mo., pp. 256.
On Good Works, 16mo., pp. 87.
Nevins's Thoughts on Popery, 16mo., pp. 156.
Letter to Syrian Clergy, 16mo., pp. 20.
Pilgrim's Progress, 12mo.
Bistany's Arithmetic.
Alexander's Evidences of Christianity.
Calhoun's Companion to the Bible.
Van Dyck's Geography, and Algebra.
Meshakah on Skepticism.
On Rites and Ceremonies.
New Testament, with references.
New Testament, pocket edition.
Genesis, 16mo., pp. 136.
Psalms of David, 12mo., pp. 276.

MODERN ARMENIAN.

One hundred and nineteen Titles.

Armenian and English Grammar, pp. 112.
Worcester's Astronomy, 16mo., pp. 104.
Abercrombie on Mental Culture, 24mo., pp. 84.
English and Armenian Grammar, 8vo., pp. 112.
Mother at Home, 16mo., pp. 292.
Dairyman's Daughter, 12mo., pp. 48.
Mary Lothrop, 16mo., pp. 96.
Pilgrim's Progress, 12mo., pp. 814.
New Testament, in the Ararat dialect, 8vo., pp. 548.
New Testament, with Ancient Armenian in parallel columns, 8vo., pp. 1020.

Book of Psalms, in the Ararat dialect, 16mo., pp. 275.
New Testament, pocket ed., 24mo., pp. 768.
New Testament, with marginal references, 12mo., pp. 948.
New Testament, 12mo., pp. 340.
Old Testament, 4 vols., 12mo., pp. 3094.
The Bible, 12mo., pp. 1406.
The Bible, with references, 8vo., pp. 804.
Concordance, 8vo., pp. 506.
Assembly's Shorter Catechism, with Proofs.
D'Aubigne's History of the Reformation, 2 vols., 8vo., pp. 1088.
Flavel on Keeping the Heart, 12mo., pp. 180.
Summary of Christian Theology, 2 vols., 8vo.
Doddridge's Rise and Progress, 12mo., pp. 450.
Work of the Holy Spirit, 12mo., pp. 173.
British Martyrology, 12mo., pp. 222.
Scripture Text Book, 12mo., pp. 838.
Whately's Evidences, 16mo., pp. 192.
Church Member's Guide, 12mo., pp. 167.
Cause and Cure of Infidelity, 12mo., pp. 277.
Hymn Book, and Church Music, pp. 149.
Twenty-two Reasons for Attending Public Worship, 12mo., pp. 20.
Protestantism not a New Religion, pp. 44.
Exposition of an Apostolical Church, pp. 48.
Protestant Confessions and Catechisms, 16mo., pp. 265.
Rule of Faith, 12mo., pp. 402.
Am I a Christian? 16mo. and 12mo., pp. 54.
Life of Zwingle, 12mo., pp. 74.
Upham's Intellectual Philosophy, pp. 60.
Bible Dictionary, 8vo., pp. 72.
Daily Meditations, and Great Truths.
Mental and Written Arithmetic, 12mo., pp. 168.
Grammar of the Modern Armenian Constantinople Dialect, 8vo., pp. 84.

ANCIENT ARMENIAN.

Six Titles.

New Testament, 16mo., pp. 836.
The Psalms, 16mo., pp. 285.
Christian Teacher, 16mo., pp. 500.
Daily Food for Christians, 16mo. pp. 62.

ARMENO-TURKISH.

Turkish in the Armenian Characters. Fifty-three Titles.

Old Testament, 12mo., pp. 2232.
New Testament, 12mo. pp. 768.
New Testament, with references, 8vo. pp. 336.
Commentary on Matthew, 8vo., 718.
Commentary on the N. Testament, pp. 128.
Chrysostom on Reading the Scriptures, 12mo., pp. 106.
Child's Book on the Soul, 16mo., pp. 168.
Natural Theology, 12mo., pp. 233.
Abbott's Young Christian, 12mo., pp. 350
Dialogues on Sin and Salvation, pp. 140.
Memoir of Dr. Capadose, 12mo., pp. 52.
False Claims of the Pope, 16mo., pp. 112.
Head of the Church, 12mo., pp. 52.
Guide to the Use of the Fathers, 16mo., pp. 318.
Good Works, 16mo., pp. 44.
Tract on Intemperance, 12mo., pp. 46.
Tract on Self-Examination, 16mo., pp. 48.
Light of the Soul, 16mo., pp. 48.
Mary Lothrop, 24mo., pp. 172.
Selections from Pike's Persuasions to Piety, 12mo., pp. 70.
The Sabbath, 16mo., pp. 116.
Spelling Book, pp. 64; Arithmetic, pp. 68.
Geography, 12mo., pp. 135.
Hymn Book, 16mo., pp. 112.
Fourteen Sermons, 8vo., pp. 316.
Bogue's Essay, 12mo., pp. 444.
Scripture Titles of Christ, 16mo., pp. 104.
Barth's Church History, 12mo., pp. 408.
Volume of Narrative Tracts, 16mo., pp. 152.
Essay on Fasts, etc., 12mo., pp. 220.
Rites and Ceremonies, 12mo., pp. 192.
Lives of Patriarchs and Prophets, pp. 428.

ARMENO-KOORDISH.

Three Titles.

The Four Gospels, 12mo., pp. 398.

GRÆCO-TURKISH.

Two Titles.

The Bible, 8vo., pp. 1128.

HEBREW-SPANISH.

Eleven Titles.

Hebrew Grammar, 8vo., pp. 183.
Hebrew Lexicon, 8vo., pp. 400.
Old Testament, 4to., pp. 1498.
Psalms, pp. 258; Hymns, pp. 20.

MODERN GREEK.

One hundred and eighty-six Titles — printed chiefly at Malta and Smyrna.

Church History, 12mo., pp. 354.
Sermons of Dr. Jonas King, preached at Athens. Athens, 1859, sm. 8vo. pp. 540.
Miscellaneous Works of Dr. King. Athens, 1859, sm. 8vo., pp. 843.

ITALIAN.

Forty-eight Titles — chiefly at Malta.

BULGARIAN.

Three Titles.

MODERN SYRIAC.

Forty-three Titles.

A Collection of Hymns.
Scripture Question Book.
The Pilgrim's Progress.
Arithmetics; Geography.
The Saints' Everlasting Rest.
Doddridge's Rise and Progress.
Barth's Church History.
A large Scripture History and Geography.
A System of Theology.
The Old Testament, with references.
The New Testament.
Grammar of the Modern Syriac.

ANCIENT AND MODERN SYRIAC.

Three Titles.

New Testament, the Peshito version, with translation into Modern Syriac, in parallel columns, large 4to.
Old Testament, the Peshito, with translation in parallel columns, large 4to., nearly 1000 pages.

MAHRATTA.

One hundred and eighty Titles.

Old Testament, pp. 942; New Test., pp. 268.
History of our Lord and Saviour Jesus Christ, 12mo., pp. 304.
Child's Book on the Soul, 12mo., pp. 211.
Arithmetic, pp. 186; Grammar, pp. 110.
Hymns, 18mo., pp. 148.

GUJARATI.

Thirty Titles.

HINDOSTANI.

Four Titles.

SANSKRIT.

Two Titles.

TAMIL.

Three hundred and seven Titles — in Ceylon and at Madras.

Coming to Christ; The True Way.
The Accepted Time; Bible Doctrines.
Scripture History, 12mo., pp. 156.
Rise and Progress, 12mo., pp. 169.
Pilgrim's Progress, pp. 370.
Instructor, 5 vols., 18mo., pp. 455.
Elementary Arithmetic, 18mo., pp. 170.
Geography of India, 12mo., pp. 206.
Hymn Book, pp. 506.
Tamil Dictionary, 8vo., pp. 897.
Anatomy, by Dr. Greene, pp. 149.
Algebra, by D. L. Carroll, pp. 252.
Manual of Private Devotion, pp. 292.
Barth's Church History, 18mo., pp. 656.
Watts's Scripture History, 12mo. pp. 458.
Body of Divinity, 12mo., pp. 600.
Rhenius's Tamil Grammar, pp. 216.
The Bible in Tamil, pp. 2158.
New Testament, 8vo., pp. 372.
English and Tamil Dictionary, 8vo., pp. 800.
Old Testament, in part, 18mo., pp. 2580.

TELUGU.

Number exceeding one hundred — at Madras.

Generally each work in both Tamil and Telugu.

CHINESE.

One hundred and fifty Titles.

A Chrestomathy, in Canton Dialect, pp. 698.
Easy Lessons in Chinese, 8vo., pp. 287.
An English and Chinese Vocabulary, in the Court Dialect, 8vo., pp. 440.
Tonic Dictionary of the Chinese Language, in the Canton Dialect, 8vo., pp. 832.
Sermon on the Mount; The Four Gospels.
Acts of the Apostles; Epistle of James.
Genesis, Chapter 1, with a Commentary.
New Testament, in the Fuhchau Dialect.
The Chinese Repository, in English, 20 vols. A part of the edition destroyed by fire in 1857.

JAPANESE.

One Title.

BUGIS.

Two Titles.

MALAY.

Three Titles.

SIAMESE.

Forty-four Titles.

Gospel of Mark, Gospel of John.
Acts of the Apostles, 2 ed., 8vo., pp. 75.
The Three Epistles of John.
The Epistle to the Colossians.
Genesis, 2 ed.; Life of Christ, pp. 168.
Geography, pp. 118.
Histories of the United States, Great Britain, France, Spain, and Portugal.
Old Testament History, in six parts.
Church History, 8vo., pp. 158.
Treatise on Midwifery, 12mo., pp. 156.

ZULU.

Thirteen Titles.

Book of Psalms; Epistle to the Romans.
Gospels of Matthew and Mark.
An Arithmetic and Geography.
A Grammar, 8vo., pp. 432.
A Zulu-Kaffir Dictionary, 8vo., pp. 459.

MPONGWE.

Twenty-one Titles.

Colloquial Sentences; Grammatical Tables.
Extracts from the New Testament, pp. 84.
Grammar, with Vocabulary, 8vo.
Gospels of Matthew and John.
Exodus, Proverbs, and Acts.

DIKĔLĔ.

Seven Titles.

GREBO.

Forty-three Titles.

Gospels of Matthew, Mark, John, 12mo., pp. 159.
Dictionary, Grebo and English, 8vo., pp. 126.
Grammar, 8vo., pp. 36.

HAWAIIAN.

Two hundred and thirty-eight Titles.

Old Testament, 2 vols., 12mo., pp. 1031.
New Testament, 12mo., pp. 520.
Child's Arithmetic, 24mo., pp. 48.
Linear Drawing, 12mo., pp. 32.
Astronomy, 12mo., pp. 12.
Mathematics, 12mo., pp. 16.
Surveying, 8vo., pp. 16.
Algebra, 8vo., pp. 96.
Logarithms, 8vo., pp. 16.
Hymn Book, 16mo., pp. 48.
Moral Philosophy, 12mo., pp. 48.
Elements of History, 12mo., pp. 60.
Scripture Evidences, 12mo., pp. 120.
Scripture History, 12mo., pp. 282.
Sacred Geography, 12mo., pp. 88.
History of Hawaii, 12mo., pp. 224.
Hawaiian Grammar, 8vo., pp. 156.
Vocabulary, pp. 96.
Trigonometry, 8vo., pp. 16.
Geography, 12mo., pp. 198.
Colburn's Arithmetic, 24mo., pp. 140.
Leonard's Arithmetic, 12mo., pp. 156.
Political Economy, 8vo., pp. 80.
Church Music, 8vo., pp. 148.
Dying Testimony of Christians and Infidels.
Keith on the Prophecies, 12mo., pp. 12.
Natural Theology, 12mo., pp. 178.
Church History, 12mo., pp. 349.
Tract for Parents, 12mo., pp. 12.
Pilgrim's Progress, 18mo., pp. 432.
Reading Book for Schools, pp. 340.
Compend of Ancient History, pp. 76.
Study of the Globes, 16mo., pp. 40.
Hawaiian and English Dictionary, pp. 40.

CHEROKEE.

Thirty-nine Titles.

Isaiah, in part, 24mo., pp. 32.
Psalms and Proverbs, in part, 24mo., pp. 34.
Genesis and Exodus, in part.
New Testament, 12mo.; Hymns, pp. 51.

CHOCTAW.

Sixty-one Titles.

The New Testament, 1848.
Joshua, Judges, Ruth, 1st and 2d Samuel, and 1st and 2d Kings.
Memoir of Catherine Brown.
Choctaw Reader; Choctaw Hymns.
The World to Come.

CREEK.

Five Titles.

OSAGE.

Two Titles.

OTTAWA.

One Title.

OJIBWA.

Fourteen Titles.

New Testament; Hymns; Spelling Book.

DAKOTA.

Fifteen Titles.

Grammar and Dictionary, 4to., pp. 338.
Dakota Scriptures—Genesis, part of Psalms, Gospels of Luke and John, Acts, Paul's Epistles, and Rev., 2 vols., pp. 528.
Hymns.

ABENAQUIS.

Two Titles.

SENECA.

Not fully reported.

Spelling Book.
Gospel of Luke.
Hymns, 1852, 16mo., pp. 230.

ADDITIONAL LIST OF PUBLICATIONS.

Sermon at the Tabernacle Church in Salem, February 6, 1812, at the Ordination of Messrs. Samuel Newell, Adoniram Judson, Samuel Nott, Gordon Hall, and Luther Rice, as Missionaries to the Heathen. By Leonard Woods, D. D.

Paul on Mars' Hill; or, A Christian Survey of the Pagan World. A Sermon preached at Newburyport, June 21, 1815, at the Ordination of Messrs. Samuel J. Mills, James Richards, Edward Warren, Horatio Bardwell, Benjamin C. Meigs, and Daniel Poor, as Missionaries to the Heathen. By Samuel Worcester, D. D.

The Duty and Reward of Missionary Labors. A Sermon preached at Newburyport in the Year 1815. By Rev. Horatio Bardwell, late Missionary at Bombay.

Idolatry of the Hindoos. A Sermon preached November 29, 1816, at the Annual Meeting of the Female Foreign Missionary Society of Franklin, Conn. By Rev. Samuel Nott, late Missionary at Bombay.

The Bible a Code of Laws. A Sermon delivered in Park Street Church, Boston, September 3, 1817, at the Ordination of Sereno Edwards Dwight, as Pastor of that Church; and of Messrs. Elisha P. Swift, Allen Graves, John Nichols, Levi Parsons, and Daniel Buttrick, as Missionaries to the Heathen. By Rev. Lyman Beecher.

Instructions from the Prudential Committee of the American Board of Commissioners for Foreign Missions, to the Rev. Levi Parsons and the Rev. Pliny Fisk, Missionaries designated for Palestine. Delivered in the Old South Church, Boston, October 31, 1819. By Samuel Worcester, D. D., Corresponding Secretary.

Sermon occasioned by the Death of the Rev. Samuel Worcester, D. D., delivered in the Tabernacle Church, Salem, Mass., July 12, 1821. By Leonard Woods, D. D.

God's Ways not as our Ways. A Sermon occasioned by the Death of the Rev. Samuel Worcester, D. D., Senior Pastor of the Tabernacle Church, in Salem, Mass. By Elias Cornelius, Surviving Pastor. 1821.

India and the Hindoos. Being a Popular View of the Geography, History, Government, Manners, Customs, and Religion, of that Ancient People; with a new and correct Map of India. By Rev. F. DeW. Ward. New York, London, and Edinburgh.

Remarks on the Best Term for *God* in Chinese. By Rev. L. B. Peet, Missionary at Fuhchou. Canton, 1852.

Discourse at the Semi-centennial Anniversary of the Institution of the American Board of Commissioners for Foreign Missions, preached at Bradford, Mass., June 29, 1860. By Samuel M. Worcester, D. D.

The following publications were in the Journal of the American Oriental Society: —

Treatise on Arab Music, chiefly from the work of Mikhâil Meshâkah, of Damascus. Translated from the Arabic, by Eli Smith. 1847.

Comparative Vocabularies of some of the principal Negro Dialects of Africa. By John Leighton Wilson. 1849.

The Zulu Language. By James C. Bryant. 1849.

The Zulu and other Dialects of Southern Africa. By Lewis Grout. 1849.

Translation of an Imperial Berât, issued by Sultân Selim III., A. H. 1215, appointing the Monk Johannes Patriarch of all the Armenians of Turkey, with Notes. By Rev. H. G. O. Dwight. 1849.

Condition of the Medical Profession in Syria. By C. V. A. Van Dyck, M. D. 1849.

Plan for a Uniform Orthography of South African Dialects. By American Missionaries. 1850.

Contribution to the Geography of Central Kûrdistan. By Azariah Smith, M. D. 1850.

Shabbathai Zevi and his Followers. By William G. Schauffler. 1851.

On Japanese Syllabaries. By Samuel Wells Williams. 1851.

Journal of a Tour from Oroomiah to Mosul, through the Kûrdish Mountains, and a Visit to the Ruins of Nineveh. By Justin Perkins, D. D. 1851.

Notes of a Tour in Mount Lebanon and the Eastern Side of Lake Hûleh. By Henry A. De Forest, M. D. 1851.

Remarks on the Mode of Applying the Electric Telegraph in Connection with the Chinese Language. By William Macy. 1852.

Catalogue of all the Works known to exist in the Armenian Language of a date earlier than the Seventeenth Century. By H. G. O. Dwight. 1853.

Notes on Ruins in the Bŭka'a and in the Belâd Ba'albek. By Henry A. De Forest, M. D. 1853.

On the Relations of the Maráthá to the Sanscrit. By Henry Ballantine. 1853.

Brief Notes on the Tamil Language. By Henry R. Hoisington. 1853.

An Essay on the Phonology and Orthography of the Zulu and kindred Dialects of Southern Africa. By Lewis Grout. 1853.

Tattuva-Kattalei, Law of the Tattuvam. A Synopsis of the Mystical Philosophy of the Hindûs, translated from the Tamil, with Notes. By Rev. Henry R. Hoisington. 1853.

Siva-Gnâna-Pōtham, Instruction in the Knowledge of God. A Metaphysical and Theological Treatise, translated from the Tamil. By Rev. Henry R. Hoisington. 1853.

Siva-Pirakâsam, Light of Sivan. A Metaphysical and Theological Treatise, translated from the Tamil, with Notes. By Rev. Henry R. Hoisington. 1854.

State and Prospects of the English Language in India. By David O. Allen, D. D. 1854.

Letters from H. Lobdell, M. D., respecting recent Discoveries at Koyunjik. 1854.

Grammar of the Modern Syriac Language, as spoken in Oroomiah, Persia, and in Koordistan. By Rev. D. T. Stoddard. 1855.

Observations on the Prepositions, Conjunctions, and other Particles of the Isizulu and its Cognate Languages. By Rev. Lewis Grout. 1858.

Translation of the Sârya-Siddhânta, a Text-Book of Hindu Astronomy, with Notes and an Appendix. By Rev. Ebenezer Burgess, assisted by the Com. of Publication. 1860.

Inverted Construction of Modern Armenian. By Elias Riggs, D. D. 1860.

On Dr. Samuel Wells Williams's Tonic Dictionary of the Chinese Language in the Canton Dialect. By Rev. William A. Macy. 1860.

The following were in the Bibliotheca Sacra and Am. Biblical Repository: —

Contributions to the Climatology of Palestine. By H. A. De Forest, M. D.

The Produce of the Vineyard in the East. By Rev. Henry A. Homes.

Description of Seleucia, Anticoh, Aleppo, etc. By Rev. William M. Thomson.

Journey from Aleppo to Mount Lebanon by Jeble El-Aala, Apamia, Riblah, etc. By Rev. William M. Thomson.

The Kingdom of Congo and the Roman Catholic Missionaries. By Rev. J. L. Wilson.

India as a Field for Inquiry and Evangelical Labor. By Rev. H. R. Hoisington.

Caste in the Island of Ceylon. By Rev. Benjamin C. Meigs, Rev. Daniel Poor, D. D., and Rev. William A. Howland.

Notes upon the Geography of Macedonia. By Rev. Edward M. Dodd.

Notes on Palestine. By Rev. William M. Thomson.

The Wines of Mount Lebanon. By Eli Smith, D. D.

Turkish Toleration. By Eli Smith, D. D.

Journal of a Visit to the Yezidees. By Rev. Thomas Laurie.

The Sources of the Jordan. By Rev. William M. Thomson.

Tour from Beirût to Aleppo in 1845. By Rev. William M. Thomson.

Life, Character, Writings, Doctrines, and Influence of Confucius. By Rev. Ira Tracy.

The Mandingo, Grebo, and Mpongwe Dialects. By Rev. John L. Wilson.

Maps of Palestine. By Rev. Samuel Wolcott.

Geographical Notes on Palestine. By Rev. Samuel Wolcott.

In most of the other accessible periodicals, to which missionaries of the American Board may be supposed to have contributed articles, the names of the writers are not usually given. Discussions of important subjects may be found appended to several of the Annual Reports of the Board; and the Missionary Herald is well known to be mainly composed of Letters and Journals from the Missionaries.

INDEX.

www.ingramcontent.com/pod-product-compliance
Lightning Source LLC
LaVergne TN
LVHW020937110826
845150LV00004B/885

* 9 7 8 1 4 2 5 5 5 1 9 2 6 *